INVENTORY THEORY
AND CONSUMER BEHAVIOR

INVENTORY THEORY AND CONSUMER BEHAVIOR

Alan S. Blinder
Professor of Economics, Princeton University

HARVESTER WHEATSHEAF

New York   London   Toronto   Sydney   Tokyo

First published 1990 by
Harvester Wheatsheaf,
66 Wood Lane End, Hemel Hempstead,
Hertfordshire, HP2 4RG
A division of
Simon & Schuster International Group

Printed and bound in Great Britain by
BPCC Wheatons Ltd, Exeter

British Library Cataloguing in Publication Data

Blinder, Alan S.
 Inventory theory and consumer behaviour.
 1. Macroeconomics
 I. Title
 339
ISBN 0-7450-0649-3

---

1 2 3 4 5 94 93 92 91 90

CONTENTS

ACKNOWLEDGEMENTS

We are grateful to the following for permission to reproduce copyright material:

Chapter 1: *American Economic Review.* Article reproduced from May 1981 issue, pp. 11–16.

Chapter 2: *Kyklos.* Article reproduced from vol. 33, fasc. 4 (1980), pp. 585–614.

Chapter 3: *Journal of Monetary Economics.* Article reproduced from November 1981 issue, pp. 277–304.

Chapter 4: *American Economic Review.* Article reproduced from June 1982 issue, pp. 334–48.

Chapter 5: *Brookings Papers on Economic Activity.* Article reproduced from issue 2 (1981), pp. 443–505.

Chapter 6: *Quarterly Journal of Economics.* Article reproduced from August 1986 issue, pp. 431–53.

Chapter 7: *Journal of Money, Credit and Banking.* Article reproduced from August 1986 issue, pp. 355–65.

Chapter 8: *Journal of Political Economy.* Article reproduced from June 1975 issue, pp. 447–75.

Chapter 9: *Journal of Political Economy.* Article reproduced from February 1981 issue, pp. 26–53.

Chapter 10: The Macmillan Press, London. Article reproduced from Modigliani, F. and R. Hemming (eds), *The Determinants of National Saving and Wealth,* International Economic Association, The Macmillan Press, London, 1983.

Chapter 11: *Annales d'Economie et de Statistique.* Article reproduced from January–March 1988 issue, pp. 77–91.

INTRODUCTION

Accident rather than design led me into a career as a macroeconomist. In graduate school at MIT, I specialized in what was then called "advanced theory." That, in itself, is a measure of how much economics has changed in less than two decades. My PhD dissertation (Blinder, 1974) was on the theory of income distribution. But when Princeton University asked if I could fill their need for someone to teach graduate macro theory, I gave the only answer a job-seeking PhD candidate can give: of course!

Teaching graduate students at Princeton drew me more deeply into macro theory than I had ever been before and kept me on top of current macro issues. Although I have periodically strayed into other fields, the bulk of my research has been in empirical and theoretical macroeconomics. This volume is a nonrandom sample of that work. In selecting items to include, I have not sought to pick out only the best papers, but rather to put together a collection with some thematic coherence – and also to include some papers that are relatively inaccessible.

Often I have wondered whether my accidental conversion to macroeconomics was a stroke of good or bad luck. On the one hand, the field has been constantly bubbling with intellectual excitement and draws you naturally into the world of public policy, where I go willingly. Furthermore, macroeconomics is a big and prominent field; so making a splash there earns you notice – or notoriety – on a wide scale. On the other hand, macroeconomic debates during my professional career have been distressingly unrelenting, acrimonious, and even ideological. The constant state of intense disputation takes a personal toll and, more importantly, inhibits scientific progress. Too much of our time, it seems to me, is spent defending obvious positions against preposterous challenges, too little doing what T. S. Kuhn called normal science. Sometimes I wonder if we are doing science at all.

Nothing in my undergraduate or graduate education (1963–71) prepared me for the tumult that was to follow. I was raised on a straight diet of Keynesian economics at Princeton and MIT just before the consensus crumbled. When I left graduate school in 1971, I thought I was joining a cadre of researchers that was pursuing a progressive research agenda started in 1936. I knew, of course, all about the Keynesian-monetarist controversy; indeed, two of my earliest papers addressed it (Blinder and Solow, 1973;

Goldfeld and Blinder, 1972). But this debate seemed to involve but a small number of people, to be greatly overblown, and to be potentially resolvable by empirical evidence. As Milton Friedman (1970) made clear, theoretical divisions among macroeconomists back then did not run deep.

The major influences on my research in the late 1970s and into the 1980s were not the Lucas critique and rational expectations, but rather real-world events. The first of these was the realization that the big recession the US experienced in 1973–5 was, in large measure, an inventory contraction.

INVENTORY BEHAVIOR

During eight years of undergraduate and graduate education, I had encountered the word "inventory" more often on store windows than in economics books and articles. None of my teachers had given me much exposure to either the theory or facts of inventory fluctuations, which therefore had no place on my early 1970s research agenda. My image of a business cycle was that of a large wave in which the inventory cycle was but a minor eddy.

A short stint at the US Congressional Budget Office (CBO) changed all that. I remember one day in the summer of 1975 when a CBO staffer returned from a congressional hearing with some amazing news. Alan Greenspan, then President Gerald Ford's chief economic adviser, had just testified that the recession was mostly an inventory correction. We all snickered at the idea that what was, up to then, the deepest recession since the Great Depression could have been "only" an inventory cycle. When I subsequently studied the data more carefully, however, I learned that Greenspan had been right. Like most of the recessions before and since, the 1973–5 contraction was dominated by changes in inventory investment. A large portion of this collection is the outgrowth of my realization that business cycles are, to a surprisingly large degree, inventory cycles.

My first papers on the macroeconomics of inventories, which are not reprinted here,[1] led me to the belief that the profession was missing something important – both theoretically and empirically, both macroeconomically and microeconomically – by ignoring inventories. Chapter 2, which originally appeared in *Kyklos* in 1980, is my first major paper on the subject. It amends the Keynesian macro model in the way suggested by the predominant micro theory of inventory behavior (the production smoothing model) and obtains several interesting results along the way – including what still seems to me the most natural explanation for the procyclical or acyclical behavior of real wages.[2] I am happy to reprint the paper here because it is not widely read, probably due to its place of publication.

A scrap of interesting (to me) intellectual history: I wrote the paper in 1976, but could not get it published in the United States because it assumed non-market-clearing and adaptive expectations. The latter was inessential to the main results, but made the paper unacceptable in my country at a time when intellectual tolerance was not running high. (At one seminar, I was actually shouted down when I insisted that adaptive expectations made no difference to the results.) While I was trying unsuccessfully to peddle the paper in the United States, Stanley Fischer and I collaborated on a related paper that used rational expectations and market clearing (reprinted here as Chapter 3). While that paper accomplished far less than the *Kyklos* paper, it ran with current fashions rather than against them and so was quickly accepted and is frequently cited. Later, I wrote, but never tried to publish, a version of the *Kyklos* model using perfect foresight instead of adaptive expectations. It naturally reached almost the same conclusions.

Chapter 1, a short paper prepared for the December 1980 meetings of the American Economic Association, summarizes my thinking up to that point and therefore serves as a good introduction to Chapters 2–4. The last of these offers a rigorous justification of the production smoothing/buffer stock model and draws out its major implication for pricing: inventories not only allow a firm to smooth production, but also to smooth prices. This contradicts the conventional view, derived from a world with no inventories, that price variability and output variability are substitutes.

As I delved more deeply into the data, however, I developed increasingly strong doubts about the validity of the production smoothing model – doubts which are expressed principally in Chapters 5 and 6. Chapter 5 offers an alternative inventory model – the (S, s) model – for retail firms, where the central assumption of the production smoothing model (convex costs) really is implausible. In the (S, s) model, inventories are held to economize on the fixed costs of placing an order. While the microeconomics of (S, s) had been known for some time, this paper was, to my knowledge, the first to draw out and test the model's implications for aggregate data.

Chapter 6 looks more closely at the discrepancies between the theory of production smoothing model and the data on US manufacturing inventories. It concludes that the theory can be salvaged by adding small cost shocks to highly serial correlated demand shocks. But it wonders out loud whether the theory is worth saving and speculates on some alternatives. Chapter 7, an econometric companion, estimates empirical counterparts to the theoretical model for 20 manufacturing industries and finds little direct evidence for important cost shocks. It also disputes Maccini and Rossana's (1984) claim that speeds of adjustment in stock-adjustment models are really much faster than earlier estimates had suggested.

CONSUMER BEHAVIOR

The last four papers in the collection are on a subject that has engaged my attention periodically throughout my career: consumer behavior. Each is empirical, at least in part, and every one is related, in one way or another, to the validity of the simple permanent income/life-cycle model. But each addresses a different specific substantive issue.

Chapter 8, the only paper in this collection that dates from the 1970s, uses the pre-rational expectations version of the permanent income hypothesis (PIH) to pose a question that has interested economists since Keynes: does the distribution of income affect aggregate consumption? The answer seems to be: not enough to show up in the US data, where time series changes in income distribution are small.

Chapter 9 uses a semi-rational expectations approach to the consumption function[3] to address a question that was hotly debated in the 1970s: do temporary changes in income taxes have smaller effects on spending than permanent ones? The permanent income hypothesis asserts that they do. But my examination of the data suggests that the truth lies roughly halfway between the strict PIH and the naive Keynesian view that only current income affects current spending.[4]

Chapter 10, written jointly with Roger Gordon and Donald Wise, is the one paper in this collection that uses cross-sectional micro data, though to examine a macro question. Our research originally intended to take the life cycle model as the maintained hypothesis and study the claim by Martin Feldstein (1974) that consumers base their spending decisions on their total wealth, including "social security wealth." But it wound up doing much more than that. The estimates we obtained actually cast a dark shadow on the validity of the life cycle model itself and, in conjunction with other evidence,[5] led me to think seriously about alternative theories of consumer spending.

Chapter 11, co-authored with Avner Bar-Ilan, is one such theory, on which I am still working. Starting from the premise that the purchaser of a new durable good incurs some fixed costs, we combine the insights of the (S, s) model of inventories with the permanent income theory to develop a new model of spending on consumer durables. Then we aggregate the resulting micro model to get a macro model and subject the macro-model to some preliminary tests. Bar-Ilan and I have continued to develop and test this model, and have written a second paper (Bar-Ilan and Blinder, 1988). In that paper, we stress the generality of the approach. Since fixed costs seem ubiquitous, the basic modeling strategy seems to apply to decisions as diverse as money demand, individual portfolio choice, business pricing, and employment.

A scholar wants little but to have his work read – praised is nice, but read is the essential thing. But I have never been presumptuous enough to suggest to anyone that my papers be collected and reprinted. I am therefore grateful to Harvester Wheatsheaf, and especially to my editor, Peter Johns, for initiating this collection. I hope the reader will find their judgment sound.

NOTES

1. Blinder (1977) is a short theoretical paper which appeared in a festschrift volume. Its main point is that the dynamics underlying the Keynesian cross – as set forth, say, in Samuelson (1947) – are logically flawed. My empirical work on inventories began with a detailed study of the US experience in 1973-6, prepared for a Brookings conference in Rome in 1977. This was subsequently expanded into a book (Blinder, 1979, especially Chapter 4).
2. A surge in demand first depletes inventories, which raises the shadow value of inventories and hence output. Thus the labor demand schedule shifts outward, which tends to push real wages up.
3. I mean by this that the approach is consistent with rational expectations but does not impose rationality in any essential way.
4. A reexamination of this question about eight years later and with a very different econometric model produced even more "Keynesian" results. See Blinder and Deaton (1985). I believe the main source of the difference is data revisions. What little we know about the effects of temporary taxes is based on precious few observations, so statistical inference is exceptionally fragile.
5. Among these are Mirer (1979), Kurz (1981), and Kotlikoff and Summers (1981).

REFERENCES

Bar-Ilan, A. and A. S. Blinder (1988) "Consumer durables and the optimality of usually doing nothing," National Bureau of Economic Research, Working Paper No. 2488, January.

Blinder, A. S. (1974) *Toward an Economic Theory of Income Distribution*, Cambridge, Mass.: MIT Press.

Blinder, A. S. (1977) "A difficulty with Keynesian models of aggregate demand," in A. S. Blinder and P. Friedman (eds), *Natural Resources, Uncertainty and General Equilibrium Systems: Essays in Memory of Rafael Lusky*, New York: Academic Press.

Blinder, A. S. (1979) *Economic Policy and the Great Stagflation*, New York: Academic Press.

Blinder, A. S. and A. S. Deaton (1985) "The time series consumption function revisited," *Brookings Papers on Economic Activity*, vol. 2, pp. 465-511.

Blinder, A. S. and R. M. Solow (1973) "Does fiscal policy matter?" *Journal of Public Economics* (November), pp. 319-37.

Feldstein, M. S. (1974) "Social security, induced retirement, and aggregate capital accumulation," *Journal of Political Economy*, vol. 82, pp. 905-26.

Friedman, M. (1970) "A theoretical framework for monetary analysis," *Journal of Political Economy*, vol. 78, pp. 193-237.

Goldfeld, S. M. and A. S. Blinder (1972) "Some implications of endogenous stabilization policy," *Brookings Papers on Economic Activity*, vol. 3, pp. 585-640.

Kotlikoff, L. J. and L. H. Summers (1981) "The role of inter generational transfers in aggregate capital accumulation," *Journal of Political Economy*, vol. 89, pp. 706–32.

Kurz, M. (1981) "The life-cycle hypothesis and the effects of social security and private pensions on family savings," mimeo, Stanford University.

Maccini, L. J. and R. J. Rossana (1984) "Joint production, quasifixed factors of production, and investment in finished goods inventories," *Journal of Money, Credit, and Banking*, vol. 16 (May), pp. 218–36.

Mirer, T. W. (1979) "The wealth-age relation among the aged," *American Economic Review*, vol. 69, pp. 43–54.

Samuelson, P. A. (1947) *Foundations of Economic Analysis*, Cambridge, Mass.: Harvard University Press.

1·INVENTORIES AND THE STRUCTURE OF MACRO MODELS

The message of this paper can be summed up in two words: *inventories matter*. They matter empirically, in the sense that inventory developments are of major importance in the propagation of business cycles; and they matter theoretically, in the sense that recognition of their existence changes the structure of a variety of theoretical macro models in some fairly important ways. This paper is mainly about the implications of inventories for the structure of theoretical macro models, but I begin by demonstrating the empirical importance of inventories in business fluctuations.

1.1 THE IMPORTANCE OF INVENTORIES IN BUSINESS CYCLES

Inventory investment is a tiny component of GNP, averaging only about 1 percent of the total, but its importance in business fluctuations is totally out of proportion to its size. As Table 1.1 shows, inventory investment typically accounts for about 70 percent of the peak-to-trough decline in real GNP during recessions.

Of course, recessions are rather special episodes. To get a broader perspective, note that real GNP (Y_t) is the sum of real final sales (X_t) and real inventory investment (ΔN_t, where N_t is the stock of inventories). After detrending each series and first differencing, we have $\Delta y_t = \Delta x_t + \Delta^2 n_t$, where lower case letters denote deviations from trend. It follows that the variance of changes in the deviations of GNP from trend can be decomposed as follows:

$$Var(\Delta y) = Var(\Delta x) + Var(\Delta^2 n) + 2\,cov(\Delta x, \Delta^2 n)$$
$$\ 90.4 \qquad 59.1 \qquad\quad 33.4 \qquad\qquad -1.8$$

where the empirical magnitudes for the United States during 1959:1–1979:4 appear below each symbol. Changes in inventory investment account for 37

I thank the National Science Foundation for research support and David Ashmore for research assistance. A slightly longer version is available as National Bureau of Economic Research Working Paper No. 515.

Table 1.1 Changes in GNP and in inventory investment in the post-war recessions

Dates of contraction		Decline in real GNP[a]	Decline in inventory investment[a]	Col. (3) as a percentage of col. (2)
Peak (1)	Trough	(2)	(3)	(4)
1948:4	1949:4	$ 6.7	$13.0	194
1953:2	1954:2	20.6	10.2	50
1957:3	1958:1	22.2	10.5	47
1960:1	1960:4	8.8	10.5	119
1969:3	1970:4	12.0	10.1	84
1973:4	1975:1	71.0	44.8	63

Note:
(a) In billions of 1972 dollars.
Source: The National Income and Product Accounts of the United States, 1929–74, and Survey of Current Business.

percent of the variance of changes in GNP. The importance of inventory fluctuations is not limited to cyclical downturns.

What types of inventories predominate in these inventory fluctuations? For the period 1959–76, unpublished quarterly data from the Bureau of Economic Analysis enable us to break down real nonfarm inventories into the six components listed in Table 1.2. The table shows that the predominant type of inventories accounting for variation in $\Delta^2 n$ are retail inventories, followed by manufacturers' inventories of raw materials and wholesalers' inventories. Neither manufacturers' finished goods nor works in progress

Table 1.2 Decomposition of the variance of $\Delta^2 n$, 1959:1 to 1976:4

Inventory component	Variance	Percent of total variance	Correlation with Δx
Total inventories ($\Delta^2 n$)	40.40	100	−0.02
Manufacturers' inventories:			
finished goods	2.15	5.3	−0.05
works in progress	2.45	6.1	+0.25
materials and supplies	5.20	12.9	−0.09
Wholesale inventories	4.77	11.8	−0.07
Retail inventories	14.18	35.1	+0.18
Other[a]	4.13	10.2	−0.11
All covariance terms	7.27	18.0	−

Note:
(a) Includes other nonfarm inventories plus statistical discrepancies that arise because the disaggregated components of manufacturers' inventories have not been revised while the total has been revised.

contribute much to the variance of $\Delta^2 n$. Note also in Table 1.2 that the correlations between Δx and the components of $\Delta^2 n$ are all pretty meager.

1.2 MICROFOUNDATIONS

The standard theory of the firm is based on nonstorable output. When output is storable, however, firms have an additional degree of freedom: they are able to make current production Y_t differ from current sales X_t, and often will find it advisable to do so. They may use inventories of finished goods to speculate on future price movements or to absorb short-run shocks to demand; they may use inventories of raw materials to hedge against future price increases. Inventory holdings may be used to spur demand (by reducing delivery lags) or to reduce production costs (through improved scheduling).[1]

The first point is fairly obvious: the existence of inventories requires a new concept of market equilibrium. Since it may well be optimal for firms to set $Y_t \neq X_t$, there is no reason to think that "equilibrium" means that the market "clears" in the usual sense ($X_t = Y_t$). Instead, an appropriate definition of equilibrium seems to be a situation in which the quantity that suppliers desire to sell equals the quantity that customers desire to buy. Note that Y_t is not even involved in this definition: it can, in principle, be anything.

The second point is that profit maximization probably dictates that the beginning-of-period inventory stock N_t affects firms' decisions. Specifically, I wish to argue that output, sales, and inventory carryover depend on N_t as follows:

$$Y_t = Y(N_t) \quad -1 < Y'(\cdot) < 0 \tag{1.1a}$$

$$X_t = X(N_t) \quad 0 < X'(\cdot) < 1 \tag{1.1b}$$

$$N_{t+1} = F(N_t) \quad 0 < F'(\cdot) < 1 \tag{1.1c}$$

These equations have several obvious macro implications, and one that is not so obvious. Equation (1.1a) implies that models of aggregate supply – such as the celebrated Lucas supply function – should allow production to depend on inventory stocks. Equation (1.1b) implies (via the law of demand), that higher inventories lead to lower prices. Taken together, (1.1a) and (1.1b) imply that GNP and final sales may sometimes exhibit rather divergent behavior during short-run business fluctuations. Equation (1.1c) suggests that inventory investment equations should have a "partial adjustment" form, even in the absence of explicit costs of changing either production or inventory levels.

While it is possible to derive results like (1.1) rigorously in the context of specific micro models, I prefer to rely on an intuitive argument because it suggests that the equations are much more general than any specific model. The basic idea can be explained with the aid of Fig. 1.1, which depicts (as point C) the equilibrium of the textbook firm with nonstorable output:

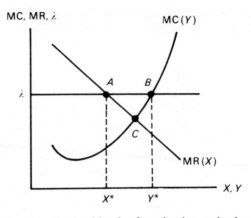

Fig. 1.1 Optimal levels of production and sales

optimal production (= sales) is determined by equating marginal revenue (MR) to marginal cost (MC). But when output is storable, the firm must operate simultaneously on *two* margins. To decide how many inputs to turn into inventories, it equates MC to the shadow value of inventories, which I call λ (point B). To decide how many inventories to withdraw for sale, it equates λ to MR (point A). Obviously, these separate decisions need not lead to X = Y.

The implications of equations (1.1) follow from Fig. 1.1. So long as MC is an increasing function of Y and λ is a decreasing function of N,[2] it is clear that Y is a decreasing function of N, in accord with (1.1a). Similarly, so long as MR decreases with X, it is clear that X is an increasing function of N, in accord with (1.1b). Rising marginal costs also imply that it is optimal to rectify inventory imbalances gradually, in accord with (1.1c).

I now come to my third point, which is the nonobvious implication of (1.1): as compared to a world with nonstorable output, prices become "sticky" when output is storable.[3] The reason, of course, is the buffer-stock role of inventories. When there is a temporary surge in demand, the necessary price increase is moderated by the fact that firms disgorge inventories. In terms of Fig. 1.1, the shadow value of inventories λ should be relatively insensitive to transitory shifts in demand (or cost) because it depends on *all* future demand and cost functions. Consequently, a shift in the MR schedule induces a larger sales response (a smaller price response) when output is storable than when it is not.

I close this section on microfoundations with a (loosely stated) general proposition about price rigidity that is prompted by these remarks:[4] prices are more "rigid," that is, respond less to demand shocks, when the costs of varying inventory levels are lower and when demand shocks are less persistent.

The following sections use these microfoundations to develop the implications of inventories for the specification and logical structure of a variety of macro models.

1.3 INVENTORIES AND OLD-FASHIONED KEYNESIAN MODELS

By including the stock of inventories in standard, old-fashioned Keynesian models, we simultaneously rid them of a serious logical flaw and of what is sometimes considered their most distressing empirical prediction – that real wages move countercyclically.

The logical flaw is quite general, but I will illustrate it with the simplest possible fixed-price model. The question is: what forces drive the economy toward an equilibrium where $Y = C + I + G$? A perfectly coherent answer is provided in most elementary textbooks. If Y, for example, exceeds $C + I + G$, inventories begin piling up, and this inventory disequilibrium signals firms to cut production. The problem is that this intuitive answer tends to get lost when models are formalized and mathematized. For example, a typical adjustment mechanism is (see, for example, Samuelson (1947), pp. 276–83):

$$\dot{Y} = \beta(X - Y), \quad \beta > 0$$

where X is final sales. This tacitly defines equilibrium as any state in which inventories are *constant* ($X = Y$), regardless of the *level* of inventories – in stark contradiction to the intuitive story just related. In my 1977 article, I explore this problem and suggest a resolution based on (1.1a) which makes the planned level of production (not the change) depend on the level of inventories (not the change).

When this basic idea is embodied in a full-fledged Keynesian model with an endogenous price level (see my 1980 paper), a number of interesting results emerge. These may be listed briefly:

1. Instead of the countercyclical behavior of real wages predicted by standard Keynesian models, search-theoretic models, and "new classical" models with rational expectations, the Keynesian model with inventories predicts that real wages move procyclically. The reason is that inventory fluctuations cause the demand curve for labor to shift along a stable labor supply function during business fluctuations.
2. The dynamic adjustment path following an increase in aggregate demand includes a period during which inflation is accelerating while output is falling. Thus inventory adjustments offer yet another instance of stagflation of the "overshooting" variety.
3. The association between inventories and output is *counter-cyclical* in the very short run, but predominately *procyclical* over business fluctuations.

1.4 INVENTORIES AND "DISEQUILIBRIUM" MODELS

The existence of inventories has profound implications for the recent wave of so-called (and badly misnamed) "disequilibrium" macro models. Indeed, I would go so far as to say that it robs them of much of their interest.

Among the fundamental notions of these models are the "min condition" of voluntary exchange and the concept of "spillovers" from one market to another. But the existence of inventories undermines both of these. For example, in simple disequilibrium models such as Barro–Grossman (1976), a firm facing a sales constraint due to a non-market-clearing price sells *and produces* the minimum of its notional supply and the constraint itself. If the constraint is binding, therefore, it cuts back on production, and hence on employment. So excess supply in the good market "spills over" into the labor market.

Now suppose that output is storable, so that production and sales can diverge. A firm confronted with a short-run sales constraint may find it optimal to produce more than it can sell, adding the un-sold balance to its inventories. So output is not the minimum of "notional" supply and sales. To the extent that firms provide *more* than the "min condition" dictates, any spillover of excess supply of goods into excess supply of labor is curtailed. Thus inventories provide a buffer stock – or, as Leijonhufvud (1973) put it, a "corridor" that limits the applicability of standard disequilibrium analysis to instances of truly severe shocks.

Recognition of the buffer-stock role of inventories also gets rid of the most embarrassing empirical prediction of the Barro–Grossman model. Under conditions of excess demand in the goods market, Barro– Grossman workers, unable to purchase all the goods they want, curtail their supply of labor. Thus excess demand for goods spills over into excess demand for labor. *Via* this mechanism, an increase in aggregate demand, starting from a position of equilibrium, will actually *reduce* output. With buffer stocks of inventories, of course, only very extreme demand shocks will render workers unable to buy the goods they want. As long as we remain in Leijonhufvud's corridor, increases in aggregate demand increase output regardless of whether the economy is initially in a state of equilibrium, of excess demand, or of excess supply (see Blinder (1980)).

1.5 INVENTORIES AND "NEW CLASSICAL" MODELS

Recent developments in macro theory have been dominated by the new classical models. The basic ingredients of these models are continuously clearing markets, rational expectations, and some variant of the Lucas supply function:

$$Y_t = K_t + \gamma(p_t - {}_{t-1}p_t) + e_t \qquad (1.2)$$

where p_t is (the *log* of) the price level, ${}_{t-1}p_t$ is its expectation formulated at time $t - 1$, and e_t is a white noise disturbance. Such models do not exhibit serially correlated output disturbances unless we assume some sort of adjustment costs or accelerator mechanism for the capital stock, and they imply that fully anticipated monetary policy has no real effects.

I think it fair to say that these models have not paid much attention to the fact that many outputs are storable. Consider what happens if we maintain the assumption of continuous market clearance, but replace (1.2) by a supply function augmented along the lines of the microfoundations suggested in Section 1.2:[5]

$$Y_t = K_t + \gamma(p_t - {}_{t-1}p_t) + \lambda(N_{t+1}^* - N_t) + e_t, \quad 0 < \lambda < 1 \qquad (1.3)$$

where N_{t+1}^* connotes the desired level of inventories. Note that (1.3) obeys the principal implication of (1.1a). Similarly, assume that in accord with (1.1c):

$$N_{t+1} - N_t = \theta(N_{t+1}^* - N_t) - \phi(p_t - {}_{t-1}p_t) + v_t, \quad 0 < \theta < 1 \qquad (1.4)$$

In this model, it is easy to see that unanticipated price-level shocks give rise to serially correlated output disturbances. A positive price surprise of one unit initially raises output by γ and reduces inventories by ϕ. If there are no further shocks, the resulting inventory shortage will be corrected gradually according to the adjustment parameter θ; and so long as inventories remain below N^* output will remain above its full-information (natural) level.

Anticipated monetary policy will have real effects *if* desired inventories are sensitive to real interest rates *and* real interest rates are sensitive to anticipated changes in money.

In addition to these theoretical propositions, (1.3) and (1.4) have implications for empirical work on the effects of unanticipated money. According to the model, the lagged effects of unanticipated money on output that Barro (1977) has found are entirely due to inventory (and unfilled orders) discrepancies caused by past unanticipated money. Empirical evidence on this implication is mixed. (See Haraf (1980), Sheffrin (1980), and Gordon (1980).)

Finally, consider the possibility that markets do not clear because prices are "sticky" in some sense. A well-known paper by McCallum (1977) pointed out that some types of price rigidity leave intact the characteristic prediction of new classical models that only unanticipated money has real effects. However, Frydman (1981) has criticized McCallum's model for foundering on the logical pitfall mentioned at the start of Section 1.3: it fails to take account of the effects of inventories on production decisions (in accord with (1.1a)). Frydman shows that a more appropriate treatment of inventories (along the lines of (1.3)) leads to the conclusion that anticipated monetary policy has real effects when prices are sticky.

NOTES

1. The theoretical analysis of this paper pertains exclusively to inventories of finished goods. Different analyses would be necessary for inventories of inputs and works in progress.
2. This negative relationship between inventories and their shadow value is slightly more subtle than might be expected. Under perfect competition, the shadow value of inventories can never diverge from the market price because firms can always sell *or buy* unlimited quantities at the going price. I therefore assume differentiated products with downward-sloping demand curves. For further details, see my 1978 paper.
3. This implication is brought out by Louis Phlips, P. Reagan, and Y. Amihud and H. Mendelson.
4. A more precise statement and a proof can be found in my 1982 paper (reprinted here as Chapter 4).
5. The following paragraphs summarize the findings of my 1981 article with Stanley Fischer (reprinted here as Chapter 3).

REFERENCES

Amihud, Y. and H. Mendelson (1980) "Monopoly under uncertainty: the enigma of price rigidity," mimeo (March).

Barro, R. J. (1977) "Unanticipated money growth and unemployment in the United States," *American Economic Review* (March), vol. 67, pp. 101–15.

Barro, R. J. and H. I. Grossman (1976) *Money, Employment and Inflation*, Cambridge: Cambridge University Press.

Blinder, A. S. (1977) "A difficulty with Keynesian models of aggregate demand," in A. S. Blinder and P. Friedman (eds), *Natural Resources, Uncertainty and General Equilibrium Systems: Essays in Memory of Rafael Lusky*, New York: Academic Press.

Blinder, A. S. (1978) "Inventories and the demand for labor," mimeo, Princeton University (March).

Blinder, A. S. (1980) "Inventories in the Keynesian macro model," *Kyklos*.

Blinder, A. S. (1982) "Inventories and sticky prices: more on the microfoundations of macroeconomics," *American Economic Review* (June), vol. 72, pp. 334–48.

Blinder, A. S. and S. Fischer (1981) "Inventories, rational expectations, and the business cycle," *Journal of Monetary Economics*, vol. 8, pp. 277–304.

Frydman, R. (1981) "A note on sluggish price adjustments and the effectiveness of monetary policy under rational expectations," *Journal of Money, Credit, and Banking*, vol. 13, no. 1 (February), pp. 94–102.

Gordon, R. J. (1980) "Discussion of William Haraf, 'Tests of a natural rate model with persistent effects of aggregate demand shocks'," paper presented to the National Bureau of Economic Research, Conference on Inventories, Princeton (March).

Haraf, W. (1980) "Tests of a natural rate model with persistent effects of aggregate demand shocks," paper presented to the National Bureau of Economic Research, Conference on Inventories. Princeton (March).

Leijonhufvud, A. (1973) "Effective demand failures," *Swedish Journal of Economics* (March), vol. 75, pp. 27–48.

McCallum, B. T. (1977) "Price-level stickiness and the feasibility of monetary stabilization policy with rational expectations," *Journal of Political Economy* (June), vol. 85, pp. 627–34.

Phlips, L. (1980) "Intertemporal price discrimination and sticky prices," *Quarterly Journal of Economics* (May), vol. 92, pp. 525–42.

Reagan, P. B. (1980) "Inventories and asymmetries in price adjustment," mimeo, Cambridge, Mass.: MIT.

Samuelson, P. A. (1947) *Foundations of Economic Analysis*, Cambridge, Mass.: Harvard University Press.

Sheffrin, S. M. (1980) "Inventories, rational expectations and aggregate supply: some estimates," paper presented to the National Bureau of Economic Research, Conference on Inventories, Princeton (March).

2 · INVENTORIES IN THE KEYNESIAN MACRO MODEL

2.1 MOTIVATION AND RELATION TO OTHER LITERATURE

If a man from Mars visited this planet and spent a year or so reading all the macroeconomic literature of the past 15–20 years, he would not come away feeling that inventories are of much importance. If we then gave him five minutes with the National Income and Product Accounts of the United States, he would quickly conclude that there was something lacking in his education. Inventories are important. Indeed, as a rough generalization, changes in the rate of real inventory investment have accounted for approximately 70 percent of the decline in real GNP during a typical postwar recession (see Table 2.1). It would seem likely, therefore, that inventories play a crucial role in the propagation of business cycles.

If our Martian read some of our leading elementary textbooks, he would again find a prominent role assigned to inventories as the principal force driving national income to its "equilibrium" level – the level at which there is no undesired inventory accumulation or decumulation.[1] But if he tried to pursue this line of reasoning in the more advanced textbooks, he would find little more.[2] And if he sought after discussions of inventories in the theoretical literature, he would come up nearly empty-handed.[3] Inventories, in a word, have been neglected by macroeconomic theorists.

In the period immediately following the publication of *The General Theory*, there was a flurry of theoretical work on inventories, culminating in Metzler's (1941) classic paper. Working with the simplest possible difference equation system, Metzler pointed out that inventory investment could conceivably destabilize an otherwise stable system. This paper extends Metzler's line of

I have benefited from the helpful comments of Costas Azariadis, William Branson, Jonathan Eaton, Ray Fair, Stanley Fischer, Robert Gordon, Herschel Grossman, Dwight Jaffee, Louis Maccini, Dennis Snower, Robert Solow, Yoram Weiss and an anonymous referee on earlier drafts. Financial support from the National Science Foundation and the Institute for Advanced Studies, Jerusalem, is gratefully acknowledged.

Table 2.1 Changes in GNP and in inventory investment in the post-war recessions

(1) Dates of contraction		(2)	(3)	(4)
Peak	Trough	Decline in real GNP[a]	Decline in inventory investment[a]	Col. (3) as a percentage of col. (2)
1948:4	1949:4	$ 6.7	$13.0	194%
1953:2	1954:2	$20.6	$10.2	50%
1957:3	1958:1	$22.2	$10.5	47%
1960:1	1960:4	$ 8.8	$10.5	119%
1969:3	1970:4	$12.0	$10.1	84%
1973:4	1975:1	$71.0	$44.8	63%

Note:
(a) In billions of 1972 dollars.
Source: The National Income and Product Accounts of the United States, 1929–74, and *Survey of Current Business.*

reasoning by showing that, in a modern Keynesian model, including inventories:

(a) a well-known condition for stability of a monetary economy due to Cagan (1956) becomes stricter on account of inventories;
(b) inventories add an additional stability condition to the model – a condition that is not innocuous since it could be violated under plausible parameter values.

But while Metzler stressed the *destabilizing* role of inventories, many other authors have stressed their *stabilizing* role. Obviously, inventories of finished goods give firms flexibility either to meet abnormally high demand by selling more than they produce, or to cope with abnormally low demand by producing more than they sell. Thus production and employment can be stabilized relative to demand when output is storable. It seems particularly important to recall this role of inventories in light of the recent work on "spillovers" by Barro and Grossman (1971, 1976) and others.

One of the bases of the Barro–Grossman analysis is that, when sticky wages and prices prevent the attainment of the full Walrasian general equilibrium in the short run, the actual quantity transacted in a market normally will be the *minimum* of supply and demand. This so-called "min condition" is based on the principle of voluntary exchange, but retains its plausibility only if output is nonstorable.[4] Consider, for example, the Barro–Grossman generalized excess supply scenario. If firms cannot sell all the output they would like to, they react by reducing production and firing workers. In this way, excess supply in the goods market "spills over" into the labor market as well. But what if output is storable at moderate costs? It seems unlikely, under these circumstances, that production cutbacks and layoffs would be a rational reaction to moderate short-run gluts in the product market. Instead, firms can – and apparently do –maintain production and store their excess output for subsequent sale. Only if poor sales performance persist for some time, or are extremely large, do firms reduce their work forces. In this way, inventories limit the spillover of excess supply from the product market to the labor markets to instances of extreme drops in demand.

Or consider the Barro–Grossman scenario of generalized excess demand. In this case, workers who are unable to purchase the commodities they desire (because these commodities are in excess demand) react by reducing their supply of labor. Why work when (at the margin) there are no goods to buy? Thus excess demand in the goods market spills over into the labor market. But once again, barring generalized stock-outs, this will not happen in an economy in which there are inventories of goods. There may well be a flow excess demand for goods; but, at least for a while, firms can meet this excess demand out of inventories. Thus it seems unlikely that excess demand for goods would lead to a drop in labor supply, except in extreme circumstances.[5] It is worth pointing out that this particular spillover mechanism accounts for what may be the most empirically distressing implication of the Barro–Grossman model: that positive shocks to aggregate commodity demand, starting from a position of equilibrium, will *reduce* real output.

The model considered here is very different from the Barro–Grossman model, though at least one of its basic aims is identical: to explain the link between aggregate demand and real output. For example, the "min condition" for the goods market does not appear here because it makes little sense in the presence of inventories. Instead, I assume that consumers always purchase their quantity demanded. Stockouts at the aggregate level are ignored. When there is excess supply, firms add the excess to their inventories; and when there is excess demand, firms meet this demand by drawing down inventories. In either case, the resulting inventory imbalance induces firms to adjust their production and employment decisions; but the adjustments are gradual, so the sharp corners of Barro and Grossman are smoothed out.[6]

Finally, since the model proposed here offers an alternative way to forge the link between aggregate demand and real output, mention should be made of the currently most popular way of doing so. In standard Keynesian analysis, money wages are assumed fixed in the short run, so higher prices (caused by higher aggregate demand) encourage employment and output by *lowering real wages*.[7] By contrast, in the main model presented here, money wages move promptly to clear the labor market, and real wages actually move *procyclically*. I make the assumption that money wages are fully flexible not for its empirical validity, but to illustrate that inventories provide a link between demand and production that does not rely on wage rigidities. Later in the paper, the assumption of instantly flexible wages is replaced by an expectations-augmented Phillips curve and a "min condition" for the labor market. It is shown that the analysis, while greatly complicated, is not altered in any essential way by these changes. In particular, the conclusion that wages move procyclically is maintained.

The plan of the paper is as follows. The next section offers a general discussion of the motives for holding inventories, noting how each motive bears on the specification of macro models. Then, choosing one particular rationale for inventories, I develop and analyze in Section 2.3 a complete macro model in which all markets "clear." Section 2.4 discusses the modifications required when the labor market does not clear, and sketches how the analysis is affected. Section 2.5 offers some brief concluding remarks.

2.2 THE SPECIFICATION OF INVENTORY BEHAVIOR

Where should inventories be brought into conventional macro-economic models? The answer depends on whether inventories are inputs or outputs, and on why firms hold them; but a wide variety of micro models suggest that higher inventory stocks lead to lower current output.

Among the major motives for holding inventories that appear in the literature is *improved production scheduling* (see, for example, Holt *et al.* (1960)). The idea is that multiproduct firms can operate more efficiently if inventories give them flexibility in scheduling production runs. So this suggests that the stock of inventories, N, should enter the production function as another factor of production in addition to employment, E: $y = f(E, N), f_N > 0$. In a model like this, inventories could either be inputs (i.e., raw materials and intermediate goods) or outputs (i.e., finished goods). The crucial question is whether and how N affects the marginal productivity of labor. The basic rationale seems to suggest that inventories raise labor's productivity; and, if so, this would stimulate employment demand. But it should also be true that, when the stock of inventories rises, the incentive to raise it further by producing diminishes (as long as there are diminishing returns to inventories). Thus, both the costs (*via* higher productivity) and the benefits of production are reduced by rising N, with consequently ambiguous effects on output.

Other models of inventory behavior seem less ambiguous regarding the effect of inventories on production. For example, it is commonly hypothesized that firms hold inventories as a *buffer stock* in the face of fluctuating demand (see, for example, Mills (1962)). In that case, inventories are probably outputs which do not directly affect the production function. Instead higher N reduces the probability of having a stock-out. Given diminishing returns to inventory-holding, this presumably leads to *lower* production.

A closely related motive for holding inventories is *speculation on future price movements*. Indeed, this is almost indistinguishable from the buffer stock motive in that expectations of high future prices relative to costs (the speculative motive) and large future sales (the buffer-stock motive) amount to more or less the same thing.

While these last two motives amount to using inventories to *smooth* production relative to demand, some firms may wish to do just the opposite: to *bunch* production relative to sales. This could happen where dramatically increasing returns to scale dictate that production be done in large "production runs," which are then put into inventory and gradually sold. In this *production run* model, it seems fairly clear that excessively high inventories will induce a postponement of the next production run, and hence a reduction in "average" output and employment over an interval of time.

Still another motive for holding output inventories, suggested by Maccini (1977) among others, is that high inventory stocks may stimulate a single firm's demand by *reducing delivery lags*. In this case, it seems appropriate to omit N from the production function, but include it in the firm's demand function. But it is not clear that N should have a similar stimulative effect on aggregate demand.

Others have suggested that input inventories are held in order to *economize on purchasing costs*. This could be either because there is a fixed cost to purchasing inputs – the assumption that underlies "optimal lot size" models, or because firms face a rising supply price of inputs which makes it economical to smooth input purchases relative to input usage.[8] In such a case, the rate at which inventories are *used* should appear in the production function, while the rate at which they are *purchased* should depend on the existing stock.

What effects, then, should inventories have on aggregate demand? Presumably, all the models agree that *desired inventory investment* should be a decreasing function of N. But there is no persuasive reason to think that N has any direct effects on the other components of aggregate demand – what are called *final sales*.

What about aggregate supply? Considering first output inventories, the production-scheduling motive suggests that $\partial y / \partial N$ might conceivably be positive. But the other motives seem strongly to suggest the opposite: the higher the level of inventory stocks, the less the firm will be inclined to produce. One would also expect high inventories to lead to price cuts.

But input inventories would have different effects. Imagine a firm whose inputs are storable, but whose outputs are not. If it finds itself with too many inventories, it will have an incentive to raise production (and employment) and cut prices. If it can store both inputs and outputs, the implication for production decisions becomes unclear. It depends on the relative costs and benefits of inventorying inputs versus outputs.

Finally, the nature of inventories has implications for the accounting identity governing inventory accumulation or decumulation, $\dot{N}$. For example, if inventories are outputs, then $\dot{N}$ is the difference between production and sales, so a rise in production (other things equal) raises $\dot{N}$. But if inventories are inputs, then N is the difference between input purchases and input usage, which will fall when production rises.

The macroeconomic model presented here is based on a very specific micro model of inventory behavior which I have presented in another paper (Blinder (1978)). The model is one of *output* inventories held for reasons of *anticipated price appreciation* or, what amounts to the same thing, as a buffer stock held because of anticipated fluctuations in demand. As I show in that paper, the level of inventories affects employment demand (and hence output) negatively:

$$E^d = E^d(w, N)$$

$$E^d_w, E^d_N < 0$$

This function has the property that $E^d(w, N*)$, where $N*$ is the desired or optimal level of inventories and w is the real wage, is equal to the inverse of the marginal productivity schedule: $f'^{-1}(w)$. For higher inventories, the labor demand schedule lies below the marginal productivity schedule; and for lower inventories, it lies above.

While I have derived it in a very specific context, let me try to explain why I believe that such a labor demand function would arise under quite general circumstances. Consider any of a family of models where the firm maximizes the discounted present value of its profits subject to (among other things) a constraint that inventory change equals production minus sales:

$$\dot{N} = f(E, \ldots) - x$$

Any of a variety of variables could enter $f(\cdot)$ without affecting the argument; similarly, sales or price could be endogenous or exogenous for present purposes. The Hamiltonian for such a problem would look like this:

$$H(E, \ldots) = \text{sales revenues} - wE - \text{other costs} + \lambda[f(E, \ldots) - x]$$

where again I need not specify the nature of sales revenues or nonwage costs. Here λ is the *shadow value of inventories*, and a well-known result of optimal control theory is that:

$$\frac{\partial J}{\partial N_0} = \lambda_0$$

where J is maximized (with respect to E and other variables) profits, and N_0 is the initial stock of inventories.

The first order condition for optimal employment is $f_E(E, \ldots) = w/\lambda$ at every instant, which has two important implications as follows:

1.   In making *production* (as opposed to sales) decisions, the firm compares its costs with λ, not with the market price. This is because it is deciding whether to turn inputs into *inventories*. Then, in deciding whether to *sell* out of inventories, it will compare λ with the market price.[9]

2. Optimal E is a decreasing function of w and an increasing function of λ. But this means that we can derive the labor demand function mentioned above by showing that λ_0 is a decreasing function of N_0. Now note that:

$$\frac{\partial \lambda_0}{\partial N_0} = \frac{\partial^2 J}{\partial N_0^2}$$

and that $\partial^2 J / \partial N_0^2$ must be negative in a wide variety of problems. (This is just a statement of diminishing returns, and is, in fact, a sufficient condition for a maximizing program to exist.)

While the labor demand function used here is therefore quite general, note that the production-scheduling model raises the possibility that $\partial y / \partial N > 0$. It should come as no surprise that models with output inventories normally will be stable only if a rise in N reduces $\dot{N} = y - x$, where x is final sales. Thus the stability of the model hinges precariously on the effects of inventories on production decisions – a question that cannot be answered by microeconomic theory, and that has barely been investigated in empirical macroeconomics.[10]

2.3 A MACROECONOMIC MODEL WITH INVENTORIES

2.3.1 Specification of the model

The demand side of the model is quite standard, except that recognition of inventories requires that a distinction be drawn between output and final sales. Thus, instead of an *IS* curve, the following expression describes real final demand:

$$x = c[y - t(y), r] + g \tag{2.1}$$

where y is GNP (or national income), $t(y)$ is real taxes, r is the real interest rate, c is real private demand, and g is real government demand. The capital stock is ignored on the grounds that it can be treated (roughly) as constant. Since the period of time that I am concerned with is quite short, this seems more legitimate than it is in many other contexts.

The demand side is completed by an *LM* curve based on the strict transactionist view of the demand for money:[11]

$$M/P = L(r + \pi, y) \tag{2.2}$$

where M is the nominal money stock, P is the price level, and π is the expected rate of inflation. Making the distinction between x and y raises interesting questions about which is the appropriate transaction variable in the demand function for money. But since this is not the subject of this paper I sweep these issues under the rug and adopt the conventional variable: gross national product. Notice that (2.2) embodies the assumption that r adjusts instantly to maintain money-market equilibrium, but (2.1) implies no such assumption about the goods market. When inventories are changing ($x \neq y$), the system is off the *IS* curve, which is:

$$y = c[y - t(y), r] + g \tag{2.1'}$$

What I call an *aggregate demand curve* can be derived from (2.1) and (2.2). First invert (2.2) to obtain:

$$r = R(y, m) - \pi \tag{2.3}$$

$$R_y = -\frac{L_y}{L_r} > 0, \quad R_m = \frac{1}{L_r} < 0$$

where $m = M/P$ is the real money stock. Then substitute (2.3) into (2.1) to obtain:

$$x = c[y - t(y), R(y, m) - \pi] + g$$

This can be written:

$$x = D(y; m, \pi, g) \tag{2.4}$$

where the function $D(\cdot)$ has the following derivatives:

$$D_y = c_y(1 - t') + c_r R_y$$

$$D_m = c_r R_m > 0$$

$$D_\pi = -c_r > 0$$

$$D_g = 1$$

The conventional assumption in *IS–LM* analysis that D_y is a positive number less than unity will be reflected in what follows. Aggregate demand is identified with sales by assuming that generalized stockouts do not occur.

The supply side of the model consists of an equation that says that the labor market clears given the (possibly disequilibrium) state of inventories:

$$E^d(w, N) = E^s(w) \tag{2.5}$$

$$E_w^s \geq 0$$

and a production function:[12]

$$y = f[E^s(w)] \tag{2.6}$$

These two equations are solved very simply for an *aggregate supply function*:

$$y = Y(N) \tag{2.7}$$

where:

$$Y_N \equiv f'(E)E_N^d \frac{E_w^s}{E_w^s - E_w^d} < 0$$

Given predetermined values for the three state variables: N, m, and π, equations (2.4) and (2.7) determine the values of x and y for any given g. Fig. 2.1 depicts one such solution on a standard "Keynesian cross" diagram. Equation (2.7) already tells us how y depends on the state variables. To obtain a similar solution function for x, substitute (2.7) into (2.4) to get:

$$x = X(N, m, \pi; g) \tag{2.8}$$

where:

$$X_N = D_y Y_N < 0$$
$$X_z = D_z, z = m, \pi, g$$

Thus, *initially* monetary or fiscal policy affects x but not y.

The position of the economy defined by (2.7) and (2.8) will not in general be an equilibrium because one or more of the state variables will change. Changes in the stock of inventories are governed by a straightforward accounting identity:

$$\dot{N} = y - x \tag{2.9}$$

Changes in the expected rate of inflation are assumed to be adaptive:[13]

$$\dot{\pi} = \beta(\dot{P}/P - \pi) \tag{2.10}$$

$$\beta > 0$$

Finally, since I assume that budget deficits are bond-financed, changes in real

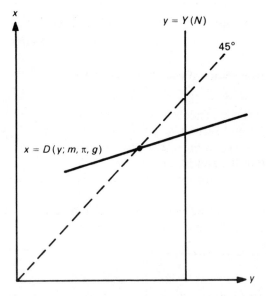

Fig. 2.1 Aggregate demand and aggregate supply

balances happen either (a) abruptly due to an open-market operation or (b) smoothly due to changes in the price level. Thus, *except at instants when there are open-market operations,*

$$\dot{m} = -m(\dot{P}/P)$$

This requires an equation for price dynamics, for which the following seems suitable:

$$\dot{P}/P = \pi + \Theta(N^* - N) \tag{2.11}$$

$$\Theta > 0$$

where N^* is the specific (optimal) level of inventories that makes $E^d(w, N^*)$ coincide with the marginal productivity schedule. In general, as shown in Blinder (1978), N^* would depend on the production function, the nature of inventory holding costs, the entire future path of expected prices (and sales constraints, if there are any), and the real rate of interest. However, I ignore all this and treat N^* as a constant in the *short run*.[14] Equation (2.11) has empirical support in that unfilled orders are the typical indicator of excess demand in product markets in recent empirical price equations (see, for example, Gordon (1975)). And for firms that *produce to order*, unfilled orders play the same role as inventories play for firms that *produce to stock*. Indeed, unfilled orders can be viewed usefully as negative inventories (see Maccini (1976)). From (2.11), the equation for changes in the real money supply follows immediately. Except at moments of open-market operations:

$$\dot{m} = -\pi m - \Theta m(N^* - N) \tag{2.12}$$

Equilibrium occurs only when (2.9), (2.10) and (2.12) are all equal to zero. That is, when GNP equals final sales, expectations are correct, and inflation is zero.[15]

2.3.2 Comparative statics of equilibrium positions

There seem to be three interesting questions to ask about what policy variables (M or g) do to endogenous variables like y or w. First, what are the instantaneous effects? Second, what are the equilibrium effects? Third, what do the paths look like in the interim period? The first question has already been answered: in the first instant, a rise in g or M increases x, but has no effect on either y or w (or on the inflation rate). I turn next to the second question.

Using (2.7) and (2.8), and imposing the requirements for equilibrium, the following equations define steady states of the model:

$$Y(N) = X(N, m, \pi; g) \quad (\dot{N} = 0)$$

$$\dot{P}/P = \pi \quad (\dot{\pi} = 0)$$

$$\pi = \Theta(N - N^*) \quad (\dot{m} = 0)$$

But the last two, in conjunction with the price equation (2.11), require that $\pi = 0$ and $N = N^*$ in equilibrium.

Thus the equilibrium version of the model can be represented by the standard *IS* curve, (2.1′); the *LM* curve with $\pi = 0$:

$$M/P = L(r, y) \tag{2.2′}$$

and a classical labor market:

$$w = f'(E^d), E^s = E^s(w), E^d = E^s$$

In its most compact form, equilibrium is defined by the single equation:

$$Y(N^*) = X(N^*, m, 0; g) \tag{2.13}$$

Thus, $y^* = Y(N^*)$ is the "natural rate" of output, and $w^* = w(N^*)$ is the equilibrium real wage. Neither of them can be *permanently* affected by policy. Nor can x, since $x = y$ in equilibrium.

2.3.3 Dynamic adjustment paths

I turn next to the dynamic paths of the important macroeconomic variables, deferring for the moment the issue of whether the dynamic system is stable. Since I ignore many variables that change in the long run, it is these short-run responses – not the steady states – that are of greatest interest.

Figure 2.2 shows the model in an initial position of equilibrium at point A. Here $x = y$, so N is unchanging; inflationary expectations are correct and equal to zero; and real balances are constant. Now suppose there is a dose of expansionary monetary $(dM > 0)$ or fiscal $(dg > 0)$ policy, shifting the demand curve upwards from D_0 to D_1.

Initially, the economy's position shifts upwards to B: sales are raised, but GNP is not. But at B, inventories are disappearing. Consequently, the supply curve starts moving to the right (see equation (2.7)). At the same time, two effects start working on the demand curve. In a stable system, the more important of these is that (2.11) implies that inflation begins, eroding real balances, and causing the demand curve to shift downwards toward D_2. The second effect is that inflation raises inflationary expectations (by (2.10)), and this reduces the real interest rate (by (2.3)), which stimulates spending. The diagram assumes that the former effect dominates, so that the position of the economy moves towards the south east, as indicated by the arrow emanating from point B.

At some point – indicated in the diagram by point C – the supply and demand curves $(S_2$ and $D_2)$ intersect on the 45° line. At this moment, the inventory decumulation is halted, and inventories begin to be replaced. So the supply curve starts shifting back toward its original position. However, while they are *rising*, inventories remain *low*, so the impetus for inflation remains. Prices keep rising while real output falls. In fact, for a period,

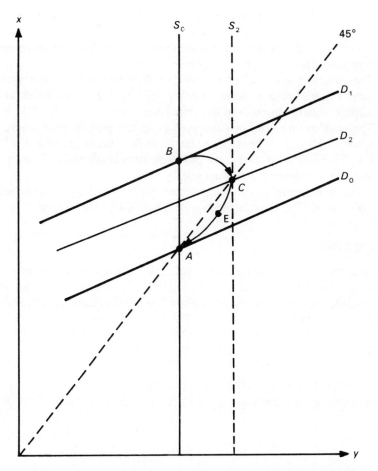

Fig. 2.2 Dynamic adjustment path to a rise in aggregate demand

inflation is *accelerating* while output is falling.[16] Whether or not this is to be called a phase of "stagflation" or not is a matter of terminological dispute. But it does create an interval of time during which changes in unemployment and changes in inflation are positively correlated – an upward sloping "Phillips curve," if you will.

Before turning to the conditions under which this stable scenario actually obtains, let me outline some of the observable consequences of the model. Following a stimulus to aggregate demand the following happens:

1. Final sales rise quickly to a peak,[17] and then decline to their original level. GNP rises much more slowly to a peak, and also declines. So the composition of GNP between final sales and inventory change varies dramatically over the cycle.

2.   Both employment and real wages follow the path of GNP, rising to a peak and then returning to their equilibrium levels. Thus, in contrast to the traditional Keynesian and search theoretic models, real wages move procyclically.

3.   The *trough* in the *level* of inventories (N) coincides with the *peak* in output (both occur at point C in Fig. 2.2). As Fig. 2.3 shows, N and y display *negative* correlation over the cycle.

4.   The peak in inventory *investment* ($\dot{N}$) lags the peak in production. (In terms of Fig. 2.2, $\dot{N}$ peaks at point E, while y peaks at point C.)[18] As Fig. 2.3 indicates, $\dot{N}$ and y are *positively* correlated, while $\dot{N}$ and $\dot{y}$ are *negatively* correlated over the cycle.

5.   Prices rise throughout the adjustment period, reaching a permanently higher level. The peak in the rate of inflation lags the peak in GNP.

2.3.4 Stability

The scenario just outlined is, of course, of interest only if the model is dynamically stable. A formal stability analysis of this system is relegated to the appendix, where it is shown that one of the three necessary and sufficient conditions for stability is:

$$1 + \beta \frac{L_r}{m} > \frac{\beta}{X_N - Y_N} \tag{2.14}$$

The right-hand side of (2.14) is a positive number which is smaller: (a) the slower the speed of adjustment of inflationary expectations; and (b) the *more*

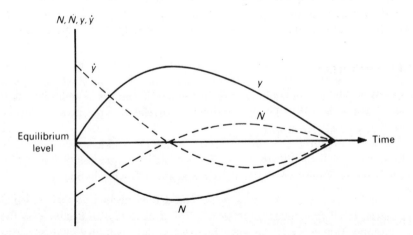

Fig. 2.3   Time patterns of output and inventories and their rates of change

negative is $Y_N - X_N$. The left-hand side is familiar from the work of Cagan (1956). Cagan found that his model (a full employment model where the "interest rate" variable in the demand for money was just π) would be stable if and only if:

$$1 + \beta \frac{L_r}{m} > 0 \tag{2.14'}$$

Here I require instead (2.14), which is stronger than (2.14').[19]

Notice the fundamental role played by Y_N. Should $Y_N - X_N = (1 - Dy)Y_N$ be zero or positive – a possibility raised by the production-scheduling model – the model is definitely unstable. Even if it is negative, the model will still be unstable unless $Y_N - X_N$ is large enough, where the precise meaning of "large enough" is spelled out in (2.14).

2.4 A MODEL WITH A NONCLEARING LABOR MARKET

The model presented in the last section includes two important features that I am unhappy about. First, the assumption that the labor market always clears in the short run means that the labor market adjusts to shocks much faster than the goods market. Second, the "Keynesian" short-run response of output to stabilization policy can occur *only* if the aggregate supply curve of labor slopes upward. Both assumptions are open to doubt, to say the least. But both can be avoided by assuming instead that the labor market does not clear, and instead wages adjust to the discrepancy between supply and demand for labour. In this section, I outline such a model. Since its formal analysis is quite complicated, involving four differential equations (for $\dot{N}$, $\dot{P}$, $\dot{\pi}$, and $\dot{w}$), interesting qualitative results are obtainable only if I suppress price expectations and assume that π is *always* at its steady state value of zero.

2.4.1 Specification

I specify a nonclearing labor market in the usual way. Actual employment is determined by the principle of voluntary exchange:

$$E = \min [E^d(w, N), E^s(w)] \tag{2.15}$$

where now the $E^s(w)$ function may well have zero or negligible slope. The production function is written:

$$y = f(E) \tag{2.6'}$$

The aggregate supply function defined by (2.15) and (2.6'),

$$y = f[\min(E^d, E^s)] = y(N, w) \tag{2.16}$$

depends on which regime we are in. Specifically:

$$y_N = E_N^d f' < 0 \quad \text{if} \quad E^d < E^s$$
$$y_N = 0 \qquad\qquad \text{if} \quad E^s < E^d$$
$$y_w = E_w^d f' < 0 \quad \text{if} \quad E^d < E^s$$
$$y_w = E_w^s f' > 0 \quad \text{if} \quad E^s < E^d$$

I also require a specification of wage dynamics, for which the following Phillips curve model seems appropriate:

$$\dot{W}/W = \pi + \gamma[E^d(w, N) - E^s(w)] \tag{2.17}$$

where W is the *money* wage and γ is a positive constant. Since I am restricting my attention to cases where π is zero, this reduces to:

$$\dot{W}/W = \gamma(E^d - E^s)$$

so that by subtracting $\dot{P}/P$ (using equation (2.11) with $\pi = 0$) I arrive at a law of motion for the real wage:

$$\dot{w}/w = \gamma[E^d(w, N) - E^s(w)] + \Theta(N - N^*) \tag{2.18}$$

Along with equations (2.9) and (2.12) for $\dot{N}$ and $\dot{m}$) of the clearing model, this constitutes the dynamics of the disequilibrium model.

The aggregate demand curve (2.4) is exactly the same as in the clearing model, except that expected inflation is now constrained to be zero. So the new solution function for x:

$$x = x(N, m, w; g) \tag{2.19}$$

is defined by:

$$x(N, m, w; g) = D[y(N, w); m, 0, g]$$

so that

$$x_N = D_y y_N$$

$$x_m = D_m$$

$$x_w = D_y y_w$$

$$x_g = 1$$

This completes the specification of the non-clearing version of the model.

2.4.2 Steady states and stability

What can we hope to learn from such a complicated model? First consider the steady state properties, which hold also in a more elaborate version of the model in which the adaptive inflationary expectations equation is maintained. As before, (2.10) implies that actual and expected inflation are equal, so that (2.11) implies that $N = N^*$. Then (2.12) implies that the equilibrium inflation rate is zero, and (2.18) implies that the labor market clears: $E^d(w, N^*) = E^s(w)$. This equation pins down the equilibrium real wage, and hence the equilibrium values of E, y and x, and allows no effect of either policy variable. The rest of the model (the full-employment *IS–LM* model) determines r and P as usual. Nothing very interesting here.

Of greater interest are the short-run responses of the variables to shocks. But before enquiring into these dynamics, it is important to know what parameter configurations render the nonclearing model stable. Appendix 2.1 shows that stability requires:

$$\Theta + \gamma E_N^d < 0 \tag{2.20}$$

which turns out to be critical to the cyclical response of real wages (see below). Hereafter I assume that (2.20) holds. Notice once again that this is an assumption that inventory effects on production are "strong enough."

2.4.3 Short-run dynamic responses

Given an initial state of disequilibrium in the labor market, what are the effects of stabilization policy on employment and wages? The answer is obtained with the aid of Fig. 2.4. Here $E^s(w)$ is the labor supply schedule, $E^d(w, N_0)$ is the labor demand schedule, and the initial real wage is assumed to be w_0 – which leads to an *excess supply* of labor (see point *B*). The initial level of inventories, N_0, could be above or below the optimal level, N^*, and, depending on where we are in the cycle, N could be either rising or falling. Irrespective of this, any increase in g or M will reduce $\dot{N}(t)$ for some interval of time, thus pushing N down *relative to what it otherwise would have been*. This is shown in Fig. 2.4 by an *upward* shift in the demand function for labor from $E^d(w, N_0)$ to $E^d(w, N_1)$ (where $N_1 < N_0$).

That the expansionary stabilization policy has two distinct effects on *the rate of change of real wages* can be seen from equation (2.18). First, a lower N raises $\dot{w}/w$ through the first term in (2.18). This represents a "tightening" of the labor market (see equation (2.17)). Second, a lower N reduces $\dot{w}/w$ through the second term in (2.18). This happens because smaller inventories lead to faster increases in product prices (see equation (2.11)).

But which effect dominates? The answer follows from stability condition (2.20): in a stable system, the first effect must be stronger so a reduction in inventories leads to an acceleration in real wage growth in the short run. Figure 2.4 shows what happens to output. In the absence of policy, wages would have fallen to some level like w_1 at time t_1, and the position of the economy would have been point *C*, with employment E_1. Expansionary policy pushes the labor demand curve outward and retards the fall in wages. Wages fall only to w'_1, and the position of the economy at time t_1 is point *D*

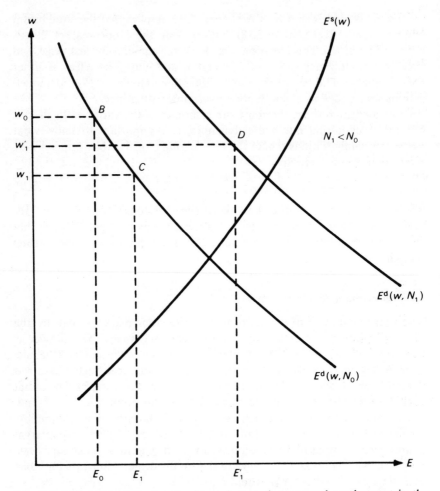

Fig. 2.4   Effects of an increase in demand on real wages and employment in the disequilibrium model

instead. The effect of policy on employment is, therefore, $E_1' - E_1$, a positive number.

Notice that this model generates an unambiguous prediction about the short-run behavior of real wages, whereas in the Barro–Grossman analysis "it all depends" on whether prices or money wages react more expeditiously to disequilibrium. How have I avoided this indeterminacy and obtained an answer that does not depend on relative adjustment speeds? The answer is that the short-run movement of w *does* still depend on relative adjustment speeds, but stability condition (2.20) places a quantitative restriction on γ and Θ that enables me to determine the sign of $\dot{w}$ in the short run.[20]

Precisely analogous arguments can be used to show that employment and wages also rise when expansionary policies are applied under conditions of excess demand or of equilibrium. In each case, a stimulus to aggregate demand leads to an interval of time in which $\dot{N}$ is more *negative* and $\dot{w}/w$ is more *positive* than it otherwise would have been. It can also be shown that output rises. Thus, just as in the clearing model, we conclude that real wages move procyclically. In addition, the present model implies a certain symmetry where Barro and Grossman found asymmetry. More demand always leads to higher real wages and higher output in the very short run, and less demand leads to lower real wages and output. However, the symmetry is only *qualitative*, not *quantitative*. Because employment is demand-determined when there is excess supply, and supply-determined when there is excess demand, the responses of w and y to policy will surely differ in the two cases. In particular, we expect a much greater output response when there is excess supply of labor than we do when there is excess demand.

2.5 SUMMARY AND CONCLUDING REMARKS

1. In a sense, the most basic conclusion of this paper may be that in-ventories really do matter in macroeconomic theory. The presence of storable output apparently can change even basic *qualitative* aspects of the behavior of macro models.

2. While the great variety of motives for holding inventories suggest a number of ways in which inventories might enter the macro model, many of them seem to suggest that output inventories should have a negative effect on the demand for labor (or supply of output). Input inventories remain an unexplored territory worthy of study.

3. While inventories play an important stabilizing role at the level of the firm, they tend to be *destabilizing* at the macro level in the sense that models with inventories are stable in a smaller subset of the parameter space than are models without inventories. This message dates back to Metzler (1941); but the mechanisms and precise stability conditions are quite different in this model than they were in Metzler's. In general, stability requires not only that inventories have a negative effect on the demand for labor, but that this effect be "large enough."

4. Because of inventory changes, short-run fluctuations in aggregate de-mand have quicker and more dramatic effects on final sales than they do on production.

5. Real wages respond positively to positive shocks to aggregate demand, because inventory changes shift the demand curve for labor. In the case of a nonclearing labor market, this conclusion hinges upon a stability condition which again states that the inventory-induced shifts in labor demand are "large enough."

As was pointed out in the introduction, this conclusion is the reverse of that reached by standard Keynesian analysis, and also by search-theoretic models. This is because those models consider a cyclically sensitive labor supply curve shifting along a labor demand curve, while the model developed here has a cyclically sensitive labor demand curve shifting along a fixed labor supply curve. If both curves were allowed to shift simultaneously, demand stimuli would have ambiguous effects on real wages. Which effect dominates in practice is an empirical issue.

It is probably apparent that other mechanisms that shift the demand for labor during the business cycle could be introduced.[21] But putting inventories into the labor demand function is not a contrivance designed to make real wages move procyclically. Quite the contrary, it seems to be an almost inescapable conclusion on both microeconomic and macroeconomic grounds. From the micro perspective, given any kind of imperfection in the market that allows the shadow value of inventories to depart from the market price, optimizing behavior seems to dictate that employment be a decreasing function of inventories in a wide variety of models.[22] From the macro perspective, it is hard to make sense of either the Keynesian cross or the *IS* curve without explicit consideration of the firm's reaction to inventory imbalances.[23]

6. Finally, the Keynesian model with inventories predicts that real output will move in the same direction as aggregate demand, regardless of whether the demand shock is administered from an initial position of equilibrium, excess supply, or excess demand. In this respect, it contrasts sharply with the implications of the Barro–Grossman model.

NOTES

1. Among the many examples that could be cited, see Samuelson (1976, pp. 222–5).
2. For example, Branson's (1979) popular text never mentions inventories once it gets past the rehash of freshman-level materials. Even Lovell (1975), himself an inventory expert, fails to give inventories any role in the elaborated *IS–LM* model.
3. A notable exception is Maccini (1976).
4. Barro and Grossman note this quite explicitly. See, for example (1971, p. 85n) or (1976, p. 41n).
5. The statement applies to the United States and other advanced industrial nations. The Barro–Grossman excess demand scenario may be applicable to centrally planned economies where consumer goods are in chronically short supply (on this, see Howard (1976)). The preceding discussion is in the spirit of Leijonhufvud (1973).
6. This has important implications for econometric specification of macro models. The Barro–Grossman model, with its many cases, would require a complex "switching regressions" approach of the sort discussed, for example, by Goldfeld

and Quandt (1976). The model that I shall present has no switches of regimes.

7. For a version of this scenario consistent with rational expectations, see Fischer (1977).

8. Alternatively, a falling supply price (e.g. quantity discounts) will give the firm an incentive to bunch its input purchases.

9. For a full discussion of when λ can or cannot differ from the market price, see Blinder (1978). Suffice it to say that some deviation from perfect markets – for example, some monopoly power – is required.

10. A notable exception is Fair's (1976) model. His equation for output (equation (10) on p. 49) can be written (if I ignore lags and dummy variables):

$$y = \text{constant} + 1.2x - 0.236N$$

which certainly shows a rather strong negative effect of inventories on output.

11. See Ando and Shell (1975).

12. Given (2.5), it does not matter whether I put E^d or E^s into the production function.

13. The expectational mechanism is not critical to any results in this paper, and is needed only to connect nominal and real interest rates. For a model with a similar, though somewhat simpler, structure that includes explicit stochastic terms and utilizes rational expectations, see Blinder and Fischer (1981), reprinted here as Chapter 3.

14. Feldstein and Auerbach (1976) have suggested that, as an empirical matter, changes in N^* proceed very sluggishly in US durable manufacturing industry.

15. Had I modeled monetary policy as fixing the growth rate, $\dot{M}/M$, rather than the level, M, inflation would be possible in equilibrium. However, my choice seems the more natural one in the context of an ultimately static model. The whole model can be transformed into a growth model with relatively little difficulty.

16. This conclusion is the only one in the chapter that depends on the assumption of adaptive expectations. Because of this, the *rate of change* of the rate of inflation is:

$$\frac{d}{dt}\left(\frac{\dot{P}}{P}\right) = \dot{\pi} - \Theta \dot{N}$$

$$= \beta\left(\frac{\dot{P}}{P} - \pi\right) > 0 \text{ at the point where } \dot{N} = 0.$$

17. In the model, they reach this peak in the "first instant," but if lags in the consumption and investment function were allowed, the "multiplier" would take some time.

18. Point E is where the slope of the trajectory, $\dot{x}/\dot{y}$, is equal to unity, for at this point $\dot{N} = \dot{x} - \dot{y} = 0$.

19. Assuming (2.14), of course, does not guarantee monotonic convergence. I depicted this case in Fig. 2.2, but nothing of consequence hinges on it; overshooting is possible.

20. An open question is whether the effect on $\dot{w}$ could be signed by a similar stability analysis of the Barro–Grossman model.

21. For example, the stock of capital or the intensity of its utilization might affect labor demand.

22. On this, see Blinder (1978) and Blinder and Fischer (1981), reprinted here as Chapter 3.

23. On this, see Blinder (1977).

24. See, for example, Gandolfo (1971, p. 241).

REFERENCES

Ando, A. and K. Shell (1975) "Demand for money in a general portfolio model in the presence of an asset that dominates money," in G. Fromm and L. R. Klein (eds) *The Brookings Model: Perspective and Recent Developments*, Amsterdam: North-Holland.

Barro, R. J. and H. I. Grossman (1971) "A general disequilibrium model of income and employment," *American Economic Review*, vol. 61 (March), pp. 82–93.

Barro, R. J. and H. I. Grossman (1976) *Money, Employment and Inflation*, Cambridge: Cambridge University Press.

Blinder, A. S. (1977) "A difficulty with Keynesian models of aggregate demand," in A. Blinder and P. Friedman (eds), *Natural Resources, Uncertainty, and General Equilibrium Systems: Essays in Memory of Rafael Lusky*, New York: Academic Press.

Blinder, A. S. (1978) "Inventories and the demand for labor," mimeo, Princeton University (April).

Blinder, A. S. and S. Fischer (1981) "Inventories, rational expectations, and the business cycle," *Journal of Monetary Economics*, vol. 8, pp. 277–304. Reprinted here as Ch. 3.

Branson, W. H. (1979) *Macroeconomic Theory and Policy*, 2nd edn, New York: Harper and Row.

Cagan, P. (1956) "The monetary dynamics of hyperinflation," in M. Friedman (ed.), *Studies in the Quantity Theory of Money*, Chicago: University of Chicago Press.

Fair, R. C. (1976) *A Model of Macroeconomic Activity. Vol. 2: The Empirical Model*, Cambridge (Mass.): Ballinger.

Feldstein, M. S. and A. Auerbach (1976) "Inventory behavior in durable goods manufacturing: the target adjustment model," *Brookings Papers on Economic Activity*, vol. 2, pp. 351–96.

Fischer, S. (1977) "Long-term contracts, rational expectations, and the optimal money supply rule," *Journal of Political Economy* (February), pp. 191–205.

Gandolfo, G. (1971) *Mathematical Methods and Models in Economic Dynamics*, Amsterdam: North-Holland.

Goldfeld, S. M. and R. E. Quandt (1976) "Techniques for estimating switching regressions," in S. M. Goldfeld and R. E. Quandt (eds), *Studies in Nonlinear Estimation*, Cambridge (Mass.): Ballinger.

Gordon, R. J. (1975) "The impact of aggregate demand on prices," *Brookings Papers on Economic Activity*, vol. 3, pp. 613–44.

Holt, C. C., F. Modigliani, J. F. Muth and H. A. Simon (1960) *Planning Production, Inventories and Work Force*, Englewood Cliffs (N.J.): Prentice-Hall.

Howard, D. H. (1976) "The disequilibrium model in a controlled economy: an empirical test of the Barro–Grossman model," *American Economic Review*, vol. 66 (December), pp. 871–9.

Leijonhufvud, A. (1973) "Effective demand failures," *The Swedish Journal of Economics*, vol. 75 (March), pp. 27–48.

Lovell, M. C. (1975) *Macroeconomics: Measurement, Theory and Policy*, New York: Wiley.

Maccini, L. J. (1976) "An aggregate dynamic model of short-run price and output behavior," *Quarterly Journal of Economics*, vol. 90, pp. 177–96.

Maccini, L. J. (1977) "An empirical model of price and output behavior," *Economic Inquiry*, vol. 15 (October), pp. 493–512.

Metzler, L. A. (1941) "The nature and stability of inventory cycles," *Review of Economic Statistics*, vol. 23.

Mills, E. S. (1962) *Price, Output and Inventory Policy*, New York: Wiley.

Samuelson, P. A. (1976) *Economics*, 10th edn, New York: McGraw Hill.

APPENDIX 2.1

Stability analysis in the clearing model

Using the solution functions given in the text for y and x, the dynamic system can be written as a system of three differential equations, the first two of which are nonlinear:

$$\dot{N} = Y(N) - X(N, m, \pi; g)$$

$$\dot{m} = -\Theta m(N^* - N) - \pi m$$

$$\dot{\pi} = \beta\Theta(N^* - N)$$

Linearizing the nonlinear equations around equilibrium ($x = y$, $N^* = N$, $\pi = \dot{P}/P = 0$) gives the following stability matrix:

$$\Delta = \begin{pmatrix} Y_N - X_N & -X_m & -X_\pi \\ \Theta m & 0 & -m \\ -\beta\Theta & 0 & 0 \end{pmatrix}$$

The Routh–Hurwitz necessary and sufficient conditions for (local) stability in this case are that:[24]

$$\text{tr}(\Delta) < 0 \tag{A2.1}$$

$$\det(\Delta) < 0 \tag{A2.2}$$

$$-\Theta(Y_N - X_N)[mX_m - \beta X_\pi] - \beta\Theta m X_m > 0 \tag{A2.3}$$

The trace,

$$\text{tr} = Y_N - X_N = (1 - D_y) Y_N$$

is negative so long as D_y (the marginal propensity to spend) is less than unity and Y_N is negative. The determinant is simply $-\beta \Theta m X_m$, which is negative so long as rising real balances stimulate demand. Only condition (A2.3) requires further analysis, and by using the definitions of X_m and X_π it can be expressed as equation (2.14) in the text.

Stability analysis in the nonclearing model

In the nonclearing model, w replaces π as the third state variable. Also, the solution functions differ and depend on whether there is excess supply or excess demand (see the text). The dynamic system is:

$$\dot{N} = y(N, w) - x(N, m, w; g)$$

$$\dot{m} = \Theta m(N - N^*)$$

$$\dot{w} = \gamma w [E^d(w, N) - E^s(w)] + \Theta w(N - N^*)$$

Linearizing it around equilibrium $(N = N^*,\ E^d = E^s)$ gives the stability matrix:

$$\Delta^* = \begin{pmatrix} y_N - x_N & -x_m & y_w - x_w \\ \Theta m & 0 & 0 \\ \gamma w E_N^d + \Theta w & 0 & \gamma w(E_w^d - E_w^s) \end{pmatrix}$$

The three Routh–Hurwitz necessary and sufficient conditions for local stability are

$$\text{tr}(\Delta^*) = y_N - x_N + \gamma w(E_w^d - E_w^s) < 0 \tag{A2.1*}$$

$$\det(\Delta^*) = \Theta m x_m \gamma w(E_w^d - E_w^s) < 0 \tag{A2.2*}$$

$$-[y_N - x_N + \gamma w(E_w^d - E_w^s)][(y_N - x_N)\gamma w(E_w^d - E_w^s) -$$
$$-(y_w - x_w)(\Theta w + \gamma w E_N^d)] - (y_N - x_N)x_m \Theta m > 0 \tag{A2.3*}$$

The first two are clearly satisfied whether the system has excess demand or excess supply in the labor market, but (A2.3*) looks different in the two cases. The excess demand case is simpler since here $y_N = x_N = 0$, $y_w - x_w = (1 - D_y)y_w > 0$. The condition reduces to:

$$\gamma w(E_w^d - E_w^s)(y_w - x_w)\ (\Theta w + \gamma w E_N^d) > 0$$

which is true if and only if:

$$\Theta + \gamma E_N^d < 0 \tag{2.20}$$

When there is excess supply in the labor market, $y_N - x_N = (1 - D_y)y_N < 0$ and $(y_w - x_w) = (1 - D_y)y_w < 0$, so a sufficient (though not necessary) condition for stability is:

$$y_N \gamma w (E_w^d - E_w^s) > y_w (\Theta + \gamma E_N^d)$$

But, looking back at (2.16), we see that $y_N E_w^d = y_w E_N^d$, so this reduces to:

$$-\gamma E_N^d f' E_w^s > \Theta f' E_w^d$$

which is true if (2.20) holds.

3·INVENTORIES, RATIONAL EXPECTATIONS, AND THE BUSINESS CYCLE

3.1 INTRODUCTION

There are doubtless many mechanisms that cooperate in producing the serial correlation of deviations of output from trend known as the "business cycle." This paper studies the role of inventories in the propagation of the business cycle in a model with rational expectations.[1]

Even a cursory look at the data indicates the importance of inventory fluctuations in the short-run dynamics of output. Table 3.1 shows peak to trough changes in both real GNP and its most volatile component – inventory investment – during the post-war recessions. The significance of inventory change is evident.

Table 3.2 focusses on the details of the 1973–6 recession and recovery.[2] During this period, there were major fluctuations in inventory investment in 1973:4, 1974:1, 1975:1, 1975:3, and 1976:1.[3] In most of these quarters, the movement in inventory investment totally dominated the movement in real GNP. Other than the tremendous drop in 1974:4 and the rapid recovery in 1975:2, rather little of the action in the GNP figures came from changes in final sales.

None of this, of course, is meant to imply that autonomous movements in inventories cause business cycles, but only to suggest that inventory dynamics play a fundamental role in their propagation.

Recent work on business cycles and monetary policy has been greatly influenced by the approach to aggregate supply due to Lucas (1972, 1973),

Written with Stanley Fischer. We are grateful for helpful comments from Costas Azariadis, Robert Barro, Martin Eichenbaum, Benjamin Friedman, John Helliwell, Bennett McCallum, and participants in seminars at the University of California, Davis, University of California, San Diego, University of Pennsylvania, Queen's University, University of Rochester, and University of Virginia. The research reported here is part of the NBER's research program in Economic Fluctuations. Financial support from the National Science Foundation and the Institute for Advanced Studies in Jerusalem is gratefully acknowledged, as is research assistance from Mark Bagnoli and Suzanne Heller. Any opinions expressed are those of the authors and not those of the National Bureau of Economic Research.

Table 3.1 Changes in GNP and in inventory investment in the post-war recessions[a]

(1) Dates of contraction		(2) Decline in real GNP[a]	(3) Decline in inventory investment	(4) Col. (3) as a percentage of col. (2)
Peak	Trough			
1948:4	1949:4	$6.7	$13.0	194%
1953:2	1954:2	20.6	10.2	50
1957:3	1958:1	22.2	10.5	47
1960:1	1960:4	8.8	10.5	119
1969:3	1970:4	12.0	10.1	84
1973:4	1975:1	71.0	44.8	63

Note:
(a) In billions of 1972 dollars.
Source: The National Income and Product Accounts of the United States, 1929–74 and *Survey of Current Business*, July 1977.

who posited an aggregate supply function such as:

$$y_t = k_t + \gamma(p_t - {}_{t-1}p_t) + e_t \tag{3.1}$$

where y is (the log of) real output, k is (the log of) the natural rate of output, p is (the log of) the price level, e_t is an independently and identically distributed error term, and the notation ${}_{t-1}x_t$ denotes the expectation that is formed at time $t-1$ of the variable x_t. These expectations are assumed to be formed rationally.

If the natural rate of output, the k_t term in (3.1), is exogenous, two strong conclusions follow immediately under the further assumption that prices always move to clear markets within the period. Since, under rational expectations, the expectational error in (3.1) must be white noise, it follows that (a) deviations of output from its natural rate are also white noise, *i.e.*, there are no business cycles, and (b) no feedback rule for monetary policy (or equivalently, no anticipated change in the money stock) can affect deviations of output from the natural rate.

Explanations for the business cycle that build on the Lucas supply function focus on the determinants of the k_t term. Lucas (1975) has shown that the inclusion of capital in the model will produce serial correlation of output, as unanticipated inflation affects current output and thereby future capital stocks. A similar mechanism has been explored in Fischer (1979). Sargent (1979, Ch. 16) has studied a model in which serial correlation of the natural rate of output follows from gradual adjustment of the labor stock by firms faced with adjustment costs.

Modifications of the basic model to allow for serial correlation of output do not necessarily modify the second conclusion – that anticipated policy actions have no real effects. However, if capital is explicitly included in the model, and if it is assumed that the rate of accumulation of capital is directly

Table 3.2 Changes in real GNP and real inventory investment, 1973–6[a]

	1973:3	1973:4	1974:1	1974:2	1974:3	1974:4	1975:1	1975:2	1975:3	1975:4	1976:1
1. Real GNP	5.2	6.3	-12.4	-5.7	-7.6	-17.2	-28.1	18.3	30.1	7.9	31.6
2. Real final sales	5.9	-5.0	-1.0	-0.9	-0.4	-22.0	-1.9	15.5	11.4	15.2	17.5
3. Real inventory investment	-0.7	+11.3	-11.5	-4.7	-7.2	+4.8	-26.2	+2.7	+18.8	-7.3	+14.1
(a) finished goods[b]	-2.9	+10.7	-6.8	-3.9	-2.0	+6.2	-21.6	+7.6	+13.9	-9.3	+12.7
(b) non-finished goods[c]	+5.7	+1.1	-4.5	-0.8	-2.2	+0.5	-6.0	-1.9	+1.0	+1.4	+3.4
(c) misc. and statistical discrepancies[d]	-3.2	-0.7	-0.1	-0.1	-3.0	-1.9	+1.8	-3.4	+4.3	+0.6	-2.2
Addendum: Levels of inventory investment											
4. Real inventory investment	14.1	25.4	13.9	9.2	2.0	6.8	-19.4	-16.7	2.1	-5.2	8.9
(a) finished goods[b]	1.5	12.2	5.4	1.4	-0.6	5.6	-15.9	-8.3	5.3	-4.0	8.7
(b) non-finished goods[c]	8.1	9.2	4.7	3.9	1.7	2.2	-3.7	-5.6	-4.5	-3.1	0.2
(c) misc. and statistical discrepancies[d]	4.6	3.9	3.8	3.8	0.7	-1.2	0.6	-2.9	1.4	2.0	0.2

Notes:
(a) Absolute changes in billions of 1972 dollars, seasonally adjusted at annual rates.
(b) The sum of retail inventories plus wholesale inventories plus finished goods inventories of manufacturers. Retail and wholesale data are from *Survey of Current Business*; manufacturing data are unpublished (and unofficial) BEA figures.
(c) Manufacturers' inventories of materials and supplies plus works-in-progress; from unpublished BEA data.
(d) Farm inventories plus nonfarm inventories not held by manufacturers, retailers, or wholesalers plus discrepancy between *Survey of Current Business* and unpublished stage-of-processing figures for manufacturing plus rounding errors at earlier stages of computation.
Source: Computed by authors from data in *Survey of Current Business* (various issues) plus unpublished (and unofficial) BEA data on real inventories in manufacturing by stage of processing. *Note:* Components may not add to totals due to rounding errors.

or indirectly a function of the anticipated rate of inflation, then the behavior of the k_t term in (3.1) can be affected by anticipated monetary changes.[4] Alternatively, a role for monetary policy in affecting cyclical behavior may be found by dropping the market clearing assumption, which changes the form of the aggregate supply function.[5]

In this paper we study how the inclusion of storable output affects the two basic conclusions arising from the combination of the Lucas supply function and rational expectations. First, we show that adding inventories to the model makes shocks persist. Second, we show that if the demand for inventories is interest elastic, anticipated monetary changes can have real effects. Of the two roles of inventories, we have no doubt that the propagation of disturbances caused by unanticipated events is much the more important. Nonetheless, it is interesting to note that the inclusion of inventories opens a potential channel for even fully anticipated monetary policy to have real effects.

In the next two sections of the paper we show that, in the presence of storable output, the aggregate supply function is modified to a form like:

$$y_t = k_t + \gamma(p_t - {}_{t-1}p_t) + \lambda(N_t^* - N_t) + e_t \tag{3.2}$$

where N_t is the stock of inventories at the beginning of the period, and N_t^* is the optimal or desired stock. Section 3.2 derives a supply function like (3.2) based on utility maximization by a yeoman farmer working in a competitive market, the case that seems closest in spirit to Lucas's analysis.[6] Section 3.3 derives a similar function in a different setting: that of a profit-maximizing firm with a downward-sloping demand curve.

The following two sections offer proofs of the assertions we have just made. In Section 3.4 we show that, even in the most stripped-down macro model with inventories that we can set up, shocks lead to persistent deviations of y_t from its natural level, i.e., to business cycles. And Section 3.5 demonstrates that, if N_t^* depends on the real interest rate, then anticipated changes in the money stock can have real effects through inventory changes. Section 3.6 contains conclusions, and some remarks on the empirical relevance of our model.

3.2 THE LUCAS SUPPLY FUNCTION REVISITED: THE CASE OF THE YEOMAN FARMER

In this section we use a framework similar to that of Lucas (1973) to examine optimal behavior for a yeoman farmer, working without any cooperating factors, who sells his output in a competitive market. Since output is assumed to be storable, he can obtain goods to sell in two ways: by working or by drawing down his inventory stocks. At first we assume that the individual knows both the aggregate price level (the average of the prices of things he buys) and the relative price of his own output. Later we follow Lucas and Phelps (1970) in allowing for confusion between the two.

We start with this model not for its realism, but because it is so close in spirit to earlier work, particularly that of Lucas and Phelps, on aggregate supply. As will become clear, however, inventories work in this model mainly through wealth effects – which is not how we imagine they work in a modern industrial economy. Further, the utility analysis to follow is plagued by the usual ambiguities arising from income and substitution effects. Little beyond the list of arguments for each demand function can in general be derived; meaningful qualitative restrictions on demand and supply functions must generally be assumed – either directly or by restricting the class of utility functions. For both these reasons, we deal briefly with this model, and then turn our attention to a model of the firm.

Consider an individual living and working for two periods,[7] whose output is identical to his labor input:

$$Y_t = L_t, \quad t = 0, 1$$

He is endowed with beginning-of-period stocks of the good, N_0, and of money, M_0, and must decide how much to produce, how much to consume, and how to carry over his wealth in the two assets available to him: N_1 and M_1. The prices of his own good and of goods in general are W_t and P_t, respectively, where we assume initially that both W_0 and P_0 are known, but W_1 and P_1 are random. It is convenient to work with transformations of W_t and P_t, namely, the individual's relative price, $w_1 = W_1/P_1$, and the purchasing power of money, $q_t = 1/P_t$.

Assuming that exogenous transfers of money and goods are received only by the young, budget constraints for periods 0 and 1 are:

$$C_0 = w_0(L_0 + N_0 - N_1) + q_0(M_0 - M_1) \tag{3.3}$$

$$C_1 = w_1(L_1 + N_1) + q_1 M_1 \tag{3.4}$$

where C_t is real consumption of goods in period t $(t = 0, 1)$. In period 0, based on expectations of w_1 and q_1, the yeoman farmer decides how much to produce, and how much to carry over to period 1 in the forms of inventories and money.[8] In period 1, w_1 and q_1 are announced, the yeoman farmer decides how much to produce, and then consumes this output plus his accumulated wealth. He is assumed to maximize a separable utility function:

$$J = U(C_0, \bar{L} - L_0) + EV(C_1, \bar{L} - L_1)$$

where both $U(.)$ and $V(.)$ are strictly concave; any time discounting is embodied in the functional form of $V(.)$.[9]

The period 1 problem is quite simple. With the carry-over stocks predetermined and the two prices known, the problem is one of certainty, with only labor supply to be chosen; that is, the yeoman farmer maximizes:

$$V(w_1 L_1 + (w_1 N_1 + q_1 M_1), \bar{L} - L_1)$$

The resultant first-order condition implies a supply function of labor with the real wage and real wealth as arguments:

$$L_1 = F(w_1, w_1 N_1 + q_1 M_1) \tag{3.5}$$

Then, using the budget constraints (3.3) and (3.4) to substitute out for C_0 and C_1, the maximand for the period 0 problem can be written as:[10]

$$\max_{\{L_0, q_0 M_1, N_1\}} = U(w_0(L_0 - N_0 + N_1) + q_0(M_0 - M_1), \bar{L} - L_0)$$

$$+ EV(w_1 F(.) + w_1 N_1 + q_1 M_1, \bar{L} - F(.)) \tag{3.6}$$

subject to $N_1 \geqq 0$, $M_1 \geqq 0$. Notice that the second argument of $F(.)$ in (3.5) is:

$$w_1 N_1 + q_1 M_1 = \frac{w_1}{w_0} w_0 N_1 + \frac{q_1}{q_0} q_0 M_1$$

By examining (3.5) and (3.6), and observing that $w_1 F(.) = w_0(w_1/w_0)^F(.)$, it is clear that the arguments of the demand functions for $L_0, q_0 M_1, N_1$ (and therefore also for C_0) must be:

(a) w_0, the current wage or relative price;
(b) $w_0 N_0 + q_0 M_0$, real wealth;
(c) the distributions of the returns on money, q_1/q_0, and on inventory holdings, w_1/w_0.

The absolute price level is not an independent argument in the behavioral functions, entering only to deflate the nominal value of money balances.

For subsequent use, we are interested particularly in the supply function for labor (which is also the supply function for output) and the demand function for inventories:

$$L_0 = L(w_0, w_0 N_0 + q_0 M_0; \phi(R_N, R_M)) \tag{3.7}$$

$$N_1 = N(w_0, w_0 N_0 + q_0 M_0; \phi(R_N, R_M)) \tag{3.8}$$

where the $\phi(.)$ notation indicates that the functions depend on the joint distribution of the two random rates of return: $R_N \equiv w_1/w_0$, and $R_M \equiv q_1/q_0$. (The consumption and real balance demand functions that are also implied by the maximization process are not of interest here.) It is a straightforward exercise in comparative statics to derive the properties of these functions from the first-order conditions for maximizing (3.6). However, we know in advance that conflicting income and substitution effects will render most derivatives ambiguous. So let us ask, instead: what are the natural assumptions to make about (3.7) and (3.8)?

First consider a change in wealth which, we note, is the only way that N_0 has effects in this simple model. If leisure is a normal good, and if demand for both assets rises when wealth increases, then it will be the case that:

$$\partial L_0/\partial N_0 < 0, \qquad 0 < \partial N_1/\partial N_0 < 1$$

In words, an increase in inventories leads to a reduction in production, and to an increase in inventory carry-over which is less than the increase in the initial inventory holdings. The latter amounts to assuming that any increment to wealth will be divided among current consumption, investment in inventories, and investment in money, with positive shares for each. Both of these results will play critical roles in the macro model. Specifically, the notion that if inventories become too large (small) for some reason, the individual will eliminate the excess (shortfall) only gradually over time, constitutes the basic source of the serial correlation of output in the macro model.

Next, consider the effects of an increase in w_0, the current relative price, on labor supply (output) and inventory carry-over. From the first argument in (3.7), production will rise if substitution effects dominate. The effects on inventory demand of an increase in w_0 are more difficult to predict. An increase in w_0, given a fixed distribution of w_1, reduces the expected return to inventory holding. This would be likely to depress inventory demand. (Production might also be depressed by rate-of-return effects, but we assume that the direct wage effect dominates.) Under these circumstances high w_0 encourages current production, and reduces inventory demand, as inventories are sold off to take advantage of a currently high relative price.

If this yeoman farmer is placed in a standard Lucas–Phelps world in which there is imperfect information about the current price level, q_0, he will react in the manner described by equations (3.7) and (3.8) to any disturbance that he believes to be an increase in the relative price of his own good. Apart from real balance effects and adjustments in his *nominal* money holdings, he will not react to changes in the aggregate price level. Thus, if he is located on a Phelpsian island, he will react to any change in the nominal price of his own output, $W_0 = w_0/q_0$, as if it were partly a relative and partly an absolute price change. That is, his reactions to an increase in the nominal price in his isolated market will be qualitatively the same as his reactions to an increase in w_0. This is nothing but a restatement of Lucas's analysis with respect to price changes. The novelty here is in the analysis of inventory holding behavior, which leads to an output equation something like (3.2) rather than to Lucas's (3.1).

3.3 INVENTORIES AND THE SUPPLY FUNCTION OF FIRMS

In the utility maximization model, we derived a demand for inventories even with perfect competition, a linear production function, and no adjustment costs. This will not be possible in a model of the firm. Accordingly, we assume a convex cost structure, i.e., increasing marginal production costs. But, for reasons explained more fully in Blinder (1978), this turns out not to be sufficient to justify an effect of the inventory stock on production decisions at the micro level since the competitive firm can always sell any "excess" inventories at the market price.

The non-existence of an effect of inventories on the production decision of the competitive firm does not, however, mean that output is independent of inventory stocks at the level of the market, but only that the effects of inventories are indirect: high inventory stocks lead to low market prices, and low prices lead to low production. However, in order to examine the role of inventories at the firm level, we turn next to a model of a firm with a downward sloping demand curve.

Consider a firm whose demand curve shifts randomly from period to period:

$$p_t = v_t P_t D(X_t) \tag{3.9}$$

where p_t is the firm's own absolute price, v_t is a serially independent disturbance in relative price, P_t is the aggregate price level (also random), and $D(X_t)$ is a downward-sloping function of the amount that the firm sells, X_t.[11] We will assume initially that the firm can observe both v_0 and P_0 before making its current output and sales decisions, while v_t and P_t ($t = 1, 2, \ldots$) are random variables. Later we shall comment on what happens if the firm cannot distinguish between v_0 and P_0.

Nominal production costs are assumed to be (a) homogeneous of degree one in the absolute price level, and (b) a convex function of output, Y_t. Specifically:

$$C_t = P_t c(Y_t), \quad c' > 0, \quad c'' > 0 \tag{3.10}$$

We assume that $\lim_{Y \to 0} c'(Y) = 0$ and $\lim_{Y \to \infty} c'(Y) = \infty$, so that the firm will always select an interior maximum for Y_t.

In the current period, the firm must decide how much to produce and how much to sell. These decisions jointly determine its inventory carry over according to:

$$N_{t+1} = N_t + Y_t - X_t \tag{3.11}$$

where N_t is the beginning-of-period inventory stock. N_0 is exogenous. Inventory carrying costs are given by a convex function, $B(N_t)$, with $B'(N_t) < 0$ for negative N_t, and $B'(N_t) > 0$ for positive N_t.[12]

The firm wants to maximize the expected discounted present value of its real profits. Thus it wants to find:

$$J_0 = \max_{(X_t, Y_t)} E_0 \sum_{t=0}^{\infty} \left\{ \frac{R(X_t, v_t)}{\prod_{s=1}^{t} (1 + r_s)} - \frac{c(Y_t)}{\prod_{s=1}^{t} (1 + r_s)} - \frac{B(N_{t+1})}{\prod_{s=1}^{t+1} (1 + r_s)} \right\} \tag{3.12}$$

where $R(.)$ is the real revenue function, defined as

$$R(X_t, v_t) = p_t X_t / P_t = v_t D(X_t) X_t$$

which we assume has the following properties: $R_X \geq 0$, $R_{XX} < 0$, $\lim_{X \to 0} R_X(X, v) = +\infty$, $D(X_t)X_t$ is bounded above.

The latter assumptions assure us that X_t will always achieve an interior maximum. The variable r_s is the one period real interest rate in period s.[13]

The problem is set up in dynamic programming form by defining:

$$\pi_t = R(X_t, v_t) - c(Y_t) - \frac{B(N_{t+1})}{1 + r_{t+1}}$$

$$J_1 = \max_{\{X_t, Y_t\}} E_1 \sum_{t=1}^{\infty} \left\{ \frac{R(X_t, v_t)}{\prod_{s=2}^{t} (1 + r_s)} - \frac{c(Y_t)}{\prod_{s=2}^{t} (1 + r_s)} - \frac{B(N_{t+1})}{\prod_{s=2}^{t+1} (1 + r_s)} \right\}$$

so that (3.12) may be rewritten:

$$J_0 = \max_{\{X_0, Y_0\}} \pi_0 + \frac{E_0 J_1}{1 + r_1} \tag{3.13}$$

It is clear from the set-up of the problem that the J_t functions depend on the initial inventory stock, N_t; the initial realizations of the two random variables, v_t and P_t; the joint distribution of all the stochastic variables; the path of real interest rates; and the functional forms of all the R, c, and B functions. Since the inventory stock is the only state variable of the firm, we shall simply write $J_t = J_t(N_t)$. Our assumptions imply that the $\pi_t(.)$ are concave, continuous, bounded functions; accordingly the J_t are concave and continuous and, given $r_s > 0$ for all s and the assumed stationarity of v_t, bounded. An optimal policy therefore exists.[14]

To solve the problem for the first-period solution, it is easiest to use (3.11) to eliminate Y_0, and treat X_0 and N_1 as the firm's decision variables. First-order conditions for an interior maximum, on which we concentrate, are then:

$$R_X(X_0, v_0) - c'(X_0 + N_1 - N_0) = 0 \tag{3.14}$$

$$\frac{E_0(J_1'(N_1)) - B'(N_1)}{1 + r_1} - c'(X_0 + N_1 - N_0) = 0 \tag{3.15}$$

The first condition states that marginal revenue is equated to marginal cost, even though production and sales may differ. The second says that the marginal value of adding one unit to inventories must be equal to the sum of the costs of producing that unit and carrying it over to the next period.

These first-order conditions imply optimal decision rules for current sales and inventory carry-over, and therefore production, of the form:

$$X_0 = X(N_0, v_0, 1 + r_1) \tag{3.16}$$

$$N_1 = N(N_0, v_0, 1 + r_1) \tag{3.17}$$

$$Y_0 = S(N_0, v_0, 1 + r_1) = X(.) + N(.) - N_0 \tag{3.18}$$

where future interest rates and the probability distribution of future vs are embodied in the functional forms. The derivatives of these functions can be worked out by the usual comparative statics technique. The following summarizes their relevant properties:

$$0 < \frac{\partial X_0}{\partial N_0} < 1, \quad \frac{\partial X_0}{\partial v_0} > 0, \quad \frac{\partial X_0}{\partial (1 + r_1)} > 0$$

$$0 < \frac{\partial N_1}{\partial N_0} < 1, \quad \frac{\partial N_1}{\partial v_0} < 0, \quad \frac{\partial N_1}{\partial (1 + r_1)} < 0 \tag{3.19}$$

$$-1 < \frac{\partial Y_1}{\partial N_0} < 0, \quad \frac{\partial Y_0}{\partial v_0} > 0, \quad \frac{\partial Y_0}{\partial (1 + r_1)} < 0$$

We are most interested in the effects of the initial stock of inventories. An increase in N_0 leads to a drop in current production, an increase in current sales (i.e., a cut in relative price), and an increase in next period's inventories, but all by less than the increase in current inventories. Thus the apparent partial adjustment feature appears here just as it did in the model of the yeoman farmer.

Turning next to the relative price shock (shift in the demand curve, v_0), the profit-maximizing firm will respond by raising both sales and output. But the sales response is greater, so inventory carry-over falls. The intuition behind these results is straightforward once we keep in mind that the firm is operating on two margins: it is deciding how much to produce for inventories, and it is deciding how much to withdraw from inventories for sale. When the firm's *relative* price increases, the rewards for selling today (rather than tomorrow) are increased. But neither production costs nor the rewards for selling tomorrow (if v_1 and v_0 are independent) are affected. So the incentive to raise sales is greater than the incentive to raise output, and inventory stocks get depleted.

Naturally, an equiproportionate change in all prices will elicit no behavioral response from the firm. But what if the firm cannot distinguish between a relative price shock (v_0) and an absolute price shock? For the same reasons as before, its reactions will be a muted version of its responses to a *known* increase in v_0.

Thus the models of a yeoman farmer and of a monopolist have almost identical predictions. Both current production and inventory carry-over depend on unanticipated inflation (interpreted as an increase in relative price), on the current relative price, on the initial stock of inventories, and on expected rates of return. The next two sections embed the conclusions from the micro models into an otherwise standard macro structure, and show that they lead to the two main results mentioned in the introduction: that unanticipated shocks have persistent effects, and that fully anticipated money can have real effects.

3.4 INVENTORIES AND PERSISTENCE

The micro models of the previous two sections imply that production, Y_t, should react negatively (though less than unit-for-unit) to the start-of-period stock of inventories, N_t, and positively to the current price-level surprise. Thus we write the supply function:

$$Y_t = K_t + \gamma(P_t - {}_{t-1}P_t) + \lambda(N_t^* - N_t) + e_{1t},$$

$$\gamma > 0, \qquad 0 < \lambda < 1 \tag{3.20}$$

Here for convenience Y_t and N_t are *levels*, while P_t is the *log* of the current price level. K_t is trend output and N_t^* are steady-state desired inventories. In terms of the micro models, N_t^* should be interpreted as the value of N_0 such that, given the values of the other variables in (3.17), $N_1 = N_0$. The supply function is taken to be linear for convenience, and the error term e_{1t} is assumed to be serially independent with expectation zero.

The demand for inventories was seen in the earlier sections to be an increasing function of the current level of inventories, with an increase in current inventories increasing desired inventories less than one-for-one. We saw also that unanticipated inflation (interpreted in part as an increase in relative price) probably causes inventories to be drawn down. We summarize these two essential elements in:

$$N_{t+1} - N_t = \theta(N_t^* - N_t) - \phi(P_t - {}_{t-1}P_t) + e_{2t}$$

$$0 < \theta < 1, \qquad \phi \geqq 0 \tag{3.21}$$

The use of a stock adjustment form for (3.21) is inessential but convenient.

It is worth noting here that $\theta > \lambda$. The reason is that the model of inventory behavior in Section 3.3 implies (see equations (3.19)) that $\partial X/\partial N_0 > 0$. Since $\partial X/\partial N_0 = 1 + \partial Y/\partial N_0 - \partial N_1/\partial N_0$, this implies – in the notation of (3.20) and (3.21) – that $1 + (-\lambda) - (1 - \theta) = \theta - \lambda$ is positive. This fact will be used later.

To provide intuitive understanding of (3.20) and (3.21), consider a situation in which inventories exceed desired inventories. In the absence of price surprises, firms will be running off their inventories slowly, selling more than they produce, and producing less than they would if inventories were at their desired level. This adjustment pattern would continue smoothly, unless there were unanticipated changes in the general price level. If there is an unanticipated change in the general price level, interpreted in part as a relative price change, firms increase sales, raising both production and sales out of inventory to do so. Hence a positive price surprise this period implies a lower stock of inventories next period.

To close the model it is necessary only to add a specification of N^*_{t+1} and an aggregate demand sector. The micro models imply that N^* depends on current and future interest rates and on the probability distribution of all future shocks.[15] To keep things simple, we write:

$$N^*_t = N^* - \delta r_t, \tag{3.22}$$

where N^* and δ are constants and r_t is the current real interest rate.

The aggregate demand sector is almost totally conventional, and so we describe it very briefly. The equations are:

$$M_t - P_t = a_1 X_t - a_2 i_t + e_{3t} \tag{3.23}$$

$$X_t = c_1 Y_t + c_2 (M_t - P_t) - c_3 r_t + e_{4t} \tag{3.24}$$

$$N_{t+1} = N_t + Y_t - X_t \tag{3.25}$$

$$i_t = r_t + {}_t P_{t+1} - P_t \tag{3.26}$$

Equation (3.23) is a standard *LM* curve except that final sales, X_t, is used instead of output as the transactions variable. Though nothing important hinges on this choice, our reason is as follows. It seems logical (and the micro models imply) that a higher initial inventory stock, N_t, should lead to a lower current price level, P_t. With X_t on the right-hand side of (3.23) this obtains since higher inventories lead to higher sales and hence to greater demand for money. With the money stock fixed, the price level must decline. By contrast, had Y_t appeared instead of X_t in (3.23), a higher level of initial inventories, by depressing Y_t, would have led to a reduction in the demand for money and hence to an increase in the price level.

Equation (3.24) defines aggregate demand as a function of production (= income), real balances, and the real interest rate. Equation (3.25), which appears to be an accounting identity, tacitly brings the assumption of market clearance into the model by stating that the amount that firms sell in (3.25) is identical to the amount that consumers demand in (3.24). Notice that equation (3.25) implies that a certain linear combination of e_{1t}, e_{2t}, e_{3t}, and e_{4t} must be zero each period.

Finally, equation (3.26) relates the nominal and real rates of interest.[16]

Solution of a rational expectations model of this complexity is a considerable task. Fortunately, it is not necessary to solve the model completely to demonstrate our two basic results. The strategy is as follows. The conclusion that output disturbances are serially correlated is straightforward and very robust. So, in the remainder of this section, we demonstrate this central result in a stripped-down version of the model that removes all interest-rate effects. This model, however, leaves no room for fully anticipated money to have real effects. So, in the next section, we restore interest rate effects, but concentrate on a version of the model in which there is no uncertainty.

Turning to the demonstration of persistence, assume that $\delta = a_2 = 0$. Equations (3.24) and (3.26) are now superfluous to the model, and it is easy to express current output (Y_t) as a function of current and past unanticipated inflation, which we denote by u_t:

$$u_t = P_t - {}_{t-1}P_t \tag{3.27}$$

First, from (3.21) with N^* a constant, the level of inventories is seen to be a function only of unanticipated inflation, and the stochastic term in the inventory demand function, e_{2t}. Then solve the difference equation (3.21), assuming the economy has an infinite past so that initial conditions can be ignored (given that the model is stable), to obtain:

$$N_t = N^* - \phi \sum_0^\infty (1 - \theta)^i u_{t-1-i} + \sum_0^\infty (1 - \theta)^i e_{2,t-1-i} \tag{3.28}$$

Equation (3.28) repeats what we already know – that an unanticipated increase in the price level leads inventories to be drawn down, and then only gradually built back to their original level, so that the effect of any burst of unanticipated inflation on the current stock of inventories is smaller the further in the past the inflation surprise occurred.

Now substitute (3.28) into (3.20) to obtain the desired expression for output:

$$Y_t - K_t = \gamma u_t + \lambda \phi \sum_0^\infty (1 - \theta)^i u_{t-1-i} + e_{1t}$$
$$- \lambda \sum_0^\infty (1 - \theta)^i e_{2,t-1-i} \tag{3.29}$$

Equation (3.29) shows that output disturbances are positively serially correlated, since unanticipated inflation in the current period pushes output above trend in the current period and in all subsequent periods. Depending on the relative magnitudes of γ and $\lambda\phi$, unanticipated inflation may have its maximal effect on output in the period it occurs, or one period later, and thereafter the effects decline geometrically. If unanticipated inflation has a small direct effect on output, so that γ is small, but leads to a large reduction in inventories, so that ϕ is large, then the inventory rebuilding effects of unanticipated inflation on output will predominate, and the maximum impact on output will occur in the period following a given unanticipated increase in the price level.

Figure 3.1 shows how the stock of inventories and level of output are affected by unanticipated inflation in this case. First, unanticipated inflation reduces the stock of inventories, as sales are increased in response to what firms regard in part as an increase in the relative price of output. Then inventories are gradually built back up; the $(1 - \theta)^i$ terms in (3.28) result from

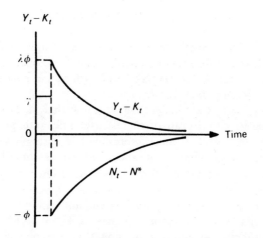

Fig. 3.1 Dynamic adjustment of output and inventories to an unanticipated increase in the money stock

the partial adjustment of inventories. Equation (3.29) shows that output is increased by current unanticipated inflation. Then in subsequent periods output is higher than it would otherwise have been, as a result of the need to rebuild depleted inventories.

Equation (3.29) also shows that systematic monetary feedback rules have no impact on the behavior of output under rational expectations for the usual reason: lagged feedback rules can produce only anticipated, not unanticipated, inflation.

For completeness, we examine also the determinants of the current price level. Combining (3.20), (3.21), (3.25) and (3.23) with $a_2 = 0$, we obtain:

$$P_t = M_t - a_1 [K_t + (\phi + \gamma)u_t$$
$$+ (\lambda - \theta)(N^* - N_t) + e_{1t} - e_{2t}] - e_{3t} \qquad (3.30)$$

The price level is accordingly proportional to perfectly anticipated increases in the money stock, and is a decreasing function of the stock of inventories since $\theta > \lambda$. It is worth noting that the price equation (3.30), derived from an equilibrium model, bears a striking resemblance to standard price adjustment equations in which the price level is reduced below its equilibrium level (which is $M_t - a_1 K_t$) in response to excess holdings of inventories.

In concluding this section, it is worthwhile emphasizing once more the basic source for the serial correlation of output. An unanticipated increase in the price level in this model leads firms to sell out of inventories at the same time as they increase production to take advantage of what is (incorrectly) perceived as an increase in relative price. Then in subsequent periods production remains high as stocks of goods are rebuilt. The serial correlation of output does not, however, imply that anticipated monetary policy has real effects.

3.5 INVENTORIES AND MONETARY POLICY

We turn now to our second objective: to show that, if desired inventory holdings are sensitive to the rate of interest, even fully anticipated changes in money will have real effects.[17] Since interest here focusses on *fully anticipated* money, nothing substantive is lost, and considerable simplification of the model is achieved, if we assume that all stochastic disturbances are always zero.

The source of the result is fairly transparent, and can hardly be surprising to anyone familiar with the seminal papers of Tobin (1965) and Mundell (1963). Fully anticipated changes in money cause changes in the (fully anticipated) inflation rate which, under conditions to be spelled out shortly, affect the real interest rate. Desired inventories then adjust according to equation (3.22), and output is (transitorily) affected by equation (3.20). We proceed now to the argument.

Using the notation L for the lag operator, it can be shown that the level of inventories, N_t, the level of output, Y_t, and the real interest rate, r_t, respectively, are given by:

$$N_t = N^* - \frac{\theta \delta L r_t}{1 - (1 - \theta)L} \tag{3.31}$$

$$Y_t = K_t - \frac{\lambda \delta (1 - L)}{1 - (1 - \theta)L} r_t \tag{3.32}$$

$r_t = \text{constant}$

$$- \frac{c_2 a_2 ({}_t P_{t+1} - P_t)}{c_3 + c_2 a_2 + \dfrac{[\theta(1 - c_2 a_1) + \lambda(c_1 - 1 + c_2 a_1)]\delta(1 - L)}{1 - (1 - \theta)L}} \tag{3.33}$$

Equation (3.33) displays the basic source of the non-neutrality of anticipated money in this model: anticipated inflation reduces the real rate of interest.[18] By looking at (3.33), we see that there are two necessary conditions for the non-neutrality of money in this model, namely that both c_2 and a_2 be non-zero. The parameter c_2 reflects the role of the real balance effect in the goods market, and a_2 reflects the interest elasticity of the demand for money.

Equation (3.31) shows that the stock of inventories is negatively related to past real rates of interest and (3.32) shows that the level of output is related to the *change* of the real interest rate. The coefficient δ that appears in (3.31) and (3.32) is likely to be small. If it were zero, neither Y_t nor N_t would be affected by fully anticipated money.

It is thus clear that the bahavior of the model depends entirely on the time path of the (fully anticipated) inflation rate. Details of the solution are relegated to the appendix.[19] Using the solution worked out there, equations (3.31)–(3.33) can be used to analyze the responses of production and inventories to a perfectly anticipated change in either the *level* or *growth rate* of the money stock beginning in period τ.

Figure 3.2 shows the dynamic adjustment of the (log of the) price level to a 1 percent permanent change in the *level* of the money stock that occurs in period τ. The rate of inflation ($P_t - P_{t-1}$) accelerates up to period τ, and thereafter slows down. Figure 3.2 shows also the implied behavior of the real interest rate, r_t, which falls as the inflation rate accelerates up to time τ, and then starts rising as the inflation rate slows down.

The corresponding behavior of the level of inventories and the level of output are shown in Fig. 3.3. Inventories build up as the real interest rate falls, and then start to decline after the increase in the money stock. The behavior of output can be understood by combining (3.20) and (3.21), with all stochastic terms set to zero, to relate the level of production to the rate of change of inventories:

$$Y_t = K_t + \frac{\lambda}{\theta}(N_{t+1} - N_t)$$

Accordingly, output is increasing up to the period before the money stock changes; thereafter output actually decreases below its steady-state value as the inventory excess is worked off. In the longest of runs, the one-time change in the money stock is neutral, resulting only in a proportionately higher price level. But the real economy is affected by the anticipation of the change in the money stock, and continues to be affected after the change has taken place.

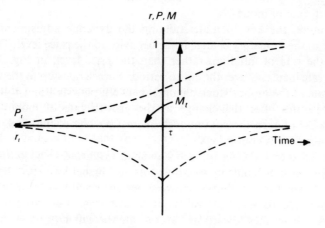

Fig. 3.2 Dynamic adjustment of the price level and real interest rate to a permanent change in the money stock

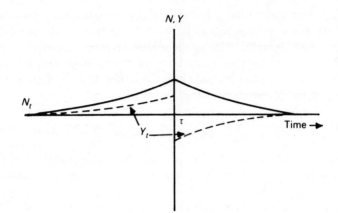

Fig. 3.3 Dynamic adjustment of the stock of inventories and level of output to a permanent change in the money stock

We turn our attention next to the effects of a permanent change in the growth rate of the money stock. Before looking at the details, it is worth thinking through the consequences of such a change. Ultimately, we expect the rate of inflation to be equal to the growth rate of money. From (3.33) we see that the real interest rate is reduced by increases in the expected inflation rate, and we should therefore expect a permanent increase in the growth rate of money to reduce the steady-state real interest rate. Equation (3.31) shows that, with the new higher rate of growth of money, the level of inventories in the steady state will be higher. From (3.32), however, we note that the level of output is affected only by the *first difference* of the real interest rate. Therefore, in the steady state, the level of output will be unaffected by the change in the growth rate of money.

Once more, the key to understanding the dynamic adjustment of the economy to the monetary change is the behavior of the price level. This time we plot the rate of inflation, rather than the price level, in Fig. 3.4. The inflation rate increases over the entire period; it accelerates up to the time the growth rate of the money stock changes (between periods τ and $\tau + 1$), and then decelerates after the change in the growth rate of money.[20] (See Appendix 3.1.) Given the continuously increasing rate of inflation, the real rate of interest falls continuously.

Figure 3.5 shows the resulting behavior of inventories and output. The stock of inventories builds up steadily to its new higher level, but the rate of increase of inventories is highest between periods τ and $\tau - 1$ and thereafter slows down. Accordingly, the level of output is at a maximum in period $\tau - 1$, and gradually declines toward its natural rate thereafter.

To sum up, the inclusion of the real interest rate in the demand function for inventories, coupled with the real balance effect on the demand for goods,

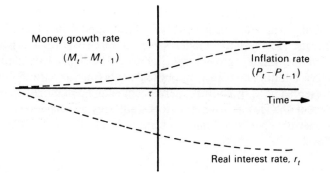

Fig. 3.4   Dynamic adjustment of the rate of inflation and real interest rate to an increase in the growth rate of the money stock

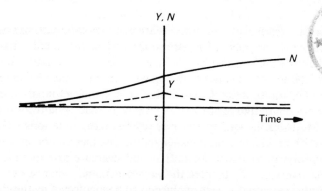

Fig. 3.5   Dynamic adjustment of the stock of inventories and level of output to an increase in the growth rate of the money stock

provides a potential route through which anticipated monetary policy can affect the behavior of output. The behavior of output depends on the change in inventories. In response to a permanent change in the stock of money, inventories build up in anticipation of the change in the money stock, and are then worked off after the change occurs. The proximate cause of the inventory changes in this case is the behavior of the real interest rate, which is in turn fundamentally determined by the expected rate of inflation. Similarly, the response to a permanent increase in the rate of growth of the money stock, which permanently reduces the real rate of interest, is that inventories are built up slowly to a new permanently higher level. Output correspondingly increases above its steady-state level, being at its highest level in the period before the growth rate of money changes, and thereafter slowly returns to its steady-state level.

The effect of anticipated money on output in this model thus differs fundamentally from that in models with fixed capital in which the Tobin effect operates. In the latter models (such as Fischer (1979)), a permanent increase in the money growth rate increases both capacity and output *permanently*, but does not cause output to deviate from its natural rate. In the model presented here, by contrast, permanent changes in money growth lead to permanent changes in inventory stocks but only to *temporary* changes in production, which persist as long as inventory stocks are not at their long-run desired levels.

3.6 CONCLUSIONS

This paper examines the way in which the inclusion of storable output modifies the aggregate supply function normally used in equilibrium models with rational expectations. The microeconomic foundations examined in Sections 3.2 and 3.3 lead to a type of "partial adjustment" mechanism for inventories, in which excess inventories are worked off only slowly over time, rather than all in one period. They are worked off in part by reducing the level of output.

Including this sort of inventory behavior changes the dynamics of the macro model substantially. In particular, in a simple rational-expectations model in which output disturbances are otherwise serially uncorrelated, inventory adjustments lead to "business cycles," that is, to long-lived effects on output. This occurs since *unanticipated* changes in the money stock simultaneously increase current output and decrease inventories, as some inventories are sold off to meet the higher demand. Then, in subsequent periods, output is raised to restore the depleted inventories. This mechanism, which we examined in Section 3.4, is the most important of this paper in that it provides a very natural vehicle for the propagation of business cycles. A look at the data suggests that this vehicle is probably of considerably empirical importance.

For example, data in Table 3.2 show how dramatic was the imprint of inventory investment on the 1973–6 business cycle. What appears to have been a negative aggregate demand shock in 1973:4 led initially to an inventory buildup followed by three quarters of diminishing rates of inventory accumulation. This same basic pattern was repeated in exaggerated form when a much larger negative shock to aggregate demand in 1974:4 caused inventories to accumulate briefly before a massive inventory liquidation began. A comparison of lines 1 and 3 shows that GNP movements were dominated by movements in inventory investment during this cycle.[21] And lines 3(a) and 4(a) show that a good deal, though certainly not all, of the "action" in the inventory series came from finished goods inventories – the central concern of this paper.[22]

Finally, in Section 3.5, we examined the effects of *perfectly anticipated* changes in the money stock on output in a model in which the desired inventory stock is a function of the real interest rate. In that case, since a permanent change in the stock of money, while ultimately neutral, alters the time path of the real interest rate, it also alters the paths of inventories and output. In particular, inventories and output are raised in anticipation of the change; and a long period of reduced output follows the monetary change, as the excess inventories are worked off. A permanent increase in the *growth rate* of money leads to a permanent increase in the stock of inventories, and to an output level that remains above capacity both before and after the change in the growth rate of money, as inventories are accumulated.

One last word. Some readers have noted that inventories cannot account for the entire postwar history of the business cycle. That we agree with this should be evident from our opening sentence. Nonetheless, we do believe that a better understanding of inventory dynamics is critical to improving knowledge of what happens to the economy during business fluctuations.

NOTES

1. For a more complete, but similar, analysis of inventory behavior in a conventional nonstochastic macro model without rational expectations, see Blinder (1980). Brunner, Cukierman and Meltzer (1980) also present a rational expectations model with inventories.

2. Data in Table 3.2 breaking down inventories by type are included for future reference.

3. Line (3) gives the *change* in inventory *investment*, which is the *second* difference of the *level* of inventories. It is this second difference that is dimensionally comparable with *first* differences in GNP and final sales. For convenience, we have included the level of inventory investment, that is, the first difference of inventory stocks in line (4).

4. Fischer (1979).

5. Fischer (1977), Phelps and Taylor (1977), and Taylor (1980). However, McCallum (1977, 1979) shows that some types of nonmarket clearing still do not permit any role for monetary policy in affecting output. See Frydman (1981) for further discussion of this point.

6. Lucas (1977, p. 18) discusses the way in which the aggregate supply function (3.1) should be modified to take account of inventory behavior, without, however, embodying the modified function in a full model.

7. It is straightforward to embed these individuals in an overlapping generations model.

8. Thus the demand for money in this model derives only from portfolio considerations, not from any special role of money as the medium of exchange.

9. Note that this set-up is consistent with multiperiod optimization.

10. Here it is convenient to treat real balances $(q_0 M_1)$ rather than nominal balances (M_1) as the choice variable.

11. $D(.)$ and the other functions introduced below do not have a time index only to economize on notation. Nothing in the nature of this problem requires that $D(.)$ or production costs or inventory holding costs be the same in each period; however, the firm's expected revenues cannot be growing too fast if an optimum is to exist.

12. Negative N_t is interpreted as a queue of unfilled orders.

13. The notation is understood to imply $\Pi_{s=\tau}^{t}(1 + r_s) = 1$ if $t < \tau$.

14. See Foley and Hellwig (1975).

15. In the yeoman farmer model, wealth is also relevant. We ignore that here.

16. In using this definition for the real interest rate, we depart slightly from the Phelpsian island paradigm in that equation (3.26) assumes that agents know the current price level. We should actually write $_t P_t$ instead of P_t in (3.26), where $_t P_t$ is the current estimate of the price level conditional on information available currently. We know that $_t P_t$ is a weighted average of the actual aggregate price level and the expectation of P_t conditional on knowledge of the aggregate price level and all other history up to and including $t - 1$. Thus any effects captured in the present version would be present in the more accurate consistent island paradigm, so long as knowledge of the current nominal interest rate does not serve to identify the current aggregate price level – as it does not in the present model in which the money demand and other disturbances prevent identification. There is, in addition, a question as to why the term $(P_t - {}_{t-1}P_t)$ appears in (3.20), once the term in N_t^* is present. The $(P_t - {}_{t-1}P_t)$ can be rationalized as resulting from one-period wage contracts. (See Fischer (1977).)

17. By "fully anticipated" we mean that the money changes being discussed have always been known about. For a more precise definition, see Fischer (1979).

18. This statement assumes that the denominator is positive. Since $\theta > \lambda$, a sufficient condition is $c_2 a_1 < 1$, which means that a \$1 increase in money *supply* raises money *demand* by less than \$1.

19. The solution is essentially as described in Fischer (1979).

20. Note that the overshooting of the inflation rate above the growth rate of money occurs *before* there is any change in monetary growth.

21. The role of inventories in this cycle is considered in much greater detail in Blinder (1979, Ch. 4), where evidence is offered to suggest that 1973:4 and especially1974:4 should indeed be considered as quarters in which negative aggregate demand shocks occurred.

22. A referee suggested that aggregate inventory movements were dominated by raw materials and goods in process, rather than by the finished goods inventories to which the theory applies. This prompted us to disaggregate the inventory data as in Table 3.2. (Details of how this was done are in footnotes to the table.) It turns out that investment in finished goods inventories (mostly of retailers and wholesalers) fluctuate a good deal more than investment in other sorts of inventories.

23. This statement requires $b_1 > \mu$, which is guaranteed if $[a_2(\theta - \lambda)(1 - c_1 - c_2 a_1) + a_2 \theta c_1 - c_3 a_1 \lambda - c_2 a_1 a_2 \lambda] > 0$, a condition we assume. It is satisfied if θ is sufficiently greater than λ, for instance.

REFERENCES

Blanchard, O. (1979) "Backward and forward solutions for economies with rational expectations," *American Economic Review*, Papers and Proceedings (May), pp. 114–18.

Blinder, A. S. (1978) "Inventories and the demand for labor," mimeo, Princeton University, Princeton, NJ.

Blinder, A. S. (1979) *Economic Policy and the Great Stagflation*, New York: Academic Press.

Blinder, A. S. (1980) "Inventories in the Keynesian Macro Model," *Kyklos*, fasc. 4. Reprinted here as Ch. 2.

Brunner, K., A. Cukierman and A. H. Meltzer (1980) "Money and Economic Activity: Inventories and Business Cycles," unpublished (Carnegie-Mellon University, Pittsburg, Pa.).

Fischer, S. (1977) "Long-term contracts, rational expectations, and the optimal money supply rule," *Journal of Political Economy* (Feb.), pp. 191–206.

Fischer, S. (1979) "Anticipations and the nonneutrality of money," *Journal of Political Economy* (April), pp. 225–52.

Foley, D. K. and M. F. Hellwig (1975) "Asset management with trading uncertainty," *Review of Economic Studies*, vol. 42 (July), pp. 327–46.

Frydman, R. (1981) "Sluggish price adjustments and the effectiveness of monetary policy under rational expectations," *Journal of Money, Credit and Banking*, vol. 13 (Feb.), pp. 94–102.

Lucas, R. E. Jr (1972) "Expectations and the neutrality of money," *Journal of Economic Theory* (April), pp. 103–24.

Lucas, R. E. Jr (1973) "Some international evidence on output-inflation tradeoffs," *American Economic Review* (June), pp. 326–34.

Lucas, R. E. Jr (1975) "An equilibrium model of the business cycle," *Journal of Political Economy* (Dec.), pp. 1113–29.

Lucas, R. E. Jr (1977) "Understanding business cycles," in: *Stabilization of the Domestic and International Economy*, Carnegie–Rochester Series on Public Policy, vol. 5, pp. 7–29.

McCallum, B. T. (1977) "Price-level stickiness and the feasibility of monetary stabilization policy with rational expectations," *Journal of Political Economy* (June), pp. 627–34.

McCallum, B. T. (1979) "A macroeconomic model with predetermined wages, markup pricing, and classical properties," mimeo (University of Virginia, Charlottesville, VA).

Mundell, R. A. (1963) "Inflation and real interest," *Journal of Political Economy*, vol. 71 (June), pp. 280–3.

Phelps, E. S. and J. Taylor (1977) "Stabilizing powers of monetary policy under rational expectations," *Journal of Political Economy* (Feb.), pp. 163–90.

Phelps, E. S. *et al.* (1970) *Microeconomic Foundations of Employment and Inflation Theory*, New York: Norton.

Sargent, T. (1979) *Macroeconomic Theory*, New York: Academic Press.

Taylor, J. B. (1980) "Aggregate dynamics and staggered contracts," *Journal of Political Economy* (Feb), pp. 1–23.

Tobin, J. (1965) "Money and economic growth," *Econometrica* (Oct.), pp. 671–84.

APPENDIX 3.1

In this appendix we solve for the behavior of the price level in the model of Section 3.5, and then briefly indicate some of the calculations underlying the dynamics discussed in that section.

Working with the model (3.20) through (3.26) with the stochastic terms set to zero, we obtain the following equation for the price level:

$$P_t = b_0 + b_1 P_{t-1} + b_{2t} P_{t+1} + b_{3t-1} P_t + b_4 M_t + b_5 M_{t-1}$$

$$\text{(A3.1)}$$

with $b_1, b_2, b_4 > 0$ and $b_3, b_5 < 0$. The coefficients b_1 through b_5 are:

$$b_1 = \xi[(1 - \theta)(c_3 + c_2 a_2 + a_2 c_3)$$
$$+ (1 + a_2)\beta\delta + a_1 a_2 c_2 (\theta - \lambda)\delta] < 0$$

$$b_2 = \xi a_2 [c_3 + \beta\delta + c_2 a_1 (\theta - \lambda)\delta] < 0$$

$$b_3 = -\xi a_2 [(1 - (1 - \theta)\theta)c_3 + \beta\delta + c_2 a_1 (\theta - \lambda)\delta] < 0$$

$$b_4 = \xi[c_3 + c_2 a_2 + \beta\delta] > 0$$

$$b_5 = -\xi[(1 - \theta)(c_3 + c_2 a_2) + \beta\delta] < 0$$

$$\xi \equiv [c_3 + c_2 a_2 + \beta\delta + a_2\{c_3 + \beta\delta + c_2 a_1 \delta(\theta - \lambda)\}]^{-1} > 0$$

$$\beta \equiv \theta(1 - c_2 a_1) + \lambda(c_1 - 1 + c_2 a_1) > 0$$

They satisfy:

$$\sum_1^5 b_i = 1 \qquad b_2 + b_4 = 1 \qquad b_1 + b_3 + b_5 = 0$$

Equation (A3.1) is a convenient form to write the price equation because it enables us to exploit a solution previously worked out in Fischer (1979).

As shown by Blanchard (1979), there are a variety of solutions for equations of the form of equation (A3.1), some of which make the price level a function only of lagged money stocks. We choose to work with a solution that makes the current price level a function of both lagged and future money stocks, since we believe it reasonable that individuals take into account the expected evolution of the money stock in forming their expectations of future price levels. The general form of a solution which takes both lagged and future behavior of the money stock into account was studied in some detail in Fischer (1979). In the case where there is no uncertainty this solution is:

$$P_t = \text{constant} + \sum_0^\infty \pi_i M_{t+i} + \alpha M_{t-1} + \mu P_{t-1} \tag{A3.2}$$

where μ is the root that is less than unity to:

$$b_2 \mu^2 + (b_3 - 1)\mu + b_1 = 0 \tag{A3.3}$$

and:

$$\pi_0 = \left[1 - \frac{b_2 \mu}{b_1} \right]\left[\frac{\mu - b_2 \mu^2}{b_1} \right] > 0 \tag{A3.4}$$

$$\pi_i = \left[\frac{b_2 \mu}{b_1} \right]^i \pi_0 \qquad i = 1, 2, 3, \ldots$$

$$\alpha = \frac{b_5 \mu}{b_1} < 0$$

and where:

$$0 < \frac{b_2 \mu}{b_1} < 1$$

The effects of a fully anticipated permanent change in the stock of money on the price level are derived as follows. It can be shown that in the period, τ, in which the money supply changes:

$$\frac{\partial P_\tau}{\partial M_\tau} = \frac{\mu(1 - b_2 \mu)}{b_1 - b_2 \mu^2} \leqq 1$$

In the earlier periods:

$$\frac{\partial P_{\tau - i}}{\partial M_\tau} = \left[\frac{b_2 \mu}{b_1} \right]^i \frac{\partial P_\tau}{\partial M_\tau} \qquad i = 0, 1, 2, \ldots$$

Thus, up to period τ, the inflation rate is given by:

$$\frac{\partial P_{\tau - i}}{\partial M_\tau} - \frac{\partial P_{\tau - i - 1}}{\partial M_\tau} = \left[\frac{b_2 \mu}{b_1} \right]^i \left[1 - \frac{b_2 \mu}{b_1} \right] \frac{\partial P_\tau}{\partial M_\tau} \qquad i = 0, 1, \ldots$$

The inflation rate therefore increases up to period τ.

In subsequent periods:

$$\frac{\partial P_{\tau+i}}{\partial M_\tau} = 1 - \frac{\mu^i(b_1 - \mu)(1 - \mu)}{b_1 - b_2\mu^2}$$

The inflation rate therefore decreases after period τ.[23]

Finally, we want to show that the maximum inflation rate occurs between periods $(\tau - 1)$ and τ. We accordingly have to show that:

$$\frac{\partial P_\tau}{\partial M_\tau} - \frac{\partial P_{\tau-1}}{\partial M_\tau} > \frac{\partial P_{\tau+1}}{\partial M_\tau} - \frac{\partial P_\tau}{\partial M_\tau} \quad \text{or}$$

$$\left[1 - \frac{b_2\mu}{b_1}\right](\mu(1 - b_2\mu)) > (b_1 - \mu)(1 - \mu) \quad \text{or}$$

$$\frac{\mu}{b_1} \frac{b_1 - b_2\mu}{b_1 - \mu} \frac{1 - b_2\mu}{1 - \mu} > 1$$

Since $b_2 < 1$, and $\mu < b_1$ (by the assumption noted in the preceding footnote), it will suffice to show that:

$$\frac{\mu(1 - b_2\mu)}{b_1(1 - \mu)} > 1 \quad \text{or}$$

$$\mu(1 - b_2\mu) > b_1(1 - \mu) \quad \text{or} \quad \mu - b_2\mu^2 - b_1 + b_1\mu > 0$$

Now, from equation (A3.3), we can substitute for $-(b_1 + b_2\mu^2)$, so we have to show:

$$\mu + (b_3 - 1)\mu + b_1\mu > 0 \quad \text{or} \quad (b_1 + b_3)\mu > 0$$

Since $b_1 + b_3 = -b_5 > 0$, the inflation rate has been shown to be at a maximum between periods $(\tau - 1)$ and τ.

To derive the behavior of N_t, r_t and Y_t, we work from (3.31) and (3.33) to obtain:

$$N_t - N^* = \sum_1^\infty \Psi_i({}_{t-i}P_{t-i+1} - P_{t-i}) \tag{A3.6}$$

$$\Psi_1 = \frac{c_2 a_2 \theta \delta}{c_3 + c_2 a_2 + \beta\delta}$$

$$\Psi_i = \left[\frac{(c_3 + c_2 a_2)(1 - \theta) + \beta\delta}{c_3 + c_2 a_2 + \beta\delta}\right]^{i-1} \Psi_1$$

$$= \left[\frac{-b_5}{b_4}\right]^{i-1} \Psi_1$$

$$r_t - \text{constant} = \frac{-c_2 a_2}{c_3 + c_2 a_2 + \beta\delta} \sum_{i=0}^\infty \xi_i({}_{t-i}P_{t+1-i} - P_{t-i}) \tag{A3.7}$$

$$\xi_0 = 1, \qquad \xi_1 = \frac{\theta \beta \delta}{c_3 + c_2 a_2 + \beta \delta}$$

$$\xi_i = \left[\frac{(c_3 + c_2 a_2)(1 - \theta) + \beta \delta}{c_3 + c_2 a_2 + \beta \delta} \right]^{i-1} \xi_1, \qquad i = 2, \ldots \infty$$

$$= \left[\frac{-b_5}{b_4} \right]^{i-1} \xi_1$$

We also use:

$$Y_t = \frac{\lambda}{\theta}(N_{t+1} - N_t) \tag{A3.8}$$

We do not give formulae corresponding to all the figures in Section 3.5, but note, using equations (A3.5) and (A3.6) that it can be shown that, in response to a fully anticipated change in the stock of money in period τ:

$$\frac{\partial(N_\tau - N^*)}{\partial M_\tau} = \frac{\Psi_1 \mu(1 - b_2)}{b_1 - b_2 \mu^2} \quad \text{and}$$

$$\frac{\partial(N_{\tau-i} - N^*)}{\partial M_\tau} = \left[\frac{b_2 \mu}{b_1} \right]^i \frac{\partial(N_\tau - N^*)}{\partial M_\tau}$$

$$\frac{\partial(N_{\tau+1} - N^*)}{\partial M_\tau} = \mu \frac{\partial(N_\tau - N^*)}{\partial M_\tau} < \frac{\partial(N_\tau - N^*)}{\partial M_\tau}$$

Next we consider the effects of an increase in the *growth rate* of money. Specifically, we assume:

$$M_t - M_{t-1} = 0 \qquad t = -\infty, \ldots, \tau$$

$$M_t - M_{t-1} = 1 \qquad t = \tau + 1, \ldots, \infty$$

Using equations (A3.2) and (A3.4) it is relatively straightforward to show:

$$\frac{\partial(P_{\tau+1} - P_\tau)}{\partial g} = \frac{\mu - b_2 \mu^2}{b_1 - b_2 \mu^2} < 1 \tag{A3.9}$$

$$\frac{\partial(P_{\tau-i+1} - P_{\tau-i})}{\partial g} = \left[\frac{b_2 \mu}{b_1} \right]^i \frac{\partial(P_{\tau+1} - P_\tau)}{\partial g} \qquad i = 1, 2, \ldots$$

$$\frac{\partial(P_{\tau+1+i} - P_{\tau+i})}{\partial g} = 1 - \frac{\mu^i(b_1 - \mu)}{b_1 - b_2 \mu^2} \qquad i = 1, 2, \ldots$$

where g is the change in the growth rate of money described above.

Looking at equation (A3.6), it is clear that inventories build up as the inflation rate increases; similarly from equation (A3.7), the real rate of interest falls continuously as the inflation rate increases. To study the behavior of output, use equation (A3.8); we leave it as an exercise to show, based on equations (A3.6) and (A3.9) that:

$$\frac{\partial N_{\tau+1}}{\partial g} = \frac{\Psi_1 \mu b_1 (1 - b_2)}{(b_1 - b_2 \mu^2)(b_1 - b_2 \mu)} \tag{A3.10}$$

$$\frac{\partial N_{\tau+1-i}}{\partial g} = \left[\frac{b_2 \mu}{b_1} \right]^i \frac{\partial N_\tau}{\partial g} \qquad i = 1, 2, \ldots$$

$$\frac{\partial N_{\tau+1+i}}{\partial g} = \frac{\partial N_{\tau+i}}{\partial g} + \frac{\mu^{i+1} \Psi_1 (1 - b_2)}{b_1 - b_2 \mu^2} \qquad i = 1, 2, \ldots$$

Accordingly:

$$\frac{\partial(N_{\tau+2} - N_{\tau+1})}{\partial g} < \frac{\partial(N_{\tau+1} - N_t)}{\partial g}$$

4 · INVENTORIES AND STICKY PRICES: MORE ON THE MICROFOUNDATIONS OF MACROECONOMICS

The phenomenon of "sticky prices," that is, the apparent insensitivity of prices to fluctuations in demand, has long intrigued both microeconomists and macroeconomists.[1] Normally, increasing production and raising prices are thought of as alternative ways for a firm to respond to an increase in the demand for its product. Thus firms that opt for large short-run quantity adjustments will display small short-run price adjustments, while firms that make small quantity adjustments will be forced to make large price adjustments.

The logic behind this common conclusion is clear from Fig. 4.1. Here y is output, $C'(y)$ is the (rising) marginal cost curve, $R'(y) + \varepsilon$ is the (falling) MR curve (with ε a random demand shock), and equilibrium is where $MR = MC$. It follows that, among firms facing the same structure of demand, those with steep MC schedules will display strong price responses and weak output responses, while those with flat MC schedules will display weak price responses and strong output responses.

The main point of this paper is that this simple conclusion may well be reversed when output is storable. Specifically, some firms may exhibit large output *and* large price responses to demand shocks while other firms have little response in either dimension. The central result is a theorem characterizing precisely what types of firms tend to fall in each category. Loosely speaking, the principal conclusion (stated precisely as Theorem 4.1 below) is that *both* price *and* output responses become smaller as demand shocks become less persistent and output becomes more "inventoriable." That is, for given MC and MR curves, "sticky" prices will tend to emerge when it is not very costly to vary inventories and when demand shocks are very transitory.

This paper is closely related to, and generalizes the results of, papers by Amihud and Mendelson (1980) and Reagan (1980), and a well-known earlier paper by Zabel (1972).[2] The two recent papers emphasize an asymmetry in

I am indebted to Yakov Amihud, Olivier Blanchard, Robert Clower, Stanley Fischer, Wolfgang Franz, Arnold Kling, Louis Maccini, Julio Rotemberg, Robert Shiller, and Lawrence Summers for useful comments on earlier drafts; to Danny Quah for outstanding research assistance; and to the National Science Foundation for financial support. This research is part of the NBER's project on inflation.

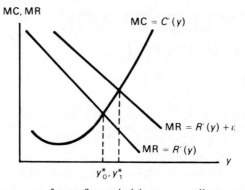

Fig. 4.1 The response of a profit-maximizing monopolist to a rise in demand

pricing behavior that results when stockouts occur by showing that prices respond more strongly to demand shocks when there are stockouts than when there are not. This asymmetry occurs in my model as well; but it is not the focus of this paper. Rather, for the most part I ignore stockouts and stress that the existence of inventories reduces the flexibility of prices in all states of demand and in both directions.

The paper is organized as follows. This introduction concludes with an intuitive explanation of the main result, which both conveys the flavor of the proof and, more importantly, suggests that the result is quite a bit more general than the model used to derive it. Section 4.1 presents the formal model, compares it to the earlier literature, and states the main theorem precisely. Section 4.2 consists of a formal proof, and Section 4.3 collects some interesting related results on inventory behavior that flow from the model. Section 4.4 shows that the main result on price "stickiness" carries over to the competitive case. Section 4.5 discusses some macroeconomic phenomena for which the model may provide microfoundations, and Section 4.6 is a summary.

Why does the existence of inventories of finished goods invalidate the simple story told by Fig. 4.1? The answer is that a firm with storable output is operating simultaneously on two margins. It must decide how much output to produce for inventory, and it must decide how much inventory to sell. While profit maximization continues to require $MC = MR$ each period, it is no longer necessary that this be done with output (y_t) equal to sales (x_t). Indeed, it will quite often be the case that optimal y_t and x_t differ, with changes in the stock of inventories (N_t) taking up the slack. Figure 4.2 illustrates the basic idea. The MC curve is $C'(y)$, and optimal output is determined by equating MC to the shadow value of inventories, denoted $\lambda(N)$, at point B. The MR curve is $R'(x) + \varepsilon$, and optimal sales are determined by equating MR to $\lambda(N)$ at point A. It is obvious that x and y need not be equal.

Now consider what happens when ε changes. Trivial algebra establishes that:

$$\frac{dy}{d\varepsilon} = \frac{1}{C''(y)} \frac{d\lambda}{d\varepsilon}$$

$$\frac{dx}{d\varepsilon} = \frac{1}{-R''(x)} \left(1 - \frac{d\lambda}{d\varepsilon} \right)$$

so it is clear that everything hinges on the response of λ to ε. If $d\lambda/d\varepsilon$ is close to unity, demand shocks will be met by substantial changes in output but small changes in sales, that is, large changes in prices. Conversely, if $d\lambda/d\varepsilon$ is close to zero, demand shocks will elicit small output responses and large sales responses, that is, small price responses. Large (small) output responses and large (small) price responses thus go together if the cross-sectional differences among firms come mainly in $d\lambda/d\varepsilon$ (rather than in $C''(y)$ and $R''(x)$).

What factors are likely to govern the size of $d\lambda/d\varepsilon$? First, intuition tells us that the shadow value of inventories will respond more strongly when shocks are expected to persist longer. A transitory shock will change λ very little; a permanent one will change it a lot. Second, it seems likely that $d\lambda/d\varepsilon$ will be larger when goods are more difficult to inventory. Finally, Fig. 4.2 suggests that the slopes of the MC and MR curves remain relevant, though not in as obvious a way as in Fig. 4.1. The essence of Theorem 4.1 below is to show that $d\lambda/d\varepsilon$ is between zero and unity, and depends on the aforementioned parameters in the ways suggested by intuition.

4.1 THE MODEL OF THE FIRM

Initially, I take the firm to be a value-maximizing monopolist, though Section 4.4 will show that the main result carries over to the competitive case. The firm knows its demand curve up to an additive stochastic disturbance and,

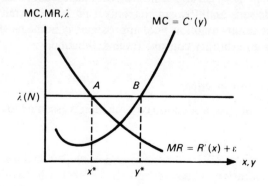

Fig. 4.2   Profit-maximizing choices of production and sales

each period, must select its price and production level *before* observing its demand shock for that period. It does, however, form (rational) expectations of the demand shock. Specifically, if the symbols X_t, Y_t, P_t, and N_t denote the firm's sales, output, price, and beginning-of-period inventory stock for period t, it seeks to maximize:

$$E_0 \sum_{t=0}^{\infty} D^t \{ \tilde{R}(X_t, \eta_t) - C(Y_t) - B(N_t) \}$$

where η_t is the demand shock, $\tilde{R}(.)$ is the revenue function, $C(.)$ is the production cost function, $B(.)$ is the inventory carrying cost function, $D \equiv 1/(1 + r)$ is a discount factor, and the expectation is taken as of time zero. Each of the functions merits some discussion.

4.1.1 Revenue function

To exploit the advantages of certainty equivalence, I assume that the demand curve is linear, so that the revenue function is quadratic. In addition, the work of Zabel (1972) makes it quite clear that there is almost no hope of deriving results unless the demand shock is additive. These considerations lead to a demand function of the form:[3]

$$X_t = 2(d_0 - dP_t + \eta'_t) \tag{4.1}$$

or in inverse form:

$$P_t = \frac{d_0}{d} - \frac{1}{2d} X_t + \eta_t \tag{4.2}$$

where $\eta_t = \eta'_t/d$ so that the revenue function is:

$$R(P_t, \eta'_t) = 2P_t(d_0 - dP_t) + 2P_t\eta'_t$$
$$\equiv R(P_t) + 2P_t\eta'_t$$

While this is a less general specification than that used by Zabel, Amihud–Mendelson, and Reagan, its only role is to permit an explicit solution. All the results to follow hold approximately in the neighborhood of equilibrium for an arbitrary concave revenue function.

4.1.2 Production cost function

For the same reason, the production cost function is assumed to be quadratic:

$$C(Y_t) = c_0 + c_1 Y_t + \frac{1}{2c} Y_t^2 \tag{4.3}$$

While this specification is less general than Zabel, who worked with an arbitrary convex cost function, it is more general than Amihud–Mendelson and Reagan, who restricted themselves to the case of constant marginal costs $(c \to \infty)$.

4.1.3 Inventory cost function

Here again, where explicit solutions are necessary, I assume that $B(.)$ is quadratic:

$$B(N_t) = b_0 + b_1 N_t + (b/2)N_t^2; \qquad b > 0 \qquad (4.4)$$

where $N_t \equiv \hat{N}_t - K$ is the deviation of actual inventories, $\hat{N}_t$, from some critical level, K. This is a more general specification than Zabel or Amihud–Mendelson, both of which assumed a linear storage cost technology $(b = 0)$. Reagan assumed no explicit storage costs. It turns out that the parameter b is absolutely critical to the analysis and that $b = 0$ is a very special case.

This cost function, which is sketched in Fig. 4.3 for the case $b_1 = 0$ admits of two possible interpretations. First, K could be zero, in which case $N = \hat{N}$ and $B(N)$ is storage costs if inventories are positive and represents the cost of holding a queue of unfilled orders if N is negative.[4] Alternatively, K could be some critical level of inventories below which production costs actually rise because it is difficult to schedule production efficiently, etc. The magnitude of K would then obviously influence the likelihood that the firm stocks out. For the most part, I assume that negative values of N (interpreted as unfilled orders) are possible; but Section 4.5 offers some brief remarks on what happens if negative N is impossible. Under either interpretation, it makes sense to assume $b_1 = 0$ since $B(N)$ reaches its minimum at $N = -b_1/b$. But the parameter b_1 is not critical in what follows.

4.1.4 Distribution of demand shocks

Each of the papers referred to above assumes that demand shocks are independently and identically distributed (*iid*). This assumption, while it

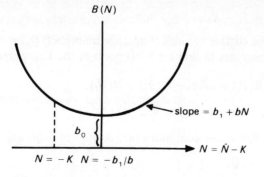

Fig. 4.3 The inventory storage cost function

simplifies things greatly, is quite unsatisfactory. We know, for example, that disturbances at the macro level are highly serially correlated, and it would be surprising indeed if this serial correlation disappeared when we disaggregated to the industry or firm levels. In this paper, I assume for the most part that the stochastic structure of demand follows an $AR(1)$ process:

$$\eta_t = \rho\eta_{t-1} + V_t; \qquad 0 \leqslant \rho \leqslant 1 \tag{4.5}$$

where V_t is a white noise disturbance term, though certain other stochastic processes will be considered as well. Obviously, *iid* disturbances are a special case of (4.5) when $\rho = 0$. At the other extreme, $\rho = 1$ denotes a random walk.

4.2 THE CENTRAL THEOREM

With the notation established, I am now in a position to state precisely the main theorem of the paper.

THEOREM 4.1. *The responses of the optimal price P_t^*, and optimal production Y_t^*, to the contemporaneous demand shock η_t, are both smaller when demand shocks are more transitory (i.e., ρ is smaller) and when marginal carrying costs of inventories are less sensitive to the level of inventories (i.e., when b is smaller).*

I proceed now to sketch the proof, whose basic idea was suggested by the intuitive analysis of the introductory section. It will be clear that the linear quadratic structure of the problem is needed only to get an explicit solution and is unlikely to be "special" in any important sense.

4.2.1 First-order conditions

The firm's optimization problem is constrained by the accounting identity relating inventory change to sales and production:

$$N_{t+1} - N_t = Y_t - X_t \tag{4.6}$$

Introducing the costate variable (Lagrange multiplier) Q_t for this constraint, the problem becomes to find a critical point of the Lagrangian:

$$E_0 \sum_{t=0}^{\infty} D^t \{ R(P_t) + 2P_t\eta_t' - C(Y_t) - B(N_t)$$
$$+ Q_t(-N_{t+1} + N_t + Y_t - X_t)\}$$

for which the first-order conditions (in addition to (4.6)) are:[5]

$$E_0 C'(Y_t) = E_0 Q_t \tag{4.7}$$

$$E_0 R'(P_t) = E_0(-2dQ_t - 2\eta_t') \tag{4.8}$$

$$E_0 B'(N_t) = E_0(Q_t - (1 + r)Q_{t-1})$$ (4.9)

To simplify the notation, let lower case Roman letters denote the expectation (conditional on the information set at time zero) of the corresponding upper case symbol. Thus, for example, $x_t = E_0 X_t$, where the information set at time zero includes all lagged data and the beginning-of-period inventory stock, N_0. And let ε_t denote the *expected* demand shock for period t, viz. $\varepsilon_t = E_0 \eta_t$. Then, under the specific functional forms introduced in Section 4.1, (4.7)–(4.9) can be written as:

$$y_t = c(q_t - c_1)$$

$$p_t = (d_0/d + q_t + \varepsilon_t)/2$$

$$q_t = (1 + r)q_{t-1} + bn_t + b_1$$

If we call the nonstochastic steady-state values of the variables $\bar{y} = \bar{x}, \bar{p}, \bar{q}$, and $\bar{n}$ and define λ_t as the deviation of q_t from its steady state, we can rewrite these equations as follows:

$$y_t - \bar{y} = c\lambda_t$$ (4.10)

$$x_t - \bar{x} = -d\lambda_t + d\varepsilon_t$$ (4.11)

$$\lambda_t - \lambda_{t-1} = r\lambda_{t-1} + b(n_t - \bar{n})$$ (4.12)

These three conditions have straightforward economic interpretations. As can readily be verified, (4.10) equates expected marginal cost to the expected shadow value of inventories, q_t, and (4.11) equates expected marginal revenue to q_t. Equation (4.12) defines optimal inventory holding by the condition that the expected (shadow) price appreciation be just equal to the sum of the expected marginal storage costs plus the implicit interest cost of carrying inventories.

A simple graphical representation of the solution is obtained by substituting (4.10) and (4.11) into the identity (4.6) to get:

$$n_{t+1} - n_t = (c + d)\lambda_t - d\varepsilon_t$$ (4.13)

For any given value of the expected demand shock, ε_t, the stationaries of the difference equation system (4.12)–(4.13) appear as in Fig. 4.4, which clearly shows that there is a unique *saddle point* solution for any fixed ε_t. The firm must select λ_0 to be on the unique stable arm, which immediately implies that λ_0 is a decreasing function of n_0.

It is important to realize that t measures *planning* time, not *calendar* time, in this model. The firm formulates a plan for $(y_0, y_1, y_2, \dots)$ and $(p_0, p_1, p_2, \dots)$, but only puts into effect the first period of this plan. Symbols such as y_1, y_2, etc. in the model connote the *current expectations* of future variables – for example, $y_2 = E_0(Y_2)$. The actual values of these future variables will be different unless there are no unanticipated events in the

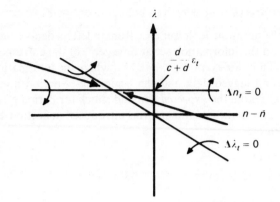

Fig. 4.4 Phase diagram for inventory and its shadow value

interim. For this reason, we really want to use equations (4.10)–(4.13) only for the case $t = 0$. Clearly, then, we must solve the model explicitly to find λ_0, the initial value of the shadow value of inventories.

The method of solution is only sketched here. See Appendix 4.1 for details. First reduce (4.12)–(4.13) to a single second-order inhomogenous difference equation:

$$\lambda_t - [2 + r + b(c + d)]\lambda_{t-1} + (1 + r)\lambda_{t-2} = -bd\varepsilon_{t-1} \qquad (4.14)$$

Letting $\beta \equiv 2 + r + b(c + d)$, the characteristic roots of (4.14) are the solutions to the quadratic equation:

$$z^2 - \beta z + (1 + r) = 0 \qquad (4.15)$$

and the solution to the homogeneous part of (4.14) takes the form:

$$\lambda_t = K_1(z_1)^t + K_2(z_2)^t$$

where z_1, z_2 are the roots of (4.15) and K_1 and K_2 are constants to be determined by the initial conditions. It is easy to show that one of the roots is less than unity while the other is greater than unity. Hence, if z_2 is the unstable root, picking λ_0 to be on the stable arm in Fig. 4.4 is tantamount to picking $K_2 = 0$. The full solution to (4.14) therefore takes the form:

$$\lambda_t = K_1 z_1^t + \phi_t, \qquad 0 < z_1 < 1 \qquad (4.16)$$

where ϕ_t is a particular solution to the inhomogenous part of (4.14). That is, ϕ_t must satisfy:

$$[1 - \beta L + (1 + r)L^2]\phi_t = -bd\varepsilon_{t-1} \qquad (4.17)$$

which makes it obvious that the form of ϕ_t depends on the time path followed by $\varepsilon_t \equiv E_0\eta_t$, which in turn depends on the nature of the stochastic process generating demand shocks.

It is shown in Appendix 4.1 that the solution for the initial value of the shadow value of inventories is:

$$\lambda_0 = \left(\frac{1 - z_1}{c + d}\right)\left[\bar{n} - n_0 + d\varepsilon_0 + \frac{\phi_1 - z_1\phi_0}{b}\right] \tag{4.18}$$

and that the so-called "forward solution" of (4.17) can be expressed as:

$$\frac{1 - z_1 L}{b}\,\phi_t = d\theta \sum_{j=0}^{\infty} \theta^j \varepsilon_{t+j} \tag{4.19}$$

where $\theta \equiv 1/z_2 < 1$. For the most part, I deal with the case of $AR(1)$ demand shocks (equation (4.5)) for which it follows that:

$$\varepsilon_0 = E_0\eta_0 = \rho\eta_{-1}$$

$$\varepsilon_t = E_0\eta_t = \rho^{t+1}\eta_{-1} = \rho^t\varepsilon_0, \quad t = 1, 2, \ldots$$

In this case, using (4.18) and (4.19) leads to the solution:

$$\lambda_0 = \left(\frac{1 - z_1}{c + d}\right)\left[\bar{n} - n_0 + \frac{d}{1 - \theta\rho}\varepsilon_0\right] \tag{4.20}$$

I note in passing that the same form of solution emerges if demand shocks follow an $ARMA(1, 1)$ process:

$$\eta_t = \rho\eta_{t-1} + V_t + mV_{t-1}$$

for in that case:

$$\varepsilon_0 = E_0\eta_0 = \rho\eta_{-1} + mV_{-1}$$

$$\varepsilon_t = \rho^t\varepsilon_0, \quad t = 1, 2, \ldots.$$

Thus (4.20) applies again with ε_0 interpreted as $\rho\eta_{-1} + mV_{-1}$ instead of merely $\rho\eta_{-1}$.

Since I have earlier shown that y_0, x_0, and n_1 all depend on λ_0, everything we need to know about the economics of the problem is embedded in (4.20). I proceed now to ferret out the implications.

PROPOSITION 1. *In response to an expected positive (negative) shock to demand, the firm increases (decreases) output, price, and expected sales, and reduces (raises) expected inventory investment.*[6]

Proof. It follows from (4.10)–(4.13) that:

$$\frac{\partial y_0}{\partial \varepsilon_0} = c\frac{\partial \lambda_0}{\partial \varepsilon_0} \tag{4.21}$$

$$\frac{\partial x_0}{\partial \varepsilon_0} = d\left(1 - \frac{\partial \lambda_0}{\partial \varepsilon_0}\right) \tag{4.22}$$

$$\frac{\partial(n_1 - n_0)}{\partial \varepsilon_0} = (c + d)\frac{\partial \lambda_0}{\partial \varepsilon_0} - d \tag{4.23}$$

and from the demand curve that:

$$\frac{\partial p_0}{\partial \varepsilon_0} = \frac{1}{2}\left(1 + \frac{\partial \lambda_0}{\partial \varepsilon_0}\right) \tag{4.24}$$

Hence the proposition is proved if we can show that:

$$0 < \partial \lambda_0/\partial \varepsilon_0 < d/(d + c)$$

This condition follows readily, once we note that by (4.20):

$$\frac{\partial \lambda_0}{\partial \varepsilon_0} = \left(\frac{d}{c + d}\right)\left(\frac{1 - z_1}{1 - \theta \rho}\right) \tag{4.25}$$

$$= \left(\frac{d}{c + d}\right)\left(\frac{z_2 - (1 + r)}{z_2 - \rho}\right)$$

where the last equality follows by multiplying both numerator and denominator by z_2 and observing that $z_1 z_2 = 1 + r$ (see equation (4.15)). Some $z_2 > 1 + r > \rho$, the proposition is proven.

There is certainly nothing surprising about Proposition 1. Our interest, of course, centers on how the derivatives referred to in the proposition vary with changes in the parameters b and ρ. Consider first the parameter b, which indicates the degree of convexity of the inventory cost function. Firms with high (low) b find it costly (cheap) to vary inventory levels. Hence b measures (with sign reversed) the "flexibility" of inventory holdings. The following proposition sums up the effects of b on the firm's adjustment procedures.

PROPOSITION 2. *As b rises, that is, as output gets less "inventoriable," demand shocks elicit: (i) larger output responses; (ii) smaller sales responses; (iii) larger price responses; and (iv) smaller (in absolute value) responses of inventory investment.*

Proof. By inspection of the derivatives of x_0, y_0, p_0, and $n_1 - n_0$ with respect to ε_0, it can be seen that the proposition follows if we can establish that:

$$d(\partial \lambda_0/\partial \varepsilon_0)/db > 0$$

Using (4.25), it follows that:

$$\frac{d}{db}\left(\frac{\partial \lambda_0}{\partial \varepsilon_0}\right) = \left(\frac{d}{d + c}\right)\left(\frac{dz_2}{db}\right)\frac{z_2 - \rho - [z_2 - (1 + r)]}{(z_2 - \rho)^2}$$

$$= \frac{d}{d + c}\frac{(1 + r - \rho)}{(z_2 - \rho)^2}\frac{dz_2}{db}$$

So the proposition follows if we can prove that dz_2/db is positive. But this can be verified by differentiating (4.15) with respect to b (recalling that $d\beta/db = d + c$).

The intuition behind this result is simple. Firms that can vary inventories painlessly (i.e., firms with low b) will use their inventories to absorb most shocks. They will therefore make small changes in output and price, while making big sales responses *via* inventory changes. Firms that lack this flexibility because b is high must rely more on output and price responses.

Before leaving this topic, it is useful to examine two special cases. As $b \to \infty$, output becomes essentially nonstorable because n cannot be changed except at prohibitive cost. In that case, it can be shown that $z_2 \to \beta \to \infty$ and therefore (4.25) implies that $\partial\lambda_0/\partial\varepsilon_0 \to d/(d + c)$. By (4.21) and (4.22) the sales and output responses both approach $dc/(d + c)$, and therefore the inventory response to shocks goes to zero. (The price response in (4.24) goes to $(d + c/2)/(d + c) < 1$.) As stated at the outset, as compared with a firm that *can* vary its inventories, a firm that *cannot* vary its inventories exhibits stronger price and output responses to a demand shock. Put differently, firms with flexible inventory storage technologies will smooth production and limit price fluctuations.

Now turn to the other extreme: a linear inventory cost function ($b = 0$), the case treated by both Zabel and Amihud–Mendelson. (Reagan assumed that carrying costs are zero for all levels of N, and hence $b = 0$ for her, too.) A glance at (4.15) shows that $z_2 \to 1 + r$ as $b \to 0$, so (4.25) says that:

$$\lim_{b \to 0} (\partial\lambda_0/\partial\varepsilon_0) = 0$$

This case is really quite special since it implies that as $b \to 0$:

$$\frac{\partial y_0}{\partial\varepsilon_0} \to 0, \quad \frac{\partial x_0}{\partial\varepsilon_0} \to d, \quad \frac{\partial p_0}{\partial\varepsilon_0} \to \frac{1}{2}$$

A firm with a linear inventory cost structure does not change its production at all in the face of fluctuations in demand, even if these fluctuations are quite persistent. This is certainly not something we expect to be true intuitively.

Now turn to the effect of ρ on the way the firm adjusts to changes in demand. Remember that ρ measures the "temporariness" of shocks. $\rho = 1$ means that shocks are permanent (a random walk), while $\rho = 0$ means that shocks are *iid*. The following proposition summarizes the results.

PROPOSITION 3. *As ρ rises, that is, as demand shocks become more persistent, these shocks elicit* (i) *larger output responses;* (ii) *smaller sales responses;* (iii) *larger price responses; and* (iv) *smaller (in absolute value) responses of inventory investment.*

Proof. Once again, the statements follow immediately if we can establish that $(d/d\rho)(\partial\lambda_0/\partial\varepsilon_0) > 0$. But now this is obvious from equation (4.25).

The intuition here is really quite straightforward. If shocks are relatively permanent, it does not pay to use inventory fluctuations to buffer them. Output and price respond strongly. On the other hand, inventories *do* play a major role in buffering relatively transitory shocks. Here price and output do not respond much, but sales do (as inventories are disgorged or accumulated).

Theorem 4.1 is simply the combination of Propositions 1–3, and hence is proven.

4.3 FURTHER RESULTS ON INVENTORIES

4.3.1 Reactions to inventory disequilibrium

The last section derived results on how the firm's output, sales, and price respond to changes in demand. This section uses the same apparatus to study how the firm responds to changes in its initial level of inventories, n_0. First we summarize the effects of n_0 on optimal y_0, x_0, p_0, and n_1.

PROPOSITION 4.[7] *Other things being equal, a higher initial level of inventories leads the firm to produce less, charge a lower price, expect to sell more, and reduce its planned inventory investment.*

Proof. We saw in Section 4.2 that the only stable path to the saddle point in Fig. 4.4 was negatively sloped. It therefore follows that:

$$\partial\lambda_0/\partial n_0 < 0 \tag{4.26}$$

Since optimal y_0 is defined by (4.10),

$$\partial y_0/\partial n_0 = c(\partial\lambda_0/\partial n_0) < 0$$

so that y_0 is a decreasing function of n_0. Since optimal x_0 is defined by (4.11),

$$\partial x_0/\partial n_0 = -d(\partial\lambda_0/\partial n_0) > 0$$

so that x_0 is increasing in n_0. Since the demand curve slopes down, this last finding also implies that p_0 is decreasing in n_0. The response of $n_1 - n_0 = y_0 - x_0$ follows by simple arithmetic.

Once again, the proposition is intuitively appealing. Firms stuck with high inventories would normally be expected to cut production and "run a sale," which is just what the proposition says. However, the proposition is a bit more fragile than might be expected. For example, suppose that inventory carrying costs are linear, as the previous studies have all assumed. Then $b = 0$, the $\Delta\lambda = 0$ locus in Fig. 4.4 is horizontal, and λ_0 is independent of n_0.[8] Quite contrary to intuition, the shadow value of inventories is independent of the amount of inventory on hand. This is one reason why extending the results to a nonlinear $B(N)$ function is crucial.

4.3.2 The concept of desired inventories

The concept of "desired inventories" has proven to be an elusive one for students of empirical inventory behavior. Often it is assumed, for no good reason, that desired inventories are an increasing linear function of expected sales:

$$N_t^* = a_0 + a_1 E_{t-1} X_t, \quad a_1 > 0 \tag{4.27}$$

I propose the following definition of desired inventories which seems natural in the context of this model.

DEFINITION. *Desired inventory, n_0^*, is the level of initial inventory holdings that would make desired inventory change exactly zero if the current demand disturbance equals its expected value.*

The linear-quadratic structure of the problem enables us to put some empirical teeth on this concept. Define n_0^* as the value of n_0 that would make optimal n_1 equal to n_0. The exact solution can be worked out by using (4.13) to find the value of λ_0 that makes $n_1 = n_0$, and then using (4.20) to find the value of n_0 that produces this value of λ_0. The answer is:[9]

$$n_0^* = \bar{n} - \frac{d(1 + r - \rho)}{(z_2 - \rho)(1 - z_1)} \varepsilon_0 \tag{4.28}$$

The two optimal inventory concepts n_0^* and $\bar{n}$ provide a rigorous basis for Feldstein and Auerbach's intuitive "target adjustment" model (1976). The long-run target $\bar{n}$ depends on production costs, inventory carrying costs, the rate of interest, and the long-run position of the firm's demand curve. It would not be expected to change very often or very quickly. This period's desired inventory stock, however, will deviate from the long-run target to reflect the current state expected of demand, and hence will move with the business cycle.

Finally, a bit more algebra gives us the "inventory investment equation" implied by the model:

$$n_1^* - n_0 = (1 - z_1)(n_0^* - n_0)$$

$$= (1 - z_1)(\bar{n} - n_0) - \frac{d(1 + r - \rho)}{(z_2 - \rho)(1 - z_1)} \varepsilon_0 \tag{4.29}$$

which clearly brings out the partial-adjustment nature of inventory investment. The positive adjustment coefficient, $1 - z_1$, depends on the convexity of the inventory carrying cost function b, the rate of interest r, the convexity of the production cost function c, and the slope of the demand curve d (see equation (4.15)). In particular, it is worth noting that since $\lim_{b \to 0} z_1 = 1$, the partial-adjustment feature of inventory change is entirely lost when marginal inventory costs are constant – the case dealt with in the earlier literature.

4.3.3 Desired inventories and the persistence of demand

There is, however, one feature of the model that is troublesome empirically. Since $z_2 > 1 > \rho$, and $z_1 < 1$, the coefficient of ε_0 in equation (4.28) is *negative*; that is, a positive expected demand shock *reduces* desired inventory holdings. In contrast, when equations like (4.27) are embedded in empirical models and estimated, the parameter a_1 is invariably estimated to be *positive*. This seems to be the one instance in which reality contradicts the model. Can the two be reconciled? The answer is yes, if we generalize the stochastic nature of the demand shock.

The reason why desired inventories are a *decreasing* function of ε_0 in (4.28) is easy to explain intuitively. If demand shocks are either $AR(1)$ or $ARMA(1, 1)$, *they are always expected to decay over time. So, for example, if* $\varepsilon_0 > 0$, then $\varepsilon_0 > \varepsilon_1 > \varepsilon_2 \ldots$. This means that a period of high anticipated demand ($\varepsilon_0 > 0$) will be a good time to *draw down* inventories because future periods are expected to have less-favorable demand curves than this period. And this is why it makes sense for desired inventories to be a decreasing function of ε_0. But this conclusion might be avoided if the stochastic process for demand allowed shocks to *build* for a while before decaying. One empirically relevant example is an $AR(2)$ process:

$$\eta_t = \rho_1 \eta_{t-1} - \rho_2 \eta_{t-2} + V_t \quad 1 > \rho_2 > 0, 1 + \rho_2 > \rho_1 > 1 \qquad (4.30)$$

It follows from (4.30) that:

$$\varepsilon_0 = E_0 \eta_0 = \rho_1 \eta_{-1} - \rho_2 \eta_{-2}$$

$$\varepsilon_1 = E_0 \eta_1 = \rho_1 \varepsilon_0 - \rho_2 \eta_{-1}$$

$$= (\rho_1^2 - \rho_2) \eta_{-1} - \rho_1 \rho_2 \eta_{-2}$$

so that it is quite possible that $\varepsilon_1 > \varepsilon_0$.[10]

The model (i.e., equations (4.18) and (4.19)) can be resolved under the assumption that demand shocks follow (4.30) instead of (4.5). The resulting expression for the shadow value of inventories is:

$$\lambda_0 = \left(\frac{1 - z_1}{c + d} \right)$$

$$\times \left[\bar{n} - n_0 + \frac{d}{1 - \theta(\rho_1 - \theta\rho_2)} \varepsilon_0 - \frac{d\rho_2}{1 - \theta(\rho_1 - \theta\rho_2)} \eta_{-1} \right] \qquad (4.31)$$

If we then follow the previous procedure to compute desired inventories, we obtain:

$$n_0^* = \bar{n} + \frac{d}{z_2^2 - \rho_1 z_2 + \rho_2} \left[\frac{\{\rho_1 - (1 + r)\} z_2 - \rho_2}{1 - z_1} \varepsilon_0 - \rho_2 z_2^2 \eta_{-1} \right]$$

$$(4.32)$$

The coefficient of ε_0 in this equation will be positive if:[11]

$$[\rho_1 - (1 + r)]z_2 > \rho_2 \tag{4.33}$$

which is certainly possible if $\rho_1 > 1$. In words, desired inventories can be an *increasing* function of the expected demand shock (holding η_{-1} constant) if demand shocks "build" strongly enough. It is interesting to note, in this regard, that many macro time-series seem to be well described by an $AR(2)$ process with $\rho_1 > 1$.

4.3.4 What kinds of firms react strongly to inventory disequilibrium?

Finally, I present and prove a theorem analogous to Theorem 4.1 that summarizes how the sensitivity of a firm's decisions (y_0, x_0, p_0 and n_1) to its initial holdings of inventories (n_0) varies with its characteristics (b and ρ).

THEOREM 4.2. *Firms whose outputs are more inventoriable, that is, which have lower b, change their optimal output, price, expected sales, and planned inventory investment less in response to inventory disequilibrium than firms whose outputs are less inventoriable. The degree of persistence of demand shocks, however, is irrelevant to the magnitude of the firm's reactions to inventory disequilibrium.*

Proof. Given the apparatus already developed, the proof is almost immediate. Start by observing that (4.10), (4.11) and (4.18) imply:

$$\frac{\partial x_0}{\partial n_0} = -d\frac{\partial \lambda_0}{\partial n_0} = \frac{d}{d+c}(1 - z_1)$$

$$\frac{\partial y_0}{\partial n_0} = c\frac{\partial \lambda_0}{\partial n_0} = -\frac{c}{d+c}(1 - z_1)$$

$$\frac{\partial (n_1 - n_0)}{\partial n_0} = \frac{\partial y_0}{\partial n_0} - \frac{\partial x_0}{\partial n_0} = -(1 - z_1)$$

$$\frac{\partial p_0}{\partial n_0} = -\frac{1}{2d}\frac{\partial x_0}{\partial n_0} = -\frac{1}{2(d+c)}(1 - z_1)$$

It can be shown that as b falls, z_1 rises toward unity. Therefore, the responses of production, price, expected sales, and planned inventory investment all fall in absolute value (without changing sign) as b falls. The rest of the proposition follows by noting that ρ appears nowhere in any of these expressions.

The intuition behind this theorem is again clear. Firms whose inventory carrying costs rise rapidly when they have excessive (or deficient) inventories will have to take decisive actions to correct their inventory disequilibrium whereas firms whose inventory cost functions are more nearly linear can afford the luxury of waiting things out.

4.4 A COMPETITIVE CASE

The central result of this paper – that the ability to hold inventories makes both prices and production "sticky" – has been derived for a monopoly producer. Does it also hold for a competitor? The answer is that it does for a competitive industry, though not for a competitive firm.

It is not hard to adapt our previous analysis to the competitive case. A competitive firm is a price taker rather than a price maker, and so it projects the price (over which it has no control) to be:

$$P_t = \bar{P}_t + \eta_t$$

which replaces the monopolist's demand curve (2). Hence the competitor's revenue function is:

$$R(X_t, \eta_t) = X_t(\bar{P}_t + \eta_t)$$

which is expressed here as a function of X_t (which the firm chooses) rather than P_t. If we carry out the same maximization as in Section 4.2, equation (4.8) will be replaced by the following first-order condition for optimal sales:

$$E_0 R'(X_t) = E_0(Q_t)$$

or: $\quad p_t - \bar{p}_t = \lambda_t$

Thus, for a competitive firm, the expected shadow value of inventories is always equal to the expected market price and does not depend on how much inventory the firm has.[12] This makes the analysis of the *firm* very different under competition than under monopoly. (Which is why I have concentrated on the case of monopoly.)

In view of the equality of $p_t - \bar{p}$ and λ_t, the remaining first-order conditions, equations (4.10) and (4.12) above, become:

$$y_t - \bar{y} = cp_t \tag{4.34}$$

$$n_t - \bar{n} = (1/b)[p_t - (1 + r)p_{t-1}] \tag{4.35}$$

Differencing (4.35) and using the identity for inventory change leads to:

$$n_{t+1} - n_t = y_t - x_t = \frac{1}{b}(p_{t+1} - p_t) - \frac{1 + r}{b}(p_t - p_{t-1})$$

So that by (4.34),

$$x_t - \bar{x} = cp_t - \frac{1}{b}(p_{t+1} - p_t) + \frac{1 + r}{b}(p_t - p_{t-1}) \tag{4.36}$$

Equation (4.36), not equation (4.34), is the competitive firm's "supply curve." It tells how much the firm decides to put on the market. For period $t = 0$, (4.36) tells us that, holding past and expected future prices constant, the slope of the supply schedule is:[13]

$$\partial x_0/\partial p_0 = c + (2 + r)/b.$$

Figure 4.5 compares y_0 and x_0 as functions of p_0 for alternative values of b, the inventory cost parameter. As is usual in competitive analysis, the market supply function comes from summing the supply functions of the individual firms. It will therefore be more elastic in an industry in which b is low, that is, an industry in which output is more inventoriable. If we now consider industry-wide reactions to a demand shock (a shift from curve D_0 to curve D_1 in Fig. 4.6), we can see clearly that when b is lower (i.e., output is more inventoriable), output and price responses are smaller while sales responses are larger. This, in essence, is the content of Theorem 4.1.

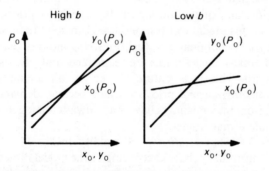

Fig. 4.5   Production and sales as functions of price

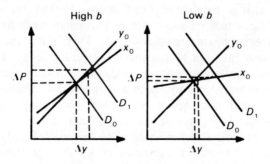

Fig. 4.6   Industry-wide responses to a rise in demand

4.5 MACROECONOMIC IMPLICATIONS

While the results presented here are micro theoretic in nature, my own interest in them is from the point of view of explaining macroeconomic phenomena. Viewed from this perspective, the model has several interesting implications.

4.5.1 Price rigidity

On the surface, it would appear that the analysis provides an explanation for price rigidity which is consistent with maximizing behavior: prices tend to move sluggishly in industries whose outputs are inventoriable. Thus industries with perishable output (for example, agriculture) are more likely to be "flexprice" industries while those with easily storable output are more likely to be "fixprice" industries.

However, such a conclusion would be a bit hasty. The macroeconomic phenomenon that needs explanation is the stickiness of *absolute* prices, while the model presented here – like those of Zabel, Amihud–Mendelson, and Reagan – provides an explanation for rigidity in *relative* prices.[14] The firm's nominal price in this model will respond less than completely to the general price level *only* if its nominal cost functions respond less than completely. Thus, it would appear, sticky prices are "explained" only by assuming sticky costs (i.e., wages). This is a feature shared by all attempts to provide microfoundations for *nominal* price stickiness because demand and supply curves derived from maximizing behavior are always homogeneous of degree zero in all nominal magnitudes.

Let us consider what *relative* price rigidity means in an inflationary environment. A firm that behaves according to the model presented here, but finds itself in an economy with a persistently rising price level, wants its *relative* price to move sluggishly. To accomplish this, it must continually raise its *absolute* price more or less in line with the overall rate of inflation. In such a world, we would not observe stickiness of *nominal prices*; they would change quite frequently. (In fact, if they did not change frequently enough, relative prices would change more than firms desire.) Instead, we would find a tendency for the actual inflation rate of particular products to gravitate toward the expected aggregate inflation rate. Then, *if* it is the case that the *expected* inflation rate can be nudged downward only by decreasing the *actual* inflation rate (a proposition which is vigorously disputed by the rational expectationists), we will have a very sluggish inflation rate which stubbornly resists disinflationary policy, but which responds quickly to permanent changes in the rate of increase of costs.

In any case, the general lesson seems to be that microfoundations of price stickiness seem only to push the question back one stage. Instead of asking: why is the inflation rate so persistent?, we must ask instead: why is so hard to reduce inflationary expectations? Looking across industries, however, the model has a clearer implication: the rate of *relative* price change will be more sluggish where output is most inventoriable (durable goods producers?) and less sluggish where output is least inventoriable (agriculture?).

4.5.2 Stockouts and downward price rigidity

It is often supposed that prices are more rigid downward than upward. If the model presented here is altered to prohibit negative inventories ("unfilled orders"), then it will generate asymmetrical price responses: prices will react more strongly to increases in demand than to decreases in demand. Since this asymmetry is the major point of the papers by Amihud̄Mendelson and Reagan, and since I am far from convinced that it is of great empirical importance, I develop it only briefly here.

For this purpose, it is natural to set K, the critical level of inventories, equal to zero (so that $N = \hat{N}$) and to impose the constraint $N(t) \geqslant 0$ for all t. When the firm does not stock out, the constraint is not binding, and the dynamic system follows the same equations as before. However, if the firm stocks out ($N_0 = 0$), and the unconstrained solution would be calling for $n_1 < N_0$, the constraint $N_1 \geqslant 0$ becomes binding. As we know, $n_1 = N_0$ only when the shadow value of inventories takes on the value $\lambda_0 = (d/(d + c))\varepsilon_0$, so that by (4.22):

$$\frac{\partial x_0}{\partial \varepsilon_0} = d\left(1 - \frac{\partial \lambda_0}{\partial \varepsilon_0}\right) = \frac{dc}{d + c}$$

By comparison, in the unconstrained case it was proven earlier that $\partial \lambda_0/\partial \varepsilon_0 < d/(d + c)$ and hence that $\partial x_0/\partial \varepsilon_0 > dc/(d + c)$. In a word, the sales response is smaller when the firm has stocked out, and hence the price response must be greater. This is the asymmetry result.

At the macro level, it appears likely that the number of firms experiencing a stockout is greater at higher levels of macroeconomic activity. Hence price responses to demand shocks should be greater at high levels of activity than at low levels.

4.5.3 Investing in flexibility

The findings of the model can be placed in a broader context. How does a firm plan for and react to fluctuations in demand? The naive view is that there is little or no advance planning and there are two ways to react when a shift in demand occurs: change price or change output. If these are the only avenues of response, then they clearly must be alternatives: the more one is used the less the other is needed.

The model presented here shows that once a third method of adjustment – building up or drawing down inventories – is allowed, sales and production can, and normally will, respond to shocks differently, and strong price responses may be associated with strong output responses rather than with weak ones. Thinking in a somewhat longer time frame, of course, firms understand the greater flexibility in dealing with unanticipated events that variable inventory stocks can buy for them, and should plan their inventory storage facilities accordingly. They should be willing to invest in acquiring flexibility (i.e., reducing b) by organizing their production and inventory procedures to make their outputs more inventoriable. How much they are willing to invest in lowering b depends, of course, on the costs and benefits of such investments.

Furthermore, inventories are not the only possible vehicle for enhancing flexibility. The phenomenon of labor hoarding has often been noted in empirical macroeconomics, especially in the context of explaining the procyclical pattern of labor productivity. Holding excess supplies of labor in reserve is another way that the firm can achieve flexibility. That is, inventories of labor may be partial substitutes for inventories of goods. Similar remarks may be made about plant and equipment. It may well be rational for firms facing stochastic demand to invest in more capacity than they expect to use in normal times so they are better positioned to take advantage of periods in which demand is higher than normal.

4.6 SUMMARY

1. When output is not storable, firms can react to increases in demand only by raising prices or by boosting production. The more they do of one, the less they have to do of the other.

2. However, when output is storable, the *same* firms that raise prices a lot may also raise production a lot, while other firms may raise both price and output little. Firms in the latter category will take up the slack by selling a lot out of inventories.

3. Firms whose marginal costs of inventory holding are relatively constant and whose demand shocks are transitory will rely heavily on inventory changes to absorb shocks, and will change price and output little. Conversely, firms with sharply rising marginal inventory costs and/or permanent demand shocks will rely less on inventories as buffer stocks and will exhibit larger price and output fluctuations.

4. The previous literature has assumed that inventory carrying costs are linear. As long as stockouts are avoided, this extreme assumption leads to the conclusion that production is totally unresponsive to fluctuations in demand. In macroeconomic terms, the critical link between fluctuations in demand and fluctuations in employment is missing in such models.

5. Other things being equal, firms with higher inventories will produce less, charge lower prices (i.e., sell more), and accumulate fewer additional inventories. Thus, at the macro level, production, employment, and prices should all respond negatively to high levels of inventories.
6. The reactions of output, price, and sales to inventory stocks are strongest when the firm's inventory carrying cost function is most convex, weakest when it is close to linear.
7. Inventory investment is characterized by the "partial adjustment" specification that is so popular in empirical work: inventory change is proportional to the gap between desired and actual inventory holdings. Desired inventories in the model are a *decreasing* function of the current demand shock.
8. The model helps provide an explanation for sluggish relative prices, not sluggish absolute prices. However, under certain circumstances, sluggish reactions of relative prices may help explain the persistence of inflation.
9. If negative inventories are impossible, and stockouts occur instead, prices will be more sensitive to positive demand shocks than to negative demand shocks.
10. Investment in inventory carrying capacity can be viewed as one of several ways for a firm to acquire greater flexibility in reacting to unanticipated events.

NOTES

1. For a recent comprehensive survey from a macroeconomic perspective, see Gordon (1981).
2. For other related work, see Maccini (1976), my article with Fischer (1981), Phlips (1980), and Reagan and Weitzman (1980).
3. The 2 is included to make d the reciprocal of the slope of the MR curve. It is not necessary to think of the firm as a pure monopolist. Suppose, for example, that the firm is a monopolistic competitor in an industry whose (average) market price will be M_t – a quantity that is random from the point of view of a particular producer. The demand for its product may be the average industry demand minus a quantity that depends on the difference between its own price, P_t, and the market price, M_t, viz.:

$$X_t = (a_0 - a_1 M_t) - a_2(P_t - M_t) + u_t$$

where u_t is a stochastic shock. This can be written $X_t = a_0 - a_2 P_t + \eta_t'$, where η_t' $= (a_2 - a_1)M_t + u_t$. This is precisely of the form (4.1). For a pure monopolist, a_2 $= a_1$. For a perfect competitor, a_2 approaches infinity.
4. The way the revenue function is structured assumes that sales made at time t earn the firm P_t, even though they are not delivered until some futute date, that is, it assumes that unfilled orders are prepaid. If, in fact, unfilled orders are paid only upon delivery, then x_t yields the firm only $P_{t+s}(1 + r)^{-s}$ where s is the delivery lag. Thus, the cost to the firm of backordering the sale is: $P_t - P_{t+s}(1 + r)^{-s}$

$= P_t[1 - \{(1 + g)/(1 + r)\}^s]$ where $P_{t+s}/P_t = (1 + g)^s$ defines g. For small g and r, this is approximately $- P_t(g - r)s$. If s is zero for positive N_t and rises in an approximately quadratic manner for negative N_t; then a quadratic function $B(N_t)$ over negative values of N_t is derived. Symmetry of $B(N_t)$ around zero is not essential.

5. The second-order conditions obviously hold since $R''(P) < 0$, $C''(Y) > 0$, and $B''(N) > 0$.

6. The proposition does not apply in the case of *iid* shocks, for in that case $\varepsilon_0 \equiv E_0(\eta_0)$ is always zero.

7. This proposition provides the microfoundations for the Blinder–Fischer model.

8. In taking the limit as $b \to 0$, it is important that the ratio b_1/b_0 approaches some finite constant.

9. Notice that if shocks are completely transitory ($\rho = 0$), then $\varepsilon_0 = 0$ and $n_0^* = \bar{n}$ every period.

10. A simple example will make this clear. Let $\eta_{-2} = 0$ and $\eta_{-1} = 1$, then $\varepsilon_0 = \rho_1$ and $\varepsilon_1 = \rho_1^2 - \rho_2$, which is larger so long as $\rho_1 > 1$ and ρ_2 is small enough.

11. The quadratic in z_2 that appears in (4.32) is always positive in the range $z_2 > 1$.

12. See also equation (4.20) and let $d \to \infty$.

13. Note that x_0 is *decreasing* in both p_{-1} and p_1. Inventory holding is essentially a matter of price speculation in this model.

14. This is easily seen by inspecting the solutions. If all nominal parameters doubled, say, the firm's price would also double and nothing real would change.

REFERENCES

Amihud, Y. and H. Mendelson (1980) "Monopoly under uncertainty: the enigma of price rigidity," mimeo (March).

Blinder, A. S. and S. Fischer (1981) "Inventories, rational expectations, and the business cycle," *Journal of Monetary Economics* (November), vol. 8, pp. 277–304.

Feldstein, M. S. and A. Auerbach (1976) "Inventory behavior in durable goods manufacturing: the target-adjustment model," *Brookings Papers on Economic Activity*, vol. 2, pp. 351–96.

Gordon, R. J. (1981) "Output fluctuations and gradual price adjustment," *Journal Of Economic Literature* (June), vol. 19, pp. 493–530.

Maccini, L. J. (1976) "An aggregate dynamic model of short-run price and output behavior," *Quarterly Journal of Economics* (May), vol. 90, pp. 177–96.

Phlips, L. (1980) "Intertemporal price discrimination and sticky prices," *Quarterly Journal of Economics* (May), vol. 92, pp. 525–42.

Reagan, P. B. (1980) "Inventories and asymmetries in price adjustment," mimeo, Massachusetts Institute of Technology (April).

Reagan, P. B. and M. L. Weitzman (1980) "Asymmetries in price and quantity adjustments by the competitive industry," mimeo, Massachusetts Institute of Technology (April).

Zabel, E. (1972) "Multiperiod monopoly under uncertainty," *Journal of Economic Theory* (December), vol. 5, pp. 524–36.

APPENDIX 4.1

Write equation (4.16) in the text for $t = 0$ and $t = 1$:

$$\lambda_0 = K_1 + \phi_0$$
$$\lambda_1 = K_1 z_1 + \phi_1$$

It follows that $K_1 = \lambda_0 - \phi_0$ and

$$\lambda_1 - \lambda_0 = K_1(z_1 - 1) + \phi_1 - \phi_0$$
$$\lambda_1 - \lambda_0 = \lambda_0(z_1 - 1) + \phi_1 - z_1\phi_0 \tag{A4.1}$$

But (4.12) for $t = 1$ says:

$$\lambda_1 - \lambda_0 = r\lambda_0 + b(n_1 - \bar{n}) \tag{A4.2}$$

And (4.13) for $t = 0$ says:

$$n_1 - n_0 = (c + d)\lambda_0 - d\varepsilon_0 \tag{A4.3}$$

Substituting (A4.3) into (A4.2) yields:

$$\lambda_1 - \lambda_0 = r\lambda_0 + b(n_0 - \bar{n} + (c + d)\lambda_0 - d\varepsilon_0)$$

Equating this expression with (A4.2) leads to:

$$\lambda_0(z_1 - 1) + \phi_1 - z_1\phi_0 = r\lambda_0 + b(n_0 - \bar{n}) + b(c + d)\lambda_0 - db\varepsilon_0$$

$$\lambda_0 = \frac{b}{1 + r - z_1 + b(c + d)}\left[\bar{n} - n_0 + d\varepsilon_0 + \frac{\phi_1 - z_1\phi_0}{b}\right] \tag{A4.4}$$

Now from the characteristic equation (4.15), it follows that (using the definition of β):

$$(z^2 - z) - (1 + r)z - b(c + d)z + (1 + r) = 0$$

or

$$(1 - z)(1 + r - z) = zb(c + d)$$

or

$$1 + r - z = \frac{z}{1 - z}b(c + d)$$

for z_1 or z_2. Substituting this with $z = z_1$ into (A4.4) yields:

$$\lambda_0 = \frac{b}{\dfrac{z}{1 - z_1}b(c + d) + b(c + d)}\left[\bar{n} - n_0 + d\varepsilon_0 + \frac{\phi_1 - z_1\phi_0}{b}\right]$$

which simplifies directly to equation (4.18) in the text.

5 · RETAIL INVENTORY BEHAVIOR AND BUSINESS FLUCTUATIONS

The enigmatic behavior of the US economy during the 1980 recession makes it more imperative than ever that some of the mystery that surrounds inventory behavior be solved. On the surface, the economy seems to have reacted quite differently to what appear to be rather similar external shocks (principally, rapid increases in oil prices) in 1973–5 and in 1979–80. However, if one abstracts from inventory behavior and focusses on final sales, the two recessions look rather similar. Several observations confirm this. First, the briefest recession in US history was also the first in which inventory investment did not swing sharply toward liquidation between the peak and the trough. Second, if one judges the contraction by real final sales instead of real GNP, the 1980 recession was actually far deeper than the "severe" 1973–5 recession.[1] And third, the way the 1980 recession was concentrated into a single quarter seems less unusual if one looks at real final sales instead of real GNP. In the 1973–5 recession, for example, fully 90 percent of the total peak-to-trough decline in real final sales happened in a single quarter (1974:4).

In a word, inventories hold the key to understanding why the 1980 recession was so different from previous ones.

Relative to its importance in business fluctuations, inventory investment must be the most underresearched aspect of macro-economic activity. A hot topic in the 1950s, research on inventory behavior apparently went out of style in the early 1960s and languished during the 1970s. But there was never any good reason for work on inventories to fall out of fashion. The importance of inventory movements in business cycles did not end in the early 1960s. Nor, despite Michael Lovell's best efforts, did economists develop such a well established and empirically validated theory of inventory investment that the

I thank Danny Quah for exceptional research assistance. I also thank Gregory Mankiw and Leonard Nakamura for research assistance and Stephenie Sigall and Phyllis Durepos for quickly and efficiently typing the paper. I am grateful to members of the Brookings panel and to a number of colleagues for helpful discussions on this research. I apologize to those I leave out when I mention Angus S. Deaton, David Germany, Wayne Gray, F. Owen Irvine Jr, Louis J. Maccini, Bennett T. McCallum, and Robert J. Shiller. The research was supported by the National Science Foundation and the Sloan Foundation, and was done mainly at the National Bureau of Economic Research.

case was closed.[2] Yet research on inventories went out like high-buttoned shoes.

Worse yet, what little attention the profession has paid to inventories over the past two decades seems to have been misplaced. Both theoretical and empirical attention appears to have congealed around applying the production smoothing-buffer stock model to the study of manufacturers' inventories of finished goods. Yet, as I demonstrate below, finished goods held by manufacturers constitute one of the least important types of inventory. Furthermore, I argue that the underlying theoretical framework is probably inappropriate and inconsistent with the facts. Obviously this leaves both the microeconomics and macroeconomics of inventory behavior in a rather unsatisfactory state.

The structure of this paper naturally follows from the preceding remarks. First, some basic facts of inventory fluctuations in the US economy are set out. This preliminary investigation (as well as data availability) leads me to concentrate on retail inventories instead of manufacturers' inventories of finished goods. Second, a variety of competing theories are examined in order to see which, if any, make sense in the light of the facts. Third, an alternative model of retail inventory investment is developed and compared with the traditional theory. Finally, empirical inventory equations are derived from this theory, and these equations are estimated econometrically and used to study recent inventory behavior.

5.1 THE IMPORTANCE OF INVENTORIES IN BUSINESS CYCLES

The overwhelming importance of inventory movements in business cycles is one of those basic facts that seems to be inadequately appreciated. Inventory investment is, on average, a tiny component of GNP (about 1 percent). Yet it has almost always accounted for a major share of the decline in GNP during recessions – and has often exceeded the decline in GNP as a whole, that is, real final sales have often risen during recessions.

5.1.1 Inventories in recessions

The top part of Table 5.1 shows the relevant data for the seven postwar recessions. Inventory change has, on average, accounted for 101 percent of the peak to trough decline in real GNP; or, keeping score a different way, the average inventory change was 60 percent of the average GNP decline.[3]

This pattern is not new. The bottom part of the table displays similar data for the inter-war period and tells a similar story. In fact, real GNP actually increased from peak to trough in two of the five inter-war recessions. Inventory investment, however, always declined.

Table 5.1 Changes in GNP and in inventory investment in recessions

Period	Change in real GNP[a]	Change in inventory investment[a]	Change in inventory investment as a percentage of change in real GNP
Post-war recessions (peak and trough)[b]			
1948:4–1949:4	−7.1	−13.0	183
1953:2–1954:2	−20.2	−9.2	46
1957:3–1958:1	−23.0	−10.5	46
1960:1–1960:4	−8.6	−18.0	209
1969:3–1970:4	−7.3	−12.3	168
1973:4–1975:1	−60.7	−38.0	63
1980:1–1980:2	−38.6	2.2	−6
Inter-war recessions			
1920–1	−3.6	−4.2	117
1923–4	1.5	−3.7	c
1926–7	1.0	−0.8	c
1929–32	−32.0	−5.6	18
1937–8	−3.1	−2.9	94

Notes:
(a) Billions of 1972 dollars for post-war recessions, billions of 1929 dollars for inter-war recessions.
(b) Peaks and troughs of real GNP, not official dates of the National Bureau of Economic Research.
(c) Real GNP rose during this recession.
Source: Post-war data are from the national income and product accounts; inter-war data are adapted from Moses Abramovitz, *Inventories and Business Cycles* (National Bureau of Economic Research, 1950), table 84, pp. 476–7.

The 1980 recession stands out as a sharp break with history. With the exception of the post-Second World War adjustment period, during which inventories were replenished while production fell, the 1980 recession is the only one since the First World War (and perhaps the only one since the American revolution) in which inventory investment moved countercyclically. Some possible reasons for this are explored at the end of the paper.

5.1.2 Decomposition of variance

Recessions are obviously atypical periods, almost by definition. It is clear that inventories play a rather minor role in economic activity when the economy is expanding smoothly. A broader picture can be obtained of the importance of inventories in business fluctuations as follows. Define Y_t as real GNP, X_t as real final sales, and N_t as real inventory stock at the beginning of the period. Then the GNP identity is:

$$Y_t = X_t + (N_{t+1} - N_t) \tag{5.1}$$

If all data are detrended and lowercase symbols are used to denote deviations from trend, the variance of GNP around trend for the 1947:2–1981:1 period can be decomposed as:[4]

$$\text{var}(y) = \text{var}(x) + \text{var}(\Delta n) + 2\text{cov}(x, \Delta n)$$
$$(678.3) \quad (514.4) \quad (43.9) \quad\quad (116.1)$$

(5.2)

Judging from equation (5.2), inventory fluctuations account for only 6.5 percent of GNP fluctuations about trend (but recall that inventory investment averages only about 1 percent of GNP). However, this calculation of the importance of inventories may understate their relevance for changes in GNP because there is a strong positive covariance between deviations of real final sales and real inventory investment from trend (the simple correlation is 0.38), and because quarterly deviations from trend are likely to be persistent. An alternative decomposition, which may be more sensitive to the importance of inventories for changes in output, can be obtained by taking the first difference of equation (5.1) and decomposing the variance of the growth of GNP for the same period as:

$$\text{var}(\Delta Y) = \text{var}(\Delta X) + \text{var}(\Delta^2 N) + 2\text{cov}(\Delta X, \Delta^2 N)$$
$$(111.5) \quad (85.3) \quad\quad (33.1) \quad\quad\quad (-6.9)$$

(5.3)

If one looks at equation (5.3), inventory fluctuations appear to account for a full 30 percent of the fluctuations in the growth of real GNP from quarter to quarter. This is an enormous amount for such a small component. Changes in final sales, however, are negatively correlated with changes in inventory investment, so that the direct contribution of inventory fluctuations may slightly overstate their importance.

A more disaggregated look at the variance of y (or of ΔY) offers some lessons about the history of business fluctuations in the post-war United States. Tables 5.2 and 5.3 display disaggregated versions of equations (5.2) and (5.3) in which the final sales variable is divided into its main components: consumption expenditures, fixed investment, government purchases, and net exports. In each table, variances are reported in boldface on the diagonal, covariances above the diagonal, and correlation coefficients below it. These tables contain some fascinating facts.

Table 5.2 displays the decomposition of var(y) – the variance of real GNP about trend. The most striking fact, though it is tangential to the concerns of this paper, is how much of the variance of x is composed of the variance of government purchases. But compared with the variances about trend of consumption and investment (both of which are much larger components of GNP), the variance of inventory investment does not look so paltry as it did in equation (5.2). Furthermore, a strong positive covariation is apparent between Δn and either consumption or investment. Thus inventory fluctuations are more significant than might appear from equation (5.2).

Inventory investment seems even more important in Table 5.3, which disaggregates equation (5.3). Inventory investment has the largest variance, measured in quarter-to-quarter changes, of any GNP component, which is

Table 5.2 Decomposition of the variance of GNP around trend, 1947:2 through 1981:1[a]

	GNP	Inventory investment	Consumption expenditure	Fixed investment	Government purchases	Net exports
GNP	**678.3**	99.1	233.2	206.0	198.9	-66.4
Inventory investment	0.58	**43.9**	34.7	37.5	-3.5	-10.7
Consumption expenditure	0.64	0.37	**199.1**	112.2	-139.4	12.2
Fixed investment	0.79	0.56	0.79	**101.4**	-36.8	-12.8
Government purchases	0.33	-0.02	-0.41	-0.16	**550.0**	-140.5
Net exports	-0.30	-0.19	0.10	-0.15	-0.70	**74.2**

Note:
(a) Variances are displayed on the diagonal; covariances and correlation coefficients are shown above and below the diagonal, respectively.
Source: Author's calculations based on national income and product accounts.

Table 5.3 Decomposition of the variance of changes in GNP, 1947:3 through 1981:1[a]

	ΔGNP	ΔInventory investment	ΔConsumption expenditure	ΔFixed investment	ΔGovernment purchases	ΔNet exports
ΔGNP	**111.5**	29.6	43.2	32.9	5.3	0.5
ΔInventory investment	0.49	**33.1**	−2.4	4.4	−1.9	−3.4
ΔConsumption expenditure	0.71	−0.07	**32.9**	15.9	−1.5	−1.7
ΔFixed investment	0.76	0.19	0.68	**16.7**	−2.2	−1.9
ΔGovernment purchases	0.15	−0.10	−0.08	−0.17	**10.6**	0.3
ΔNet exports	0.02	−0.22	−0.11	−0.17	0.04	**7.1**

Note:
(a) See Table 5.2, note (a).
Source: Author's calculations based on national income and product accounts.

quite surprising when one recalls that, on average, consumption spending is about seventy times as large as inventory investment. The case is probably made; inventories really do matter in business fluctuations.

5.1.3 Inventory fluctuations by type

A natural next question to ask is, which sorts of inventories are responsible for all this fluctuation? From 1959 on there are good data on real inventories by sector and by stage of processing. Table 5.4 reports a decomposition of the overall variance of both nonfarm inventory investment (ΔN) and the change in nonfarm inventory investment ($\Delta^2 N$). Two results are striking. First, manufacturers' inventories of finished goods, the component of inventories that has received the lion's share of both theoretical and empirical attention, are the least important type of inventories in cyclical fluctuations. Second, retail inventories are the most important component of total inventories in terms of cyclical variability. Although less important than total manufacturing inventory investment in accounting for variations around trend, retail inventory investment is far more important than any of the three components of manufacturers' inventories. And when it comes to the variance of changes in inventory investment, retail inventories are more important than even total manufacturing inventories.[5]

5.1.4 The inventory-sales ratio as a cyclical indicator

The most commonly used indicator of the state of inventory equilibrium or disequilibrium is the ratio of inventories to sales in manufacturing and trade. This ratio moves countercyclically, rising in recessions. But the meaning of this empirical regularity is far from clear.

Letting N^* denote desired inventories, the ratio can be expressed as:

$$\frac{N}{X} = \frac{N}{N^*} \times \frac{N^*}{X}$$

In most journalistic interpretations of the business cycle, N^*/X is regarded as relatively constant, and observed fluctuations in N/X are taken to reflect changes in inventories relative to desired inventories, that is, inventory disequilibrium. In this view, N/N^* rises in recessions because firms accumulate unwanted stocks and falls in booms because sales outstrip expectations and stocks are drawn down.

An opposing interpretation is that N/N^* is always approximately unity, with firms always keeping their inventories more or less where they want them. In this view, it is N^*/X that rises in recessions and falls in booms. Why? Suppose desired inventories depend on long-run average sales, X^*, and N^*/X^* is constant. Then, in a recession, X falls relative to X^*, so N^*/X rises. For similar reasons, N^*/X falls in a boom. Movements in N/X, in this view,

Table 5.4 Decomposition of the variance of inventories, quarterly, 1959–80

Inventory component	Inventory level at the end of 1980[a]	Percentage of total level	Variance of inventory investment[b]	Percentage of total variance	Variance of change in inventory investment[c]	Percentage of total variance
Total nonfarm	297.6	100.0	44.45	100.0	36.90	100.0
Manufacturers	145.0	48.7	15.76	35.5	10.58	28.7
materials and supplies	51.0	17.1	5.28	11.9	5.70	15.4
work in progress	50.4	16.9	3.87	8.7	2.99	8.1
finished goods	43.5	14.6	2.10	4.7	2.40	6.5
Retail trade	64.6	21.7	9.07	20.4	14.56	39.5
automobiles	15.3	5.1	4.57	10.3	9.91	26.9
Wholesale trade	64.7	21.7	3.39	7.6	4.77	12.9
All other	23.4	7.9	1.22	2.7	1.82	4.9
All covariance terms	—	—	15.01	33.8	5.17	14.0

Notes:
(a) In billions of 1972 dollars, seasonally adjusted.
(b) From 1959:2 through 1980:4.
(c) From 1959:3 through 1980:4.
Source: Author's calculations based on national income and product accounts.

do not indicate inventory disequilibrium. These different interpretations of the same basic fact lead to strikingly different specifications and interpretations of econometric equations explaining inventory investment, and these are explored below.

5.2 THE PRODUCTION SMOOTHING-BUFFER STOCK MODEL OF INVENTORY BEHAVIOR

Firms hold inventories for transactions, speculative, or precautionary reasons. A clothing store must display goods on the racks to sell them; a furniture store needs floor samples to show customers (both transactions motives). Manufacturers may hold stocks of raw materials because they think their prices will rise (speculative motives). A department store holds inventories to avoid running out of stock and therefore losing customers (a precautionary motive). There are other motives as well. For example, manufacturers may hold inventories of finished goods because they want to smooth production in the face of fluctuating sales. Manufacturers may find inventories of work in progress useful in scheduling production.

Although it is easy to invent micro theoretic rationales for holding inventories, only one model has provided the micro foundations for any substantial amount of empirical work. That model is the production smoothing-buffer stock model, which was first extensively used in empirical work by Lovell and has provided the basis for most empirical work since then.[6]

Production smoothing arises when sales are variable over time and marginal costs of production are rising; it has nothing inherently to do with uncertainty. Even without randomness anywhere, firms with variable sales and rising marginal costs will find it optimal to smooth production relative to sales, accumulating inventories when demand is weak and liquidating inventories when demand is strong. In addition to being variable, sales may also be random. In this case a buffer-stock element arises: firms may hold inventories against the contingency that demand will be unexpectedly high.

The production smoothing-buffer stock model is typically represented empirically by the following stock-adjustment equation:

$$N_{t+1} - N_t = \lambda(N_t^* - N_t) - \beta(X_t - X_t^e) + \varepsilon_t \tag{5.4}$$

where X_t^e is expected sales and ε_t is a random error. That the first term represents the production-smoothing motive while the second represents the buffer stock can be seen by using the identity (equation (5.1)) to rewrite (5.4) as:

$$Y_t = X_t^e + (1 - \beta)(X_t - X_t^e) + \lambda(N_t^* - N_t) + \varepsilon_t \tag{5.5}$$

The first two terms reflect the use of inventories as a buffer stock. If production decisions are made before actual sales are known and $N_t = N_t^*$, firms will produce X_t^e. Under these circumstances, β will be unity; inventory movements will completely buffer production from sales surprises. If, however, firms desire and are able to alter production plans within the period as they learn about X_t, β can be less than unity. In the extreme case, $\beta = 0$, production reacts fully to realized sales, and inventories do not serve as a buffer at all. Thus the size of β measures the degree of buffering. The value of β obviously should depend, among other things, on the length of the observation period.

The last term in (5.5) represents intended inventory accumulation, and production-smoothing considerations will result in a value of λ between 0 and 1, which is what leads to the stock-adjustment feature.[7]

To make the model represented by equation (5.4) operational, N_t^* is typically expressed as a linear function of X_t or X_t^e or a related variable, and some proxy for expectations is introduced. When this is done, the following sorts of empirical results typically emerge from quarterly data.[8]

First, the estimated coefficient β is practically zero. This means that sales surprises do not affect inventories, so that such surprises must have nearly one-for-one effects on output. That is, the estimated coefficient suggests that the buffer stock motive is unimportant.

Second, the coefficient λ is normally so small that it seems implausible to interpret it as a parameter measuring speed of adjustment. When even the biggest swings in inventories amount to no more than one or two weeks of sales, it is hard to understand why λ would be around 0.1 or 0.2, that is, why only 10 or 20 percent of the deviation of inventories from target would be corrected within a quarter.[9]

A third piece of evidence, which is difficult to reconcile with the notion of production smoothing, is the observation that the variance of Y over time exceeds that of X in a wide variety of sectors and subsectors, and also in the entire economy.

Finally, as just shown, retail inventories play a more prominent role in cyclical fluctuations than manufacturers' inventories of finished goods, for which the production smoothing-buffer stock model was designed.

The stock-adjustment model can be applied to retailing, with empirical results that in general turn out to be quite similar to those for manufacturing.[10] The problem is that a persuasive rationale for partial inventory adjustment by retailers is lacking. The variable Y_t for a retailer represents deliveries from manufacturers, and it seems unlikely that the typical retailer faces rising marginal costs of purchasing. In fact, because of quantity discounts and related phenomena, retailers probably face constant or declining marginal costs. Under such conditions, the production-smoothing model falls apart. Just as a manufacturer with declining marginal costs will want to produce output in large lots (production runs), a retailer with falling marginal costs will want to "bunch" orders to reduce costs.

5.3 THE S, s MODEL OF INVENTORY BEHAVIOR

This simple idea is the basis for the model I explore in this paper. In particular, suppose there are no quantity discounts but there is a substantial fixed cost of placing an order or receiving a delivery. That is, suppose a retailer's cost of acquiring Y_t units from the manufacturer in period t is given by:

$$C(Y_t) = A + c Y_t \quad \text{if } Y_t > 0$$
$$C(Y_t) = 0 \qquad \quad \text{if } Y_t = 0$$

(5.6)

where A is fixed cost and c is (constant) marginal cost.

This cost function has been studied extensively in the operations research literature. It leads to an inventory strategy called the "S, s rule," meaning that inventories are allowed to dwindle to some minimum level, s, at which time a purchase restores inventories to their maximum level, S. The basic idea behind the S, s strategy is that, owing to the fixed costs, it pays for a firm to place fewer orders, make each order larger, and store more inventories than it would if fixed costs did not exist.

There are many reasons for such a cost structure. Some originate with the retailer. There may be transportation and warehousing costs that are lumpy (for example, it may cost little more to receive a truckload of television sets than to receive a dozen). Bookkeeping costs probably depend far more on the number of orders than on the quantity of goods ordered. Perhaps most important, and most often ignored, is the scarcity of managerial time and attention. One way to economize on this scarce resource is to place orders less frequently and make each one larger.

Although somewhat contrary to standard neoclassical economic thought, this factor is probably pervasive and important. Why, for example, when workers take stationery from the office supply cabinet, do they not just take what they need for the next day (or hour or minute)? It is not because there is a large transportation cost or because there is bookkeeping to do. Rather, it is because each trip to the cabinet occupies some of the workers' time – valuable time that they could spend on something else. The same is certainly true for business managers.[11]

Other sources of fixed costs originate with manufacturers. They, too, may incur substantial costs in processing an order, getting the goods together, and shipping them out. They certainly face the same scarcity of managerial time and energy that retailers do. These factors may induce the manufacturer to adopt a pricing structure like that represented in equation (5.6). Indeed, the fact that most manufacturers refuse to deal directly with consumers placing small orders suggests that the fixed costs, elusive as they may be, are probably very important in practice. Thus the cost technology that underlies the S, s model is appealing on *a priori* grounds. The fixed cost, A, may represent a fee the manufacturer charges, a cost the retailer incurs, or both.

5.3.1 Background

The S, s model, which is allegedly in common use in industry, has a long and venerable history in the operations research and management science literature. The interest of economists in S, s inventory strategies seems to have been sparked by the pioneering paper of Arrow, Harris, and Marschak (1951). Many articles on specific S, s models were published in the ensuing years, and Scarf finally proved that fixed costs of ordering make S, s rules of one type or another optimal under a wide variety of circumstances.[12]

Because I make use of several examples of S, s models with particular simplifying assumptions, it is worth emphasizing that the basic S, s rule emerges as the optimal inventory strategy under a wide variety of assumptions about such matters as what is random and what is deterministic, when information on sales becomes available to firms, whether it is possible to accept unfilled orders, whether there are delivery lags, whether time is continuous or discrete, and so on. However, three features of the firm's economic environment seem to be critical to the optimality of the S, s rule. First, the cost of acquiring goods from the manufacturer must be precisely like that given in equation (5.6). It can be shown that this equation does in fact lead to the S, s rule, and also that such a rule will not be optimal if either A equals zero or c is not constant.[13] Second, a firm's sales and prices must be exogenous. To my knowledge, no S, s models have been developed in which the firm can exercise control over its sales – for example, by varying its selling price. Furthermore, it is doubtful that S, s behavior is optimal once the probability distribution of sales comes under the firm's control (even though the fixed cost element will continue to induce firms to order infrequently). Third, the parameters underlying the firm's optimization problem (its cost functions, probability distribution of sales, and so on) must be constant through time. Every S, s model that I know about has been solved under the assumption of stationarity, including the assumption that sales are independently and identically distributed over time. Such assumptions are very stringent and empirically inaccurate. For example, aggregate retail sales are highly serially correlated, and it would be surprising indeed if this serial correlation disappeared at the level of the firm.

It is easy to see what happens qualitatively in a nonstationary environment. It can be shown that if the underlying parameters vary over time, the firm will adhere to an S_t, s_t strategy in which the trigger points change each period.[14] For example, if sales disturbances are serially correlated, information on past sales will be used in setting S_t and s_t for this period.

5.3.2 An example

To understand the factors determining S and s, it is helpful to have an example of an explicit solution. None exists for the nonstationary case, which is the case of greatest empirical interest. Nonetheless, a specific example will help clarify the nature of the S, s trigger points. Hadley and Whitin (1963) show that the following square root rule is optimal or approximately optimal in a variety of different models in which firms have exogenous (but random) sales and minimize long-run costs in a stationary environment:[15]

$$S - s = \sqrt{\frac{2\bar{X}}{r+d}\left[\frac{A}{c} + \frac{\delta}{c}q(s)\right]}$$

$$1 - H(s) = \frac{S-s}{\bar{X}} \cdot \frac{c}{\delta}(r+d)$$

(5.7)

where:

$\bar{X}$ = mean sales
$H(X)$ = cumulative distribution function of sales
$H(s)$ = the probability that sales will be less than s in a given period
r = real rate of interest
d = storage cost per period (as a percent)
δ = a penalty cost for having an order unfilled per unit
$q(s)$ = mean number of unfilled orders, which will depend on s and on $H(X)$.

Obviously, if the structure of cost or demand changes, so will S and s.

The system of equations in (5.7) implicitly defines the trigger points S and s, and hence the width of the inventory range, as functions of the following parameters with the following derivatives:

$$S = S\left(r, \; d, \; \frac{A}{c}, \; \frac{\delta}{c}, \; H(X)\right)$$
$$\quad\;\; -\;\; -\;\; ?\;\;\; +\;\;\;\; +$$

$$s = s\left(r, \; d, \; \frac{A}{c}, \; \frac{\delta}{c}, \; H(X)\right)$$
$$\quad\;\; -\;\; -\;\; -\;\;\; +\;\;\;\; +$$

(5.8)

$$S - s = \sigma\left(r, \; d, \; \frac{A}{c}, \; \frac{\delta}{c}, \; H(X)\right)$$
$$\quad\;\;\;\;\; -\;\; -\;\; +\;\;\; ?\;\;\;\; +$$

These derivatives have straightforward interpretations. If either interest costs or storage costs rise, firms reduce both S and s. But they change S more, so the optimal lot size, $S - s$, falls. If the fixed cost of ordering rises relative to the marginal cost, firms reduce s and increase the optimal lot size; the effects on S are ambiguous. An increase in the penalty for running out of stock causes both S and s to move up, but the effect on the lot size is indeterminant.

Finally, the derivative with respect to $H(X)$ is heuristic notation to indicate that if the density function of sales shifts to the right, that is, if sales increase, firms raise both S and s and increase the optimal lot size. All these results make good intuitive sense.

The empirical work reported in the next section is based on the notion that each of the exogenous variables listed in equation (5.8) influences the firm's choice of S and s. The rate of interest, r, the manufacturer's price, c, and the distribution of sales, $H(X)$, are all captured by specific empirical variables. The fixed costs, A, and storage costs, d, are treated as unobservables.

5.3.3 Dynamic adjustments by a single firm

Suppose now that a firm has selected its trigger points, S and s. How will its inventories move through time? For simplicity, I assume that S and s are constant and an order placed within a period is received at the end of the period.

Figure 5.1 traces the inventory holdings of a firm that starts with stock N_0 at time $t = 0$, sells at the exogenously determined rate X_0 for the first week (between $t = 0$ and $t = 1$), and then sells at the rate X_1 for the second week (between $t = 1$ and $t = 2$).

Because inventories decline at the rate X except at the points at which a firm receives delivery, the rate of sales, X_0, is shown as the slope of the line emanating from point N_0. In this example, inventories fall below s, the lower trigger point, during period 1, so the firm places an order at the end of period 1 and a delivery is made replenishing the firm's stock so that it begins the next period with exactly S. Then inventories decline at rate X_1 until the end of the second week (point N_2 on the diagram).

Consider how this firm's behavior would differ if its sales in the second week were better than those assumed in Fig. 5.1, that is, suppose the line emanating from point N_1 were steeper. If it were only slightly steeper, N_2 would be lower than indicated in the figure. However, if it were substantially steeper, the firm would sell enough to justify placing an order during the second week, and so N_2 would end up at S. In general one cannot determine whether stronger sales lead to higher or lower end-of-period inventories. This is an interesting finding. It contrasts sharply with the stock-adjustment model in which it is always true that higher sales lead to lower end-of-period inventories.[16] It also shows that firms that appear to be quite similarly situated might nonetheless exhibit divergent behavior patterns.

This example illustrates a general point: the S, s model permits a far richer variety of dynamic behavior patterns than does the conventional stock-adjustment model. It may also help us to understand why inventory dynamics are so hard to predict.

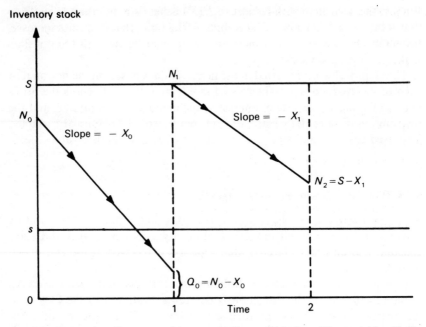

Fig. 5.1   Dynamic adjustment of inventories by a single firm. The variables N, X, and Q denote real inventory stock, final sales, and carry-over stock respectively.

5.3.4 Aggregation across firms

If firms have a technology that makes the S, s rule optimal, aggregation across firms is inherently difficult.[17] Indeed, it is precisely this difficulty that has prevented the S, s model from being used in empirical work to date. It is clear that the convenient fiction of the "representative firm" cannot be adopted because the essence of the S, s rule is (a) that firms that are otherwise identical will react very differently to the same demand shock if they have different initial inventories, (b) that firms may react very differently to large demand shocks (which push inventories below s) than to small ones (which do not induce them to place an order), and (c) that Y_t is not a continuous function of X_t for a single firm. Hence one must be extremely careful about aggregation.

As a first step toward that aggregation, note that the S, s rule in discrete time can be expressed as follows:[18]

If $N_t - X_t > s$, then $Y_t = 0$

If $N_t - X_t \leq s$, then $Y_t = S + X_t - N_t$

It is convenient to introduce the variable $Q_t = N_t - X_t$. This variable, sometimes called the "carry-over stock" in the inventory literature, is the inventory stock the firm has at the end of the period if it does not receive a delivery at that time.[19] Using this new variable, the S, s rule can be expressed more succinctly as:

If $Q_t > s$, then $Y_t = 0$

If $Q_t \leq s$, then $Y_t = S - Q_t$ (5.9)

Now consider an industry in which there are a large number of small firms with the same costs and technology that face the same random distribution of demand shocks. All firms select the same s and S points. However, during any particular period, each firm inherits a different initial inventory stock, N_t, and receives a different drawing, X_t, from the (common) sales distribution. Hence the composite variable, $Q_t = N_t - X_t$, differs across firms according to some density function, which itself varies over time as initial inventory stocks change. I denote this function by $f_t(Q_t)$.

Using the notation $\bar{Y}_t$ to denote the average of Y_t across firms, I average over the density of Q_t. Then the S, s rule (equation (5.9)) implies:

$$\bar{Y}_t = \int_{s - X_1}^{s} (S - Q_t) f_t(Q_t) \, dQ_t \tag{5.10}$$

where X_1 is the largest possible realization of sales. Integrating this equation by parts and simplifying yields:

$$\bar{Y}_t = (S - s) F_t(s) + \int_{s - X_1}^{s} F_t(Q_t) \, dQ_t \tag{5.11}$$

where $F_t(Q_t)$ is the cumulative distribution function corresponding to density $f_t(Q_t)$.

If mean sales are subtracted from both sides of (5.11), one has an equation for inventory investment as a function of the distribution of sales, the distribution of initial inventories as captured in the distribution across firms of carry-over stock, and the parameters S and s, which together indicate the desired inventory range. This inventory investment equation is quite different in spirit from the standard stock-adjustment specification. It is not only the means, but also the shapes, of the distributions of X_t and N_t that determine the mean of Y_t. For example, for any given distribution of sales and mean level of initial inventories, $\bar{Y}_t$ will be larger if the distribution of inventories has a concentration near s.

The dynamics inherent in (5.11) are easy to explain but difficult to analyze. The distribution of inventories at the start of each period, coupled with the distribution of sales for the same period, together induce some distribution of Q_t for that period. Given $f_t(Q_t)$, mean deliveries for period t follow directly from (5.11) and mean inventory investment is simply $\bar{Y}_t - \bar{X}_t$. The end-of-period inventory position of each firm is determined by the dynamics depicted in Fig. 5.1. The distribution of closing inventories for period t then becomes the distribution of opening inventories for period $t+1$, and the problem repeats.

5.3.5 Implications at the industry level

Equation (5.11) is hardly suitable for econometric implementation as it stands. It is highly nonlinear and includes variables whose values cannot be observed. My estimation strategy is first to linearize the equation and then to introduce observable proxies for as many of the unobservable variables as possible. This subsection explains how the first step in this strategy is implemented. Most of the formal mathematics are relegated to Appendix 5.1; the text illustrates the dynamics of the inventory behavior for a firm and for an aggregation of firms using a simple numerical simulation model that, although a special case, does a better job of conveying the nature of the results.

A simulation model
Consider an economy consisting of four firms with identical cost and demand structures, but whose ordering cycles are completely out of phase. Specifically, suppose each firm uses as trigger points $S = 16$ and $s = 2$ and, initially, sells four units every period. Table 5.5 shows the steady-state inventory cycle of one such firm; each of the others goes through the same ordering cycle, though with different timing. Say the economy consists of one firm that orders in periods 0, 4, 8, . . . ; a second firm that orders in periods 1, 5, 9, . . . ; a third that orders in periods 2, 6, 10, . . . ; and a fourth ordering in periods 3, 7, 11, . . . (as in Table 5.5). The aggregate economy then exhibits the steady-state behavior summarized in Table 5.6. Inventory stocks are constant at 40, and deliveries (which match sales) are 16 every period. Table 5.6 is an example

Table 5.5 Simulated steady-state inventory cycle for a single firm[a]

Period, t	Initial inventory, N_t	Sales, X_t	Carry-over stock, Q_t	Deliveries, Y_t	Inventory investment, $N_{t+1} - N_t$
0	16	4	12	0	−4
1	12	4	8	0	−4
2	8	4	4	0	−4
3	4	4	0	16	12
4	16	4	12	0	−4
5	12	4	8	0	−4
6	8	4	4	0	−4
7	4	4	0	16	12
[b]					

Notes:
(a) The trigger points are $S = 16$ and $s = 2$.
(b) Cycle repeats in subsequent periods.
Source: Simulations by the author.

Table 5.6 Simulated steady state for a four-firm economy

Period, t	Initial inventory, N_t	Sales, X_t	Deliveries, Y_t	Inventory investment, $N_{t+1} - N_t$	Inventory– sales ratio
0	40	16	16	0	2.5
1	40	16	16	0	2.5
2	40	16	16	0	2.5
3	40	16	16	0	2.5
a					

Note:
(a) All values are stable in subsequent periods.
Source: Simulations by the author.

of the steady state of equation (5.11). In the paragraphs below, I consider how the system adjusts if it is subjected to a variety of different shocks.

Experiment 1: a temporary rise in sales
Suppose there is a purely transitory sales fluctuation that does not induce firms to change their expectations about future sales or their target inventory range. Table 5.7 shows the response of the firm in Table 5.5 if sales are 6 in period 0 and then return to 4 thereafter. Inventories are drawn down more quickly than normal in period 0, which induces the firm to place its next order in period 2 rather than period 3. Thereafter, it returns to its normal four-period cycle, but now its orders come in periods 2, 6, 10, . . . instead of in periods 3, 7, 11, ... A one-time shock leaves a permanent imprint on the firm.

But different firms react differently to the same sales shock if they are at different stages in their replacement cycles. Indeed, a firm that is pushed

Table 5.7 Effects of a temporary rise in sales on a single firm

Period, t	Initial inventory, N_t	Sales, X_t	Carry-over stock, Q_t	Deliveries, Y_t	Inventory investment, $N_{t+1} - N_t$
0	16	6	10	0	−6
1	10	4	6	0	−4
2	6	4	2	14	10
3	16	4	12	0	−4
4	12	4	8	0	−4
5	8	4	4	0	−4
6	4	4	0	16	12
7	16	4	12	0	−4
a					

Note:
(a) Cycle repeats in subsequent periods.
Source: Simulations by the author.

below its trigger point will respond to this same shock by building up inventories in period 0 instead of drawing them down.

Table 5.8 shows what happens in the four-firm economy if all firms have sales of 6 in period 0. Inventories accumulate at first, and the one-time shock converts the smooth behavior shown in Table 5.6 into a rather unusual inventory cycle in which stocks decline from 44 to 28 every fourth period and then return to 44. Similarly, both deliveries and inventory investment go through a four-period limit cycle. This is because the transitory shock created a degree of synchronization of orders among firms that was not present before.

Naturally, one does not expect the entire economy to behave this way forever. There are many reasons. Most obviously, shocks are not likely to be so perfectly correlated. Furthermore, prices would adjust to smooth the orders. For example, manufacturers would probably start posting higher prices in periods 4, 8, 12, . . . when orders are 32 and lower prices in periods 3, 7, 11, . . . when orders are zero so as to encourage some retailers to adjust their ordering schedules. A simple way to avoid this artificial problem in the simulations is to assume that the economy consists of four sectors, each of which behaves exactly as shown in Table 5.8, but that each is completely out of phase with the others. Sector A experiences the sales shock in period 0, and hence behaves as in Table 5.8; sector B experiences the shock in period 1, and so lags behind by one period; and so on.

Table 5.8 Effects of a temporary rise in sales on a four-firm economy[a]

Period, t	Initial inventory, N_t	Sales, X_t	Deliveries, Y_t	Inventory investment, $N_{t+1} - N_t$
0	40	24	32	8
1	48	16	14	-2
2	46	16	14	-2
3	44	16	0	-16
4	28	16	32	16
5	44	16	16	0
6	44	16	16	0
7	44	16	0	-16
8	28	16	32	16
9	44	16	16	0
10	44	16	16	0
11	44	16	0	-16
b				

Notes:
(a) All firms are assumed to have sales of 6 in period 0.
(b) Cycle repeats in subsequent periods.
Source: Simulations by the author.

Table 5.9 Effects of a temporary rise in sales on a four-sector, 16-firm economy[a]

Period, t	Initial inventory, N_t	Sales, X_t	Deliveries, Y_t	Inventory investment, $N_{t+1} - N_t$	Inventory-sales ratio
0	160	72	80	8	2.22
1	168	72	78	6	2.33
2	174	72	76	4	2.42
3	178	72	60	−12	2.47
4	166	64	60	−4	2.59
5	162	64	62	−2	2.53
6	160	64	64	0	2.50
7	160	64	64	0	2.50
b					

Notes:
(a) It is assumed that sector A experiences an increase in sales in period 0, sector B in period 1, and so on.
(b) All values are stable in subsequent periods.
Source: Simulations by the author.

Table 5.9 shows the implied behavior of the four-sector (16-firm) economy. In this more heavily populated economy a noncyclical steady state does reemerge beginning with period 6. But note the interesting aggregative behavior. A four-period rise in sales induces inventory accumulation at first, followed by some rather abrupt inventory liquidation. This behavior – which is only one of a variety of possible patterns – is precisely the opposite of that predicted by the stock-adjustment model. In that model, a transitory and unexpected rise in sales leads to involuntary inventory decumulation followed by a gradual rebuilding of stocks.

Because this example is contrived, one should not try to draw general conclusions from it. In particular, it should not be concluded that transitory sales increases always lead to inventory accumulation. But the example does show that this outcome is quite possible and that the dynamics buried in equation (5.11) are both interesting and complex.

To derive more general results about how the economy responds to a transitory sales shock, one must return to equation (5.11) and consider the effects of a shift parameter, γ_1, which denotes a uniform rightward shift of the density function of sales (an increase in sales). What effect would this have on average deliveries, $\bar{Y}_t$? The mathematics of this problem is presented in Appendix 5.1; the answer is:

$$\frac{\partial \bar{Y}_t}{\partial \gamma_1} = (S - s)f(s) + F(s) \equiv 1 + \theta > 0 \tag{5.12}$$

This equation has a straightforward intuitive interpretation. The $F(s)$ indicates the number of firms placing an order in period t. If all firms experience a unit increase in sales, each of these firms raises its order by one unit. This accounts for the second term in 12. The first term represents the firms that are just pushed below the s trigger point by the increase in demand. There are $f(s)$ such firms, and they each order $S - s$. Equation (5.12) expresses the increase in aggregate orders as the sum of these two components.

The sign of θ is critical in what follows. For example, because aggregate inventory investment is $\bar{N}_{t+1} - \bar{N}_t = \bar{Y}_t - \bar{X}_t$, the effect of a transitory increase in mean sales on mean inventory investment is:[20]

$$\frac{\partial \Delta \bar{N}_t}{\partial \bar{X}_t} = \frac{\partial \bar{Y}_t}{\partial \bar{X}_t} - 1 = (1 + \theta) - 1 = \theta$$

So whether inventories rise or fall depends on whether θ is positive or negative.

Figure 5.2 depicts two density functions, each with particular values of S and s, corresponding respectively to cases in which $\theta > 0$ and $\theta < 0$. In each panel of the figure the area representing $(S - s)f(s)$ is shaded horizontally and the area representing $F(s)$ is shaded vertically.[21] The sum of these two areas is $1 + \theta$, and the area under the density function is 1.0. It is clear that the shape of the density function and the values of S and s are crucial to the value of θ. In principle these are related since the distribution of carry-over stocks reflects the interaction of the distribution of sales and the S, s policy, which itself depends on the distribution of sales.

In the top panel of Fig. 5.2 the density function of carry-over stocks, $f(Q)$, has a shape similar to a normal density and most firms have carryover stocks below s. It is clear that the areas labeled $F(s)$ and $(S - s)f(s)$ add up to more than the area under the density function. Thus θ is positive. Economically, this means that the additional orders from those firms that place orders overwhelm the declining stocks of the firms that do not place orders. Hence a rise in sales leads to an increase in average inventories.

The bottom panel of Fig. 5.2 shows the other case. Here the density function of Q displays a strong negative skewness. The S, s model makes such a shape quite plausible because it implies that the density function of initial inventories always has a mass of probability at S. In this panel $F(s)$ is rather small, and the horizontally shaded areas, $(S - s)f(s)$, are less than $1 - F(s)$. Hence θ is negative.

Both cases are possible. All that is known on *a priori* grounds is that θ must exceed -1 because $1 + \theta$ must be positive.

Notice also that θ need not be constant over time. Even if S and s are constant, the distribution function $F(Q)$ changes over time, reflecting fluctuations in sales, and hence so does θ. In most of my empirical work, θ is treated as a constant; information on changes in the shape of the distribution of carry-over stocks is simply not available.

Finally, recall from the simulation model that the derivative (equation (5.12)) is only the tip of the iceberg; it indicates the impact effect of a transitory sales shock. But such a shock sets in motion a complex dynamic inventory

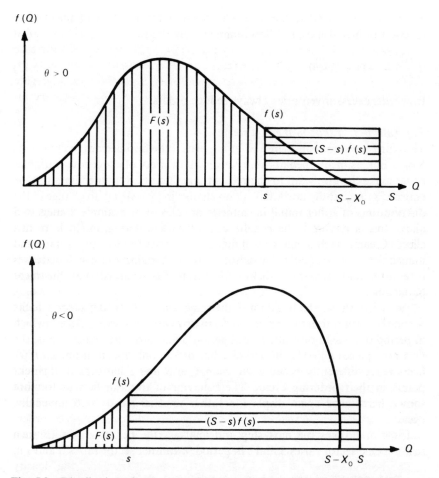

Fig. 5.2   Distribution of carry-over stocks across firms. The θ is the effect of mean sales on mean inventory investment. The Q is the carry-over stock.

adjustment process that may well be cyclical. This must be taken into account in the econometric formulation.

Experiment 2: a rise in initial inventories
Consider what will happen if each firm discovers that it has some additional units in inventory and that nothing has happened to make it want to change either S or s. Empirically this is meant to capture the firm's reactions to above-average inventories that arise from mistakes or are the legacy of a past sales shock that triggered an order. (For example, in experiment 1, firms accumulated inventories for a while and then liquidated stocks.)

Because the critical variable for the firm is $Q = N - X$, a positive shock to N is just like a negative shock to X – the case just analyzed. Thus, if the shift parameter γ_2 is used to connote a uniform rightward shift of the density function of inventories, it follows immediately that:

$$\frac{\partial \bar{Y}_t}{\partial \gamma_2} = -(1 + \theta) < 0 \tag{5.13}$$

In words, excess inventories always reduce orders.

Experiment 3: a shift in the S, s range
Thus far I have not considered what happens if the firm decides to change its S or s. But, as mentioned above, changes in a variety of exogenous variables could make the firm want to change its trigger points. Suppose, first, that the entire S, s range shifts upward, with no change in $(S - s)$ and no change in the distributions of either initial inventories or sales. (For example, I suggested above that a rise in δ, the penalty cost of back ordering, might have this effect.) Clearly, such a change will make inventories too low on average and induce firms to accumulate inventories, thus changing the distributions of inventories and carry-over stocks in the future. But what will the adjustment pattern be?

Table 5.10 shows the behavior of the same firm that was depicted in Table 5.5 on the assumption that both S and s rise by two units, to $S = 18$ and $s = 4$, in period 0. Instead of waiting until period 3 and ordering sixteen units, the firm now places an order in period 2 but orders only fourteen units. Other firms react differently because the change in S and s happens at different points in their ordering cycles. The behavior of the four-firm sector (not shown here) once again displays a rather unusual steady-state inventory cycle.

Table 5.11 takes the next step and analyzes the behavior of four such sectors. One sector raises S and s in period 0; another sector raises S and s in

Table 5.10 Effects of a rise in S and s on a single firm[a]

Period, t	Initial inventory, N_t	Sales, X_t	Carry-over stock, Q_t	Deliveries, Y_t	Inventory investment, $N_{t+1} - N_t$
0	16	4	12	0	−4
1	12	4	8	0	−4
2	8	4	4	14	10
3	18	4	14	0	−4
4	14	4	10	0	−4
5	10	4	6	0	−4
6	6	4	2	16	12
7	18	4	14	0	−4
[b]					

Notes:
(a) The rise is two units, to $S = 18$ and $s = 4$, in period 0.
(b) Cycle repeats in subsequent periods.
Source: Simulations by the author.

Table 5.11 Effects of a rise in S and s on a four-sector, 16-firm economy[a]

Period, t	Initial inventory, N_t	Sales, X_t	Deliveries, Y_t	Inventory investment, $N_{t+1} - N_t$	Inventory-sales ratio
0	160	64	80	16	2.50
1	176	64	78	14	2.75
2	190	64	76	12	2.97
3	202	64	60	−4	3.16
4	198	64	60	−4	3.09
5	194	64	62	−2	3.03
6	192	64	64	0	3.00
7	192	64	64	0	3.00
b					

Notes:
(a) Sector A is assumed to raise S and s in period 0, sector B in period 1, and so on.
(b) All values are stable in subsequent periods.
Source: Simulations by the author.

period 1; and so on. Here the jagged edges are smoothed out, and a clear pattern emerges that resembles overshooting. Such overshooting in response to a rise in desired inventories can never occur in a stock-adjustment model. But Table 5.11 shows that it can occur in an S, s model even though no firm ever allows its inventories to exceed S.

More formally, if shift parameter γ_3 denotes a change in an exogenous variable that moves S and s equally, and does not change $F(Q)$, equation 5.11 implies:

$$\frac{\partial \bar{Y}_t}{\partial \gamma_3} = 1 + \theta > 0 \tag{5.14}$$

This derivative is equal and opposite to equation (5.13), which makes sense. If, for some reason, $\bar{N}_t$, S, and s all increase equally at the same time, there will be no effect on $\bar{Y}_t$.

Experiment 4: a widening of the S, s range
Not all changes in the firm's price and cost structure will induce it to move S and s equally. For example, as mentioned, an increase in the fixed cost of purchasing, A, would raise $S - s$, lower s, and have an unclear effect on S. So it is worth exploring what happens if either s or S, but not both, changes. Let γ_4 denote a change in some parameter that moves S but leaves s unchanged. Then, by equation (5.11),

$$\frac{\partial \bar{Y}}{\partial \gamma_4} = F(s) > 0 \tag{5.15}$$

Alternatively, if γ_4' denotes a change in some parameter that moves s but leaves S unchanged, then:

$$\frac{\partial \bar{Y}}{\partial \gamma_4'} = (S - s)f(s) > 0 \tag{5.15a}$$

Either sort of shift raises inventory investment initially, and then has subsequent effects by changing the distribution of carry-over stocks in future periods.

Clearly, among the three shift parameters $-\gamma_3$, γ_4, and γ_4' – one is redundant because γ_3 is just the sum of γ_4 and γ_4'. In what follows I work with γ_3 – which represents equal changes in both S and s and with γ_4 – which represents a rise in S and s fixed.

Experiment 5: an anticipated rise in sales

Now I come to the source of variation in deliveries that I believe is predominant in the data actually observed. Suppose that most sales fluctuations experienced by retailers are anticipated, so that a higher X_t is preceded by a higher S, s, or both. In this case, each rightward shift of the distribution of sales (as in experiment 1) is accompanied by a rightward shift in the distribution of initial inventories (as in experiment 2).[22] Hence the effects of an expected, and presumably persistent, increase in sales can be captured by combining the experiments conducted above. Specifically, the shift parameter denoting an anticipated rise in sales, γ_5, is composed of the following combination of shift parameters already discussed: a one-unit rise in γ_1 (an increase in sales), a b unit increase in γ_2 (an increase in initial inventories), either an a_1 unit increase in γ_4 (a widening of the S, s range) or an a_2 unit increase in γ_3 (an upward shift of the S, s range).

The new parameters introduced here have fairly clear intuitive meanings. The parameters a_1 and a_2 are like marginal inventory sales ratios; they represent the sensitivity of desired inventories to expected sales. The derivatives in equation (5.8), which are for a specific example, lead one to expect S, s, or both to respond positively to anticipated sales. Notice that this presumption does not quite follow from the mathematics. Hadley and Whitin (1963) derive equation (5.7) for a firm whose sales each period are drawn from an unchanged probability distribution. The derivatives in equation (5.8) thus compare different firms with different but stationary sales distributions. I use these results to predict the response of a firm that anticipates a change in its own sales distribution for the next period. For this reason, I imagine that, in addition to the factors enumerated in (5.7), the parameters a_1 and a_2 depend in an important way on how persistent, and hence how predictable, demand fluctuations are. More persistent fluctuations, I surmise, lead to higher values of a_1 or a_2.

The parameter b, which measures the responsiveness of initial inventories, N_t, to expected sales, X_t^e, should depend on all the factors that influence a_1 or a_2 and in addition on the degree of uncertainty firms attach to the forecasts and on how risk averse they are.

In what follows I deal with two different models, corresponding to two different ways in which the S, s range may be affected. In *model 1*, changes in the target inventory range are assumed to take the form of equal movements in S and s. So the effect of shift parameter γ_5 on mean orders is:

$$\frac{\partial \bar{Y}}{\partial \gamma_5} = \frac{\partial \bar{Y}}{\partial \bar{X}^e} = 1 + \theta - b(1 + \theta) + a_2(1 + \theta) = (1 - b + a_2)(1 + \theta)$$

where the $1 + \theta$ term comes from the shift in the distribution of sales; the $b(1 + \theta)$ term comes from the shift in the distribution of initial inventories; and the $a_2(1 + \theta)$ term comes from the shift in S and s. In *model 0*, shocks to desired inventory holdings are assumed to correspond to changes in S with s fixed, widening or narrowing the S, s range. Thus the effect of the composite shift parameter γ_5 is:

$$\frac{\partial \bar{Y}}{\partial \gamma_5} = \frac{\partial \bar{Y}}{\partial \bar{X}^e} = 1 + \theta - b(1 + \theta) + a_1 F(s) = (1 - b)(1 + \theta) + a_1 F(s)$$

where the sales and initial inventory terms are the same as in *model 1* and the $a_1 F(s)$ term comes from the shift in S. To economize on notation, I introduce the parameter λ, which takes on the value $\lambda = 1$ for *model 1* and $\lambda = 0$ for *model 0*, and write the two expressions more succinctly as:

$$\frac{\partial \bar{Y}}{\partial \gamma_5} = \frac{\partial \bar{Y}}{\partial \bar{X}^e} = (1 + \theta)(1 - b) + \lambda a_2(1 + \theta) + (1 - \lambda)a_1 F(s) \equiv K_1$$

(5.16)

Experiment 6: an unanticipated rise in sales
There is one other type of composite shock that appears to have empirical relevance: a change in the mean of the sales distribution that was not anticipated. By definition, an unanticipated sales shock cannot affect beginning-of-period inventories. However, as long as the random process generating sales is not independently and identically distributed, sales shocks contain information relevant to predicting future sales and hence induce firms to alter their S, s target range. Hence I consider an unanticipated rise in sales, X_t^u, to be a composite of a unit increase in γ_1 (a rise in sales) and either an a_3 unit increase in γ_4 (a rise in S alone) in model 0 or an a_4 unit increase in γ_3 (a rise in both S and s) in *model 1*.

So, if one denotes the shift parameter representing an unanticipated sales shock γ_6 and once again uses the convenient variable λ to capture both models in a single expression, the following relation is implied:

$$\frac{\partial \bar{Y}}{\partial \gamma_6} = \frac{\partial \bar{Y}}{\partial \bar{X}^u} = 1 + \theta + \lambda a_4(1 + \theta) + (1 - \lambda)a_3 F(s) \equiv K_2 \qquad (5.17)$$

where the $\lambda a_4(1 + \theta) + (1 - \lambda)a_3 F(s)$ terms come from the appropriate changes in the S, s range. Note that K_2, which is the effect of a unit increase in $\bar{X}_t^u$ on mean deliveries, may be greater than or less than K_1, which is the effect of a unit increase in X_t^e. In versions of the S, s models in which delivery lags are unimportant, there is no particular implication about whether expected or unexpected sales should have the stronger effect on inventory investment. This, once again, stands in sharp contract to the stock-adjustment model.

As pointed out above, equations like (5.16) and (5.17) indicate only the impact effects of increases in sales, but there are also complicated dynamic adjustments inherent in (5.11). These dynamics need to be captured in the econometric specification.

5.4 EMPIRICAL IMPLEMENTATION OF THE S, s MODEL

To create regression equations from this analysis it is necessary to relate the theoretical shift parameters to empirical variables. One must also assume that parameters like K_1 and K_2, which in principle vary, are constant through time. It will be easiest first to write down the two-equation empirical model that is meant to represent the theoretical model and then to explain it by components. Thus:

$$Y_t = K_1 X_t^e + K_2 X_t^u + K_3(\eta_{t+1} - \eta_t) - (1 + \theta)u_t + \varepsilon_t \tag{5.18}$$

$$N_t = b X_t^e + \eta_t + u_t \tag{5.19}$$

The first term on the right-hand side of each equation represents the effects of anticipated increases in sales. According to experiment 5, a unit increase in X_t^e raises Y_t by an amount K_1 and raises N_t by b.

Experiment 6 is interpreted as an unexpected increase in sales, X_t^u. It was shown that a unit increase in X_t^u moves Y_t by K_2 units, but does not affect N_t. This is reflected in equations (5.18) and (5.19).

The variable η_t represents exogenous variables other than X_t^e and X_t^u that influence S and s. As has been shown above in an explicit example, interest rates, manufacturer's prices, and fixed costs are among these variables.

A concrete example may help clarify the nature of η. One of the determinants of S and s is the fixed cost of making a purchase. An increase in A is expected to widen the S, s range. Suppose this happens by raising S with s fixed.[23] Let ω denote the derivative dS/dA. Then, according to experiment 3, an increase in A by $1/\omega$ units would push S up by one unit and raise Y_t by $1 + \theta$ units. Hence, if A were the only factor determining S and s, one would simply define η as A/ω. Other variables that influence S and s, such as interest rates and storage costs, can be handled similarly. In the empirical work, η_t is actually a vector of variables. The units of measurement for the elements of η are chosen to make unity the coefficient of η_t in equation (5.19). Variable η_t is dated so that η_t captures the influences on beginning-of-period inventories and $\eta_{t+1} - \eta_t$ captures the change in these influences during the period. The model therefore implies that a unit increase of η raises Y_t by $(1 + \theta)$ units in *model 1* (equal increases in S and s) or by $F(s)$ units in *model 0* (a rise in S alone). Once again I can economize on notation by defining the coefficient of $\eta_{t+1} - \eta_t$ in equation (5.18) as:

$$K_3 = \lambda(1 + \theta) + (1 - \lambda)F(s) \equiv F(s) + \lambda(S - s)f(s)$$

which encompasses both models.

The most difficult variable to explain in equations (5.18) and (5.19) is u_t, which is something akin to undesired inventories. But that description is not really accurate because the micro model implies that firms only have a desired inventory range, not level, and that they always keep inventories within this range. The best way to understand u_t is to recall the complicated dynamic adjustments in the simulation model. After a shock there is always a period that has the earmarks of inventory disequilibrium, even though each individual firm always has its inventories where it wants them, given its past history and its S, s trigger points. This disequilibrium is particularly clear, for example, in Table 5.11 in which there appears to be overshooting following a rise in S and s. The variable u_t in equations (5.18) and (5.19) is meant to embody the legacy of all past shocks and errors; it is the way these apparently simple equations accommodate the complex dynamics of the S, s model.[24]

Equation (5.19) amounts to a definition of u_t. The terms $bX_t^e + \eta_t$ can be thought of as the steady-state level of average inventories – corresponding, for example, to the entry 192 in Table 5.11. Then u_t measures the deviation of actual inventories from this steady state, period by period. To decide on the proper coefficient for u_t in equation (5.18), one must connect it with one of the experiments in the previous section. The most natural one seems to be experiment 2, which deals with a shift of the distribution of N_t when all the determinants of S and s are held constant. Hence the coefficient $-(1 + \theta)$ is assigned to u_t in equation (5.18).

Plainly, there are no data on u_t to permit estimation of (5.18) and (5.19) directly. There are two routes that can be followed in deriving an estimating equation. The most obvious, but I will argue inappropriate, procedure is to solve (5.19) for u_t and substitute into (5.18) to obtain:

$$\begin{aligned}Y_t = &[(1 + \theta)(1 - b) + a_1 F(s)]X_t^e + [1 + \theta + a_3 F(s)]X_t^u \\ &- (1 + \theta)N_t + (1 + \theta)\eta_t + F(s)[\eta_{t+1} - \eta_t] + \varepsilon_t\end{aligned} \tag{5.20}$$

in *model 0* ($\lambda = 0$), or:

$$\begin{aligned}Y_t = &(1 + a_2)(1 + \theta)X_t^e + (1 + a_4)(1 + \theta)X_t^u \\ &- (1 + \theta)N_t + (1 + \theta)\eta_{t+1} + \varepsilon_t\end{aligned} \tag{5.21}$$

in *model 1* ($\lambda = 1$). These equations, which may look complicated, are actually rather conventional. If one treats η_t as a stochastic disturbance, either (5.20) or (5.21) can be written as:

$$Y_t = A_1 X_t^e + A_2 X_t^u + BN_t + error$$

with suitable interpretations of A_1, A_2, and B. This is exactly the econometric specification normally used to represent the stock-adjustment model (compare equation (5.5)). The only difference is that the parameters have very different interpretations.

However, there is a problem with the error terms in (5.20) and (5.21). It is most obvious in (5.20), in which η_t is part of the error term, while (5.19) implies that N_t and η_t have a positive covariance. Thus the coefficient of N_t in (5.20) should be biased. The same problem arises in (5.21) if η_t is serially correlated. There can be little doubt that it is. In the empirical work, η_t is represented by:

$$\eta_t = \alpha R_t + v_t \tag{5.22}$$

where R_t is a vector of measurable variables that influence S and s such as interest rates and manufacturers' prices, and v_t is the truly unobservable component. Thus v_t reflects, among other things, changes in the cost technology (storage costs and the ratio A/c), changes that one expects to be persistent and perhaps even permanent – that is, v_t may well be a random walk.

A better way of deriving an estimating equation is found by using the model to eliminate u_t from equation (5.18). This is done in Appendix 5.2; there it is shown that the model can be reformulated as:

$$\begin{aligned}
\Delta N_t = {}& -\theta \Delta N_{t-1} + [\theta + a_1 F(s)](X_t^e - X_{t-1}^e) \\
& + [\theta + a_3 F(s)](X_t^u - X_{t-1}^u) + (1 + \theta)z_{t-1} \\
& + F(s)[z_t - z_{t-1}] + \varepsilon_t - \varepsilon_{t-1}
\end{aligned} \tag{5.23}$$

in *model 0* ($\lambda = 0$), or

$$\begin{aligned}
\Delta N_t = {}& -\theta \Delta N_{t-1} + [\theta + a_2(1 + \theta)](X_t^e - X_{t-1}^e) \\
& + [\theta + a_4(1 + \theta)](X_t^u - X_{t-1}^u) + (1 + \theta)z_t + \varepsilon_t - \varepsilon_{t-1}
\end{aligned} \tag{5.24}$$

in *model 1* ($\lambda = 1$), where I introduce the new symbol, z_t, as shorthand for $\eta_{t+1} - \eta_t$.

Equation (5.24) has some chance of being a legitimate equation for estimation. The econometric error term in this equation is:

$$(1 + \theta)(v_{t+1} - v_t) + (\varepsilon_t - \varepsilon_{t-1})$$

The first term is assumed to be uncorrelated with all the variables in the equation, and will be almost independently and identically distributed if v_t is close to a random walk, which is a plausible case. The second term will also be uncorrelated with all the variables in the model. But it will be highly serially correlated if ε_t is serially independent. On the other hand, if ε_t is approximately a random walk, $\varepsilon_t - \varepsilon_{t-1}$ will be approximately "white noise".

The error term in (5.23) potentially has a rather complicated serial correlation structure, even if one is willing to assume that v_t is a random walk. However, it will still be orthogonal to all the variables in the equation. Thus estimation of (5.23) and (5.24) by ordinary least squares seems likely to give unbiased coefficient estimates, even if they are inefficient.

To make (5.23) or (5.24) operational, it is only necessary to specify the variables in the vector R_t (see equation (5.22)) and to obtain a time series on expected sales. The latter is explained below. For the former, I have tried interest rates and the ratio of manufacturers' prices, c_t, to retail prices, p_t.

5.5 THE DATA

Because a firm's optimal choices of S and s are sensitive to its cost and demand structures, firms in different industries are expected to make quite different choices of S and s and of the parameters a_1 through a_4 above. Thus I decided to work at a level that was as disaggregated as the data permitted. In practice, this meant dividing retailing into eight subsectors. In addition, results are reported for all retailing. However, as shown below, automobiles dominate the results for all retailing.

5.5.1 Sales and inventories

The basic data on the sales and inventories of retailers are unpublished and have only recently become available. The data are monthly and seasonally adjusted, covering the period from January 1959 through December 1980.[25] Both sales and inventories are deflated by the US Bureau of Economic Analysis and are expressed in 1972 prices at monthly rates.[26]

A word on the overall trend in these data is in order. In the period before the first OPEC shock, inventories in most sectors were growing faster than sales. Despite all the talk about improved inventory control and economies of scale in inventories, the inventory-sales ratio was generally increasing in retailing. (See Fig. 5.3, which pertains to all retailing.) This basic fact is sometimes read as evidence against the S, s model because the square root rule is thought to suggest that inventories should grow as the square root of sales. There is no contradiction, however. For example, if economic growth is characterized mainly by more firms or by firms expanding the number of products they handle rather than by firms with fixed product lines growing larger, the square root rule would not be relevant to the trend movement in inventories.

Table 5.12 offers some descriptive statistics on these data, intended to give an idea of the relative sizes of the various sectors and how much of the overall variance comes from each sector. It can be seen that there are only two large sectors in terms of inventory holding: automobile dealers and general

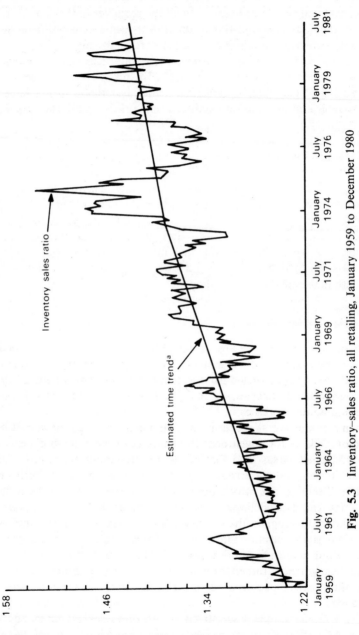

Fig. 5.3 Inventory–sales ratio, all retailing, January 1959 to December 1980

Table 5.12 Descriptive statistics on sales and inventory data, by sector, January 1959 to December 1980

| Sector | Sales | | Inventories | | |
	mean[a]	variance about trend[b]	mean inventory stock[c]	variance of inventory investment about trend	mean inventory sales ratio
All retailing	34.20	1.3200	46.50	0.1338	1.34
Durables					
automobiles	6.45	0.3320	10.14	0.0741	1.53
furniture and appliances	1.66	0.0067	3.58	0.0016	2.12
lumber and hardware	1.75	0.0208	3.83	0.0013	2.22
other durables	1.16	0.0169	3.22	0.0033	2.83
Nondurables					
food	7.69	0.0439	5.39	0.0028	0.70
apparel	2.02	0.0076	4.80	0.0030	2.39
general merchandise	4.88	0.0405	8.89	0.0191	1.80
other nondurables	8.59	0.0436	6.69	0.0062	0.78

Notes:
(a) Billions of 1972 dollars, at a monthly rate.
(b) Data are detrended by the procedure outlined in note 4.
(c) Billions of 1972 dollars.
Source: Computed by the author from unpublished data from the US Bureau of Economic Analysis.

merchandise stores (primarily department stores). It can also be seen that the sectors vary widely in how much inventory they hold relative to sales. The inventory-sales ratio is highest in the apparel and other durables categories, lowest in food and other nondurables. The range of time is impressive: from 21 days to 85 days of sales.

When one looks at variances in the detrended data, the real dominance of the automobile sector is revealed. The variance around trend of automobile sales is $7\frac{1}{2}$ times larger than that of the next largest sector, and in fact far exceeds the sum of the variances of all other sectors. In terms of inventory investment, the dominance of the automobile industry is even more complete. Except for general merchandise, the variance about trend of automobile inventory investment is at least 12 times greater than that in any other sector. In a word, cyclical inventory variability is essentially a matter of automobile dealer and department store behavior.

It is thus worth considering the *a priori* plausibility of the S, s model for automobile dealers and department stores. Department stores appear to be an industry in which the S, s rule should apply well. Deliveries presumably come in by the truckload, whereas sales are made continuously. The automobile industry presents a less obvious case. A truckload of automobiles is not a very large number, which suggests that the lot size, $S - s$, may be quite small relative to monthly sales for a typical dealer. This diminishes the importance of the S, s rule. The need to have a variety of models on display and ready for immediate delivery may be a more important factor in explaining the size of automobile inventories. Furthermore, the distinction between manufacturers' inventories of finished goods and retail inventories is a slippery one in this industry. While dealers are generally independent, and quite competitive firms, they are sometimes thought to be captives of the automobile makers. It may be that the makers rather than the dealers decide the inventory holdings of automobile dealers.

I have stressed repeatedly that the S, s model has very different empirical implications from the stock-adjustment model. Table 5.13 helps to distinguish between the two models. It displays, for each retail sector, a decomposition of the variance of Y around trend similar to that presented above for more aggregated data. Several generalizations can be made. First, except for the other durable goods sector, the variance of deliveries to retailers, y, exceeds the variance of retail sales, x. Second, the covariance between sales and inventory change is never a substantial negative number; it is either positive or virtually zero. These two facts make it very difficult to believe that the main role of retail inventories is to serve as a buffer stock.[27] If firms want to use inventories to cushion y_t against fluctuations in x_t, it seems odd that var(y) > var(x). It seems even odder, if inventories are primarily a buffer, that Δn and x do not covary negatively.

5.5.2 Sales expectations

The model requires that sales be divided into expected and unexpected components. I started with a variety of proxies for expectations. However,

Table 5.13 Decomposition of the variance of deliveries to retailers around trend, by sector, January 1959 to December 1980[a]

Sector	var(y)	var(x)	var(Δn)	2cov(x, Δn)	$\dfrac{\text{var}(y)}{\text{var}(x)}$	$\dfrac{\text{var}(\Delta n)}{\text{var}(x)}$
All retailing	1.620	1.320	0.134	0.1410	1.15	0.10
Durables	0.794	0.636	0.088	0.0824	1.25	0.14
automobiles	0.454	0.332	0.074	0.0491	1.37	0.22
furniture and appliances	0.009	0.007	0.002	0.0090	1.31	0.24
lumber and hardware	0.023	0.021	0.001	0.0015	1.10	0.06
other durables	0.013	0.017	0.003	−0.0007	0.76	0.19
Nondurables	2.600	2.030	0.370	0.0919	1.28	0.18
food	0.047	0.044	0.003	−0.0004	1.07	0.06
apparel	0.010	0.008	0.003	−0.0003	1.35	0.39
general merchandise	0.067	0.041	0.019	0.0051	1.65	0.47
other nondurables	0.046	0.044	0.006	−0.0023	1.06	0.14

Note:
(a) Sales and deliveries are in billions of dollars, at monthly rates.
Source: Same as Table 5.12.

since they all led to roughly the same results, I report equations based on only one. Specifically, in the estimates presented here, firms are assumed to estimate (or know) a demand curve,

$$X_t = a(L)X_{t-1} + b(L)P_t + c(L)PI_t + error \qquad (5.25)$$

where the first term is a fourth-order distributed lag on past sales, the second is a distributed lag on the industry's relative price (relative to the personal consumption deflator), and the third is a distributed lag on real personal income.[28] The $b(L)$ and $c(L)$ parameters were estimated initially as free distributed lags, with lags going back as far as one year. Then, using a series of F-tests, the lag length was reduced if there was no deterioration in the fit.

In order to use (5.25) to generate forecasts, it is necessary to forecast the contemporaneous values of relative price and real personal income. Relative prices are forecast by an autoregression. Personal income is forecast in two ways: by an autoregression and by an autoregression supplemented by publicly available macroeconomic forecasts. Two sources of real GNP forecasts were tried: the consensus forecast of the National Bureau of Economic Research-American Statistical Association and that of Wharton-Econometric Forecasting Associates, Inc.[29] However, I found that neither forecast was a significant determinant of PI after controlling for $PI_{t-1}, PI_{t-2}, \ldots$. For this reason, the macro forecasts were discarded, and personal income was predicted by an autoregression.[30]

5.5.3 Interest rates

One long-standing problem in the empirical inventory literature has been the inability to uncover significant interest rate effects, even though every theory of inventory holding insists that they should be present.[31] The usual intertemporal substitution variable in optimizing models of inventory behavior (and the S, s model is no exception) is the so-called own real interest rate, that is, the nominal interest rate minus the expected rate of inflation of the firm's product. The reason for this is quite straightforward. A decision to hold a finished good in inventory for one period entails forgoing the current price, P_t, today to receive the expected future price, P_{t+1}^e, one period later. If the nominal interest rate is i_t, the effective cost of this storage activity (ignoring explicit storage costs) is:

$$\frac{(1 + i_t)P_t - P_{t+1}^e}{P_t} = (1 + i_t) - (1 + \pi_t) = i_t - \pi_t$$

where π_t is the anticipated rate of nominal capital gain. Therefore intertemporal substitution can be captured by including $i_t - \pi_t$ in the equation.

However, there is at least one theoretical consideration that points toward using the nominal interest rate instead. Many retailers (and perhaps manufacturers as well) are thought to follow a first in, first out (FIFO) pricing strategy:

once a finished good is placed on the shelves, it is given a price tag that remains on the item regardless of what subsequently happens to the price of newly produced goods. Everyone has at one time or another bought some durable good that was the last one at a given price because the next shipment would have higher priced merchandise. To many economists the rationality of this practice has seemed dubious. But Arthur Okun recently suggested that FIFO pricing may be rational when there are long-standing customer relations.[32] If FIFO pricing really is prevalent, the real interest rate is not the appropriate intertemporal price. If a firm pays i_t to hold a commodity in inventory but does not earn the price appreciation, π_t, when it sells the commodity (because the old price tag remained on the commodity), the nominal interest rate is the "correct" cost of capital. For this and other reasons, I use the nominal interest rate and the expected rate of inflation as separate variables rather than using the difference between them.[33]

What about taxes? Suppose first that the real interest rate specification is the correct one. Since inventories of retailers are, by definition, part of their normal business, price appreciation on inventory holdings is taxable as ordinary income under FIFO accounting. So the real after-tax cost of capital under FIFO is:

$$(1 - \tau_t)(i_t - \pi_t) \tag{5.26a}$$

where τ_t is the marginal corporate income tax rate. But if firms use last in, first out (LIFO) accounting, they can essentially escape taxation on their nominal capital gains, making the cost of capital:

$$(1 - \tau_t)i_t - \pi_t \tag{5.26b}$$

Finally, suppose the nominal interest rate specification is the correct one because firms are FIFO pricers. Then the relevant after-tax cost of capital would be:

$$(1 - \tau_t)i_t \tag{5.26c}$$

Since the statutory corporate income tax rate has been changed only slightly (and infrequently) since 1959, not much is lost by treating τ as constant in empirical work. Once this is done, all three versions of equation (5.26) can be handled by simply allowing the nominal rate of interest and the expected rate of inflation to enter the regression separately as determinants of η, and embedding the factor $(1 - \tau)$ in the appropriate slope coefficients.

The nominal interest rate is measured by the bank prime lending rate. Expected inflation rates are obtained by fitting autoregressions to the levels of absolute prices in each sector, using these to compute one-month-ahead forecasts, and then converting the forecasts into monthly inflation rates. (The prime rate is also entered as a monthly rate.)

5.5.4 Manufacturers' prices

Among the variables that the S, s model suggests should influence the target inventory range is the ratio of the manufacturers' selling price, c_t, to the retailers' selling price, p_t. This ratio is computed separately for each sector by matching up the retail sectors with corresponding components of the producer price index. (The matchup is presented and discussed in Appendix 5.3.) Relative prices were normalized to 1.00 in 1972.

5.5.5 Stock-adjustment regressions

Before looking at the empirical results for my rather unconventional model of inventory behavior, it may be useful to investigate first what happens when these data are used to estimate a standard stock- adjustment model. I argued above that this model lacks a persuasive theoretical rationale for retailers and that the coefficient of N_t will be afflicted by least-squares bias if the S, s model is correct.

Table 5.14 displays estimates of the stock-adjustment model described in equation (5.4) for all retailing and for eight subsectors:

$$N_{t+1} - N_t = \lambda(N_t^* - N_t) - \beta X_t^u + \varepsilon_t$$

where:

$$N_t^* = a + bX_t^e + c_1 i_t + c_2 \pi_t$$

which together imply:

$$Y_t = \lambda a + (1 + \lambda b)X_t^e + (1 - \beta)X_t^u - \lambda N_t$$
$$+ \lambda c_1 i_t + \lambda c_2 \pi_t + \varepsilon_t \tag{5.27}$$

Several observations summarize the results. First, the model does rather well in goodness of fit,[34] but in some sectors (especially automobiles) there is an indication of autocorrelation in the residuals. Second, the estimates of λ, the speed of adjustment, are totally implausible. The highest is merely 0.14 (14 percent a month!) while the lowest is 0.03. These simply do not make sense. Third, the coefficients of expected and unexpected sales are sometimes quite close together.[35] This finding makes little sense in the context of equation (5.27) since the coefficient of X_t^e should exceed the coefficient of X_t^u by $\lambda b + \beta$. Fourth, interest rate effects are of the correct (negative) sign in all sectors except one, but are significant in only two sectors.[36] And fifth, the expected rate of inflation performs much worse, with the correct (positive) sign in only four of the eight sectors and a significantly positive coefficient only for general merchandising. The hypothesis that the coefficients of the nominal interest rate and the inflation rate are equal and opposite, in other words, that it is the real rate of interest that matters, does not seem to hold for any sector except general merchandise.

Table 5.14 Stock-adjustment regressions, by sector, February 1960 to November 1980[a]

Sector	Coefficient					Summary statistic		
	X_t^e	X_t^u	N_t	i_t	π_t	R^2	standard error of estimate	Durbin-Watson
All retailing	1.12 (0.03)	0.94 (0.06)	−0.06 (0.02)	−0.401 (0.208)	−0.060 (0.081)	0.998	0.342	1.57
Durables								
automobiles	1.13 (0.04)	1.08 (0.07)	−0.10 (0.03)	−0.000 (0.146)	−0.061 (0.030)	0.983	0.263	1.56
furniture and appliances	1.25 (0.05)	1.00 (0.08)	−0.08 (0.02)	−0.071 (0.020)	0.011 (0.010)	0.996	0.037	1.97
lumber and hardware	1.08 (0.03)	1.02 (0.05)	−0.05 (0.01)	−0.060 (0.017)	−0.002 (0.003)	0.993	0.035	2.17
other durables	1.07 (0.06)	0.84 (0.10)	−0.03 (0.02)	−0.037 (0.030)	0.000 (0.013)	0.990	0.056	1.73
Nondurables								
food	1.04 (0.02)	0.97 (0.03)	−0.12 (0.03)	0.028 (0.026)	0.001 (0.010)	0.998	0.053	2.20
apparel	1.04 (0.05)	0.90 (0.09)	−0.06 (0.03)	−0.045 (0.030)	0.005 (0.004)	0.986	0.052	2.15
general merchandise	1.25 (0.06)	0.97 (0.10)	−0.10 (0.03)	−0.076 (0.078)	0.081 (0.038)	0.991	0.132	1.92
other nondurables	1.05 (0.03)	1.03 (0.07)	−0.14 (0.04)	−0.050 (0.041)	−0.018 (0.007)	0.998	0.078	2.08

Note:
(a) The dependent variable is Y_t, deliveries from manufacturers. The regressions also include a constant, a time trend, and a second time trend beginning in October 1973. Expected and unexpected sales are denoted by X_t^e and X_t^u, respectively; N_t denotes initial inventories; i_t is the nominal interest rate; and π_t is the anticipated rate of nominal capital gains. The numbers in parentheses are standard errors.
Source: Same as Table 5.12.

The S, s model offers an explanation of the puzzling results found in these tables and also provides a way to assess the quantitative importance of the aforementioned least squares bias. The regressions in Table 5.14 seem to suggest a simple model of the form:

$$Y_t = AX_t + BN_t + error \tag{5.28}$$

with A somewhat larger than unity and B a small negative number. Viewed as estimates of equation (5.27), these results do not make much sense. But suppose instead that the data were generated by the S, s model. Could one then make sense of the parameter estimates?

To answer this question, consider a simplified version of the S, s model – equations (5.18) and (5.19) – in which $K_1 = K_2$ (so that only X_t, not its division into $X_t^e + X_t^u$, matters) and in which u_t is zero every period:[37]

$$Y_t = K_1 X_t + K_3 (\eta_{t+1} - \eta_t) + \varepsilon_t \tag{5.29}$$

$$N_t = bX_t + \eta_t \tag{5.30}$$

It is a straightforward but tedious computation to use (5.29) and (5.30) to calculate the variances and covariances among the variables X, Y, and N, and then to put these into the standard formulas for the ordinary least squares regression coefficients in (5.28). The results are:

$$\text{p}\lim \hat{A} = K_1 + (1 - \rho)bK_3$$

$$\text{p}\lim \hat{B} = -(1 - \rho)K_3$$

where ρ is the simple correlation coefficient between η_{t+1} and η_t. Recall that I have argued that ρ should be close to 1.0. If ρ is high, then $\hat{B}$ in equation (5.28) is a badly biased estimate of $-K_3$ while A in (5.28) is a nearly unbiased estimate of K_1. These *a priori* notions seem quite consistent with the empirical results, which show small negative $\hat{B}$ and $\hat{A}$ in excess of unity. In summary, if the S, s model is correct, the least squares bias afflicting (5.28) could well be strong enough to produce the results that were actually found.[38]

5.5.6 S, s model regressions

The S, s model derived above is represented by equations (5.23) and (5.24) for *model 0* and *model 1*, respectively. To these are added, for empirical purposes, $z_t = \eta_{t+1} - \eta_t$ and:

$$\eta_{t+1} = \alpha_1 i_t + \alpha_2 \pi_t + \alpha_3 \left(\frac{c_t}{p_t} \right) + v_{t+1} \tag{5.31}$$

The equations are clearly nonlinear in the parameters, and so were estimated by nonlinear least squares. Results for *model 0* and *model 1* are reported in Tables 5.15 and 5.16, respectively. Before looking at the details, some broad generalizations are possible.

First, the fit of the equations is quite good, despite their small R^2. The left-hand variable in these regressions is inventory investment, $Y_t - X_t$, whereas in the stock-adjustment regressions it was just Y_t. Hence the standard errors of the two sets of regressions are comparable, not their R^2. The standard errors in Tables 5.15 and 5.16 are almost as low as those in Table 5.14 despite the absence of the variable N_t from the S, s regressions.[39] Second, there is a surprising absence of serial correlation in the residuals. In terms of the underlying model, this suggests either that ε_t can be modeled well as a random walk or that the variance of ε_t is trivial compared to the variance of v_t (which, in turn, is nearly a random walk). Third, estimates using other proxies for expectations (not reported here) show that the parameters are quite insensitive to the way expectations are measured. Fourth, those parameters that are common to the two models (such as θ) have more or less the same point estimates in *model 0* and *model 1*.

I turn now to the parameter estimates, beginning (because it is slightly simpler) with *model 1*, which assumes that changes in interest rates, cost conditions, and so forth always move S and s equally.

The most important parameter in the model is θ, which was defined in equation (5.12). The one restriction on θ is that $1 + \theta > 0$, and all the estimates easily satisfy this restriction. As indicated in Fig. 5.2, *a priori* reasoning cannot determine the sign of θ, but does suggest that very large negative θ are unlikely. In fact, the estimate of θ is positive in four sectors and negative in the other four. None of the point estimates seems implausible. Note that $1 + \theta$ is analogous to the speed-of-adjustment parameter in the stock-adjustment model.[40] In these estimates, $1 + \theta$ ranges from 0.67 to 1.19. These are quite rapid monthly adjustment speeds.

Unlike the parameter θ, which arises from the aggregation process and has no counterpart at the micro level, the parameters a_2 and a_4 do have clear economic interpretations. Each is like a marginal inventory-sales ratio. Specifically, a_2 is the marginal effect on S and s of a unit increase in expected sales, and a_4 is the corresponding effect of a unit increase in unexpected sales. Hence one expects each to be positive and, if some inventories are required for display purposes, to be less than the average inventory-sales ratio.

Viewed from this perspective, most of the estimates of a_2 are reasonable. The $\hat{a}_2$ never exceeds the average inventory-sales ratio (which was reported in Table 5.12). Of the nine cases in the table, $\hat{a}_2$ is positive in six; the only really bothersome sector appears to be food, where the estimated a_2 is significantly negative. The results for a_4 are not as good. The estimated a_4 is always below the average inventory-sales ratios, but $\hat{a}_4$ is negative in five of nine cases, including all the nondurable goods sectors.

Parameter α_1 measures the marginal effect of the monthly rate of interest in percentage points on the steady-state inventory level (see equation (5.31)). It

Table 5.15 Nonlinear least squares estimates of *model 0*, by sector, March 1960 to November 1980[a]

	Coefficient							Summary statistic		
Sector	θ	$F(s)$	a_1	a_3	α_1	α_2	α_3	R^2	standard error of estimate	Durbin-Watson
All retailing	-0.32 (0.06)	0.36 (0.11)	0.85 (0.36)	0.72 (0.31)	0.335 (0.991)	-0.168 (0.174)	-22.43 (9.34)	0.132	0.349	2.03
Durables										
automobiles	-0.24 (0.06)	0.40 (0.14)	0.67 (0.34)	0.71 (0.34)	0.353 (0.684)	-0.094 (0.060)	2.70 (4.55)	0.083	0.267	2.00
furniture and appliances[b]	-0.11 (0.06)	0.33 (0.25)	0.95 (0.86)	0.25 (0.36)	0.100 (0.087)	0.016 (0.016)	-0.59 (1.02)	0.050	0.041	2.06
lumber and hardware	0.01 (0.07)	0.28 (0.34)	0.41 (0.63)	0.11 (0.33)	0.037 (0.069)	-0.004 (0.004)	0.26 (0.17)	0.033	0.037	2.00
other durables	-0.20 (0.07)	0.10 (0.33)	0.32 (1.94)	-0.07 (1.04)	0.045 (0.129)	-0.010 (0.016)	-1.94 (1.23)	0.063	0.057	2.04
Nondurables										
food	0.20 (0.07)	0.76 (0.20)	-0.29 (0.13)	-0.31 (0.11)	0.069 (0.081)	0.004 (0.011)	-0.63 (0.20)	0.079	0.052	2.04
apparel[b]	0.06 (0.07)	0.45 (0.69)	-0.45 (0.74)	-0.42 (0.65)	-0.134 (0.097)	-0.001 (0.005)	-0.08 (0.57)	0.025	0.054	1.98
general merchandise	-0.03 (0.07)	0.67 (0.16)	0.19 (0.30)	-0.10 (0.15)	0.479 (0.266)	0.125 (0.062)	-0.64 (1.45)	0.050	0.138	1.99
other nondurables	0.10 (0.07)	0.91 (0.29)	0.03 (0.12)	-0.09 (0.10)	-0.046 (0.139)	-0.013 (0.008)	-1.68 (1.10)	0.039	0.083	2.08

Notes:
(a) The dependent variable is ΔN_t, inventory investment. See text for a description of the model and parameters. The numbers in parentheses are asymptotic standard errors.
(b) Based on detrended data.
Source: Same as Table 5.12.

Table 5.16 Nonlinear least squares estimates of *model 1*, by sector, March 1960 to November 1980[a]

Sector	Coefficient						Summary statistic		
	θ	a_2	a_4	α_1	α_2	α_3	R^2	standard error of estimate	Durbin-Watson
All retailing	−0.33 (0.06)	0.47 (0.16)	0.41 (0.14)	0.854 (0.871)	−0.023 (0.092)	−13.20 (6.76)	0.122	0.350	2.04
Durables									
automobiles	−0.25 (0.06)	0.38 (0.15)	0.41 (0.14)	0.489 (0.594)	−0.015 (0.031)	3.95 (0.281)	0.082	0.266	1.98
furniture and appliances	−0.10 (0.07)	0.37 (0.16)	0.08 (0.11)	−0.003 (0.074)	0.004 (0.009)	−0.239 (0.754)	0.041	0.040	2.04
lumber and hardware	0.02 (0.07)	0.11 (0.10)	0.03 (0.08)	0.043 (0.060)	0.001 (0.002)	0.248 (0.152)	0.029	0.037	1.99
other durables	−0.21 (0.07)	−0.01 (0.22)	−0.02 (0.13)	0.176 (0.124)	−0.009 (0.012)	0.005 (0.901)	0.057	0.057	2.03
Nondurables									
food	0.19 (0.06)	−0.16 (0.06)	−0.19 (0.05)	0.061 (0.073)	0.002 (0.006)	−0.407 (0.150)	0.070	0.052	2.05
apparel	0.07 (0.07)	−0.20 (0.15)	−0.18 (0.08)	−0.066 (0.083)	0.000 (0.003)	0.170 (0.486)	0.023	0.053	1.98
general merchandise	−0.04 (0.06)	0.13 (0.20)	−0.06 (0.10)	0.501 (0.240)	0.061 (0.031)	−0.888 (1.377)	0.047	0.138	1.99
other nondurables	0.10 (0.07)	0.03 (0.10)	−0.07 (0.08)	−0.058 (0.128)	−0.010 (0.005)	−1.41 (0.77)	0.038	0.081	2.00

Note:
(a) See Table 5.15, note a.
Source: Same as Table 5.12.

obtains the correct (negative) sign in only three sectors and is never significantly negative. One cannot help wondering whether the positive coefficients do not reflect reverse causation (borrowing to finance inventory investment raises the prime rate). But, in any case, the coefficients are all quite small. For example, the coefficient of approximately 0.85 in the all-retailing equation in Table 5.16 means that a 1 percentage point rise in the annual rate of interest (a 1/12th percentage point rise in the monthly rate of interest) adds about $71 million in 1972 dollars to steady- state retail inventory stocks. This is a trivial sum.

The results for the expected rate of inflation (parameter α_2) are no better. Here the theoretically correct (positive) sign emerges in five of the nine cases, but the only sector that yields a correctly signed and statistically significant inflation effect is general merchandise. The coefficient is trivially small, however. It implies that a 1 percentage point rise in the steady-state annual rate of inflation would add only about $5 million to the steady-state level of inventory holdings.

Finally, the impact of the nominal interest rate is generally far stronger than that of the expected rate of inflation. This reinforces *a priori* expectations and also the findings of Irvine (1981).[41]

The last parameter, α_3, indicates the impact of the ratio of buying prices to selling prices (that is, the retailer's margin) on desired inventory stocks. This variable, c_t/p_t, has the correct (negative) sign in the aggregate and in four of the eight sectors, and its effect is roughly statistically significant in the aggregate and in the food and other nondurable sectors. More important, the estimated effects are large enough to be economically important. The point estimate of roughly -13.2 for retailing as a whole means that a rise of 0.1 in the ratio of buying to selling prices (roughly a 10 percent decline in retailers' margins) reduces inventory investment by $884 million at a monthly rate, or $10.6 billion at an annual rate in the first month. This is a substantial impact. However, the effect dwindles, and the ultimate effect of a permanent decline of 0.1 in c_t/p_t is to reduce steady-state inventories by only $1.32 billion.

A much briefer description of the estimates of model 0 (Table 5.15) can be given because most of the parameters are common to the two models. The θ, for example, has virtually the same point estimates in the two models.[42]

The important new parameter is $F(s)$, which has no counterpart in *model 1* and provides another test of the model's validity because values outside the (0, 1) range are theoretically inadmissible. In fact, all nine of the point estimates fall comfortably within this range, and many differ significantly from both 0 and 1.

In this model, a_1 and a_3 play the role of marginal inventory-sales ratios, but their interpretations are slightly different from a_2 and a_4 in *model 1*. Specifically, a_1 indicates the marginal effect on S of a unit increase in expected sales, and a_3 indicates the corresponding effect of a unit increase in un-expected sales. Here, because s is held fixed, a_1 and a_3 are analogous to double the marginal inventory sales ratio,[43] and so one expects them to be about twice as large as a_2 and a_4 in *model 1*. In a rough way, the point estimates confirm this expectation. Using the standard that a_1 and a_3 should always be less than *twice* the average inventory-sales ratio, no instances are found in which either a_1 or a_3 is too large. However, just as in *model 1*, negative values of a are common in the nondurable sectors.

The interest rate and relative price variables do not perform any better in *model 0* than in *model 1*.

Econometric results such as these are always like bottles half full and half empty. My own view is that the results are, on balance, favorable to the model. Unlike the stock-adjustment regressions, where almost none of the estimated parameters make sense in the light of the theory, most, though certainly not all, of the estimated parameters of the S, s model are consistent with the underlying theory.

5.5.7 Additional tests

A number of further tests of the model yield generally favorable results. First, the model is estimated with detrended data, with results that are quite similar to those presented here. Hence the estimates are not dominated by common trends. Second, an examination of equations (5.23) and (5.24)–along with equation (5.31), which defines η_t – shows that while (5.24) is exactly identified, (5.23) is overidentified, reflecting the fact that both z and Δz are included in the equation. Specifically, as compared to an unconstrained linear regression, *model 0* places two overidentifying restrictions on the data. These restrictions can be tested directly by a standard χ^2-test.[44] When this is done, the overidentifying restrictions are never rejected; the data and the model are compatible.

One final issue is worth exploring. Recall that the central parameter θ is defined as $\theta \equiv (S - s)f(s) - (1 - F(s))$, where $f(\cdot)$ is the density function of $Q = N - X$ and $F(\cdot)$ is the corresponding cumulative distribution function. There is no reason to think that θ is constant through time. Yet, as an expedient to permit estimation, θ has been assumed to be constant.

I have tried only one way to improve this procedure by allowing θ to depend on some observable variable. My candidate is last period's sales surprise, X_{t-1}^u, which should have important effects on this period's initial inventories, N_t. The problem is that there is no *a priori* notion about which way this effect might go. On the one hand, a positive sales surprise makes some firms carry fewer inventories into the next period than they would otherwise. On the other hand, firms that are pushed below the s trigger point by the sales surprise take more inventories into the next period. The net result is unclear.

Nonetheless, as an experiment, I ran a set of regressions for each model on the assumption that θ depends linearly on X^u_{t-1}, namely,

$$\theta = \theta_0 + \theta_1 X^u_{t-1}$$

Since θ appears in almost all the slope coefficients in (5.23) and (5.24), this amendment complicates the estimating equations. Rather than show a complete set of results – which, for the most part, look just like Tables 5.15 and 5.16 – I simply report that the χ^2-test rejected the null hypothesis $\theta_1 = 0$ for all retailing and for the automobile sector, but for no other sector.

Examination of the estimated equations (not reported here) shows that the parameter estimates for the all-retailing sector changed little even though θ_t was significantly negative (meaning that a positive sales surprise last period reduces this period's θ). However, the estimates for the automobile sector did change noticeably. Because this industry is so important in terms of cyclical activity, Table 5.17 compares the regression results with and without the extra parameter θ_1. In *model 0* the parameter $F(s)$ rises from 0.40 to 0.82, and

Table 5.17 Estimated equations for the automobile industry, with and without the θ_1 parameter[a]

Model 0			*Model 1*		
parameter and summary statistic	estimate[b]		parameter and summary statistic	estimate[b]	
	with θ_1	without θ_1		with θ_1	without θ_1
θ_0	−0.24	−0.29	θ_0	−0.25	−0.32
	(0.06)	(0.06)		(0.06)	(0.06)
θ_1	0.00[c]	−0.00038	θ_1	0.00[c]	−0.00039
		(0.00013)			(0.00010)
$F(s)$	0.40	0.82	—	—	—
	(0.14)	(0.48)			
a_1	0.67	0.41	a_2	0.38	0.56
	(0.34)	(0.30)		(0.15)	(0.17)
a_3	0.71	0.41	a_4	0.41	0.55
	(0.34)	(0.27)		(0.14)	(0.16)
α_1	0.353	0.694	α_1	0.489	0.733
	(0.684)	(0.620)		(0.594)	(0.570)
α_2	−0.094	−0.017	α_2	−0.015	−0.035
	(0.06)	(0.032)		(0.031)	(0.033)
α_3	2.70	3.75	α_3	3.95	5.87
	(4.55)	(3.69)		(2.81)	(2.95)
Standard error of estimate	0.267	0.263	Standard error of estimate	0.266	0.260
R^2	0.083	0.114	R^2	0.082	0.132
Durbin-Watson	2.00	2.02	Durbin-Watson	1.98	2.08

Notes:
(a) See Table 5.15, note a.
(b) Asymptotic standard errors are in parentheses.
(c) Constrained.
Source: Same as Table 5.12.

the parameters a_1 and a_3 fall from 0.67, 0.71 to 0.41, 0.41, respectively. Parameter changes in *model 1* are smaller.

5.6 INVENTORY BEHAVIOR IN 1979 AND 1980

Can the events of 1979–80 be explained using this knowledge of inventory behavior? As will be seen, the S, s model is not quite up to the task, although it does better than the stock-adjustment model.

There are three main puzzles about inventory behavior during the 1979–80 episode (see Table 5.18). First, real inventory investment peaked in 1979:2, a full three quarters before real GNP peaked, and then troughed in 1980:1, which was the GNP peak. By contrast, inventory investment has typically peaked in the same quarter as GNP, or perhaps one quarter before, in previous recessions. The second puzzle is that inventory investment rose (slightly) during the recession, which is somewhat unprecedented. And the third is that inventories were liquidated while sales were expanding briskly in the second half of 1980.

Much of this unusual behavior of aggregate inventory investment can be traced to retail inventory investment. Clearly, both the decline in inventory investment from 1979:2 to 1980:1 and the rise from 1980:1 to 1980:2 came mainly from the retail sector. However, the sharp turn toward liquidation late in 1980 did not come from retailing, where inventory stocks were fairly constant after March. Hence I focus on the 1980 recession period and on the first two puzzles.

Two hypotheses about inventory behavior during the recession appear frequently in the news media but receive little support from the data.

Table 5.18 Real inventory investment, 1979:1 to 1980:4 (billions of 1972 dollars)[a]

Year and quarter	Entire economy	Retail sector[b]
1979:1	15.4	0.0
2	18.4	6.0
3	7.6	−1.1
4	−0.7	−5.3
1980:1	−0.9	−7.5
2	1.3	−0.6
3	−5.0	1.3
4	−7.2	−1.9

Notes:
(a) At seasonally adjusted annual rates.
(b) Aggregated from monthly data.
Sources: Data for the entire economy are from the national income and product accounts; the retail sector is based on unpublished data from the Bureau of Economic Analysis.

According to the first of these, firms suffered so much during the 1973–5 recession that they permanently changed their inventory management techniques and kept their inventories trimmer relative to sales than previously. The other hypothesis agrees that inventory management procedures changed permanently during the 1970s but attributes the shift to computerization rather than to the recession.[45]

The data do not support these hypotheses, however. Figure 5.3 shows the time series behavior of the inventory-sales ratio in retailing; the downward deflection at OPEC-1 was quite trivial. The picture for the entire economy is even more damaging to the hypothesis. The ratio of real inventories to final sales shows a pronounced downward trend until about 1966, a pronounced upward trend between 1966 and 1970, and no trend since then. Inventory-sales ratios have averaged about the same since OPEC-1 as they did between 1969 and 1973.

An alternative hypothesis is that the 1980 recession, unlike earlier recessions, was forecast far in advance. (Indeed, many forecasters were predicting a recession a year or more before it actually began.) As a consequence, firms kept inventories lean and did not experience the traditional surprising drop in sales that leads to an unwanted buildup in inventories and a subsequent liquidation. According to this hypothesis, it was the absence of any need to liquidate inventories at the trough that enabled the economy to get through what was actually a severe recession in terms of final sales with such a small rise in unemployment and in such a short time. The data in Table 5.18 seem quite consistent with this hypothesis, especially for retailing. Note in particular that inventories were being reduced sharply even though final sales were growing in 1979:4 and 1980:1. This behavior seems consistent with the idea that retailers were anticipating a recession.

To tell the story of 1979–80 in terms of the model, I use the time series on expected sales, X_t^e, and unexpected sales, X_t^u, to generate the predicted values of inventory investment from the equations in Table 5.14 for the stock-adjustment model, Table 5.15 for *model 0*, and Table 5.16 for *model 1*. However, since the evidence indicates that X_{t-1}^u was a significant determinant of θ in all retailing and in the automobile sector, the equations having this augmented specification were used for these sectors.

Table 5.19 shows what actually happened to retail sales and inventory investment between April 1979 and June 1980, which seems to be the interesting period, and what the three models predict.

The table gives two overall impressions: first, that none of the models does a very good job of accounting for inventory behavior during this period (even though it was part of the sample period); second, that the stock-adjustment model behaves quite sluggishly. It seems quite incapable of predicting large inventory movements even when there are large sales surprises.

The period from April to July 1979 was one of rapid inventory accumulation by retailers, and Table 5.19 shows that this accumulation was poorly

Table 5.19 Retail sales and inventory investment, April 1979 to June 1980 (millions of 1972 dollars)[a]

	Sales		Inventory investment			
				prediction		
Year and month	actual, X_t	unexpected, X_t^u	actual, ΔN_t	stock-adjustment model	model 0	model 1
1979, April	46,646	− 360	348	106	190	174
May	46,800	301	731	− 8	180	188
June	46,312	− 296	429	− 18	496	462
July	46,422	195	1,064	− 88	177	163
August	47,620	883	− 86	− 146	301	322
September	48,223	626	− 1,262	− 95	− 225	− 132
October	47,125	− 646	477	43	− 263	− 160
November	47,389	262	− 483	− 149	161	179
December	47,565	273	− 1,313	− 89	− 133	− 105
1980, January	47,997	900	− 1,048	− 90	− 561	− 511
February	46,917	− 714	− 538	94	− 197	− 98
March	45,482	− 927	− 291	− 89	− 178	− 54
April	44,225	− 1,383	276	− 124	18	− 83
May	43,880	− 487	− 296	− 249	13	− 204
June	44,407	73	− 130	− 179	− 123	− 143

Note:
(a) Monthly rates.
Sources: Actual sales and inventory investment are based on unpublished data from the Bureau of Economic Analysis; model predictions, on simulations by the author.

predicted by all the models. The stock-adjustment model predicts no net change in inventory levels during these months. The S, s model does far better, but still underpredicts the amount of accumulation – especially in July, when the equation residuals are about $2\frac{1}{2}$ standard errors. Thus there was some unusual inventory accumulation going on during these months, especially in July. Disaggregated data show that a good deal of this unusual behavior was accounted for by automobile dealers, though other retailers were heavily involved in June and July.

August 1979 was, according to my expectations measure, a period in which there was a big, positive, sales surprise. In view of how large and how abrupt the sales increase was, the amount of inventory liquidation was quite small in the aggregate (although automobile inventories declined more). The stock-adjustment model does fairly well here, while the S, s model misses by about one standard error.

In September 1979 there was another positive sales surprise according to my model, and inventory decumulation was severe. In fact, virtually all of this astonishingly large inventory disinvestment ($15.1 billion at an annual rate) was done by automobile dealers, and the equations do not predict this behavior at all. Sales then dropped sharply in October and inventories accumulated – suggesting involuntary inventory investment. None of the models captures this behavior.

The most stunning and, from the point of view of the 1980 recession, most significant behavior occurred in December 1979 and January 1980. In December, although sales were strong and fairly well predicted, inventories were drawn down at an astounding rate ($15.8 billion at annual rates). A good deal of this disinvestment, once again, came from the automobile industry. The equations do not capture this liquidation well; residuals are over two standard errors. Then, in January 1980, sales shot upward rapidly and, according to the model, unexpectedly. The rate of inventory decumulation in January exceeds the rate of unexpected sales, which suggests involuntary disinvestment. The S, s models do reasonably well in predicting this disinvestment, but the stock-adjustment model misses it entirely.

Then sales went sour after February 1980, and the recession was on. According to the model, the declines in sales in February, March, and April were mostly unexpected. And casual observation of what went on during this time buttresses this view. (Recall that the Federal Reserve enforced credit controls in March 1980, and final sales went into a tailspin.) Despite this, retailers managed to trim inventories in February and March and accumulated only in April. The S, s model predicts this behavior better than the stock-adjustment model, but none does very well.

Thus retailers appear to have shed inventories rapidly both in December 1979 (for reasons that are unclear) and in January 1980, mostly because sales spurted ahead unexpectedly. As a consequence, they entered the recession with very low stocks. In addition, they were able to trim inventories further in February and March – which they wanted to do, according to the S, s model – even though sales were collapsing. Thus, when final sales bottomed out in May 1980, retailers were not loaded with excess inventories, and so the painful inventory liquidation that normally prolongs and deepens recessions did not have to take place.

What features of this episode, then, were predictable from the models and what features are unexplained? One largely unexplained phenomenon is the high rate of stock building from April to July 1979, and especially in July. It may well have been a mistake that retailers rectified with rapid inventory decumulation in September.

But the main event in Table 5.19 is surely the huge inventory liquidation in December 1979 and January 1980. Less than a third of this is predicted by the S, s model; almost none is predicted by the stock-adjustment model; and the rest is unexplained. Whatever its cause, this period of rapid inventory liquidation left retailers with lean stocks at the onset of the recession. In sum, the sharp drop in inventories in December 1979 and January 1980 (mostly automobiles), which was caused in part by a spurt in sales, may have prevented the 1980 recession from rivaling or even surpassing the 1973–5 recession.

5.7 A SUMMING UP

Inventory fluctuations are important in business cycles; indeed, to a great extent, business cycles are inventory fluctuations. A surprisingly large fraction of the variability of aggregate inventory investment comes from the retail sector; little comes from manufacturers' inventories of finished goods.

But retail inventory investment has received little empirical and theoretical attention. The empirical work that has been done on retail inventory behavior has generally adopted the stock-adjustment model that Michael Lovell designed for explaining manufacturing inventories. However well this model does in explaining manufacturers' inventories, it seems unsuited to retailing both on theoretical grounds (why should retailers want to smooth deliveries?) and on empirical grounds (the estimates do not make sense).

There is a workable alternative – the S, s model – which has a long and venerable history in the operations research literature, and which is allegedly in common use in industry today. The difficulties of deriving aggregate implications from a model in which inventory behavior is so discontinuous, and the complex dynamics that the S, s model implies, pose barriers to empirical implementation of the theory. This paper offers one way to overcome these barriers.

The empirical model described here as a representation of the S, s theory – equations (5.23) and (5.24) – may not be the only one possible, but it is a beginning. When it is applied to the data, most of the estimated parameters are consistent with the implications of the theory.

The estimates presented in Tables 5.15 and 5.16 offer an alternative interpretation of the anomalous results obtained with stock- adjustment models that suggests far faster speeds of adjustment; they do not offer much support for the view that inventory investment is highly sensitive to the cost of capital; and they indicate a rather low sensitivity of S and s to current sales, whether expected or unexpected.[46]

NOTES

1. Real GNP declined $60.7 billion from peak to trough in the 1973–5 recession, versus only $38.6 billion in the 1980 recession. However, the respective declines in real final sales were $22.7 billion and $40.8 billion.
2. See Lovell (1961).
3. Note that the peaks and troughs are defined here by real GNP. They do not always correspond to official NBER dates. One common objection to data like those in Table 5.1 is that other components of GNP might show a similarly dramatic pattern. They do not. In fact, the only component that comes close is fixed investment, which has been procyclical in all seven recessions. A table like Table 5.1 for fixed investment would have entries in the third column ranging from a high of 95 percent to a low of 1 percent, and averaging only 55 percent.

4. Because of a strong *a priori* notion (based on observations of plotted data) that there was a break in the trend of most macro aggregates after the first OPEC shock, real final sales, real GNP, and real inventory stocks (not changes) were all detrended according to the following model of the trend component:

$$\log Z_t = a_0 + a_1 TIME + a_2 DTIME + \varepsilon_t$$

where *TIME* is a linear time trend and *DTIME* is a linear time trend beginning at 1 in 1973:4 in quarterly data or October 1973 in monthly data. Estimation was by generalized least squares, allowing for second order autocorrelation in ε_t. The antilogs of the fitted values from the detrending regressions were subtracted from the actual data to define the detrended data. Because the detrending of each series was done in logs independently, the identity (equation (5.1)) does not hold exactly for the detrended data; but it comes close.

5. However, a good deal of the variability of retail inventory investment comes from the automobile industry, where the distinction between retail inventories and manufacturers' inventories of finished goods may not be very sharp.

6. See Lovell (1961).

7. See Blinder (1982).

8. See Feldstein, Auerbach (1976) and Irvine (1981).

9. This point was emphasized by Feldstein and Auerbach (1976).

10. See Lovell (1969) and Irvine (1981).

11. Indeed, Michael Lovell suggests to me that part of the appeal of the S, s inventory strategy in practice is that, once the trigger points S and s are set, there is little need for managerial attention and decision-making.

12. See G. Hadley and T. M. Whitin (1963); Arrow, Harris and Marschak (1951), Arrow, Karlin and Scarf (1962); Arrow, Karlin and Scarf (1958); and Scarf (1960).

13. An appendix showing this and other technical results is available from the author upon request.

14. This is demonstrated in the appendix mentioned above, available from the author. See also Easley and Spulber (1979).

15. In the Hadley–Whitin examples, firms that run out of stock retain unfilled orders for the next period, though there is a penalty cost for doing so. See Hadley and Whitin (1963).

16. Strictly speaking, this statement is true only if X_t is an independently and identically distributed random variable. If not, a rise in sales might lead the firm to increase its desired inventory level. However, the same is true of the S, s model. If sales are serially correlated, "good" sales in the first week would lead the firm to raise S and s for the second week. Implicitly, Fig. 5.1 assumes that sales are independently and identically distributed.

17. George A. Akerlof has applied the S, s model to aggregate money holdings in Akerlof (1979).

18. This formulation assumes either that X_t is known at the start of period t or that there are no delivery lags. If orders must be placed before sales are known, Y_t can only depend on X_t^e, not on X_t.

19. See Fig. 5.1 for an example of Q.

20. Here and throughout the paper the symbol ΔN_t denotes $N_{t+1} - N_t$.

21. Since X_0 denotes the minimum possible value of sales, S is necessarily larger than $S - X_0$ unless $X_0 = 0$.

22. The firms that do place orders will have a higher S_t and will thus place larger orders, resulting in higher initial inventories the following period. If firms adjust s_t upward, more firms find themselves tripping the lower barrier and hence placing orders.

23. In fact, in the example given above for firms that have exogenous sales and minimize long-run costs in a stationary environment, the widened range is accompanied by a reduction in s.

24. The evolution of u_t through time is governed by a difference equation that is derived in Appendix 5.2.

25. In principle, seasonally unadjusted data would have been preferable, but these are not available in real terms.

26. The deflation procedure for inventories is a complex one using, among other things, information on LIFO (last in, first out) versus FIFO (first in, first out) accounting procedures. The documentation by the US Bureau of Economic Analysis explaining the procedures in detail is still in preparation.

27. In fact, it was data like these that first led me to investigate the S, s model as an alternative to the buffer stock model.

28. In fact, equation (5.25) was estimated on detrended data, and then the trend component of sales was added back.

29. In each case I interpolate monthly forecasts from the quarterly data. I would like to thank Victor Zarnowitz for providing the NBER-ASA forecasts and Jeffrey Green for providing the Wharton forecasts.

30. The other proxies for expectations were simpler. One was a fourth-order auto-regression in sales – that is, equation (5.25) with $b(L)$ and $c(L)$ constrained to zero. The other was the retailer proxy forecast, a simple rule of thumb suggested by Irvine (1981).

31. See, however, a series of recent papers on the subject by F. Owen Irvine Jr: Irvine (May, July, September and Winter, 1981). See also Rubin (1979–80); and Lieberman (1980).

32. See Okun (1981). Okun also made the intriguing suggestion that the desire to use a FIFO pricing strategy (so as not to break a trust with the firm's regular customers) may explain why firms use FIFO accounting.

33. For discussion of these other reasons and some evidence that the coefficients of i_t and π_t are not equal and opposite, see Irvine, "Merchant Wholesaler Inventory Investment."

34. This is hardly surprising with trend-dominated data. However, even when the regressions were performed on detrended data, the R^2 ranged from 0.66 to 0.95.

35. By a standard F-test, the null hypothesis that the coefficients of expected and unexpected sales are equal – that is, that only actual sales appears on the right-hand side – can be rejected in only four of the eight sectors. It can, however, be argued that there is an econometric bias when expectations are measured with error. This would bias the coefficient of unexpected sales toward the coefficient of expected sales. The argument is fully presented in Germany (1981).

36. Because the interest rate coefficient in these tables shows the effect of the monthly rate of interest (in percentage points) on the monthly rate of deliveries, it also shows (approximately) the effect of the annual rate of interest on the annual rate of deliveries. For example, in the equation for all retailing in Table 5.14, the -0.401 coefficient means that a 1 percentage point rise in the nominal interest rate would decrease annual deliveries by $401 million at annual rates.

37. This is not really legitimate. I do it only for the following reason. If u_t were included, all the expressions I present below would have complicated additional terms involving the variance of u_t and its covariances with other variables. These expressions are always of indeterminate sign, and so it is never clear how they would affect the results presented here.

38. But see note 37.

39. I have just argued that N_t is correlated with the error term and hence is not a legitimate regressor.

40. Experiment (2) above shows that one unit of unwanted inventories leads firms to reduce orders by $1 + \theta$ units.
41. See Irvine, "Merchant Wholesaler Inventory Investment and the Cost of Capital."
42. However, *model 0*, unlike *model 1*, has convergence problems in several sectors. I believe this is due to extreme multicollinearity in the data. To avoid the problem, I estimate the *model 0* equation for the furniture and appliances and apparel sectors with detrended (and hence far less collinear) data. The results with detrended data are reported in Table 5.15 for these two sectors.
43. If inventories were distributed uniformly on the interval $[s, S]$ – a condition not implied in the present model – average inventories would be:

$$\bar{N} = s + \frac{S - s}{2}$$

Thus with s fixed the marginal inventory sales ratio would be

$$\frac{\partial \bar{N}}{\partial \bar{X}} = \frac{1}{2} \frac{\partial S}{\partial \bar{X}} = \frac{1}{2} a_1$$

44. The χ^2-test for nonlinear regressions is described in Goldfeld and Quandt (1972).
45. On the latter, see Beman (1981).
46. An open question is whether the estimated sensitivity of S and s to sales is too small from the point of view of the theory. This cannot be addressed until there is some explicit S, s theory for a nonstationary world.

REFERENCES

Abramovitz, M. (1950) *Inventories and Business Cycles*, Cambridge, Mass.: National Bureau of Economic Research.

Akerlof, G. A. (1979) "Irving Fisher on his head: the consequences of constant threshold-target monitoring of money holdings," *Quarterly Journal of Economics*, vol. 93 (May), pp. 169–88.

Arrow, K. J., T. Harris, and J. Marschak (1951) "Optimal Inventory Policy," *Econometrica*, vol. 19 (July), pp. 250–72.

Arrow, K. J., S. Karlin, and H. Scarf (eds) (1962) *Studies in Applied Probability and Management Science*, Stanford: Stanford University Press.

Arrow, K. J., S. Karlin, and H. Scarf (1958) *Studies in the Mathematical Theory of Inventory and Production*, Stanford: Stanford University Press.

Beman, L. (1981) "A big payoff from inventory controls," *Fortune* (July 27), pp. 76–80.

Blinder, A. S. (1982) "Inventories and sticky prices: more on the micro-foundations of macroeconomics," *American Economic Review*, vol. 72, no. 3 (June), pp. 334–48.

Cyert, R. M. and J. G. March (1963) *A Behavioral Theory of the Firm*, Englewood Cliffs: Prentice Hall.

Easley, D. and D. F. Spulber (1979) "Optimal policies and steady state solutions for inventory problems with Markovian uncer- tainty," Providence: Brown University.

Feldstein, M. and A. Auerbach (1976) "Inventory behavior in durable-goods manufacturing: the target-adjustment model," *Brookings Papers on Economic Activity*, no. 2, pp. 351–96.

Germany, J. D. (1981) "Unanticipated money growth, inventories, and the business cycle," PhD dissertation, Cambridge, Mass.: Massachusetts Institute of Technology.

Goldfeld, S. M. (1976) "The case of the missing money," *Brookings Papers on Economic Activity*, no. 3, p. 686.

Goldfeld, S. M. and R. E. Quandt (1972) *Nonlinear Methods in Econometrics*, Amsterdam: North-Holland.

Gordon, R. J. (1979) "The 'end of expansion' phenomenon in short-run productivity behavior," *Brookings Papers on Economic Activity*, no. 2, pp. 447–61.

Hadley, G. and T. M. Whitin (1963) *Analysis of Inventory Systems*, Englewood Cliffs: Prentice Hall.

Holt, C. C. *et al.* (1960) *Planning Production, Inventories and Work Force*, Englewood Cliffs: Prentice Hall.

Irvine, F. O. Jr (1981) "Retail inventory investment and the cost of capital," *American Economic Review*, vol. 71 (September), pp. 633–48.

Irvine, F. O. Jr (1981) "The influence of capital costs on inventory investment: time series evidence for a department store," *Quarterly Review of Economics and Business*, vol. 21, no. 4 (Winter), pp. 25–44.

Irvine, F. O. Jr (1981) "Merchant wholesaler inventory investment and the cost of capital," *American Economic Review*, vol. 71 (May, *Papers and Proceedings, 1980*), pp. 23–9.

Irvine, F. O. Jr (1981) "A study of automobile inventory investment," *Economic Inquiry*, vol. 19 (July), pp. 353–79.

Klein, L. R. and J. Popkin (1961) "An econometric analysis of the postwar relationship between inventory fluctuations and changes in aggregate economic activity," in Joint Economic Committee, *Inventory Fluctuations and Economic Stabilization*, 87 Cong. 1 sess., Washington DC: US Government Printing Office, pt. 3, pp. 71–89.

Lieberman, C. (1980) "Inventory demand and cost of capital effects," *Review of Economics and Statistics*, vol. 62 (August), pp. 348–56.

Lovell, M. (1961) "Manufacturers' inventories, sales expectations, and the acceleration principle," *Econometrica*, vol. 29 (July), pp. 293–314.

Lovell, M. (1969) "Department store inventory, sales, order relationships," in J. S. Duesenberry *et al.* (eds) *The Brookings Model: Some Further Results*, Amsterdam: North-Holland, pp. 18–38.

Lovell, M. C. and A. A. Hirsch (1969) *Sales Anticipations and Inventory Behavior*, New York: Wiley, Ch. 5, pp. 112–92.

Mack, R. P. (1961) "Changes in ownership of purchased materials," in Joint Economic Committee, *Inventory Fluctuations and Economic Stabilization*, 87 Cong. 1 sess., Washington DC: US Government Printing Office, pt. 2, pp. 59–87.

Mills, E. S. (1962) *Price, output, and inventory policy, a study in the economics of the firm and industry*, New York: Wiley.

Modigliani, F. and O. H. Sauerlender (1955) "Economic expectations and plans of firms in relation to short-term forecasting," in National Bureau of Economic Research, *Short-Term Economic Forecasting*, Studies in Income and Wealth, vol. 17, Princeton: Princeton University Press.

Okun, A. M. (1981) *Prices and Quantities: A Macroeconomic Analysis*, Washington DC: Brookings Institution.

Rubin, L. S. (1979–80) "Aggregate inventory behavior: response to uncertainty and interest rates," *Journal of Post Keynesian Economics*, vol. 2 (Winter), pp. 201–11.

Scarf, H. (1960) "The optimality of (S, s) policies in the dynamic inventory problem," in K. J. Arrow, S. Karlin, and P. Suppes (eds) *Mathematical Methods in the Social Sciences*, Stanford: Stanford University Press, pp. 196–202.

Stanback, T. M. Jr (1962) *Postwar Cycles in Manufacturers' Inventories*, Cambridge, Mass.: National Bureau of Economic Research.

Whitin, T. M. (1953) *The Theory of Inventory Management*, Princeton: Princeton University Press.

APPENDIX 5.1

COMPARATIVE STATICS OF THE ANALYTICAL MODEL

The expression for aggregate deliveries, equation (5.11) in the text, is repeated here for convenience:

$$\bar{Y} = (S - s)F(s, \gamma) + \int_{s - X_1}^{s} F(Q, \gamma)\, dQ$$

where the vector of parameters γ has been added because some of these parameters affect the distribution function $F(Q)$.

The first comparative statics experiment considered in the text was a uniform rightward shift of the distribution of sales by γ_1 units (an increase in demand). Since $Q = N - X$, such a change would shift the distribution function of Q_t uniformly to the left by γ_1 units, that is, from $F(Q, 0)$ to $F(Q, \gamma_1) = F(Q + \gamma_1, 0)$. Thus for an infinitesimal move of γ_1:

$$\frac{\partial F(Q, \gamma_1)}{\partial \gamma_1} = f(Q + \gamma_1)$$

Evaluated around $\gamma_1 = 0$, this is:

$$\frac{\partial F(Q)}{\partial \gamma_1} = f(Q)$$

Such a shift leaves S, s, and $\bar{N}$ unchanged and moves $\bar{X}$ and X_1 by one unit. Using all this information in taking the derivative of equation (5.11) leads to:

$$\frac{\partial \bar{Y}}{\partial \gamma_1} = (S - s)f(s) + \int_{s - X_1}^{s} f(Q)\,dQ = (S - s)f(s) + F(s) \qquad (A5.1)$$

which is equation (5.12) in the text.

Comparative statics experiment 2 in the text considered a uniform rightward shift in the distribution of initial inventories, N_t, with no change in the distribution of X_t and no change in S or s.

For convenience, I calibrate the shift parameter γ_2 so that $d\bar{N}/d\gamma_2 = 1$. Since the random variable Q_t is the difference between N_t and X_t, the effect of γ_2 on $F(Q)$ is equal and opposite to the effect of γ_1 on $F(Q)$, that is:

$$\frac{\partial F(Q)}{\partial \gamma_2} = -\frac{\partial F(Q)}{\partial \gamma_1} = -f(Q)$$

Using this information in equation (5.11) leads to:

$$\frac{\partial \bar{Y}}{\partial \gamma_2} = -(S - s)f(s) - F(s) \equiv -(1 + \theta) \qquad (A5.2)$$

which is equation (5.13) in the text.

The next shift parameter to be considered is γ_3, which raises S and s equally but has no effect on the distributions of either N_t or X_t, and hence no effect on $f(Q)$. It follows directly from equation (5.11) that:

$$\frac{\partial \bar{Y}}{\partial \gamma_3} = (S - s)f(s) + F(s) \equiv 1 + \theta \qquad (A5.3)$$

which is equation (5.14) in the text. Equations (5.15) and (5.15a) are derived similarly.

APPENDIX 5.2

DERIVATION OF THE ESTIMATING EQUATIONS

The u_t can be eliminated from equation (5.18) as follows. Solve equation (5.19) for u_t and take the difference forward to obtain $u_{t+1} - u_t$. Then use the accounting identity to replace $N_{t+1} - N_t$ by $Y_t - X_t = Y_t - X_t^e - X_t^u$, and simplify. The result is:

$$(1 + \theta L)u_{t+1} = -bX_{t+1}^e + (K_1 - 1 + b)X_t^e$$
$$+ (K_2 - 1)X_t^u + (K_3 - 1)z_t + \varepsilon_t \qquad (A5.4)$$

where L is the lag operator and $z_t = \eta_{t+1} - \eta_t$. This is the exact definition of u_t.

Next subtract X_t from both sides of equation (5.18) to obtain:

$$Y_t - X_t = (K_1 - 1)X_t^e + (K_2 - 1)X_t^u - (1 + \theta)u_t + K_3 z_t + \varepsilon_t$$

and apply the operator $(1 + \theta L)$ to both sides of this equation. After some algebraic manipulations, this yields:

$$\Delta N_t = -\theta \Delta N_{t-1} + [K_1 - 1 + b(1 + \theta)](X_t^e - X_{t-1}^e)$$
$$+ (K_2 - 1)(X_t^u - X_{t-1}^u) + K_3(z_t - z_{t-1})$$
$$+ (1 + \theta)z_{t-1} + \varepsilon_t - \varepsilon_{t-1}$$

Application of the assumptions of *model 0* and *model 1* gives equations (5.23) and (5.24), respectively, in the text.

APPENDIX 5.3

MANUFACTURERS' PRICE INDEXES

One variable used in the regressions is the ratio of the retailers' buying price (the manufacturers' selling price) to the retailers' selling price. Retail sales price indexes are available for each of the sectors (unpublished data from the Bureau of Economic Analysis), but there are no data on buying prices.

I attempted to match each retail sector with a corresponding producer price subindex designed to represent the buying price of that sector as follows:

Retail sector	*Manufacturing sector, producer price index*
All retailing	Finished consumer goods
Durables	
automobiles	Passenger cars
furniture and appliances	Furniture and household durables
lumber and hardware	Lumber and wood products
other durables	Finished consumer durables
Nondurables	
food	Processed foods and feeds
apparel	Textile products and apparel
general merchandise	Consumer nondurable finished goods (other than food)
other nondurables	Consumer nondurable finished goods (other than food)

In most cases the match is quite good. One minor problem is that the producer price subindex matched to "other durables" is actually the price index appropriate to *all* durables; it does not remove the prices of automobiles, furniture and appliances, and lumber and hardware. A similar problem is that the index matched to "other nondurables" fails to remove the prices of apparel and general merchandise items.

There is, however, one problem that is much more serious. The producer price index matched to the general merchandise sector – non-durable finished goods excluding food – includes energy prices and hence must have little resemblance to the prices actually paid by department stores in the post-OPEC period. There is no easy solution to this problem. I tried to create a synthetic index by using this index for the pre-OPEC period and using the index for consumer finished goods excluding food and energy (but including durables) for the post-OPEC period. But this variable performed very poorly in the regressions.

6 · CAN THE PRODUCTION SMOOTHING MODEL OF INVENTORY BEHAVIOR BE SAVED?

6.1 INTRODUCTION

The production smoothing model of inventory behavior has a long and venerable history.[1] Its theoretical foundations seem very strong. All that is necessary to create a production smoothing motive for holding inventories is that demand vary through time and either that the short-run cost function be convex (*i.e.*, the short-run production function be concave) or that there exist costs of changing output, or both. If, in addition, there is a random element to demand, inventories will also serve as a buffer stock.

These conditions appear to be very weak – so weak, in fact, that it is hard to imagine how they could fail to hold. In addition, the production smoothing model has been used with some success in empirical work on inventories.[2] Under the special assumption that costs are quadratic, it leads (approximately) to the "stock adjustment" model that dominates empirical work on the subject.[3]

Yet the production smoothing model is in trouble. Certain overwhelming facts seem not only to defy explanation within the production smoothing framework, but actually to argue that the basic idea of production smoothing is all wrong. First, firms do not in fact smooth production; production is actually more variable than sales. Second, if inventories are used to buffer output against shocks to demand, then inventories should fall when sales spurt and rise when sales slump; but, in fact, the covariance between sales and inventory change is not negative.[4] Third, the standard way to implement the production smoothing model empirically is the stock-adjustment specification; yet when stock-adjustment equations are estimated econometrically, estimated adjustment speeds are typically very low, even though the apparent reaction to unanticipated sales is very rapid.[5]

I am indebted to Douglas Holtz-Eakin for extensive and superb research assistance, to the National Science Foundation and Alfred P. Sloan Foundation for financial support, and to Olivier Blanchard, John Carlson, Michael Lovell, Louis Maccini, Angelo Melino, Kenneth West, and anonymous referees for useful comments on earlier drafts.

Taken as a whole, these three facts seem to spell bad news for the production smoothing-buffer stock model. Yet, as I just indicated, the theory that underlies this model requires very weak assumptions about technology. There seems to be more than a little tension here between theory and fact. This paper asks, first, whether this tension can be resolved without jettisoning the basic technological assumptions that underlie almost all neoclassical theory[6] and, second, whether the data are consistent with this explanation. The answers turn out to be "yes" and "maybe," respectively.

The paper is organized into three sections. Section 6.2 documents the relevant stylized facts. Section 6.3 rigorously derives a version of the production smoothing-buffer stock model based on convex production costs, explains how this model can be made consistent with the facts, and looks to see whether the data have the basic characteristics needed to "rescue" the theory. Section 6.4 summarizes briefly and suggests some alternative explanations of the stylized facts.

6.2 THE STYLIZED FACTS ABOUT MANUFACTURING INVENTORIES

The data analyzed here are monthly, seasonally adjusted data on sales and inventories in billions of 1972 dollars, provided by the Bureau of Economic Analysis (BEA). Inventories are broken down by stage of processing (materials and supplies, work in progress, and finished goods) and by industry (10 durable sectors and 10 nondurable sectors). The period of study runs from February 1959 (the first month for which opening stocks of inventories are available) through December 1981.

Before looking at the data, it is wise to get some accounting identities straight. When the only inventories are finished goods, the basic accounting identity relating inventories, production, and sales is:

$$Y_t = X_t + N_{t+1} - N_t \tag{6.1}$$

where Y is production, X is sales, and N_t is the stock of inventories at the beginning of period t. If lower case symbols are used to denote the detrended values of the corresponding upper case symbols, this identity leads to the following decomposition of the variance of Y about trend:

$$\text{var}(y) = \text{var}(x) + \text{var}(\Delta n) + 2\,\text{cov}(x, \Delta n) \tag{6.2}$$

The first two facts of interest pertain to equation (6.2).

Figure 6.1 will help adapt these identities to the actual data. In this schema, F denotes the stock of finished goods, and W denotes the stock of works in progress. It indicates the following:

1. Items that are started within the period might be counted as work in progress (path a), finished goods (path b), or shipments to customers (path c) by the end of the period.

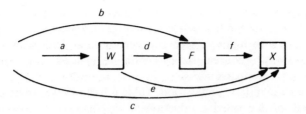

Fig. 6.1 Stages of processing

2. Items that began the period as work in progress might still be in progress, or might be recorded as finished goods (path d), or as sales (path e) by the end of the period.
3. Items that started the period as finished goods either are sold within the period (path f) or remain in inventory.

Adding up these possibilities (using obvious notation), we see that sales are given by:

$$X = c + e + f \tag{6.3}$$

while a natural definition of output (not value added) is:[7]

$$Y = a + b + c \tag{6.4}$$

Similarly, the change in the stock of finished goods is:

$$\Delta F = b + d - f \tag{6.5}$$

and the change in the stock of work in progress is:

$$\Delta W = a - d - e \tag{6.6}$$

Adding up (6.5) and (6.6) gives:

$$\Delta F + \Delta W = a + b - (e + f)$$

which, according to (6.3) and (6.4), is exactly equal to $Y - X$. So we see that the concept of inventories that satisfies (6.1) is the sum of finished goods plus work in progress. I shall henceforth denote this sum by the symbol N, in accord with (6.1).

Data on shipments and inventories of finished goods and work in progress were used, in conjunction with identity (6.1), to create a series on production for each industry.[8] Then all the series were detrended by the following model of the trend component:

$$\log(Z_t) = a_0 + a_1 TIME + a_2 DTIME + a_3 D66 + u_t$$

where *TIME* is a time trend beginning at 1 in January 1959, *DTIME* is a second time trend beginning at 1 at the first OPEC shock (October 1973), and *D66* is a dummy variable equal to 1 for all observations in 1966–82. (*D66* is motivated by a data revision that went back only to 1966.) To get more efficient estimates of the trends, estimation was by generalized least squares with u_t assumed to follow a second-order autoregressive scheme.[9] This is exactly the same procedure I used earlier on the retailing data (Blinder, 1981), which facilitates comparisons.

With these definitions understood, Table 6.1 shows the decomposition of the variance of detrended production as in equation (6.2). A number of conclusions are apparent.

First, and most important, the variance of production is generally larger than the variance of sales, and sometimes much larger. Primary metals is the only industry in which sales has a bigger variance than production. The ratio of $var(y)/var(x)$ ranges from a high of 2.40 to a low of 0.95, and is 1.14 for manufacturing as a whole.

This remarkable fact seems to be remarkably robust. It has been known for a long time at the aggregate level, where y stands for real GNP and x stands for real final sales.[10] In Blinder (1981), I showed that $var(y) > var(x)$ for retailing as a whole and for seven of eight two-digit retail industries, with an average ratio of $var(y)/var(x)$ of 1.15. Recently, West has used a more elaborate version of this inequality to derive a test of the validity of the production smoothing model in several nondurable manufacturing industries – with mostly negative results. Blanchard (1983) has found that it holds for the automobile industry.

Second, notice from (6.2) that $var(y)$ cannot possibly be less than $var(x)$, unless the covariance between x and Δn is negative enough to overwhelm the variance of Δn. In the durables sector, this covariance is negative in only two of 10 industries; and the only nontrivial negative value occurs in primary metals (where $\rho = -0.22$). By contrast, large positive covariances are found in electrical machinery ($\rho = 0.33$), non-electrical machinery ($\rho = 0.45$), and transportation equipment ($\rho = 0.29$). Things are more mixed in the nondurables sector: the covariance is positive half the time and negative half the time, but generally of trivial magnitude. This stylized fact is also robust. The covariance between sales and inventory change is strongly positive for GNP as a whole (that is, inventory investment is strongly procyclical) and weakly positive in the retail sector.[11]

Believers in a buffer stock role for inventories will raise several questions about this finding. Recall that:

$$cov(x, \Delta n) = cov(x, \Delta f) + cov(x, \Delta w)$$

Could it be that a negative covariance between sales and changes in finished goods inventories (evidence for a buffer stock role for inventories) is hidden by an even stronger positive covariance between sales and changes in work in progress? Regrettably, the answer is no. The correlation between x and Δf is negative in only seven of 20 industries, and more negative than -0.10 in only three industries.

Table 6.1 Summary of variances and covariances

Sector	var(y)	var(x)	var(Δn)	2cov(x, Δn)	ρ(x, Δn)	$\frac{\text{var}(y)}{\text{var}(x)}$	$\frac{\text{var}(\Delta n)}{\text{var}(x)}$
All manufacturing	10.22	8.90	0.177	0.999	0.40	1.14	0.020
Durable goods	6.23	5.21	0.147	0.775	0.44	1.20	0.028
primary metals	0.244	0.257	0.011	−0.024	−0.22	0.95	0.042
fabricated metals	0.146	0.131	0.012	0.0049	0.06	1.11	0.092
electrical machinery	0.197	0.163	0.0097	0.026	0.33	1.21	0.060
non-elect. machinery	0.230	0.154	0.021	0.051	0.45	1.49	0.138
transportation equipment	0.802	0.657	0.041	0.096	0.29	1.22	0.063
lumber & wood products	0.0146	0.0130	0.0019	−0.00027	−0.03	1.12	0.148
furniture & fixtures	0.0046	0.0036	0.00064	0.00032	0.10	1.27	0.176
stone, clay and glass products	0.0098	0.0086	0.00103	0.00015	0.02	1.14	0.120
instruments and related products	0.0096	0.0057	0.0030	0.0012	0.14	1.69	0.537
miscellaneous manufacturing industries	0.0037	0.0025	0.00093	0.00017	0.06	1.46	0.371
Nondurable goods	0.728	0.694	0.032	0.0029	0.01	1.05	0.046
food & kindred products	0.0449	0.0365	0.0108	−0.0025	−0.06	1.23	0.296
tobacco manufacturing	0.00133	0.00056	0.00078	0.000005	−0.00	2.40	1.405
textile mill products	0.0134	0.0124	0.0012	−0.00064	−0.08	1.08	0.098
apparel products	0.0208	0.0149	0.0042	0.0015	0.09	1.40	0.283
leather & leather products	0.00130	0.00097	0.00029	0.000056	0.05	1.34	0.300
paper & allied products	0.00958	0.00917	0.00051	−0.000078	−0.02	1.04	0.056
printing & publishing	0.0162	0.0136	0.0020	0.00014	0.01	1.18	0.149
chemical & allied products	0.0538	0.0522	0.0048	−0.0030	−0.09	1.03	0.092
petroleum & coal products	0.0207	0.0207	0.0016	−0.0012	−0.11	1.00	0.078
rubber & plastic products	0.0181	0.0162	0.0010	0.00066	0.08	1.12	0.064

Alternatively, would the buffer stock role of finished goods inventories look more important if we replaced the deviation of sales from trend by the change in sales, or by unexpected sales? Only a little. Cov(Δx, Δf) is negative in only nine of 20 industries. The same is true of cov(x^u, Δf), where x^u is a proxy for unexpected sales based on a twelfth-order autoregression. We do slightly better with innovations from sixth-order bivariate autoregressions for x and Δf. Innovations in x are negatively correlated with innovations in Δf in 11 of 20 industries; but only five of these negative correlations are below -0.1, and only two (primary metals and chemicals) are below -0.2.

The third empirical problem pertains to the way the theory is normally made operational for econometric purposes, and was mentioned in the introduction. If a stock-adjustment model of inventory behavior is estimated in the form,

$$N_{t+1} - N_t = \beta_1(N_{t+1}^* - N_t) - (1 - \beta_2)(X_t - {}_{t-1}X_t) + u_t \tag{6.7}$$

where ${}_{t-1}X_t$ is expected sales, N_{t+1}^* is (some proxy for) desired inventories, and u_t is a stochastic disturbance term, estimates of β_1 normally turn out to be extremely low, implying implausibly slow adjustment.

A final fact worth mentioning, though it is not developed here, is that the three types of inventory change – finished goods, work in progress, and materials and supplies – display rather little covariance. Each type of inventory movement seems to have a life of its own.[12] This suggests seeking separate empirical, and perhaps also theoretical, explanations for each type of inventory.

6.3 THE THEORY OF PRODUCTION SMOOTHING

6.3.1 Concepts and notation

The model used here is a generalization of Blinder (1982), and uses the notation employed there. Specifically, consider a value-maximizing firm with linear demand curve:

$$X_t = 2d_0 - 2dP_t + 2d\eta_t \tag{6.8}$$

where P_t is the price in period t and X_t is the quantity sold. The demand shock η_t has a complex structure that will be specified presently.

A motive for production smoothing is generated by appealing to convex costs, rather than to costs of changing output. Specifically, production costs are:

$$C(Y_t) = c_0 + (c_1 + \Gamma_t)Y_t + (1/2c)Y_t^2 \tag{6.9}$$

where Y_t is output and Γ_t is a cost shock representing stochastic disturbances to either technology or factor prices. The curvature parameter c is critical to the production smoothing issue. A low value of c connotes a steeply increasing marginal cost curve, and hence a strong motive to smooth production.

The model treats only inventories of finished goods, the costs of holding which are:

$$B(N_t) = b_0 + b_1 N_t + (b/2)N_t^2 \tag{6.10}$$

The curvature parameter b is again critical to the production smoothing issue. A large value of b makes it costly to vary inventories, and hence will discourage the firm from using inventory movements to smooth production.

There are several possible definitions of production smoothing. One obvious definition is:

DEFINITION 1. *A firm is said to smooth production if the (unconditional) variance of production is less than the (unconditional) variance of sales:* $\text{var}(Y) < \text{var}(X)$.

For obvious reasons, I call this "long-run production smoothing." The stylized facts show that firms do not smooth production by this definition. For "short-run production smoothing," I offer the following definition:

DEFINITION 2. *A firm is said to smooth production if its production responds less to a sales shock than it would if it could not carry inventories:*

$$\frac{\partial Y}{\partial \eta} < \left(\frac{\partial Y}{\partial \eta}\right)^*$$

where the asterisk denotes a firm that cannot carry inventories. If either inequality is reversed, I shall say that there is production "bunching" instead.

6.3.2 The informational structure

Because expectations are assumed to be rational, the information structure is critical to the solution. I assume that the firm observes its current cost shock before making its decisions on production and price. This seems a natural specification if cost shocks represent fluctuations in input prices, but not so natural if they represent stochastic aspects of the technology.

For the demand shock, I employ a general structure that admits of several interpretations. Specifically, the demand shock is assumed to have two independent components:

$$\eta_t = \eta_t^1 + \eta_t^2 \tag{6.11}$$

which differ only in that the firm can observe η_t^1, but not η_t^2, before it makes its decisions on P_t and Y_t. The idea is that what the econometrician, using monthly or quarterly data, labels as "unanticipated sales" is only partly unanticipated by the firm, which actually knows η_t^1.

Two polar cases are evident. If the η_t^2 shock is absent, then the firm knows its demand curve before making its decisions, and the sales "surprise" is a surprise only to the econometrician. If the η_t^1 shock is absent, the firm must make its decisions before it knows its demand curve, and sales surprises really are surprises.[13] The distinction between these two versions of "unanticipated" sales turns out to be critical to reconciling the theory with the data. I shall interpret the empirical evidence as suggesting that η_t^1 shocks are far more important than η_t^2 shocks.

To recapitulate briefly, the firm inherits an opening stock of inventories (N_t), which is the legacy of the past. It then observes its cost shock (Γ_t) and part of its demand shock (η_t^1) before choosing its level of production (Y_t), price (P_t), and expected sales. After these decisions are made, the rest of the demand shock (η_t^2) is observed and actual sales (X_t) are determined. The beginning-of-period inventory for period $t+1$ then follows from the identity (6.1), and the whole process repeats.

6.3.3 The solution: optimal inventory policy

Details of the solution are presented in a mathematical appendix available on request. Here I confine myself to establishing the notation and stating the results. First, for the variables, X_{t+s}, Y_{t+s}, N_{t+s}, and P_{t+s}, let lower case symbols denote the expectations of the corresponding upper case symbols, all expectations being conditional on the information available when the period t decision is made. For example:

$$y_{t+s} = E_t Y_{t+s}$$

where the information set available at time t includes N_t, Γ_t, η_t^1, and all variables dated $t-1$ or earlier. Similar definitions hold for x_{t+s}, p_{t+s}, and η_{t+s}. Analogously, let the new symbols:

$$\gamma_{t+s} = E_t \Gamma_{t+s}$$
$$\varepsilon_{t+s}^i = E_t \eta_{t+s}^i, \qquad i = 1, 2$$

denote the expected values of the period $t+s$ shocks.

As is typical in such problems, the dynamics are governed by a second-order differential equation with one stable and one unstable root. The roots are defined by:

$$z^2 - [2 + i + b(c+d)]z + (1+i) = 0 \qquad (6.12)$$

where i is the rate of interest. I take z_1 to be the stable root, z_2 to be the unstable root, and define $\theta = 1/z_2 < 1$.

Although I shall deal with more particular cases shortly, I begin by assuming that both demand shocks are $ARMA(1, 1)$ processes:

$$\eta_t^i = \rho \eta_{t-1}^i + m v_{t-1}^i + v_t^i \quad i = 1, 2$$

and the cost shock is $AR(1)$:

$$\Gamma_t = r\Gamma_{t-1} + w_t$$

Under these assumptions, the solutions for production, sales, and inventory change are:

$$Y_t - \bar{Y} = \frac{c(1-z_1)}{c+d}(\bar{N} - N_t) + \left(\frac{dc}{c+d}\right)\left(\frac{1-z_1}{1-\theta\rho}\right) \tag{6.13}$$

$$\times [E_t\eta_t + m\theta v_t^1] - \left(1 - \frac{c}{c+d}\frac{1-z_1}{1-\theta r}\right)c\Gamma_t$$

$$X_t - \bar{X} = \frac{-d(1-z_1)}{c+d}(\bar{N} - N_t) \tag{6.14}$$

$$+ d\left(1 - \frac{d}{d+c}\frac{1-z_1}{1-\theta\rho}\right)E_t\eta_t - \frac{d}{d+c}\frac{1-z_1}{1-\theta\rho}dm\theta v_t^1$$

$$+ 2dv_t^2 - \frac{cd}{c+d}\frac{1-z_1}{1-\theta r}\Gamma_t$$

$$N_{t+1} - N_t = (1-z_1)(\bar{N} - N_t) - d\left(\frac{1+i-\rho}{z_2-\rho}\right)E_t\eta_t$$

$$+ d\left(\frac{1-z_1}{1-\theta\rho}\right)m\theta v_t^1 - c\left(\frac{1+i-r}{z_2-r_2}\right)\Gamma_t - 2dv_t^2 \tag{6.15}$$

where a bar over a variable denotes its nonstochastic steady state value and:

$$E_t\eta_t = \varepsilon_t = \eta_t^1 + \rho\eta_{t-1}^2 + mv_{t-1}^2$$

Equation (6.15) is the basis for the effort to reconcile the theory with the stylized facts.

6.3.4 Short-run production smoothing

We now know enough to study short-run production smoothing. From Definition 2, a natural quantitative measure of the degree of production smoothing is:

$$S_y = 1 - \frac{\partial Y}{\partial \eta} \bigg/ \left(\frac{\partial Y}{\partial \eta}\right)^*$$

where the asterisk denotes a firm with no inventories. (Such a firm simply solves a static profit maximization problem and equates marginal cost with expected marginal revenue each period.) Performing the relevant computations in both numerator and denominator leads to:

$$S_y = 1 - \left(\frac{cd}{c+d} \right) \frac{\partial Y_t}{\partial v_t}$$

By (6.13), this is readily seen to be:

$$S_y = 1 - \frac{c+d}{cd} \left(\frac{cd}{c+d} \right) \frac{1-z_1}{1-\theta\rho} (1+m\theta)$$

$$= \frac{z_1 - \theta\rho - m\theta(1-z_1)}{1-\theta\rho} \text{ for } v_t^1 \text{ type shocks;}$$

$S_y = 1$ for v_t^2 type shocks.

Thus, production smoothing is complete for truly unexpected sales, but production bunching is actually possible for the econometrician's version of "unexpected sales." Remembering that $\theta = 1/z_2$ and observing (from (6.12)) that $z_1 z_2 = 1 + i$, we see that some smoothing will take place if and only if:

$$1 + i - \rho > m(1 - z_1) \tag{6.16}$$

which must be true for $AR(1)$ demand shocks ($m=0$), but can be false if m is large enough.

The intuition behind this result is as follows. Consider the implied moving average coefficients when the stochastic process is $ARMA(1, 1)$:

$$\eta_t = \rho\eta_{t-1} + mv_{t-1} + v_t$$

We have:

$$\frac{\partial \eta_t}{\partial v_t} = 1$$

$$\frac{\partial \eta_{t+1}}{\partial v_t} = \rho + m$$

$$\frac{\partial \eta_{t+2}}{\partial v_t} = \rho(\rho + m)$$

$$\vdots$$

So if $\rho + m > 1$, the response pattern "builds" at first before decaying.

Suppose that a firm sees a positive value of v_t, connoting a good period for sales. If the shock is $AR(1)$, the firm will expect the ensuing periods also to be good, but not quite so good as period t. Hence it has an incentive to sell out of inventory, i.e., to smooth production. However, if the shock is $ARMA(1, 1)$, the firm will expect next period to be even better than this period (if $\rho + m > 1$). If $\rho + m$ exceeds 1 by enough (as defined by (6.16)), the firm will actually want to build inventories for future sale. So it will bunch, rather than smooth, production.

Naturally, a firm that smooths production will "bunch" sales, and conversely. Equally naturally, a firm will smooth its price behavior only if it bunches its sales; that is, only if it also smooths its production.[14] Thus, condition (6.16) is pivotal to the firm's behavior. If it holds, as it must unless demand shocks have a strong moving-average component, the firm smooths both production and sales and plans to draw down inventories when demand is high. These reactions are just what we expect. But if (6.16) fails to hold, the firm's optimal behavior is counterintuitive. It smooths sales, not production (nor price), and plans to build inventories in periods when demand is unusually high.

With this analysis complete I turn to the stylized facts.

6.3.5 var(Y) exceeds var(X)

I begin with the most striking of the stylized facts mentioned in the introduction: that detrended output is more variable than detrended sales. From (6.15), N_t can be expressed as a function of current and lagged shocks. Then, by using (6.15) to eliminate N_t from (6.13) and (6.14), it is possible to do the same for X and Y. Algebraic manipulations, sketched in the appendix, yield closed-form, but complicated, expressions for the unconditional variances of X and Y, and for the covariance cov($X, \Delta N$).

The first question is, can these expressions ever rationalize the fact that var(Y) > var(X)? The answer is that they can if cost shocks are big enough. More specifically, the appendix establishes the following:

PROPOSITION 1. *In a simplified version of the model with no demand shocks and r = 0 (serial correlation of the cost shock is an unnecessary complication for this purpose), var(Y) > var(X) for any admissible values of the parameters.*

The economic intuition is clear. In the usual case (such as my 1982 paper), there are demand shocks, but no cost shocks; so inventories are used to smooth production relative to sales, leading to var(X) > var(Y). However, if instead there are cost shocks, but no demand shocks, inventories are used to exploit intertemporal substitution possibilities in production, making var(Y) > var(X).

Hence cost shocks are always a potential explanation of the fact that var(Y) > var(X), if the variance of cost shocks is large enough relative to the variance of demand shocks. However, this explanation comes perilously close to assuming the conclusion (production is variable if it is variable!), and for this reason is not very satisfying.

The remaining propositions pertain to a model in which cost shocks are absent.

PROPOSITION 2. *In a simplified version of the model with no cost shocks and a serially independent demand shock that the firm sees before deciding on production,* $\mathrm{var}(X) > \mathrm{var}(Y)$ *for any admissible values of the parameters. However, as* z_1 *approaches zero, the ratio* $\mathrm{var}(X)/\mathrm{var}(Y)$ *approaches 1.*[15]

Together, Propositions 1 and 2 provide a potentially more satisfying explanation of the fact that $\mathrm{var}(Y) > \mathrm{var}(X)$. Suppose that the technology makes z_1 very small, so that, in the absence of cost shocks, $\mathrm{var}(X)$ would be only slightly larger than $\mathrm{var}(Y)$. Then even relatively minor cost shocks could tip the balance and turn $\mathrm{var}(Y) > \mathrm{var}(X)$.

The problem with this explanation is that the empirical evidence suggests slow adjustment speeds, and hence high values of z_1.[16] According to the logic of Proposition 2, a high value of z_1 will leave $\mathrm{var}(X)$ substantially larger than $\mathrm{var}(Y)$. An alternative explanation would be desirable. One is provided by the next proposition.

PROPOSITION 3. *In a simplified version of the model with no cost shock and an AR(1) demand shock that is known before output is set,* $\mathrm{var}(X) > \mathrm{var}(Y)$ *for any admissible parameter values. However, the ratio* $\mathrm{var}(X)/\mathrm{var}(Y)$ *approaches 1 as the autoregressive parameter approaches 1; that is, as demand shocks become permanent. This holds for any value of* z_1.[17]

The intuition behind Proposition 3 is clear. As the stochastic structure of the demand shock gets closer to a random walk, demand disturbances become more permanent. Hence the firm is more likely to adjust production fully.[18]

Propositions 1 and 3 together provide a potentially better explanation of the fact that $\mathrm{var}(Y) > \mathrm{var}(X)$. The speed of adjustment can be as slow as we please. But as long as ρ is close to unity, as it is empirically, $\mathrm{var}(Y)$ will be nearly as large as $\mathrm{var}(X)$. In that case, only minor cost shocks are necessary to make $\mathrm{var}(Y)$ greater than $\mathrm{var}(X)$.

For example, in a numerical example with $z_1 = 0.85$, no cost shocks, $d = c$, $b = 0.013c$, and a zero rate of interest, $\mathrm{var}(Y)/\mathrm{var}(X)$ is only 0.55 when $\rho = 0.9$. But if ρ gets as high as 0.98, $\mathrm{var}(Y)/\mathrm{var}(X)$ rises to 0.95.

To summarize, a combination of a rapid speed of adjustment (i.e., low z_1) and high serial correlation in demand disturbances (i.e., high ρ) can leave $\mathrm{var}(Y)$ so close to $\mathrm{var}(X)$ that it takes only very minor cost shocks to make $\mathrm{var}(Y) > \mathrm{var}(X)$.

6.3.6 Sales and inventory change do not covary negatively

The fact that $\mathrm{cov}(X, \Delta N)$ is typically zero or positive is the hardest to deal with, because conflicting factors produce theoretically ambiguous results. The reader is spared the detailed analysis. Suffice it to say that a positive

$cov(X, \Delta N)$ can be produced by cost shocks or by demand shocks that are seen before sales decisions are made and that "build" before decaying. Other types of demand shocks produce a negative $cov(X, \Delta N)$. Thus, $cov(X, \Delta N)$ can have either sign, depending on which types of shocks dominate.

6.3.7 Puzzling regression estimates

Finally, there is the problem that econometric inventory investment equations like:

$$N_{t+1} - N_t = \beta_1(N^*_{t+1} - N_t) - (1 - \beta_2)(X_t - {}_{t-1}X_t) + u_t \qquad (6.7)$$

tend to produce low estimates of the parameter β_1 and high estimates of the parameter β_2. It is useful to compare the theoretical equation (6.15), derived from my version of the production smoothing model, to this empirical stock adjustment model.[19]

Notice first that (6.15) does have the partial adjustment form assumed in (6.7). In the absence of shocks, inventory change is a fixed fraction of the gap between $\bar{N}$ and N_t. This fraction – "the speed of adjustment" – depends on the curvatures of the revenue and cost functions, and on the rate of interest (see (6.12)). Low estimated adjustment speeds, therefore, suggest a high value of z_1.

The similarity is even greater once we realize that $\bar{N}$ is not the firm's desired inventory stock. A natural definition of the desired inventory stock, call it N^*_{t+1}, is the value of N_t that makes desired inventory change equal to zero, conditional on the information available at time t. Equating the expectation of the right-hand side of (6.15) to zero, we can express N^*_{t+1} as a function of $\bar{N}$ and the stochastic shocks that are known at time t. If this definition of N^*_{t+1} is then substituted back into (6.15), a little algebra gives:

$$N_{t+1} - N_t = (1 - z_1)(N^*_{t+1} - N_t) - (\eta_t - E_t\eta_t)$$

which differs from (6.7) only in that the unexpected demand disturbance replaces unexpected sales.

Next consider the parameter β_2 in (6.7). The model offers two possible theoretical interpretations of "unexpected sales." The most natural definition is $2dv_t^2$ – the difference between what the firm sells and what it expected to sell when it made its production and price decisions. By this definition, unexpected sales enters the theoretical inventory equation with a coefficient of exactly -1. However, the econometrician's version of "unexpected sales" is likely to include both v_t^1 and v_t^2. As noted earlier, the theoretical coefficient of a v_t^1 shock is negative if and only if (6.16) holds.

Putting all this together, we have the following potential explanation for the puzzling regression estimates:

1. Technological conditions produce a high value of z_1, that is, a slow speed of adjustment. This will occur if $b(c + d)$ is fairly small, which means

either that inventory storage costs are nearly linear or that the marginal cost or marginal revenue schedules are quite steep.
2. Much of what looks like unexpected sales to the econometrician is not actually unexpected by the firm, and condition (6.16) fails to hold. The empirical coefficient $1 - \beta_2$ will then be a weighted average of -1 and the (positive) coefficient of a v_t^1 demand shock. Therefore, with v_t^1 shocks quantitatively more important than v_t^2 shocks, it would not be surprising to find a very small estimated value of $1 - \beta_2$ – which is what regressions like (6.7) typically give.

6.3.8 The stylized facts: summary

In summary, then, the version of the production smoothing–buffer stock model considered here seems compatible with all the stylized facts under the following circumstances, none of which seems outlandish:

1. Cost shocks are present, though they need not be large – a seemingly unobjectionable hypothesis.
2. Most demand shocks are seen by firms before they make their production and pricing decisions. While we cannot know for sure that firms see their demand shocks before econometricians do, it seems a tenable hypothesis.
    Some (extremely) rough evidence can be culled from the time series as follows.[20] If firms are better at seeing good sales prospects coming than econometricians are, their knowledge ought to be reflected in their inventory behavior. If so, inventory investment in finished goods should have predictive power for sales, given the past history of sales; that is, inventory investment should Granger-cause sales. Does it? I addressed this question using twelfth-order (or, when the data did not reject the specialization, sixth-order) bivariate autoregressions for x and Δf. The appropriate F tests suggested Granger causality running from Δf to x at the 10 percent significance level in 10 of the 20 industries (in only seven industries at the 5 percent level). This can hardly be construed as overwhelming evidence in favor of the assumption, but neither is it hostile to the idea.
3. Demand shocks build before they decay. ($ARMA(1, 1)$ and $AR(2)$ processes are simple examples.) Again, demand disturbances are not observable, but actual shipments are.[21] When 12th-order autoregressions are fit to data on shipments for each of the 20 two-digit manufacturing industries, the implied moving average representation shows rising coefficients at short lags in almost every case.
4. Either the technology parameters dictate a rapid speed of adjustment, or demand disturbances have strong positive serial correlation. As noted earlier, stock adjustment estimates almost always show slow adjustment speeds. But the data on shipments display such high serial correlation

that it is hard to imagine that the demand disturbances are not highly serially correlated.

Most important for this paper, none of these requirements forces us to jettison the basic idea that the production function is concave. In this respect, then, the production smoothing–buffer stock model is "saved," though with rather little emphasis on the buffer stock aspects.

6.4 CONCLUSION

It is easy enough to see why the production smoothing model looks so bad at first blush. Consider a trivially simple fixed-price macro model of aggregate supply and demand based on the production smoothing idea:

Supply: $Y = \alpha + \beta X$

Demand: $X = \bar{X} + e$

where Y is production and X is sales. Here e is the random demand shock that drives the model, and $\beta < 1$ captures the idea that production is smoothed relative to sales. In this model, $\text{var}(Y)/\text{var}(X) = \beta^2$, which is certinaly less than unity. Further, since inventory change is:

$$\Delta N = Y - X = \alpha + (\beta - 1)\bar{X} + (\beta - 1)e$$

X and N are perfectly negatively correlated in the model. In the data, as we know, $\text{var}(Y)$ exceeds $\text{var}(X)$, and X and ΔN are nearly orthogonal. The contradiction between the model and reality could hardly be more complete.

This paper has shown, however, that it is possible to amend the production smoothing model in ways that make it consistent with the facts. The two critical ingredients are serially persistent demand disturbances of a particular type and the addition of a cost shock. It is easy to see how these amendments help. Adding a cost shock changes the model to:

Supply: $Y = \alpha + \beta X + u$

Demand: $X = \bar{X} + e$

and Section 6.3 showed that, for any given cost structure, serial correlation in demand disturbances has the effect of pushing β toward unity. Assuming that u is independent of e at all lags, trivial calculations establish that:

$$\text{var}(Y)/\text{var}(X) = \beta^2 + \tau^2$$

$$\text{cor}(X, \Delta N) = \frac{\beta - 1}{[\tau^2 + (1 - \beta)^2]^{1/2}}$$

where τ^2 is the ratio $\text{var}(u)/\text{var}(e)$. Now, if τ is big enough, the variance ratio can exceed unity; and the correlation between X and ΔN, while still negative, can at least be small. At some level, therefore, the exercise must be judged a success. The production smoothing model, or at least the concavity of the production function, has been saved.

Yet there are some lingering doubts. A skeptic may recall that Ptolemaic astronomy was "saved" many times by the addition of epicycles specifically designed to accommodate each new fact. In addition, empirically estimated stock adjustment models often give unsatisfactory results. One suspects that Copernicus may be waiting in the wings.

Certainly there are other models of inventory behavior that might be used to explain the stylized facts. For example, the (S, s) model was mentioned in note 6, but judged implausible on *a priori* grounds. An alternative technological assumption would be that the production function is convex at low output levels and then becomes concave, giving rise to the U-shaped cost curves of elementary textbooks.[22] In that case, small shifts in the demand curve can, at times, cause production to jump substantially. Another possibility arises if inventories are held to avoid stockouts. A paper by Kahn (1985) shows that, if firms can backlog some of their unsatisfied demand when they run out of stock, sales will be smoothed relative to (underlying) demand and possibly also relative to production.

But perhaps the explanation for the puzzling behavior of inventories does not lie in inventory behavior at all. To see what I mean, consider the following trivial "Keynesian cross" model in which demand creates its own supply and inventories never change:

Supply: $Y = X$

Demand: $X = a + bY + e$

Obviously, in this model $\mathrm{var}(Y)/\mathrm{var}(X) = 1$. And since there are no changes in inventories, $\mathrm{var}(\Delta N) = 0$, and $\mathrm{cov}(X, \Delta N) = 0$ in a trivial sense. Clearly, this model cannot be quite right because it ignores some empirically important movements in inventories. Nonetheless, it makes a promising start at "explaining" the stylized facts.

It does not take much imagination to integrate the Keynesian specification of aggregate demand with the production smoothing model of aggregate supply to get:

Supply: $Y = \alpha + \beta X + u$

Demand: $X = a + bY + e$

In this hybrid model, the critical variance ratio is:

$$\frac{\mathrm{var}(Y)}{\mathrm{var}(X)} = \frac{\mathrm{var}(u) + \beta^2 \mathrm{var}(e)}{b^2 \mathrm{var}(u) + \mathrm{var}(e)}$$

This expression clearly shows that demand shocks lead to a variance ratio smaller than one (depending on the degree of production smoothing), while supply shocks lead to a variance ratio larger than one (depending on the MPC). The variance ratio can fall on either side of unity. More important, the covariance between sales and inventory change is:

$$\text{cov}(x, \Delta N) = \frac{b(1-b)\,\text{var}(u) - (1-\beta)\,\text{var}(e)}{(1-b\beta)^2}$$

which can have either sign – an empirically pleasing prediction, given the mixed results in the data.

Thus, it would appear that attaching a Keynesian demand side to our production-smoothing supply side may help the latter account for the stylized facts. Metzler probably knew this 40 years ago.

NOTES

1. See, for example, Holt, Modigliani, Muth, and Simon (1960).
2. Lovell (1961) began this tradition, and many have followed.
3. For a precise derivation, see Blinder (1982). A notable exception is Blanchard (1983), which is based on a cost of changing output and therefore includes a strong role for lagged output.
4. These two facts are documented carefully in the next section.
5. This problem was noticed by Orr (1967), and received prominent attention from Carlson and Wehrs (1974) and from Feldstein and Auerbach (1976).
6. There are also approaches based on different technological assumptions. For example, in an earlier paper on retail inventories (Blinder, 1981; reprinted here as Chapter 5), I suggested that the technology of the retail firm is not in fact convex, and nominated the (S, s) model as a replacement for the production smoothing model. This model, which is based on a large fixed cost element plus constant marginal costs, has little trouble accounting for the stylized facts; but the technology that underlies the (S, s) model is far less appealing on *a priori* grounds for manufacturers than it is for retailers.
7. This is not the only possible definition of output for a multistage production process. For example, we could define output as the sum of $b + c + d + e$, or we could count a portion of a and a portion of d as production. However, this is the definition of output used by the BEA in constructing the price indexes used to deflate inventory stocks, and hence is the only definition of Y consistent with the data.
8. In doing this, data an inventory stocks were adjusted to reflect the fact that one dollar of inventory stock represents more physical units than one dollar of shipments because inventories are valued at cost rather than market. Part of the appropriate adjustment to convert the data from real values into physical units is presented and explained by West (1983). The rest is described in Blinder and Holtz-Eakin (1983).
9. However, detrending by ordinary least squares led to very similar results, as did entirely different detrending procedures.
10. For the period 1947:2–1981:1 (quarterly data), Blinder (1981, p. 446) reports that the variance of real GNP around trend is 32 percent larger than the variance of real final sales around trend.
11. See Blinder (1986).

12. More details can be found in the working paper version of this chapter (National Bureau of Economic Research Working Paper no. 1257, January 1984) or in Reagan and Sheehan (1985).
13. This is the case dealt with in Blinder (1982), which is reprinted here as Chapter 4.
14. This statement summarizes succinctly the main point of Blinder (1982).
15. In the case of a v_t^2 demand shock that is unknown to the firm when it makes its production decision, the ratio $\text{var}(X)/\text{var}(Y) \to (1 + (d/c)) + (d/c) > 1$ as $z_1 \to 0$. If d is much smaller than c, this will not exceed 1 by much.
16. Feldstein and Auerbach (1976), for example, reported adjustment speeds between 5 percent and 7 percent per quarter for finished goods inventories in durable manufacturing. This was fairly typical of work up to that time. Auerbach and Green (1980) got much faster adjustment speeds (from 12 percent to 85 percent per quarter) using data on four two-digit industries and a model that treated finished goods and work in progress separately. Blanchard's (1983) study of the divisions of US auto firms found adjustment speeds ranging from 0 percent to 35 percent per month. Maccini and Rossana (1984) estimate much faster adjustment speeds but, for reasons explained in Blinder (1986; reprinted here as Chapter 7), I believe that is entirely attributable to the estimation technique they employ.
17. This proposition does not apply to a v_t^2 demand shock which is unknown to the firm when it makes its production decision. If demand shocks are of this type, $\text{var}(X)/\text{var}(Y)$ exceeds 1 even as ρ approaches 1.
18. If demand shocks have a strong moving average component, production can respond more than demand, as proved earlier. This led me to suspect that $\text{var}(Y)$ could exceed $\text{var}(X)$ with an $ARMA(1, 1)$ demand shock and no cost shock. However, that is not true, as West (1986) proves.
19. Other production smoothing models, such as Blanchard's (1983), do not lead to the stock adjustment equation.
20. I owe this suggestion to Olivier Blanchard.
21. The time series properties of sales depend on both cost and demand disturbances, however, so we cannot easily infer the time series representation of v from that of X.
22. I owe this idea to a discussion with Geoffrey Heal.

REFERENCES

Auerbach, A. J. and J. R. Green (1980) "Components of manufacturing inventories," NBER Working Paper no. 491 (June).

Blanchard, O. J. (1983) "The production and inventory behavior of the American automobile industry," *Journal of Political Economy*, XCI (June), pp. 365–400.

Blinder, A. S. (1981) "Retail inventory behavior and business fluctuations," *Brookings Papers on Economic Activity*, vol. 2, pp. 443–505. Reprinted here as Chapter 5.

Blinder, A. S. (1982) "Inventories and sticky prices," *American Economic Review*, LXXII (June), pp. 334–48. Reprinted here as Chapter 4.

Blinder, A. S. (1986) "More on the speed of adjustment in inventory models," *Journal of Money, Credit and Banking*, vol. 18, no. 3 (August), pp. 355–65. Reprinted here as Chapter 7.

Blinder, A. S. and D. Holtz-Eakin (1983) "Constant dollar manufacturers' inventories: a note," Princeton Univerisity (September), mimeo.

Carlson, J. and W. Wehrs (1974) "Aggregate inventory behavior," in George Horwich and P. A. Samuelson (eds) *Trade Stability and Macroeconomics: Essays in Honor of L. A. Metzler*, New York: Academic Press, pp. 311–32.

Feldstein, M. S. and A. Auerbach (1976) "Inventory behavior in durable goods manufacturing: the target adjustment model," *Brookings Papers on Economic Activity*, vol. 2, pp. 351–96.

Holt, C. C., F. Modigliani, J. Muth, and H. A. Simon (1960) *Planning Production, Inventories and Work Force*, Englewood Cliffs: Prentice Hall.

Kahn, J. (1985) "Stockouts, backlogs, and the variance of production," unpublished manuscript, MIT (August).

Lovell, M. C. (1961) "Manufacturers' inventories, sales expectations, and the acceleration principle," *Econometrica*, vol. XXIX (July), pp. 293–314.

Maccini, L. J. and R. J. Rossana (1984) "Joint production, quasi-fixed factors of production and investment in finished goods inventories," *Journal of Money, Credit and Banking*, vol. XVI (May), pp. 218–36.

Orr, L. (1967) "A comment on sales anticipations and inventory investment," *International Economic Review* (Oct), pp. 368–73.

Reagan, P. and D. P. Sheehan (1985) "The stylized facts about the behavior of manufacturers inventories and backorders over the business cycle: 1959–1980," *Journal of Monetary Economics*, vol. XV (March), pp. 217–46.

West, K. D. (1983) "A note on the econometric use of constant dollar inventory series," *Economics Letters*, pp. 337–41.

West, K. D. (1986) "A variance bounds test of the linear quadratic inventory model," *Journal of Political Economy*, vol. 94, no. 2 (April), pp. 374–401.

7 · MORE ON THE SPEED
OF ADJUSTMENT IN
INVENTORY MODELS

7.1 INTRODUCTION

Applied econometricians estimating stock adjustment models of inventory investment have long bemoaned the fact that estimated adjustment speeds turn out to be "implausibly slow."[1] Other applications of stock adjustment models, such as the demands for money and for consumer durables, also turn up slow adjustment speeds.[2] In a thought-provoking paper, however, Maccini and Rossana (1984) claim that the slow adjustment is an artifact of inappropriate estimation procedures which fail to correct for autocorrelation. Using a two-step procedure due to Hatanaka (1974), they obtain econometric inventory equations for finished goods with very fast adjustment speeds.

While Maccini and Rossana are correct that failure to correct for autocorrelation can bias estimated adjustment speeds downward, their application to manufacturers' investment in finished goods inventories produces estimates that are inappropriate in a very subtle sense. In particular, I show below that the types of models estimated by Maccini and Rossana – and perhaps most stock adjustment models – have two local minima in the sum of squared residuals (henceforth SSR) function, and that the Hatanaka technique that they use typically picks out the "wrong" local minimum.

This short paper has two purposes. The first is methodological. Since partial adjustment models are commonly estimated for all kinds of economic variables, it seems important to reemphasize the potential identification problem first pointed out by Griliches (1967): that it may be quite difficult to distinguish between partial adjustment and serial correlation. This is done in Section 7.2, where I explain why the existence of two local minima should be expected to be the norm, not the exception.

The second purpose is substantive. The empirical work reported in Section 7.3 strongly suggests that the estimates obtained by Maccini and

I am indebted to Douglas Holtz-Eakin for extensive and superb research assistance, to the National Science Foundation and Alfred P. Sloan for financial support, and to John Carlson, Michael Lovell, Louis Maccini, Angelo Melino, and Kenneth West for useful comments on an earlier draft.

Rossana – which feature high serial correlation and rapid adjustment – are not, in fact, the global minima of the SSR functions. Instead the global minima for most manufacturing industries are characterized by little autocorrelation but slow adjustment. Thus, if the partial adjustment model is accepted as the maintained hypothesis, the best estimates of the speed of adjustment in inventory models remain "implausibly slow."[3]

7.2 THE DIFFICULTY OF IDENTIFYING THE SPEED OF ADJUSTMENT

To make the point as starkly as possible, I start with a stripped-down model far simpler than those estimated either by Maccini and Rossana or by myself. The model is a special case of the one dealt with by Betancourt and Kelejian (1981). Let N_t denote the inventory stock (or any other stock) at the *beginning* of the period, and suppose that desired inventories, N^*, are constant. Then the stock adjustment model is simply:

$$N_{t+1} - N_t = \beta(N^* - N_t) + u_t \tag{7.1}$$

If the error term follows an $AR(1)$ process:

$$u_t = \rho u_{t-1} + e_t \tag{7.2}$$

the natural procedure is to quasi-difference (7.1) before estimating to get:

$$N_{t+1} = \beta(1-\rho)N^* + (\rho - \beta + 1)N_t - \rho(1-\beta)N_{t-1} + e_t \tag{7.3}$$

This is an $AR(2)$ model for the stock of inventories.[4] But notice the fundamental identification problem. Suppose the econometric estimate of (7.3) is:

$$N_{t+1} = \mu_0 + \mu_1 N_t + \mu_2 N_{t-1} \tag{7.4}$$

where the μs are the estimated coefficients. We find the implied estimates for ρ and β by solving:

$$\mu_1 = \rho + 1 - \beta \tag{7.5}$$

$$\mu_2 = -\rho(1-\beta) \tag{7.6}$$

which yields:

$$\rho^2 - \rho\mu_1 - \mu_2 = 0. \tag{7.7}$$

Clearly, equation (7.7) offers two solutions for ρ:

$$\rho = \frac{\mu_1}{2} \pm \sqrt{\frac{\mu_1^2}{4} + \mu_2} \tag{7.8}$$

and two corresponding solutions for β.

An example that is germane to the inventory problem is where ρ and β are approximately equal. Then the two coefficients in (7.3) are approximately 1 and $\beta(\beta-1)$. Hence, we cannot tell β from $1-\beta$. For example, if either $\rho = \beta = 0.9$ or $\rho = \beta = 0.1$, then the coefficients in (7.3) are respectively 1.0 and -0.09. Exact equality between ρ and β is not necessary, of course. If (7.4) is:

$$N_{t+1} = 1.1N_t - 0.1425N_{t-1} + constant,$$

which is pretty typical in the inventory application, the two solutions of (7.8) are:

$$\rho = 0.95, \beta = 0.85 \tag{a}$$

$$\rho = 0.15, \beta = 0.05 \tag{b}$$

Hereafter, I will refer to solutions like (a) as the "high ρ" solution and solutions like (b) as the "low ρ" solution. The general point is that, as Griliches pointed out years ago, any estimation technique will have trouble distinguishing between a model with strong serial correlation and fast adjustment and one with little serial correlation but slow adjustment.[5]

In the simple example of (7.1) and (7.2), both parameters are literally unidentified. Actual empirical models such as those of Maccini and Rossana, or the regressions presented in the next section, include a variety of other regressors and hence are identified in the formal sense. But identification hinges precariously on regressors which are often of minor empirical importance. Hence, while it is not *impossible* to distinguish between a "high ρ, high β" model and a "low ρ, low β" model, it is *difficult*.

All the equations reported in the next section were fit by nonlinear least squares under the assumption that the error term was $AR(1)$.[6] If the disturbances are normal, this is a maximum likelihood procedure. In many cases, two local minima of the sum of squared residuals function were found. In such cases, one of the minima always had high ρ and rapid adjustment while the other had low ρ and slow adjustment, precisely as suggested by this simple argument. This point is important because the extremely high adjustment speeds found by Maccini and Rossana (1984) result from an estimation technique that settles on the local minimum with high ρ. (They report estimated values of ρ from the two-step Hatanaka procedure ranging from 0.67 to 0.97.) The nonlinear estimation method used here shows, however, that the low ρ solution is typically the global minimum.

7.3 ECONOMETRIC INVENTORY EQUATIONS

This section presents econometric estimates of stock-adjustment models for inventory investment in finished goods. I concentrate on finished goods because that is the only type of inventory for which we have a coherent and operational theory.[7]

The data presented in Table 7.1 are monthly, real, and seasonally adjusted, and (after allowing for lags) span the period December 1960–March 1981.[8] Each two-digit industry is treated separately. However, for direct comparison with Maccini and Rossana, I also present results for all manufacturing and for the durable and nondurable sectors. The theoretical stock adjustment model was made operational as follows.

Demand disturbances were proxied by two variables: expected sales, X_t^e, is the one-period-ahead forecast from a 12th order autoregression fit to each industry's actual data on shipments; and unexpected sales, X_t^u, is the residual from this autoregression. Thus expectations are assumed to be "rational," albeit in a limited sense. Experimentation with other expectational proxies led to substantially identical results. In 13 of the 20 industries, data on new orders are available. For these industries, the collinearity between the two sales measures is almost always too great to include both, so two versions of the regressions were run. Normally, a better fit was obtained using shipments.

Cost disturbances were treated by including both the real product wage, w, and the real cost of raw materials, c, in each regression. The nominal wage series is the average hourly earnings series specific to that industry or sector. The nominal materials cost series is the *PPI* for Crude Materials for Further Processing (and is the same for every industry). Each nominal factor price is deflated by an industry-specific price index.

In addition, the interest rate is included as a potentially important determinant of the desired steady-state level of inventories. For reasons described in Blinder (1981), the nominal interest rate, R (bank prime rate), and the expected rate of inflation, π (generated by an autoregression), are entered as separate variables rather than combined into a real interest rate.

The theoretical model in Blinder (1986) recognizes the existence of only one type of inventory. But, in fact, there are three types and Maccini and Rossana have convincingly demonstrated the importance of stock interactions. Many industries also have backlogs of unfilled orders. Preliminary regressions showed clearly that investment in finished goods inventories reacts differently to the initial stock of each kind of inventory, so Table 7.1 presents estimates of the following flexible accelerator model of finished goods inventories:

$$\Delta F_t = \beta_1 F_t + \beta_2 W_t + \beta_3 M_t + \beta_4 U_t + \alpha_1 X_t^e + \alpha_t X_t^u$$
$$+ \gamma_1 R_t + \gamma_2 \pi_t + \delta_1 w_t + \delta_2 c_t + u_t \tag{7.9}$$

where:

F_t = stock of finished goods (beginning of period)
W_t = stock of work in process
M_t = stock of materials and supplies
U_t = stock of unfilled orders

Table 7.1 Simple stock adjustment regressions, 1960:12 to 1981:3.

	Coefficient (absolute t ratio) of											
	Initial stock of			sales								
Sector	finished goods	work in progress	materials & supplies	unfilled orders	expected	unexpected	interest rate	expected capital gains	wages	materials costs	$\hat{\rho}$	R^2
All manufacturing	−0.080 (3.3)	0.006 (0.4)	0.029 (2.8)	0.002 (0.7)	0.003 (0.4)	−0.052 (3.2)	−128 (0.7)	−9.9 (0.1)	15.9 (4.5)	−9.4 (3.4)	0.13 (1.8)	0.19
Durable goods	−0.061 (2.6)	−0.002 (0.2)	0.018 (2.3)	0.001 (0.4)	0.005 (0.6)	−0.039 (2.7)	8.8 (0.1)	−20 (0.3)	10.3 (1.3)	−3.7 (2.2)	0.12 (1.7)	0.12
primary metals	−0.271 (4.7)	0.151 (3.5)	−0.051 (2.6)	0.008 (1.3)	−0.057 (2.8)	−0.133 (7.6)	−82 (2.4)	−31 (3.4)	6.0 (2.6)	−4.0 (4.4)	0.42 (5.0)	0.37
fabricated metals	−0.257 (5.7)	0.056 (2.9)	0.034 (4.5)	0.001 (0.4)	−0.001 (0.1)	0.025 (0.9)	−10 (0.4)	−9.2 (1.0)	1.7 (1.5)	−0.69 (2.1)	−0.10 (1.3)	0.21
electrical mach.	−0.112 (2.8)	0.013 (1.2)	0.000 (0.0)	−0.010 (1.8)	0.037 (2.3)	0.004 (0.1)	−28 (0.8)	83 (4.1)	5.0 (2.8)	−0.52 (1.3)	0.03 (0.4)	0.12
nonelectrical[a] machinery	−0.106 (3.9)	0.026 (1.2)	0.029 (1.8)	−0.005 (1.0)	0.010 (0.9)	−0.033 (2.3)	1.2 (0.0)	7.7 (0.4)	4.9 (1.8)	−2.0 (3.4)	0.01 (0.1)	0.17
transportation equipment	−0.049 (1.7)	0.001 (0.2)	−0.027 (2.0)	0.002 (1.3)	0.027 (3.4)	0.017 (1.4)	−56 (1.5)	104 (3.1)	−1.5 (0.9)	0.17 (0.3)	−0.14 (2.0)	0.12
lumber & wood products	−0.106 (3.0)	0.036 (0.9)	0.040 (1.8)	—	−0.044 (2.2)	0.061 (1.5)	14 (1.0)	1.3 (0.5)	−0.05 (0.1)	−0.55 (2.0)	−0.03 (0.4)	0.08
furniture and fixtures	−0.115 (3.9)	0.040 (1.2)	0.024 (2.4)	0.009 (1.3)	−0.020 (0.7)	0.070 (1.8)	−1.6 (0.3)	11.3 (2.6)	−0.18 (0.3)	−0.16 (1.6)	−0.23 (3.4)	0.18
stone, clay, & glass products	−0.179 (4.0)	0.107 (1.1)	0.005 (0.3)	−0.008 (0.9)	0.071 (2.9)	−0.103 (2.8)	25 (1.7)	8.8 (0.8)	0.22 (0.4)	−0.48 (2.1)	0.09 (1.2)	0.16
instruments and related prods.	−1.04 (16.4)	0.167 (4.5)	0.068 (2.4)	0.074 (1.7)	0.030 (0.3)	0.002 (0.0)	29 (0.7)	−13.2 (1.7)	−4.6 (1.4)	1.32 (2.3)	0.98 (80.5)	0.15
miscellaneous manufacturing indust.	−0.221 (4.9)	0.103 (2.0)	0.045 (2.5)	0.021 (0.9)	0.137 (3.2)	−0.016 (0.3)	−13 (0.9)	−1.4 (0.3)	0.44 (1.3)	0.23 (1.0)	0.29 (3.7)	0.19

Nondurable goods	-0.142 (3.8)	0.184 (1.9)	0.054 (2.3)	0.017 (0.3)	-0.026 (1.1)	-0.067 (2.0)	98 (1.1)	14.5 (0.3)	12.3 (2.2)	-10.5 (4.0)	0.15 (2.0)	0.15
food and kindred products	-0.785 (10.1)	0.293 (1.3)	0.115 (1.8)	—	0.285 (3.7)	0.237 (0.6)	-99 (0.7)	-21.8 (1.9)	10.8 (2.1)	-1.85 (0.4)	0.91 (25.0)	0.12
tobacco manufacturing	-0.382 (4.5)	0.076 (0.8)	0.020 (2.8)	—	0.209 (1.6)	-0.047 (0.6)	1.7 (0.2)	1.6 (0.4)	0.58 (2.4)	-0.24 (1.1)	0.13 (1.2)	0.18
textile mill prods.	-0.999 (15.2)	0.319 (3.4)	0.109 (2.3)	-0.057 (2.6)	0.064 (0.9)	0.013 (0.4)	6.9 (0.2)	-20.6 (2.7)	3.1 (2.7)	-0.68 (1.2)	0.98 (68.0)	0.17
apparel products	-0.248 (4.3)	0.027 (0.5)	0.134 (3.9)	—	0.033 (0.7)	0.111 (2.4)	-12 (0.4)	-53 (1.6)	1.8 (1.0)	-0.51 (1.4)	0.26 (2.8)	0.17
leather & leather products	-0.177 (4.4)	0.092 (1.2)	0.052 (1.9)	-0.048 (2.8)	-0.042 (1.1)	-0.032 (0.6)	-8.4 (1.3)	-52 (2.1)	0.31 (1.1)	0.05 (0.6)	-0.14 (1.8)	0.17
paper & allied products	-0.237 (5.0)	0.160 (2.1)	0.056 (3.8)	0.001 (0.1)	-0.001 (1.1)	-0.074 (2.2)	27 (2.8)	-3.4 (0.8)	2.4 (3.3)	-0.54 (2.9)	0.11 (1.3)	0.21
printing and publishing	-0.151 (4.6)	-0.014 (0.4)	0.031 (3.3)	-0.081 (3.4)	0.068 (3.0)	0.041 (1.1)	-28 (1.9)	-1.0 (0.3)	0.08 (0.1)	0.03 (0.1)	-0.02 (0.2)	0.11
chemicals & allied products	-0.081 (2.9)	0.093 (1.3)	0.009 (0.4)	—	0.021 (1.1)	-0.251 (6.5)	43 (1.5)	3.0 (0.0)	2.2 (2.0)	-2.6 (4.0)	0.10 (1.5)	0.27
petroleum & coal products	-0.123 (3.3)	-0.248 (2.7)	0.133 (1.5)	—	0.008 (0.4)	-0.159 (3.2)	26 (1.5)	-9.2 (3.4)	0.84 (1.8)	-1.3 (2.5)	0.02 (0.3)	0.16
rubber & plastic products	-0.076 (3.3)	-0.041 (0.5)	0.048 (2.9)	—	0.015 (0.5)	-0.006 (0.2)	-34 (2.4)	0.32 (0.1)	1.66 (3.4)	-0.76 (3.2)	0.09 (1.3)	0.14

Notes:
Estimation was by nonlinear least squares, with allowance for first-order autocorrelation. All regressions also included a constant, not shown here.
(a) For this industry *only*, new orders are use to measure sales.

and the error term, u_t, is assumed to be generated by (7.2). The model is similar to that of Maccini and Rossana. (In Table 7.1, t-ratios are in parentheses.)

First, note that the opening stock of finished goods always enters with a significant negative coefficient, indicative of partial adjustment. However, in accord with much previous work, but in contradiction to Maccini and Rossana, most of the estimated speeds of adjustment are rather slow. Among the 17 industries for which the "low ρ" solution was the global minimum, the speeds of adjustment range from 5 percent to 38 percent per month. These speeds are slightly faster than, but not out of line with, those typically found in work at a more aggregative level.[9] But they are much slower than those reported by Maccini and Rossana (1984), using very similar data and a similar specification. The difference between my results and theirs is entirely attributable to the estimation method. In the three industries in which the "high ρ" solution is the global minimum (instruments, food, and textiles), I get extremely rapid adjustment (104 percent, 79 percent, and 100 percent per month, respectively).[10]

It is worth noting that aggregation seems to bias the estimated speed of adjustment downward. The adjustment speeds for durables and non-durables as a whole are lower than those of most of the constituent industries. This helps explain why more highly aggregated studies find slower adjustment.

The cross-adjustment coefficients, β_2 and β_3, are more novel and display a rather consistent pattern across industries. High opening stocks of either works in progress (W_t) or raw materials (M_t) usually are associated with higher investment in finished goods inventories, that is, with higher production. Whether or not this empirical regularity implies causation, of course, is another matter entirely. For example, higher planned production could induce stockpiling of works in progress and materials.

Studies that merge all three types of inventory into a single stock necessarily produce an estimated "adjustment speed" that is an amalgam of the three adjustment coefficients, β_i. Since one of these is negative and the other two are positive, we would expect this procedure to understate the speed of adjustment if the three types of inventories covary positively. To test this idea, a version of (7.9) was run in which all three types of inventory were lumped together into a single aggregate. The results were as expected: estimated adjustment speeds generally declined, sometimes dramatically.

Turning to specifics, the coefficient of works in progress is positive in 17 of 20 industries, though significantly positive in only four of these. The petroleum refining industry is the only important exception; here, high stocks of work in progress apparently lead to lower levels of output.

The coefficient of the opening stock of materials and supplies inventory is positive in 18 of 20 industries, and significantly positive in 10 of these. The only exceptions are the primary metals and transportation equipment industries, where high levels of raw materials apparently lead to cutbacks in production. Maccini and Rossana also found significant effects of raw materials inventories, though not in nondurables.

In contrast to these rather good results, the stock of unfilled orders performs poorly. Among the 13 industries reporting data on unfilled orders, the estimated coefficient is positive seven times (the "correct" sign, it seems to me) and negative six times. Only three coefficients are significant; and they are all negative.

As noted already, sales are measured alternatively by shipments and, in those industries offering such data, unfilled orders. Fortunately, the estimated equations proved quite insensitive to the choice of a sales measure. Since shipments perform slightly better than new orders, and are available for all industries, Table 7.1 reports only the results with shipments.

In general, results for the sales variables are disappointing and not always in line with *a priori* expectations. For example, many of the coefficients are insignificantly different from zero, suggesting either that production reacts virtually one-for-one to sales (whether expected or unexpected) or that the difference between production and sales shows up mostly in works in progress rather than in finished goods.[11]

Specifically, the coefficient of expected sales X_t^e, is normally quite small (values of 0.05 or less are typical) and insignificantly different from zero. Its sign is positive in 14 cases and negative in six, and only eight of the 20 industries (all in durables) display significant coefficients.

The unexpected sales variable is significant in only seven industries. A positive coefficient for this variable is impossible to interpret in the context of the model; taken literally, it implies that inventories of finished goods rise when there is an unexpected surge in sales. Presumably, a positive coefficient means that the sales fluctuations which we label "unexpected" are really expected by firms, in accord with the discussion in Blinder (1986). Yet the point estimate is positive in 11 of 20 industries. There is evidence of a strong negative effect of X_t^u on ΔF_t in only six industries.

Interest rates, represented here by the (monthly) nominal interest rate (R_t) and the (monthly) industry-specific expected rate of inflation (π_t) do not perform as the theory suggests. The expected signs are negative for R_t and positive for π_t; but only four of 20 industries display this pattern. Taking the two variables individually, we see that R_t gets the expected negative coefficient in only 10 of 20 cases and π_t gets the expected positive coefficient in only nine of 20 cases. Only five of the 19 correctly-signed coefficients are significant; as are five of the 21 incorrectly-signed coefficients. This is not much better than what you would expect if the coefficients were randomly distributed around zero, so the overall conclusion seems to be that interest rates do not matter. This finding is consistent with older empirical work on inventory investment, and with Maccini and Rossana, but contradictory to some other work in which significant interest rate effects have been found.[12]

The wage rate is probably the least successful variable of all. Of the 20 industries, only four estimates get the expected negative sign. Of the 16 positive coefficients, nine are significantly different from zero. The results here strongly suggest reverse causation running from higher production to higher wages, perhaps due to overtime premia. Thus, I conclude that wage rates are not good representations of cost shocks.

Raw materials costs are far more successful in this role. The estimated coefficient of c_t is negative in 15 of 20 cases, and is significant in about half the industries. And many of the coefficients are of an economically meaningful size. For example, the coefficient for all manufacturing indicates that a 10 percent rise in raw materials prices (the variable c_t is an index number with January 1972 = 100) will lower the desired stock of finished goods inventories by $2 billion (in 1972 dollars), or about 5 percent of the mean inventory stock. The strong estimated effect of raw materials prices echoes the finding of Maccini and Rossana (1984).

Finally, I note in passing that the fits of the regressions – as measured by R^2 – are modest at best. Time series analysis of noisy, virtually trendless series like ΔF_t encourages humility.

One objection to the standard stock adjustment model is that it assumes that all the right-hand variables enter only contemporaneously. But if there are lags in adjustment, lagged values of variables like interest rates and raw materials costs may also matter. In fact, Irvine (1981c) argued that omission of such variables may bias estimated adjustment speeds downward, and Maccini and Rossana's equations include distributed lags.

There are so many possible combinations of distributed lags that might be added to (7.9) that I adopted a sequential search procedure to economize on computing costs. The reader is spared the laborious details of the many regressions that were run.[13] Suffice it to say that, while distributed lags of at least one variable were found to be significant in most industries, the basic findings on adjustment speeds were not changed. However, it is worth reemphasizing that, because of the two local minima in the sum of squared residuals, our ability to pin down the speed of adjustment is not nearly so good as the t-statistic suggests.[14]

7.4 CONCLUSION

When empirical stock-adjustment models of manufacturers' inventories of finished goods are estimated, there appear to be two local minima in the sum of squared residuals functions. At one local minimum, the estimated adjustment speed is typically quite high; at the other, it is typically quite low. That, in itself, means that we have precious little ability to pin down the speed of adjustment empirically – certainly far less than indicated by the standard errors of the estimated coefficients.

Furthermore, finding two sets of estimates that fit the data almost equally well does not appear to be a quirk of this particular application. Rather, it stems from a fundamental identification problem that afflicts partial adjustment models of all kinds. For example, it has become common to use the partial-adjustment specification in studies of the demand for money, and the estimated equations typically have surprisingly slow adjustment speeds.[15] It may be that money demand equations also have two local maxima.[16]

Hence this paper stands as a generic warning to users of stock adjustment models to use estimation methods that do not mechanically select a particular local maximum. There appears to be no better procedure than to search thoroughly over alternative values of ρ and to select the maximum maximorum. If there is more than one local maximum, standard errors estimated in the usual way will certainly overstate the precision of the point estimates, but by an amount that will remain unknown until some basic econometric theory relevant to such problems is developed.

In the specific context of explaining changes in manufacturers' inventories of finished goods, the two-step procedure employed by Maccini and Rossana (1984) seems to pick out the solution with rapid adjustment (and high serial correlation in the disturbances) whereas the solution with slow adjustment (and little serial correlation) is more often the global minimum. Thus I am afraid that Maccini and Rossana (1984), despite admirable efforts and a number of interesting innovations, have not succeeded in explaining why estimated adjustment speeds in stock-adjustment models of inventory behavior are "implausibly slow."

NOTES

1. This problem has been emphasized by, for example, Carlson and Wehrs (1974) and Feldstein and Auerbach (1976).
2. Regarding demand for money, c.f. Goldfeld (1976). Regarding consumer durables, c.f. Bernanke (1985). There are numerous other examples.
3. Of course, it is possible to question the validity of the stock adjustment model for inventories. See, for example, Blinder (1986).
4. Lovell (1976) shows that an $AR(2)$ model can be derived in other ways, e.g., from adaptive expectations.
5. Betancourt and Kelejian (1981) pointed out the possibility of multiple roots in a more general setting and argue that it can lead the standard Cochrane–Orcutt procedure astray.
6. Experiments with more complicated error structures bore little fruit.
7. For a derivation and discussion, see Blinder (1986).
8. Had they been available, I would have preferred to use data that were not seasonally adjusted, since the production-smoothing model presumably applies to seasonal fluctuations in sales. However, such data are not available.
9. Feldstein and Auerbach (1976), for example, reported adjustment speeds between 5 percent and 7 percent per quarter for finished goods inventories in durable manufacturing. Lovell's (1961) original adjustment speed for finished goods was

18 percent. Auerbach and Green (1980) got much faster adjustment speeds (from 12 percent to 85 percent per quarter) using data on four two-digit industries and a model that treated finished goods and work in progress separately. Blanchard's (1983) study of the divisions of US auto firms found adjustment speeds ranging from 0 percent to 35 percent per month.

10. Maccini and Rossana (1984, note 20) observe that ordinary least squares regressions (which constrain $\rho = 0$) produce slow estimated adjustment speeds.

11. Because $Y_t - X_t = \Delta F_t + \Delta W_t$, if F_{t+1} does not change when X_t rises, then either Y_t must rise or W_{t+1} must fall.

12. The earlier literature, summarized for example by Irvine (1981a), found little evidence for a significant effect of interest costs on inventory holdings. However recent work by Irvine (1981a, 1981b) has detected such effects for retailers and merchant wholesalers, while Rubin (1980) and Akhtar (1983) have found aggregate inventories to be interest sensitive. Only Lieberman (1980), using micro data on a small sample of firms and a specially-constructed cost of capital variable, has found any evidence for interest sensitivity in manufacturing.

13. Full details are available on request.

14. For example, if we constrain $\rho = 1$ (by estimating the equation in first-difference form), estimated adjustment speeds are extremely high; indeed, many are above 100 percent.

15. Goldfeld's (1973) exhaustive empirical survey began with a "conventional equation" whose adjustment speed is 28 percent per quarter. He observed that "while this is not dramatically rapid, it is certainly more plausible than the 0–10 percent estimates that some writers have reported" (p. 583).

16. Hafer and Hein (1984) reported quarterly adjustment speeds even slower than Goldfeld's. But, mindful of Betancourt and Kelejian's (1981) warning, they establish these to be the global maxima.

REFERENCES

Akhtar, M. A. (1983) "Effects of interest rates and inflation on aggregate inventory investment in the United States," *American Economic Review*, vol. LXXIII (June), pp. 319–28.

Auerbach, A. J. and J. R. Green (1980) "Components of manufacturing inventories," NBER Working Paper no. 491 (June).

Bernanke, B. (1985) "Adjustment costs, durables, and aggregate consumption," *Journal of Monetary Economics*, vol. 15 (January), pp. 41–68.

Betancourt, R. and H. Kelejian (1981) "Lagged endogenous variables and the Cochrane–Orcutt procedure," *Econometrica*, vol. 49 (July), pp. 1073–8.

Blanchard, O. J. (1983) "The production and inventory behavior of the American automobile industry," *Journal of Political Economy* (June), pp. 365–400.

Blinder, A. S. (1986) "Can the production smoothing model of inventory behavior be saved?" *Quarterly Journal of Economics*, vol. 101 (August), pp. 431–53.

Blinder, A. S. (1981) "Retail inventory behavior and business fluctuations," *Brookings Papers on Economic Activity*, vol. 2, pp. 443–505.

Carlson, J. and W. Wehrs (1974) "Aggregate inventory behavior," in G. Horwich and P. A. Samuelson (eds) *Trade, Stability and Macroeconomics: Essays in Honor of L. A. Metzler*, New York: Academic Press, pp. 331–2.

Feldstein, M. S. and A. Auerbach (1976) "Inventory behavior in durable goods manufacturing: the target adjustment model," *Brookings Papers on Economic Activity*, vol. 2, pp. 351–96.

Goldfeld, S. M. (1973) "The demand for money revisited," *Brookings Papers on Economic Activity*, vol. 3, pp. 683–730.

Goldfeld, S. M. (1976) "The case of the missing money," *Brookings Papers on Economic Activity*, no. 3, pp. 683–739.

Griliches, Z. (1967) "Distributed lags: a survey," *Econometrica*, vol. 35 (January), pp. 16–49.

Hafer, R. W. and S. E. Hein (1984) "Financial innovations and the interest elasticity of money demand: some historical evidence," *Journal of Money, Credit, and Banking*, vol. 16 (May), pp. 247–52.

Hatanaka, M. (1974) "An efficient two-step estimator for the dynamic adjustment model with autoregressive errors," *Journal of Econometrics*, vol. 2 (September), pp. 199–220.

Irvine, F. O. (1981a) "Retail inventory investment and the cost of capital," *American Economic Review*, vol. 71 (September), 633–48.

Irvine, F. O. (1981b) "Merchant wholesaler inventory investment and the cost of capital," *American Economic Review* (May), pp. 23–9.

Irvine, F. O. (1981c) "Specification errors and the stock-adjustment model: why estimated speeds-of-adjustment are too slow in inventory equations," Federal Reserve Working Paper (January).

Lieberman, C. (1980) "Inventory demand and cost of capital effects," *Review of Economics and Statistics*, vol. 62 (November), pp. 348–56.

Lovell, M. (1976) "Comments and discussion," *Brookings Papers on Economic Activity*, vol. 2, pp. 399–405.

Lovell, M. (1961) "Manufacturer's inventories, sales expectations, and the acceleration principle," *Econometrica*, vol. 28 (July), pp. 293–314.

Maccini, L. J. and R. J. Rossana (1984) "Joint production, quasi-fixed factors of production, and investment in finished goods inventories," *Journal of Money, Credit, and Banking*, vol. 16 (May), pp. 218–36.

Rubin, L. S. (1979–80) "Aggregate inventory behavior: its response to uncertainty and interest rates," *Journal of Post-Keynesian Economics* (Winter), pp. 201–11.

8 · DISTRIBUTION EFFECTS AND THE AGGREGATE CONSUMPTION FUNCTION

8.1 INTRODUCTION

Does the manner in which a given amount of income is distributed affect the fraction of it that is consumed? In the early post-Keynesian days it was commonly assumed, presumably on the basis of Keynes's own intuition, that it does – in particular that equalization of the income distribution would increase consumption. With the publication of Kuznets's (1942) and Goldsmith's (1955) data, and the ascendancy of the Friedman (1957) and Modigliani and Brumberg (1954) models of consumer behavior, this view fell into disrepute in academic circles. It was supplanted by the view that marginal, and perhaps even average, propensities to consume are constant over the income distribution. Of course, this "modern" view does not accord very well with intuition. It does, after all, seem "obvious" to most people, especially those not schooled in macroeconomics, that the rich save proportionately more than the poor, even at the margin.

While what is "obvious" is not always true, I was somewhat shocked to discover that the notion that aggregate consumption is independent of the income distribution has never been subjected to a direct empirical test. That is, the hypothesis that the *size distribution* of income does not affect consumption has never been treated as a special case of a more general class of consumption function and tested by standard statistical techniques. I propose to do so in this paper.

Let me begin with a confession. At the outset of this research I hoped to establish:

PROPOSITION A. *The marginal propensity to consume of an individual falls as his disposable income rises.*

I would like to thank, without implicating, Robert Barro, William Branson, Michael Darby, Ray Fair, Malcolm Fisher, Milton Friedman, Stephen Goldfeld, Michael Hurd, James MacKinnon, and Michael Rothschild for helpful comments which materially improved the content of this paper. The research reported herein has been generously supported by the National Science Foundation.

And therefore:

PROPOSITION B. *Out of any given total disposable income, a larger share is spent on consumption when income is more equally distributed.*

As it turns out, while both theory and empirical evidence lend at least some support to A, they do not support B. In fact, as I explain shortly, Proposition B does not follow from Proposition A. What does follow is the similar-sounding proposition:

PROPOSITION C. *If income is taken from one individual and given to another individual who is identical in all relevant respects save that his income is higher, then total consumption will decline.*

The next section develops the theoretical equipment necessary to investigate the effects of redistribution on aggregate consumption. I derive a plausible condition on individual utility functions which is sufficient to guarantee Proposition A, and then establish (as should be obvious) that A implies C. Section 8.3 explains why I view previous tests of the effect of income inequality on aggregate consumption as inconclusive, and derives a model for testing Proposition B in the context of the permanent income theory. Section 8.4 explains some compromises that had to be made because of weaknesses in the data, and presents the empirical results I have obtained with a compromise model. These results suggest that a rise in income inequality, disposable income held constant, would either have no effect on consumption or would actually *increase* it. That is to say, while Propositions A and C may be true, the obverse of B is given at least mild support by post-war American data. Section 8.5 offers a variety of possible explanations for this result, and the last section is a brief summary.

8.2 THE IMPLICATIONS OF PURE THEORY

8.2.1 Optimal life-cycle consumption

By now the derivation of the aggregate consumption function from a Fisherian model of intertemporal utility maximization, as pioneered by Modigliani and Brumberg (1954) and Friedman (1957), has achieved widespread acceptance. In this theory, the consumer chooses the time path for consumption, $c(t)$, which maximizes lifetime utility, subject to the constraint that the present discounted value of all consumption, plus the present discounted value of the bequest (if any), is equal to lifetime disposable resources, W. That is:

$$\int_0^T c(t)e^{-rt} + K_T e^{-rt} = W \tag{8.1}$$

where t is age, r is the rate of interest, T is the length of life, K_T is the bequest, and W is defined as the sum of the inheritance plus the present discounted value of earned income.[1] In order to get the typical "life cycle" or "permanent income" result that consumption at each instant is proportional to W, the lifetime utility functional must be of the form:

$$U = \int_0^T \frac{c(t)^{1-\delta}}{1-\delta} e^{-\rho t} dt + \frac{bK_T^{1-\beta}}{1-\beta}: \quad \delta, \beta > 0; b \geq 0 \qquad (8.2)$$

with the further stipulation that $\delta = \beta$.[2] Thus (8.2) represents a minor generalization of the Modigliani–Brumberg–Friedman (henceforth MBF) model – a generalization with important consequences for the question of distribution effects.

The maximization of (8.2) subject to (8.1) is a well-known problem, which was first studied by Strotz (1955–6). A heuristic method of solution is given in Appendix 8.1. For present purposes, it suffices to note that the optimal plan is given implicitly by the following equations:

$$c(t) = c_0 e^{gt}, \text{ where } g \equiv (r - \rho)/\delta \qquad (8.3)$$

$$c_0 = \phi(r, \rho, \delta, T)(W - K_T e^{-rT}) \qquad (8.4)$$

$$K_T = (be^{rT})^{1/\beta} c_0^{\delta/\beta}, \qquad (8.5)$$

where $\phi(\cdot)$ is a known function specified in Appendix 8.1.

The strict MBF model holds that consumption at each instant is proportional to W, with the constant of proportionality dependent on age (t), the length of life (T), the rate of interest (r), and tastes. This result follows from (8.3)–(8.5) under two sets of circumstances. The first is $b = 0$. This is the strict life-cycle model of Modigliani–Brumberg–Ando (MBA). If there is no utility from bequests, then the optimal K_T will be zero for every person, as is clear from (8.5). By (8.3) and (8.4), then, c_0 (and hence all $c[t]$) will be proportional to W. Specifically, $c(t) = \phi e^{gt} W$. The second condition is $\delta = \beta$. This is a modification mentioned by Modigliani and Ando (1960). In this case K_T is proportional to c_0 by (8.5), so that (8.3)–(8.5) can be solved to yield:

$$c(t) = \left(\frac{\phi e^{gt}}{1 + \phi b^{1/\delta} e^{rT(1-\delta)/\delta}} \right) \cdot W$$

It is important to note that these are the *only* two cases which give rise to strict proportionality, that is, a constant lifetime marginal propensity to consume (MPC). Extending the life-cycle model to allow for the bequest motive destroys the proportionality property unless $\delta = \beta$. The lifetime MPC in the more general case can be found by implicit differentiation in (8.3)–(8.5). The answer turns out to be:

$$\frac{\partial c^*}{\partial W} = \left(1 + \frac{\delta}{\beta} b^{1/\beta} e^{rT(1-\beta)/\beta} \phi^{\delta/\beta} c^{*(\delta/\beta)-1} \right)^{-1}$$

where:

$$c^* \equiv \int_0^T c(t)e^{-rt}\,dt$$

is lifetime consumption. In words, the lifetime MPC is smaller than unity as long as $b > 0$, and is decreasing with W if $\delta > \beta$ or increasing with W if $\beta > \delta$.

What do these conditions mean? If β, the elasticity of the marginal utility of bequests, exceeds δ, the elasticity of the marginal utility of consumption, then consumption is the luxury good, that is, has a wealth elasticity greater than unity. Conversely, if $\delta > \beta$, then bequests are the luxury good. It seems plausible, to me at least, that bequests should be the luxury good,[3] but, in the absence of the requisite empirical evidence, each reader is free to make his own judgment. My only purpose here is to establish that it is possible, within the basic MBF model, to have an MPC which either rises or falls with income.

8.2.2 The effect of redistribution on aggregate consumption

I shall now prove that, if the MPC declines with W, an increase in income inequality must reduce consumption. Conversely, if the MPC actually rises with W, a rise in inequality will increase consumption.

Consider a population of individuals identical in every respect save permanent income. Let y denote permanent income, defined as the flow equivalent of the stock of lifetime resources, so that y is proportional to W. Then the model of consumption behavior just developed implies $c = c(y)$, $1 > c'(y) > 0$, and $c''(y) \gtreqless 0$, according as $\delta \lesseqgtr \beta$. Let the distribution of permanent income be given by a density function $f(y, d)$, where d is a very general indicator of inequality to be explained shortly; and let $F(y, d)$ be the corresponding cumulative distribution function. Finally, let μ, a, and b denote, respectively, the average, lowest, and highest permanent income in the population.

It is easily established that:[4]

$$\mu = b - \int_a^b F(y, d)\,dy \tag{8.6}$$

The parameter d represents what Rothschild and Stiglitz (1970) have termed a "mean preserving spread." That is, a rise in d signifies a sequence of transfers from poorer persons to richer ones (called "regressive transfers") which leave the mean unchanged. I add the further stipulation (solely for convenience) that the maximum and minimum incomes are also unaffected, so that a change in d must satisfy the folowing:

$$\frac{\partial a}{\partial d} = \frac{\partial b}{\partial d} = 0 \tag{8.7a}$$

$$F_d(y, d) \text{ is continuous on the interval } a \leq y \leq b \tag{8.7b}$$

there is some y^* in the interval (a, b) such that:

$$F_d(y, d) \geq 0 \quad \text{for} \quad a \leq y \leq y^* \quad \text{and} \tag{8.7c}$$

$$F_d(y, d) \leq 0 \quad \text{for} \quad y^* \leq y \leq b$$

$$\frac{\partial \mu}{\partial d} = - \int_a^b F_d(y, d) dy = 0 \tag{8.7d}$$

The last requirement, that shifts in d leave the mean unchanged, follows from (8.6).

With the preliminaries thus established, the proof is quite direct.[5] Aggregate consumption is defined as:

$$C = \int_a^b c(y) f(y, d) dy$$

so that the effect of an increase in inequality on aggregate consumption is:

$$\frac{\partial C}{\partial d} = \int_a^b c(y) f_d(y, d) dy$$

Integrating this by parts yields:[6]

$$\frac{\partial C}{\partial d} = - \int_a^b c'(y) F_d(y, d) dy \tag{8.8}$$

First consider (8.8) in what I take to be the more plausible of the two cases the case where $c'(y)$ is falling. By (8.7), F_d is a continuous function which is positive when y is "low," is negative when y is "high," and integrates to zero over its entire range. The integral in (8.8) attaches higher weights to the (positive) values of F_d which occur when y is low than it does to the (negative) values of F_d which occur when y is high. Thus the integral must be positive, and $\partial C / \partial d$ must be negative. Conversely, if $c'(y)$ were a rising function of y, $\partial C / \partial d$ would be positive. Of course, if $c'(y)$ is constant, (8.7d) immediately implies that $\partial C / \partial d = 0$. In words, I have established:

PROPOSITION D. *A mean-preserving spread in the income distribution will decrease, leave unchanged, or increase aggregate consumption according as δ is greater than, equal to, or less than β.*

Of course, Propositions A and C follow from D only with the added assumption that $\delta > \beta$.

It is worth pausing at this juncture to consider what has *not* been proven. Proposition D refers only to transfers within a group which is identical in all relevant respects save income. It is not applicable to transfers from one socioeconomic group to another (*e.g.*, whites to blacks; men to women) if there is any reason to believe that tastes may differ in the two groups. Nor is it applicable to transfers where the age distribution of the donors differs from the age distribution of the recipients. Finally, the fact that the population consists of many age cohorts poses still another problem. Suppose $\delta > \beta$, and there is a decline in inequality in the older (donor) cohorts. As just noted, this would lead to greater average consumption within these cohorts. However, it would lead to lower average bequests, and hence to reduced consumption within the younger (recipient) cohorts. The macro consumption function will reflect both these changes.[7]

The practical implication of all this, of course, is that Proposition D gives no basis for predicting the effect on aggregate consumption of most real-world redistributions.[8] That is, it certainly does *not* establish Proposition B.

8.3 TESTING FOR DISTRIBUTION EFFECTS

8.3.1 The definition of income distribution

In the typical test for distribution effects in the aggregate consumption function, the income variable in the model is disaggregated into two or more components, and the hypothesis that the two (or more) regression coefficients are equal is tested. Suppose, for example, that the maintained hypothesis is represented by the estimating equation:

$$C_t = aY_t + bC_{t-1} + u_t \tag{8.9}$$

where Y_t is current disposable income (real or nominal; total or per capita) and C_t is consumer expenditures (defined symmetrically). A typical test is to divide Y_t into labor income (L_t) and property income (P_t), reformulate the model as:

$$C_t = a_1 L_t + a_2 P_t + bC_{t-1} + u_t$$

and test $a_1 = a_2$ against the alternative $a_1 > a_2$. Generally the null hypothesis of no distribution effects cannot be rejected.[9]

What is the rationale for this test? The theory outlined in Section 8.2 suggests that MPCs might differ by income bracket, not by source of income. Presumably there is no reason for an individual to spend a different fraction of the marginal dollar, depending on whether it accrues in the form of wages or dividends. Suits (1963), in a review of the early literature on this question, suggested one possible justification: "... since functional shares vary by income bracket, taking account of functional distribution makes some allowance for the curvature in the consumption function. ... " That is, distributive shares might be a proxy for the distribution of income by size. This assumes, for example, that an increase in labor's share is reliably associated with an equalization in the size distribution.

How accurate is this assumption? The reader familiar with American income distribution statistics since the Second World War will be immediately suspicious, since labor's share has steadily increased while most conventional measures of inequality in the size distribution have either been constant or exhibited some upward drift. In point of fact, the division of national income between labor and capital has only a tenuous relation to the size distribution. Table 8.1 presents the distribution of four components of total income in the United States in 1962. Except in the highest decile the distributions of wages and salaries and of business and property income are not radically different in the sense that knowing whether a given dollar went to "labor" or to "capital" conveys relatively little information about where that dollar landed in the size distribution. In fact, it is not unambiguously clear that "nonlabor income" is distributed more unequally than "labor income," for the Lorenz curves cross. If pensions and annuities are grouped with business and property income, the resemblance is even stronger. Thus, testing whether aggregate consumption is sensitive to the *factor share* distribution is not a fair test of whether aggregate consumption is sensitive to the *size* distribution. This is the first error I set out to correct.

8.3.2 The definition of consumption

The second error is the utilization of a theory of consumption to explain the behavior of *consumer expenditures*.[10] It is quite conceivable that the marginal propensity to *consume* could be falling with rising income while the marginal propensity to *spend on consumer goods and services* could be constant, or conversely.

To distinguish the various concepts of consumption, I introduce the following notation: C = consumption; CE = consumer expenditures, as de-

Table 8.1 US income distribution in 1962 by components

	Share (%) in:			
Decile group	wages and salaries	business and property income	pensions and annuities	other income
Lowest	0	0	11	4
Second	1	2	19	16
Third	3	4	16	24
Fourth	5	4	17	13
Fifth	8	6	4	9
Sixth	10	6	9	4
Seventh	13	6	5	7
Eighth	15	9	6	9
Ninth	18	13	4	9
Highest	27	51	8	5

Source: Projector, Weiss, and Thoresen (1969, table 4, p. 128).

fined in the national income accounts; CD = expenditures on consumer durables; and UD = use value of the stock of consumer durables, defined as the sum of depreciation plus imputed income. Then the following relation holds: $CE = C + CD - UD$, from which it follows that:

$$\frac{\partial^2 CE}{\partial Y^2} = \frac{\partial^2 C}{\partial Y^2} + \frac{\partial^2 CD}{\partial Y^2} - \frac{\partial^2 UD}{\partial Y^2} \qquad (8.10)$$

It is clear from this equation that a theoretical model which implies $\partial^2 C/\partial Y^2 < 0$ carries no obvious prediction about the sign of $\partial^2 CE/\partial Y^2$; in particular, it is possible for $\partial^2 CE/\partial Y^2$ to be zero or even positive. One objective of the present research was thus to test for distribution effects using aggregate *consumption*, rather than *consumer expenditures*. Fortunately, such a time series (complete with a consistent definition of disposable income)[11] has been constructed by the builders of the MIT–Penn–SSRC (MPS) econometric model.[12]

8.3.3 A statistical model deduced from the theory

While the theoretical bases of Friedman's permanent income model and Modigliani–Brumberg's life-cycle model are identical, the empirical formulations differ. I have followed Friedman's model (which expresses consumption as a function of current income and lagged consumption), rather than MBA's (which expresses consumption in terms of current *labor* income and net worth) solely because of data limitations. While there are several annual time series on the distribution of income, there are no time series on the distribution of wealth, and the distribution of labor income can only be guesstimated from the available data. (Example: How do you decompose income of the self-employed into "labor" and "property" components?)

The model of Section 8.2 implies that permanent consumption, c^*, is some (nonlinear and complicated) function of permanent income: $c^* = \psi(y^*)$. To make the problem tractable, I assume that $\psi(\cdot)$ is approximately linear *within* each income class. That is, if i is the index of income class, I assume $c_{it}^* = \gamma_i + k_i y_{it}^*$, where the γ_is and k_is may depend on interest rates. Allowing for some transitory consumption which is uncorrelated with permanent income, the expression for measured consumption in the ith income group is:

$$c_{it} = \gamma_i + k_i y_{it}^* + u_{it} \qquad (8.11)$$

where u_{it} is the transitory component. Summing over i to obtain aggregate consumption yields:

$$c_t = \sum_i c_{it} = \gamma + \sum_i k_i y_{it}^* + v_t \qquad (8.12)$$

where:

$$\gamma \equiv \sum_i \gamma_i \quad \text{and} \quad v_t \equiv \sum_i u_{it}$$

Were data on permanent income by income class available, (8.12) could be estimated directly. However, in the absence of such data, it is necessary to have proxies for the permanent income of each group. Following Friedman's suggestion, I assume:

$$y_{it}^* = (1 - \lambda_i)[y_{it} + (1 + m_i)\lambda_i y_{i,t-1} + (1 + m_i)^2 \lambda_i^2 y_{i,t-2} + \ldots]$$

where m_i is an extraneously estimated growth rate and $0 \le \lambda_i \le 1$. Under this assumption, (8.11) can be expressed as:

$$c_{it} = \gamma_i[1 - (1 + m_i)\lambda_i] + k_i(1 - \lambda_i)y_{it} + (1 + m_i)\lambda_i c_{i,t-1} + \eta_{it} \tag{8.13}$$

where $\eta_{it} = u_{it} - (1 + m_i)\lambda_i u_{i,t-1}$. Lacking data on consumption by income class, I am forced to assume that λ is the same for each income group. While m_i could easily be made different for each income class, the actual differences are so trivial that I ignore them. Summing (8.13) over i with $\lambda_i = \lambda$ and $m_i = m$ leads to:

$$C_t = \gamma[1 - (1 + m)\lambda] + (1 - \lambda)\sum_i k_i y_{it} + (1 + m)\lambda C_{t-1} + \eta_t$$

where:

$$\eta_t = \sum_i \eta_{it}$$

Note that if the model is well specified, the u_{it} in (8.11) will not display much serial correlation, but η_t will.[13] Also, it seems likely that the u_{it} (and hence η_t) would be heteroskedastic. If the standard deviation of the u_{it} grows proportionately with aggregate disposable income, a more efficient estimating equation would be:

$$\frac{C_t}{Y_t} = \frac{\gamma^*}{Y_t} + (1 - \lambda)\sum_i k_i\left(\frac{y_{it}}{Y_t}\right) + (1 + m)\lambda\frac{C_{t-1}}{Y_t} + \varepsilon_t \tag{8.14}$$

where $\gamma^* \equiv \gamma[1 - (1 + m)\lambda]$, $\varepsilon_t \equiv \eta_t/Y_t$, and Y_t is aggregate disposable income. In words, (8.14) requires regressing the average propensity to consume (APC) on the inverse of disposable income, the shares of each income group,[14] and the lagged APC adjusted for growth, $C_{t-1}/Y_t = (C_{t-1}/Y_{t-1})(Y_{t-1}/Y_t)$. If each k_i also depends on the rate of interest, r_t, then interaction terms between r_t and each income share should also be included. Since with five quintile shares this would involve nearly as many coefficients as observations, the constraint that $k_i = w_i + \xi r_t$ is imposed. That is, w, but not ξ, is permitted to vary across income classes.

8.4 EMPIRICAL RESULTS

8.4.1 The data

The average propensity to consume was obtained by dividing consumption (MPS definition) by disposable income (also MPS definition). Continuous time series (annually from 1947 to 1972) on the shares received by each quintile of families were obtained from the Bureau of the Census.[15]

The rate of interest posed the most complex measurement problem. What is wanted for a consumption function, presumably, is the *real* opportunity cost of a *consumer*. I first constructed a nominal savings rate, annually from 1949 to 1972, as a weighted average of the rates paid by commercial banks on time deposits, by savings and loan associations, and by mutual savings banks.[16] To obtain a real rate, I then subtracted a proxy for the expected rate of inflation. Following conventional procedures, I assumed an adaptive expectations mechanism:

$$\Pi_t = \theta \frac{\Delta P_t}{P_{t-1}} + (1 - \theta)\Pi_{t-1} \tag{8.15}$$

where Π_t is the expected rate of inflation and P_t is the actual price level (the deflator for personal consumption expenditures). To be sure that initial conditions did not influence the series, I started the series by assuming $\Pi_t = \Delta P_t / P_{t-1}$ for $t = 1930$, used the recursion formula (8.15) to generate Π_t from 1931 forward, and then discarded all the data prior to 1949.[17] The value of θ was chosen from the set $[0, 0.1, 0.2, \ldots, 1.0]$ so as to minimize the standard error of each regression. This is approximately equivalent to maximizing the likelihood function over θ, and the optimal value of θ is reported (without a standard error) with each regression.

8.4.2 Discussion of a failure

In brief, the regression is of the form:

$$\frac{C_t}{Y_t} = \frac{a_0}{Y_t} + a_4 + a_1 F_{1t} + a_2 F_{2t} + a_3 F_{3t} + a_5 F_{5t}$$

$$+ a_6 r_t + a_7 \frac{C_{t-1}}{Y_t} + \varepsilon_t \tag{8.16}$$

where F_{it} is the share of total income received by the ith quintile (counting from the bottom) of families. Note that since:

$$\sum_{i=1}^{5} F_{it} = 1$$

for all t, one quintile has to be omitted in order to avoid exact multicollinearity. The choice is arbitrary, and I selected the fourth quintile because it had the least variability.[18]

There are three obvious reasons why I was doomed to failure. First, with only 24 annual observations it is asking a lot of the data to estimate eight coefficients (seven parameters in (8.16) plus the autocorrelation coefficient). Second, as is well known, the income distribution has been relatively stable since the Second World War; and this means the Fs have very modest variances. Finally, even with one share omitted, considerable collinearity remains, since $F_{1t} + F_{2t} + F_{3t} + F_{5t} = 1 - F_{4t}$, for all t, and F_{4t} is nearly constant through time.

For what it is worth, the regression is reported in column 2 of Table 8.2. A constrained regression, which assumes equal MPCs for all income classes, is presented in column 1 for comparison. Even this latter regression allows for distribution effects of sorts. Recall that the MBF model has distribution effects unless $\delta = \beta$, and, when this equality holds, the consumption function should be strictly proportional. Since the constant (i.e., the coefficient of $1/Y$) in column 1 is significant at the 2 percent level (by a two-tail test), we can

Table 8.2 Regressions with quintile shares, 1949–72

| Variable | Coefficients (*t*-ratios) | | | | |
	(1)	(2)	(3)[a]	(4)	(5)
$1/Y$	57.51	46.28	42.80	46.36	44.77
	(2.6)	(2.1)	(2.1)	(2.2)	(2.3)
Constant	0.616	0.066	0.113	0.130	0.264
	(16.0)	(0.2)	(0.3)	(0.4)	(1.5)
r	−0.0019	−0.0022	−0.0021	−0.0018	−0.0022
	(−2.2)	(−2.1)	(−2.5)	(−2.4)	(−2.9)
C_{-1}/Y	0.253	0.290	0.312	0.312	0.295
	(3.4)	(3.8)	(4.1)	(3.9)	(4.1)
F_1	—	0.692	0.796	0.837	0.515
		(0.8)	(1.1)	(1.2)	(1.9)
F_2	—	0.168	—	—	—
		(0.1)			
F_3	—	0.997	0.908	0.837	0.515
		(1.2)	(1.1)	(1.2)	(1.9)
F_5	—	0.721	0.645	0.621	0.515
		(1.5)	(1.7)	(1.8)	(1.9)
$\hat{\rho}$	0.93	0.92	0.92	0.92	0.92
	(12.1)	(11.5)	(11.4)	(11.6)	(11.5)
θ	0.8	0.8	0.9	1.0	0.9
R^2	0.944	0.953	0.952	0.952	0.952
SE	0.00351	0.00364	0.00356	0.00344	0.00336

Notes: Estimation was by the Cochrane–Orcutt iterative technique; $\hat{\rho}$ is the estimated autocorrelation coefficient; *t*-ratios are in parentheses; as the standard errors are only valid under the assumption that θ is known, these ratios are indicative only; θ is the weight given to actual inflation in forming inflationary expectations (see eq. (8.15)).
(a) The equation with $\theta = 0.5$ had virtually the same standard error.

reject strict proportionality. On the basis of an extraneous estimate of the growth rate of real disposable income (FMP concept) of 3.83 percent per annum, it is possible to identify the underlying parameters. The implied estimate of λ is 0.24, a rather faster speed of adjustment than found by Friedman. Similarly, the long-run MPC (which, in this equation, is smaller than the APC) is 0.81 evaluated at the mean value of r;[19] this is, of course, lower than Friedman's estimate.

Although there is a hint of distribution effects, column 2 shows that equation (8.16) does not capture them at all well: the standard error of the regression exceeds that for column 1, and the estimated short-run MPCs are very suspect, ranging from 1.06 to 0.07. Clearly there is too much multi-collinearity among the F_is and too little data to get accurate estimates of subtle differences in MPCs.

One obvious approach is to omit one or more of the shares. This already compromises the theoretical model by imposing the constraint that some quintile has the same MPC as the fourth. For want of a better criterion, I omitted the quintile whose estimated MPC was closest to that of F_4; this led to the regression reported in column 3 of Table 8.2. The resulting standard error of estimate is still larger than in column 1 and autocorrelation is no less severe. As before, computed standard errors for individual shares are very high, suggesting multicollinearity.[20] I then imposed the further constraint that the first and third quintiles have identical MPCs to arrive at the regression in column 4. Here at last the standard error of the regression is reduced below that of the no-distribution-effects case, but the distribution variables are not very important.[21] Finally, using the same criterion, I omitted still another variable, leaving a single distributional variable in the regression. Column 5 is equation (8.16) subject to the constraints $a_2 = 0$, $a_1 = a_3 = a_5$.

Of all the regressions reported in Table 8.2, only column 5 can really be said to be an improvement over column 1. The lone distribution variable, $F_1 + F_3 + F_5$, has a coefficient nearly twice as large as its standard error.[22] This equation implies that the short-run MPCs (evaluated at the mean interest rate) are 0.26 for the second and fourth quintiles and 0.78 for the first, third, and fifth. The corresponding long-run MPCs are 0.36 and 1.09. The pattern is not entirely believable but is probably the best job of estimating quintile-specific MPCs that can be done in the absence of quintile-specific consumption data. In any event, there is certainly no indication that MPCs decline in higher income brackets, as is commonly assumed. Precisely what they do is not illuminated very well by Table 8.2.

8.4.3 The first compromise model

It is clear from these results that some compromise with the theory must be made if any estimation is to be done. And it is not clear that omitting variables (i.e., constraining certain MPCs to be equal) is the ideal compromise. I therefore tried two other approaches which at least have the virtue of allowing every distributional shift to affect aggregate consumption. The first involves constraining the way the MPC varies by income class and is explained in this subsection. The second entails replacing the quintile shares by one or another aggregate index of inequality and is discussed in the following subsection.

The basic model which I would like to estimate is essentially:

$$c_{it} = \gamma_i + (k_0^i + k_1^i r_t)y_{it} + \lambda c_{i,t-1} + u_{it} \tag{8.17}$$

The problem is that collinearity among the y_{it} precludes accurate estimation of the k_0^i and the k_1^i. Taking a cue from the technique introduced by Almon (1965) to cope with a similar problem in the case of distributed lags, one possibility is to assume a functional form for the dependence of k_0^i and/or k_1^i on i. I report below regressions based on the assumption that both of these coefficients are linear functions of i, but I also ran equations with ks assumed to be either quadratic or logarithmic functions of i. The results were essentially identical. Appending to equation (8.17) the constraints $k_0^i = m_0 + m_1 i$ and $k_1^i = n_0 + n_1 i$, summing over i, and simplifying leads to:

$$C_t = \gamma + m_0 Y_t + n_0 r_t Y_t + m_1 \sum_{i=1}^{5} iy_{it} + n_1 r_t \sum_{i=1}^{5} iy_{it} + \lambda C_{t-1} + V_t$$

where:

$$\gamma = \sum_{i=1}^{5} \gamma_i, \quad V_t = \sum_{i=1}^{5} u_{it}, \quad Y_t = \sum_{i=1}^{5} y_{it}$$

Dividing through by Y_t, and denoting the distributional variable

$$\sum_{i=1}^{5} i\left(\frac{y_{it}}{Y_t}\right)$$

by D_t, leads to the estimating equation:

$$\frac{C_t}{Y_t} = \frac{\gamma}{Y_t} + m_0 + n_0 r_t + m_1 D_t + n_1 r_t D_t + \lambda \frac{C_{t-1}}{Y_t} + v_t \tag{8.18}$$

where $v_t = V_t/Y_t$. Unfortunately, multicollinearity has still not been purged from the equation. Since D_t is relatively constant, r and rD are almost perfectly correlated, so I had to estimate one of two alternative models:

$$\frac{C_t}{Y_t} = \frac{\gamma}{Y_t} + m_0 + n_0 r_t + m_1 D_t + \lambda \frac{C_{t-1}}{Y_t} + v_t \quad (n_1 = 0) \tag{8.19a}$$

$$\frac{C_t}{Y_t} = \frac{\gamma}{Y_t} + m_0 + n_1 r_t D_t + m_1 D_t + \lambda \frac{C_{t-1}}{Y_t} + v_t \quad (n_0 = 0) \tag{8.19b}$$

Both variants are reported in Table 8.3. Once again, the expectations parameter in the definition of the real interest rate (θ) was chosen to minimize

Table 8.3 Regressions with constrained
MPCs, 1949–72

Variable	Coefficients (t-ratios)	
	(1)	(2)
$1/Y$	49.64	49.51
	(2.6)	(2.6)
Constant	0.283	0.279
	(1.2)	(1.2)
C_{-1}/Y	0.240	0.240
	(3.7)	(3.7)
r	−0.0028	—
	(−2.8)	
D	0.092	0.093
	(1.5)	(1.5)
rD	—	−0.0007
		(−2.8)
$\hat{\rho}$	0.92	0.92
	(11.6)	(11.6)
$\hat{\theta}$	0.7	0.7
R^2	0.947	0.947
SE	0.00352	0.00352

Note: See general note to Table 8.2.

the standard error; only the results with the optimal choice of θ are given in the table.[23]

It is obvious from Table 8.3 that the choice between (8.19a) and (8.19b) is a matter of indifference. The regressions tell a story which is rather similar to that of Table 8.2. Even if the value of θ were known *a priori* (so that the t-ratios reported in the table were valid), the null hypothesis of no distribution effects (*i.e.*, the null hypothesis that the coefficient of D or rD is zero) could not be rejected at the 10 percent level (two-tail test). But the point estimate suggests that increasing inequality actually increases consumption. To give the reader some feeling for magnitudes, when both r_t and D_t are at their mean values, the predicted short- and long-run MPCs are 0.63 and 0.82, respectively. If D should then rise by 10 percent, these figures would increase to 0.67 and 0.87. While these are not dramatic changes, they are substantial relative to typical year-to-year fluctuations in the observed APC. Were the point estimate of the distributional coefficient more precise, I would be tempted to conclude that there are moderate distributional effects which are opposite in direction to those normally assumed. However the large standard error makes this temptation easy to resist.

8.4.4 The second compromise model

My second compromise approach is to give up on estimating separate MPCs by income class in favor of estimating the effect of income inequality on aggregate consumption directly, using some conventional measure of inequality such as the Gini ratio or the variance of the logarithms. The great advantage of this approach is, of course, that it saves on degrees of freedom without constraining any particular MPCs to be equal. The disadvantage is that it embodies a weaker "no distribution effects" assumption of its own. For example, by employing the Gini ratio as the measure of inequality, I essentially impose the constraint that all possible redistributions which raise the Gini ratio by 0.01 have the same effect on consumption. Obviously, this need not be true, but it seems more innocuous than assuming away any distribution effects whatever. In any case, I prefer to view this model as a crude approximation to the true model – an approximation dictated by the weakness of the data.

The permanent income hypothesis is generally specified for regression purposes as:

$$C_t = \alpha_0 Y_t + \alpha_4 C_{t-1} + v_t \tag{8.20}$$

Friedman derived this by assuming that consumption is proportional to permanent income and that permanent income is a Koyck lag on measured income. But since this is the general framework in which I have tested for distribution effects throughout, it is worth noting that (8.20) can arise in other models as well. For example, (8.20) could represent Brown's (1952) habit-persistence model. Also, a regression very close to (8.20) could represent Duesenberry's (1949) relative income hypothesis, since, in annual data for the postwar era, "previous peak income" and lagged income are almost always identical.

The pure theory of consumer behavior implies that α_0 should be a function of the rate of interest, r_t, and I simply propose to add the inequality in the size distribution of income, d_t, to the list of arguments. That is, $\alpha_0 = \alpha_1 + \alpha_2 d_t + \alpha_3 r_t$. The null hypothesis to be tested is $\alpha_2 = 0$ against the two-tailed alternative: $\alpha_2 \neq 0$. The regression to be estimated, then, is:[24]

$$C_t = \gamma + (\alpha_1 + \alpha_2 d_t + \alpha_3 r_t) Y_t + \alpha_4 C_{t-1} + v_t \tag{8.21}$$

I again correct for heteroskedasticity by dividing (8.21) through by Y_t and estimate:

$$\frac{C_t}{Y_t} = \frac{\gamma}{Y_t} + \alpha_1 + \alpha_2 d_t + \alpha_3 r_t + \alpha_4 \frac{C_{t-1}}{Y_t} + e_t \tag{8.22}$$

where $e_t = v_t / Y_t$.

Several time series on overall income inequality, d_t, are available. Since it is by no means clear which measure best captures the relevant distributional shifts, I have run regressions with each of them. The measures are as follows:

G = the Gini concentration ratio of the distribution of money income (CPS concept) among families and unrelated individuals. This series is available for 1948–68 (with 1953 missing) in Budd (1970).

σ^2 = the variance of the logarithms of CPS money income among all persons with income over 14 years of age. This is available over 1947–70, as computed by Schultz (1971).

σ_M^2 = same as σ^2, but restricted to males.

σ_F^2 = same as σ^2, but restricted to females.

σ_{25}^2 = same as σ_M^2, but restricted to men at least 25 years of age. This has been calculated over 1949–69 by Chiswick and Mincer (1972).

σ_{64}^2 = same as σ_{25}^2, but excluding men over 65.

Following a suggestion made by Lubell (1947), I tried each variant of d in both current and lagged form. Regressions using current d are reported in Table 8.4, and regressions using lagged d are reported in Table 8.5.

Note that the period of estimation differs somewhat, depending on which variant of d is employed. Because of the paucity of data, I used every available data point rather than confine myself to a common sample period (which would have been 1949–52, 1954–68).

If σ^2, the variance of logarithms over the entire adult population, is used as the inequality measure, it does not matter much whether d_t or d_{t-1} enters the regression. In either the current or the lagged version the impact of inequality is apparently measured with some precision, and an increase of 0.03 in σ^2 (which is a fairly typical year-to-year change) would increase the average propensity to consume by about 0.3 of a percentage point in the short run and about 0.5 of a percentage point in the long run. These two equations are also notable for the absence of autocorrelation (a rare finding in this study)

Table 8.4 Regressions with current inequality measures

	Inequality measure					
Variable	σ^2 (1)	σ_M^2 (2)	σ_F^2 (3)	σ_{25}^2 (4)	σ_{64}^2 (5)	G (6)
$1/Y$	10.18	52.35	47.13	51.30	57.38	−9.48
	(1.3)	(2.2)	(2.0)	(2.1)	(2.5)	(−3.0)
Constant	0.347	0.567	0.594	0.596	0.630	0.371
	(7.4)	(11.9)	(9.4)	(12.8)	(17.3)	(4.1)
r	−0.0030	−0.0022	−0.0022	−0.0021	−0.0020	−0.0035
	(−3.5)	(−2.6)	(−2.6)	(−2.6)	(−2.51)	(−3.5)
C_{-1}/Y	0.509	0.290	0.307	0.293	0.244	0.631
	(7.0)	(3.4)	(3.7)	(3.6)	(3.4)	(10.9)
d	0.083	0.012	−0.014	−0.004	0.012	0.072
	(2.5)	(0.5)	(−0.4)	(−0.1)	(2.1)	(0.3)
$\hat{\rho}$	0.19	0.92	0.92	0.93	0.94	0.14
	(0.9)	(11.0)	(11.0)	(11.4)	(12.8)	(0.6)
$\hat{\theta}$	1.0	0.9	0.9	0.9	0.8	1.0
R^2	0.942	0.946	0.946	0.956	0.958	0.947
SE	0.00381	0.00366	0.00367	0.00338	0.00313	0.00392

Note: See general note to Table 8.2. The periods of estimation are: for σ^2, σ_M^2, and σ_F^2, 1949–70; for σ_{25}^2 and σ_{64}^2, 1949–69; for G, 1949–52, 1954–68.

Table 8.5 Regressions with lagged inequality measures

	Inequality measure					
Variable	σ^2 (1)	σ_M^2 (2)	σ_F^2 (3)	σ_{25}^2 (4)	σ_{64}^2 (5)	G (6)
$1/Y$	16.98	35.27	47.28	−8.94	−9.70	53.24
	(2.0)	(2.2)	(2.2)	(−3.1)	(−4.2)	(2.3)
Constant	0.353	0.521	0.562	0.395	0.393	0.641
	(8.5)	(10.7)	(8.6)	(7.3)	(8.5)	(7.8)
r	−0.0021	−0.0026	−0.0022	−0.0032	−0.0034	−0.0070
	(−2.2)	(−3.2)	(−2.7)	(−3.4)	(−3.8)	(−3.2)
C_{-1}/Y	0.457	0.340	0.311	0.580	0.588	0.220
	(5.6)	(5.5)	(4.0)	(8.0)	(9.3)	(3.4)
d_{-1}	0.099	0.034	0.010	0.060	0.071	0.066
	(3.1)	(1.5)	(0.3)	(1.8)	(2.8)	(0.4)
$\hat{\rho}$	0.07	0.91	0.92	0.29	0.19	0.93
	(0.4)	(10.2)	(11.4)	(1.4)	(0.8)	(10.6)
$\hat{\theta}$	1.0	0.8	0.9	1.0	1.0	0.3
R^2	0.940	0.948	0.947	0.928	0.940	0.961
SE	0.00382	0.00353	0.00359	0.00414	0.00376	0.00334

Note: See general note to Table 8.2. The periods of estimation are: for σ^2, σ_M^2, and σ_F^2, 1949–71; for σ_{25}^2 and σ_{64}^2, 1950–70; for G, 1949–53, 1955–69.

and for the slow speed of adjustment. In fact, inspection of the tables reveals a systematic relationship: the equations with slow adjustment speeds do not have autocorrelated residuals.

The only other measure which is "significant"[25] in both the current and the lagged specification is σ_{64}^2, the log variance among males aged 25–64. The current version exhibits trivially small distribution effects, and the lagged version has much larger ones. Other than these, only the regression with lagged σ_{25}^2 indicates significant distribution effects (at the 10 percent level in a two-tailed test). However, the persistent sign pattern is suggestive. Except for two trivially small coefficients, the point estimates all say that a rise in an inequality index leads to higher consumption. The next section is devoted to interpreting this conclusion and convincing the reader that it is not quite so outlandish as it may seem.

8.5 CAN THE RESULTS BE RIGHT?

I began this paper by contrasting what might be called the educated layman's view (that more equal income distributions give rise to more consumption) with the view that is now dominant among macroeconomists (that the income distribution does not matter). The empirical results certainly contradict the layman's view. Instead, they suggest either that consumption is independent of the income distribution or that distributions with less measured inequality give rise to somewhat less consumption. Is the latter possibility believable?[26]

To begin with pure theory, I showed in Section 8.2 that – in the optimal life-cycle consumption model – transfers from poor to rich will actually increase consumption if the elasticity of the marginal utility of bequests, β, exceeds the elasticity of the marginal utility of consumption, δ. So one interpretation of the data – an interpretation which I do not find particularly appealing – is that the rich actually consume a larger fraction of their lifetime resources because bequests have a wealth elasticity less than unity.[27]

Duesenberry's relative income hypothesis gives an alternative theoretical rationale for the empirical findings. In his model, utility attaches not to consumption but to the *ratio* of own consumption to a weighted average of consumption of others. The weights reflect the frequency of contact with individuals in other consumption classes, and Duesenberry hypothesizes that more contacts with individuals with higher consumption will increase the fraction of income that is consumed. Thus, *it is possible* that an equalization of the income distribution could reduce the number of contacts which most people have with persons much better off than themselves, and therefore reduce aggregate consumption (Duesenberry, 1949, pp. 44–5).[28]

A third explanation of the findings, and the one I find most satisfying, rests on the distinction between the kind of "ideal" redistributions that pure theory envisions and the actual redistributions that are reflected in post-war US data. Table 8.6 shows the net change over the entire sample period in each of the six measures of income inequality. The variable G is conceptually different from the other variables in two ways. First, it is a Gini ratio, not a log variance. But, more important, it uses families and unrelated individuals (pooled) as the recipient unit, whereas all the others are based on individuals. Thus, the six measures tell the following story. The distributions of income among *families*, and among males over 24 years old, hardly changed in the

Table 8.6 Post-war changes in income inequality

Measure	Initial value[a]	Final value[b]
σ^2	0.785	1.406
σ_M^2	0.668	1.187
σ_F^2	0.670	1.169
σ_{25}^2	0.742	0.729
σ_{64}^2	0.653	0.581
G	0.424	0.406

(a) 1947 for σ^2, σ_M^2, and σ_F^2; 1948 for G; and 1949 for σ_{25}^2 and σ_{64}^2.
(b) 1968 for G; 1969 for σ_{25}^2 and σ_{64}^2; 1970 for σ^2, σ_M^2, and σ_F^2.

post-war period; the decline in inequality was very slight. However, inequality fell much more noticeably among prime-age males (25–64 years old)[29] – suggesting that the gap between old and prime-age men widened. Further, among all individuals above 14 years of age, inequality rose substantially in the total population, among males, and among females. This suggests that substantial increases in the labor force participation of young people and women may have raised inequality by adding many new income recipients to the lower tail of the distribution.

A more detailed look at these phenomena can be obtained by consulting Tables 8.7–8.10. Tables 8.7 and 8.8 analyze the age–sex composition of the population which underlies each of the income distribution measures other than G, that is, all persons with income. It is clear from Table 8.7 that the distribution included many more teenage boys, and females of all ages except 35–44, in 1972 than it did in 1948. There are two principal reasons for such changes over time: demographic shifts in the age–sex composition of the population as a whole, and changes in labor force participation rates.[30] Table 8.8 shows that it is the former that accounts for the increased importance of teenage boys; their participation rate actually fell. Similarly, exogenous demographic factors appear to play the major role in the increased numbers of very young and very old women having income. However, for women aged 20–64, it appears that their increased importance in the income distribution is largely attributable to higher labor force participation.

Tables 8.9 and 8.10 contain similar information for shares in *income*, rather than in population. Table 8.9 highlights the increased importance of women over 20 in the overall income distribution. While they received only 17.2 percent of all income in 1948, this share rose to 24.4 percent by 1972. And Table 8.10 shows that this was accomplished despite a widening in the

Table 8.7 Fractions of all persons receiving income, by age-sex group

	Males		Females	
Age group	1948	1972	1948	1972
14–19	3.8	5.7	3.0	4.9
20–24	7.2	6.6	4.3	5.8
25–34	15.4	11.0	6.6	7.4
35–44	14.0	8.9	6.1	6.1
45–54	11.7	9.1	4.8	6.5
55–64	8.9	7.2	3.5	5.8
65 and up	6.6	6.8	4.1	8.3

Note: Totals may not add to 100% as a result of rounding.
Source: Computed by the author from data in US Bureau of the Census (1967, table 14; 1973, table 47).

Table 8.8 Labor force participation rates, by age-sex group

Age group	Males 1948	Males 1972	Females 1948	Females 1972
14–19	54.2	46.9	32.7	35.8
20–24	85.7	85.9	45.3	59.1
25–34	96.1	95.9	33.2	47.6
35–44	98.0	96.5	36.9	52.0
45–54	95.8	93.3	35.0	53.9
55–64	89.5	80.5	24.3	42.1
65 and up	46.8	24.4	9.1	9.3

Source: Figures for 14–19 age group were computed by the author from data in US Office of the President (1974, table A-1). Other figures came directly from that source.

Table 8.9 Shares in total money income, by age and sex

Age group	Males 1948	Males 1972	Females 1948	Females 1972
14–19	1.1	1.3	0.9	0.8
20–24	6.0	5.2	2.5	3.0
25–34	19.4	16.7	4.2	5.0
35–44	21.4	17.0	4.0	4.3
45–54	17.2	17.4	3.3	4.8
55–64	11.5	11.7	1.8	3.7
65 and up	5.1	5.7	1.4	3.6

Note: Totals do not add to 100% as a result of rounding
Source: Computed by the author from data in US Bureau of the Census (1967, tables 14, 36; 1973, table 47).

relative income gap between men and women. In fact, it is apparent from Table 8.10 that all groups except elderly women lost ground relative to prime-age males during this period.

In a word, these tables suggest the following anatomy of the rise in *measured* inequality *among persons with income* over the postwar period:

1. Purely demographic forces[31] led to a substantial increase in the number of teenagers and elderly women receiving income. Since these groups generally have low mean incomes (and, in the case of teenagers, also relatively high within-group variance), this alone would tend to raise inequality. Compounding this, the mean income of teenagers relative to prime-age males fell so sharply that their share in total income actually declined.[32]

Table 8.10 Relative mean incomes, by age and sex[a]

	Males		Females	
Age group	1948	1972	1948	1972
14–19	0.20	0.12	0.20	0.09
20–24	0.54	0.42	0.38	0.27
25–34	0.83	0.79	0.41	0.35
35–44	1.00	1.00	0.42	0.37
45–54	0.95	0.99	0.44	0.39
55–64	0.84	0.85	0.35	0.23
65 and up	0.51	0.44	0.23	0.29

Note:
(a) Ratio of mean income in each group to mean income of males aged 35–44.
Source: Same as for Table 8.7.

2. Marked increases in labor force participation of women between 20 and 64 years of age added a great number of relatively low incomes to the distribution, thus raising inequality as conventionally measured. This alleged rise in inequality strikes me as particularly illusory, since it is attributable to an artifact in construction of the data, that is, to defining the population as "all persons with income" rather than "all persons." Presumably, if all the "zeros" in both years had been included in the income distribution, the growth of the female labor force would have *reduced* measured inequality.

3. Incomes of males aged 20–24 and over 64, as well as all but the oldest women, declined relative to prime-age males. This represents a bona fide increase in inequality by most reasonable criteria, but it is very far afield from the idealized "regressive transfers" discussed in Section 8.2.2.

If these were the underlying changes in the income distribution, the regressions in Section 8.4 could be associating greater inequality with greater consumption if any of the following are true: (*a*) elderly women have higher-than-average marginal propensities to consume, (*b*) women have greater MPCs than men, or (*c*) prime-age males have lower-than-average MPCs.

Of these possibilities, the theory of optimal life-cycle consumption gives every reason to believe that (*a*) and (*c*) would be true. Given a typical "humped" income profile, consumer units will dissave while very young and very old, and save during the prime earning years. However, there seems to be no theoretical reason to believe in the veracity of (*b*).[33] Indeed, the theory of the household gives every reason to believe that the consumption behavior of married women and married men should be essentially identical.[34] And it is the married women (in particular, those married with spouse present) who have registered the greatest gains in labor force participation over this period.[35]

Finally, the only other study known to me which included the *size* distribution of income in the consumption function also obtained the "odd" result that increased inequality led to increased consumption. Metcalf (1972) was rather puzzled by the finding and noted that "while a number of significant relationships were uncovered, it is not yet clear how the results should be interpreted" (pp. 148–9). The distributional variable in his preferred consumption function is the ratio of income at the ninetieth percentile to mean income, and he concluded that "the higher the top decile income relative to the mean, the higher the marginal propensity to consume" (p. 152).[36]

8.6 SUMMARY

In this chapter I have shown that the established theory of consumer behavior carries definite implications as to the effect of a sequence of regressive transfers on aggregate consumption. Such an increase in inequality must reduce *consumption* if bequests are a luxury good (or increase consumption if own consumption is the luxury good). However, this does *not* say that such a redistribution would necessarily reduce *consumer expenditures*. Nor does it say that aggregate consumption must fall as a result of the kinds of redistributions that have taken place in the post-war United States. Finally, the theory (and the facts) give no reason to believe that a shift in the *factor share* distribution will have any particular effect upon consumption.

The only rigorously correct way to test for the existence of distribution effects in the aggregate consumption function is to estimate directly separate marginal propensities to consume by income class. Unfortunately, the data are too weak to allow this, so several "second best" procedures were adopted. First, various MPCs were constrained to be equal to one another; then a method similar to the Almon lag technique was used to constrain the variation in MPCs; finally, the MPCs were ignored and an aggregate measure of inequality was inserted in the consumption function. The upshot of all this appears to be that equalizing the income distribution will either have no bearing on or (slightly) reduce aggregate consumption.

Several reasons for the latter possibility were suggested. Of these, I find two most appealing. First, if the kinds of "demonstration effects" stressed by Duesenberry are at all important, disequalization can conceivably lead to more rather than less consumption. Second, income inequality in the post-war United States increased largely because of demographic shifts and increased labor force participation of women. Had these women been counted as "zeros" in the income distribution while out of the labor force, rather than omitted, income inequality might well have fallen. Thus the observed positive effect of certain inequality measures on consumption may be misleading.

As a by-product, this study has shed some additional light on other properties of the consumption function. In all specifications, I find an absence of money illusion, a very small negative interest elasticity, and a rather fast adjustment of inflationary expectations to actual inflation.

NOTES

1. Equation (8.1) is the budget constraint only under the assumption of a perfect capital market. This same assumption allows me to collapse all gifts to heirs into a single number, K_T. That is, an *inter vivos* gift of G given at age t is *equivalent* – for both donor and recipient – to a gift of $Ge^{r(T-t)}$ at death.
2. This is implied by some results of Yaari (1964) and is developed in some detail in Blinder (1974, ch. 2).
3. Becker's recent analysis of intergenerational transfers (1974) provides some theoretical support for the notion that $\delta > \beta$. Consider, for simplicity, a two-generation family. Letting c_i denote lifetime consumption, W_i denote lifetime wealth, and m_i denote the part of W_i not inherited, the budget constraints for generations $i = 1, 2$ would be $c_1 + k = W_1$ and $c_2 = W_2 \equiv m_2 + k$, where k is the bequest from generation 1 to generation 2, and all quantities are discounted to a common date ($c_2 = W_2$, since generation 2 leaves no bequest). Becker observes that the two budget constraints can be collapsed to $c_1 + c_2 = W_1 + m_2 \equiv S$, where S is what he calls "social income." He then shows that if the elasticity of c_1 (and therefore also of c_2) with respect to S is approximately unity, the elasticity of k with respect to W_1 (which is my δ/β) must exceed unity. The proof is almost immediate. Let η_{xy} denote the elasticity of x with respect to y. The budget constraint for generation 1 implies that a weighted average of $\eta_{c_1 W_1}$ and η_{kW_1} equals unity. But $\eta_{c_1 S} = 1$ implies that $\eta_{c_1 W_1} = (W_1/S)\eta_{c_1 S} < 1$. It is thus clear that $\eta_{kW_1} > 1$. QED.
4. *Proof:* By definition:

$$\mu = \int_a^b yf(y, d)dy$$

Integrating this by parts yields:

$$\mu = yF(y, d)\Big|_a^b - \int_a^b F(y, d)dy$$

Equation (8.6) follows by noting that $F(b, d) = 1$, $F(a, d) = 0$
5. The proof follows a suggestion by Rothschild and Stiglitz (1970, p. 237 n).
6. Again I use the fact that $F(b, d) = 1$, $F(a, d) = 0$.
7. I owe this last point to Robert Barro.
8. The theory does, however, have testable implications that are not given in Proposition D. For example, *ceteris paribus*, a transfer from the young to the old will increase consumption (assuming g is positive).
9. The most recent example of this is Taylor (1971), who cannot reject $a_1 = a_2$ but does find significantly different MPCs out of transfers and other types of income.
10. This difficulty is noted by Mayer (1972, pp. 12–16), who nonetheless uses consumer expenditures in his tests.
11. As Mayer (1972, p. 15) notes, this is important. The few previous studies of the consumption function which used C, rather than CE, as the dependent variable failed to use a consistent concept of disposable income.

12. It should be noted that the MPS model does not classify residential structures as a consumer durable. Thus neither consumption nor disposable income includes the imputed yield on owner-occupied houses.

13. Worse yet, η_t is a first-order moving average rather than an autoregressive process. Strictly speaking this makes standard procedures for dealing with autocorrelation inappropriate. However, Shaman (1969) has shown that the inverse of the covariance matrix of a first-order moving average is best approximated by the inverse covariance matrix of a first-order autoregressive. This provides a pragmatic justification for my use of the Cochrane–Orcutt technique in the subsequent estimation. I am indebted to Michael Hurd for a valuable discussion on this point.

14. Note that using the Koyck representation of permanent income makes it appropriate to use the shares in *measured*, rather than *permanent*, income for the estimation of distribution effects in (8.14).

15. I wish to thank the Bureau of the Census for furnishing me with the data prior to publication. The distributions, of course, are based on the Current Population Survey (CPS) definition of total money income. It should be noted that the shares were tabulated from ungrouped data from 1958 through 1972, but from grouped data from 1947 through 1958. In using these series I averaged the two figures for 1958. See US Bureau of the Census (1973, table 16).

16. The three constituent rates were obtained from the MPS model data file and are only available from 1949 on. The weights used were 7/16 for time deposits, 6/16 for savings and loan shares, and 3/16 for mutual savings bank shares. I adopted this weighting scheme from Springer (1973).

17. It is hard to defend the notion that expectations are strictly adaptive in historical episodes that include drastic events such as the Great Depression and the Second World War. However, my estimated θ is always so high that the influence of 1930–47 price behavior on 1949–72 expectations is negligible.

18. Analogous regressions were run using the shares received by unrelated individuals as well. The results were always similar, but slightly inferior to those reported below.

19. The estimated short- and long-run MPCs are actually quite insensitive to r. The interest elasticity of consumption (evaluated at the means) in col. 1 is -0.0027 in the short run and -0.0035 in the long run. Other equations gave similarly trivial elasticities.

20. In view of the way the hypothesis is obtained from the data, these standard errors are purely indicative and cannot be used for hypothesis testing. In particular, the ratio of a coefficient to its "standard error" certainly does not have a t-distribution.

21. An "F-test" of the null hypothesis that both distribution variables have zero coefficients fails to reject the null hypothesis at the 5 percent level, but just barely. The computed F-value is 3.04, as compared to a critical 5 percent point in the $F(2, 17)$ distribution of 3.59. As noted in note 20 above, the test statistic does not really have an F-distribution because the restrictions $a_2 = 0$ and $a_1 = a_3$ were obtained from the data. The "test" is meant to be heuristic only.

22. The reader is again reminded of the caveat raised in note 20 above.

23. Other results are available on request. In view of the interest in money illusion elicited by Branson and Klevorick's paper (1969), I experimented with an alternative specification using the inverse of *nominal* disposable income in place of the inverse of *real* disposable income. In every case, the real specification gave a better fit, indicating an absence of money illusion.

24. Equation (8.21) cannot be offered as an accurate representation of Friedman's model for the following reason. Adding distribution effects to Friedman's model in the way I have suggested gives $C_t = (k_0 + k_1 d_t + k_2 r_t) Y_t^*$, where Y^* is permanent

income. Adopting the Koyck lag for permanent income, as Friedman suggested, gives $Y_t^* - \lambda Y_{t-1}^* = (1 - \lambda) Y_t$, but applying the same Koyck transformation to C_t gives:

$$
\begin{aligned}
C_t - \lambda C_{t-1} &= k_t Y_t^* - \lambda k_{t-1} Y_{t-1}^* \\
&= k_t (Y_t^* - \lambda Y_{t-1}^*) + \lambda Y_{t-1}^* (k_t - k_{t-1}) \\
&= k_t (1 - \lambda) Y_t + \lambda Y_{t-1}^* (k_1 d_t - k_1 d_{t-1} + k_2 r_t - k_2 r_{t-1})
\end{aligned}
$$

Since Y_{t-1}^* is not observable, this equation is not suitable for empirical analysis. Thus equation (8.21) was adopted instead. Note that this difficulty would arise even without distribution effects, as long as the rate of interest is allowed to affect the MPC.

25. As noted, significance tests are valid only on the assumption that θ is known *a priori*.

26. To be sure, the arguments I am about to give are not terribly convincing on *a priori* grounds. They are offered as conceivable explanations of a counterintuitive result which gets at least mild support from the data.

27. Becker's (1974) analysis shows that $\delta \leq \beta$ implies that the intergenerational distribution of consumption shifts in favor of the current generation as the economy gets richer. See note 3 above.

28. While this is possible, the reverse could also happen, as was pointed out by Johnson (1951).

29. Shultz (1971, p. 11) actually finds a 17 percent *rise* in the log variance of income among males aged 25–64 over the period 1947–70. But most of this occurs between 1947 and 1949.

30. This ignores any changes in the fraction of each age-sex group receiving property (but not labor) income.

31. This phrase is not meant to deny that there may have been economic reasons behind these phenomena. It simply connotes that the variable itself (age–sex distribution) is a demographic one rather than an economic one like labor-force participation rates).

32. The drop in relative incomes may well have been caused by the increase in relative labor supplies, but that is beyond the scope of this paper.

33. This, of course, does not prove that (b) is false. It would be true, for example, if wives typically entered the labor force to finance the acquisition of specific consumer durables which the family wished to purchase.

34. In March 1972, 58.4 percent of the females in the labor force were married with a husband present. The remainder included single, widowed, divorced, and separated women (see US Office of the President 1974, table B-1).

35. Labor force participation among "married, spouse present" women rose from 22 percent in 1948 to 41.5 percent in 1972, while participation rates were virtually trendless for other categories of women. (See US Office of the President 1974, table B-2.)

36. A further possibility, which I regard more as an intellectual curiosum than as a practical explanation of the results, is that the log variance could conceivably *increase* while inequality is actually falling by the mean-preserving spread criterion. To show this, I follow Atkinson's (1970) approach to inequality measurement, which assumes an additive social welfare function, $W = \int u(y) f(y) dy$, where $u(y)$ is the social welfare significance of a person's receiving income y, and $f(y)$ is the income density function. The specific utility function implicit in using the variance of logarithms, $V \sim \int (\log y - k)^2 f(y) dy$, where $k \equiv E(\log y)$, as the inequality measure is clearly $u(y) = (\log y - k)^2$. As first noted by Atkinson (1970, p. 13), this function is not concave over its entire range; therefore a sequence of *regressive*

transfers might actually *raise* social welfare (Rothschild and Stiglitz (1973)). Since five of the six inequality measures are variances of logarithms, they may not be correct indicators of the direction of change in inequality.
37. Assuming $U(\cdot)$ and $B(\cdot)$ are strictly concave, these are also sufficient. Also the assumptions

$$\lim_{c(t) \to 0} U'[c(t)] = \infty \quad \text{and} \quad \lim_{K(T) \to 0} B'[K(t)] = \infty$$

rule out the possibility of corner solutions.

REFERENCES

Almon, S. (1965) "The distributed lag between capital appropriations and expenditures," *Econometrica*, vol. 33 (January), pp. 178–96.

Atkinson, A. B. (1970) "On the measurement of inequality," *Journal of Economic Theory*, vol. 2 (September), pp. 244–63.

Becker, G. S. (1974) "A theory of social interactions," *Journal of Political Economy*, vol. 82, no. 6 (November/December), pp. 1063–93.

Blinder, A. S. (1974) *Toward an Economic Theory of Income Distribution*. Cambridge, Mass.: MIT.

Branson, W. H., and A. K. Klevorick. (1969) "Money illusion and the aggregate consumption function," *American Economic Review*, vol. 59 (December), pp. 832–49.

Brown, T. M. (1952) "Habit persistence and lags in consumer behavior," *Econometrica*, vol. 20 (July), pp. 355–71.

Budd, E. C. (1970) "Postwar changes in the size distribution of income in the US," *American Economic Review*, vol. 60 (May), pp. 247–60.

Chiswick, B. R., and J. Mincer (1972) "Time series changes in personal income inequality in the United States from 1939, with projections to 1985," *Journal of Political Economy*, vol. 80, no. 3, pt. 2 (May/June), pp. S34̄66.

Duesenberry, J. S. (1949) *Income, Saving, and the Theory of Consumer Behavior*, Cambridge, Mass.: Harvard University Press.

Friedman, M. (1957) *A Theory of the Consumption Function*, Princeton, N.J.: Princeton University Press.

Goldsmith, R. (1955) *A Study of Saving in the United States*, vol. 1, Princeton, N.J.: Princeton University Press.

Johnson, H. G. (1951) "A note on the effect of income redistribution on aggregate consumption with interdependent consumer preferences," *Economica*, vol. 18 (August), pp. 295–7.

Kuznets, S. (1942) *Uses of National Income in Peace and War*, New York: National Bureau of Economic Research.

Lubell, H. (1947) "Effects of redistribution of income on consumers' expenditures," *American Economic Review*, vol. 37 (March), pp. 157–70.

Mayer, T. (1972) *Permanent Income, Wealth, and Consumption*, Berkeley: University of California Press.

Metcalf, C. E. (1972) *An Econometric Model of the Income Distribution*, Chicago: Markham.

Modigliani, F., and A. Ando (1960) "The 'permanent income' and the 'life cycle' hypothesis of saving behavior: comparisons and tests," In I. Friend and R. Jones (eds), *Proceedings of the Conference on Consumption and Saving*, vol. 2, Philadelphia: University of Pennsylvania.

Modigliani, F., and R. Brumberg (1954) "Utility analysis and the consumption function: an interpretation of cross-section data," In K. K. Kurihara (ed.), *Post-Keynesian Economics*, New Brunswick, N.J.: Rutgers University Press.

Projector, D. S., G. S. Weiss, and E. T. Thoresen (1969) "Composition of income as shown by the survey of financial characteristics of consumers," In L. Soltow (ed.) *Six Papers on the Size Distribution of Wealth and Income*, New York: Columbia University Press.

Rothschild, M., and J. E. Stiglitz (1970) "Increasing risk. I. A. definition," *Journal of Economic Theory*, vol. 2 (September), pp. 225–43.

Rothschild, M. and J. E. Stiglitz (1973) "Some further results on the measurement of inequality," *Journal of Economic Theory*, vol. 6 (April), pp. 188–204.

Schultz, T. P. (1971) "Long term changes in personal income distribution: theoretical approaches, evidence and explanations," paper presented at the meetings of the American Economic Association, New Orleans (December).

Shaman, P. (1969) "On the inverse of the covariance matrix of a first order moving average," *Biometrika*, vol. 56, pp. 595–600.

Springer, W. L. (1973) "Windfalls, temporary income taxes, and consumption behavior," PhD dissertation, Princeton University.

Strotz, R. H. (1955–6) "Myopia and inconsistency in dynamic utility maximization," *Review of Economic Studies*, vol. 23, no. 3, pp. 165–80.

Suits, D. B. (1963) "The determinants of consumer expenditure: a review of present knowledge," In *Impacts of Monetary Policy, Commission on Money and Credit*, Englewood Cliffs: Prentice-Hall.

Taylor, L. D. (1971) "Saving out of different types of income," *Brookings Papers on Economic Activity*, vol. 2, no. 2, pp. 383–407.

US Bureau of the Census (1967) *Trends in the Income of Families and Persons in the United States, 1947–1964*, Technical Paper no. 17, Washington: Government Printing Office.

US Bureau of the Census (1973) *Current Population Reports*, ser. P-60, no. 90. *Money Income in 1972 of Families and Persons in the United States*, Washington: Government Printing Office.

US Office of the President (1974) *Manpower Report of the President*, Washington: Government Printing Office.

Yaari, M. E. (1964) "On the consumer's lifetime allocation process," *International Economic Review*, vol. 5 (September), pp. 304–17.

APPENDIX 8.1

SOLUTION OF THE OPTIMAL CONSUMPTION PROBLEM WITH A BEQUEST MOTIVE

The problem is to pick a time pattern of consumption, $c(t)$, and a level of terminal assets, $K(T)$, so as to maximize:

$$\int_0^T U[c(t)]e^{-\rho t}dt + B[K(T)] \tag{A8.1}$$

subject to the lifetime budget constraint:

$$\int_0^T c(t)e^{-rt}dt + K(T)e^{-rt} = W \tag{A8.2}$$

Defining the functional,

$$L[c(t), K(T)] = \int_0^T U[c(t)]e^{-\rho t}dt + B[K(T)]$$
$$+ \lambda\left[W - \int_0^T c(t)e^{-rt}dt - K(T)e^{-rt}\right]$$

the first-order conditions are:[37]

$$\frac{\partial L}{\partial c(t)} = U'[c(t)]e^{-\rho t} - \lambda e^{-rt} = 0 \text{ for all } t \tag{A8.3}$$

$$\frac{\partial L}{\partial K(T)} = B'[K(T)] - \lambda e^{-rT} = 0 \tag{A8.4}$$

Equation (A8.4), of course, is simply the transversality condition, since $\lambda e^{-rT} = U'[c(T)]e^{-\rho T}$ by (A8.3). Solving (A8.3) under the specific functional form $U[c(t)] = [c(t)^{1-\delta}]/(1-\delta)$ gives:

$$c(t)^{-\delta} = \lambda e^{-(r-\rho)t} \tag{A8.5}$$

from which it follows that λ is related to the initial level of consumption by:

$$c(0)^{-\delta} = \lambda \quad \text{or} \quad c(0) = \lambda^{-1/\delta} \tag{A8.6}$$

Therefore (A8.5) becomes:

$$c(t) = \lambda^{-1/\delta}e^{[(r-\rho)/\delta]t} = c(0)e^{[(r-\rho)/\delta]t}$$

by (A8.6), which is equation (8.3) in the text.

Now use (A8.6) and the specific functional form:

$$B[K(T)] = \frac{bK(T)^{1-\beta}}{1-\beta}$$

to express (A8.4) as $bK_T^{-\beta} = c(0)^{-\delta}e^{-rT}$, or $K_T = (be^{rT})^{1/\beta}c(0)^{\delta/\beta}$, which is equation (8.5) in the text.

Finally, return to the budget constraint, equation (A8.2), to write:

$$W - K(T)e^{-rT} = \int_0^T c(t)e^{-rt}\,dt$$

$$= c(0)\int_0^T e^{[(r-\rho)/\delta]t}e^{-rt}\,dt$$

$$= c(0)\int_0^T e^{\{[r(1-\delta)-\rho]/\delta\}t}\,dt$$

which is equation (8.4) in the text with:

$$\phi(r, \rho, \delta, T) \equiv \left[\int_0^T e^{\{[r(1-\delta)-\rho]/\delta\}t}\,dt\right]^{-1}$$

9 · TEMPORARY INCOME TAXES AND CONSUMER SPENDING

In 1968, faced with a classic case of demand inflation, Congress enacted a temporary increase in personal income tax payments to curb aggregate demand. In 1975, near the trough of our worst postwar recession, Congress enacted a tax rebate and other temporary decreases in taxes and increases in transfer payments designed to stimulate aggregate demand. Questions have been raised about the effectiveness of both measures.

The questions have both theoretical and empirical roots. On theoretical grounds, the permanent income–life cycle hypothesis seems to argue that temporary income tax changes should have little effect on consumer spending in principle. On empirical grounds, data on consumer behavior seem to suggest that the impacts of the two temporary taxes on spending were also small in practice. In 1968, the savings rate fell from 7.5 percent in the quarter immediately preceding the tax surcharge (1968:2) to only 5.6 percent in the first quarter of the surtax, suggesting that consumers kept spending despite the tax. In 1975, the savings rate ballooned from 6.4 percent just prior to the rebate to a stunning 9.7 percent in the quarter of the rebate (1975:2), suggesting that little of the rebate was spent.

The purpose of this paper is to study these two temporary tax changes in some detail. Precisely what prediction does economic theory make about the relative effectiveness of temporary versus permanent tax changes? And what conclusions can be reached from US time-series data? The fact that the Carter

This paper benefited from seminar presentations at Princeton, Hebrew University of Jerusalem, Tel-Aviv University, and the University of Pennsylvania, and from helpful suggestions from Walter Dolde, Marjorie Flavin, Roger Gordon, Levis Kochin, Robert Solow, James Trussell, and a referee of the *Journal of Political Economy*. Most of the laborious computations were done expertly by Suzanne Heller; additional research assistance was provided by David Card, Robin Lindsey, and William Newton. Stephen Goldfeld and Richard Quandt generously guided this novice through the intricacies of their nonlinear optimization routines. Financial support from the National Science Foundation and from the Institute for Advanced Studies in Jerusalem, where part of this work was done, is gratefully acknowledged. This research is part of the National Bureau of Economic Research's program in economic fluctuations, but any opinions expressed herein are those of the author, not of the NBER.

administration asked for (but did not get) a repeat performance of the rebate in 1977 suggests that there is more than academic interest in the answers to these questions.

Section 9.1 outlines the theoretical issues, beginning with an idealized life-cycle model and proceeding to introduce some important "real world" considerations. Since the discussion shows quite clearly that the issue is an empirical one, Section 9.2 reviews previous empirical work on the subject very briefly. Section 9.3 explains the underlying basis of the empirical model of this paper, relating it to recent literature on rational expectations and the permanent income hypothesis (PIH), and then Sections 9.4 and 9.5 show how this basic conceptual framework was converted into an operational empirical model. The estimates are presented and analyzed in Section 9.6, and Section 9.7 summarizes the main conclusions.

9.1 THE IMPLICATIONS OF THEORY: PURE AND IMPURE

9.1.1 The pure permanent income-life-cycle theory

As Eisner (1969) pointed out some time ago, the PIH casts doubt on the effectiveness of income tax changes that are labeled as temporary because such measures have only minor effects on permanent income. To develop a theoretical benchmark for the marginal propensity to consume (MPC) that the PIH suggests might apply to a temporary tax, consider a rarefied world in which consumers with exogenous earnings streams select consumption paths to maximize lifetime utility. If capital markets are perfect, only the discounted present values of the earnings streams matter, so suppose all households earn a constant income y per year. Assume further that households differ only in age, a; that the real rate of interest is zero; and that the subjective rate of time discounting is also zero.[1] The question is, if income taxes are raised by z per capita for the period from $t = 0$ to $t = t_1$, how much less will consumers spend over this interval?

In answering this question, there are three population groups to keep track of. People who are "alive" (in the economic sense) at $t = 0$ and who live past the expiration of the tax suffer an income loss of $t_1 z$ over the period. If T denotes the length of life, then each such person of age a consumes a fraction $t_1/(T - a)$ of this loss during the years in which the temporary tax is in effect. Thus the change in consumption per capita is $\Delta C_1 = z t_1^2/(T - a)$.

Old people who are alive at $t = 0$, but die before $t = t_1$, lose only $(T - a)z$ in income. However, since they have MPCs of unity during the surtax period as a whole, their change in consumption per capita is $\Delta C_2 = (T - a)z$.

Finally, we must worry about people who are born between $t = 0$ and $t = t_1$. If a, a negative number between 0 and $-t_1$, denotes the age of such a person, and he lives for $t_1 + a < t_1$ years during the period $0 \leqslant t \leqslant t_1$, his income loss is $(t_1 + a)z$. Since he spends a fraction $(t_1 + a)/T$ of this income during the period $0 \leqslant t \leqslant t_1$, the change in his consumption is $\Delta C_3 = [z(t_1 + a)^2]/T$.

To derive the aggregate change in per capita consumption, weigh these groups by the age distribution, considering the ages $-t_1 \leqslant a \leqslant T$. In the simplest case of a uniform age distribution, $f(a) = 1/T$, the change is:

$$\Delta C = \int_0^{T-t_1} \frac{\Delta C_1}{T}\, da + \int_{T-t_1}^{T} \frac{\Delta C_2}{T}\, da + \int_{-t_1}^{0} \frac{\Delta C_3}{T}\, da$$

Working out the integrals and dividing by the total income that is taxed away during the period ($t_1 z$ per capita), we obtain:

$$\text{MPC} = \frac{t_1}{T}(\log T - \log t_1) + \left[1 - \frac{T}{2t_1} + \frac{(T-t_1)^2}{2Tt_1} \right] + \frac{t_1^2}{3T^2}$$

where the three terms show the contributions of the three different population groups.

To take a concrete example, suppose the typical lifetime of a household head as a household head is $T = 50$ years. Then, according to this formula, the MPC for a 1 year tax ($t_1 = 1$) is 0.09, while that for a 2 year tax ($t_1 = 2$) is 0.15.2 The MPC = 0.09 for a 1 year temporary tax is only a rough benchmark representing the pure PIH, and there are a number of reasons why the theory probably systematically understates the responses of consumers to temporary taxes (see below), so we should not take this number too seriously. Still, there are two lessons worth drawing from this simple exercise – lessons that have often been forgotten in the temporary-tax debate.

1. Income gains and losses from temporary taxes will eventually be spent just like any other increment or decrement to lifetime resources: if less is spent at first (because $t_1 < T$), then more will be spent later. Thus, if we want to inquire about the "effectiveness" of temporary taxes, we must specify a time horizon. Over a long enough run, they must be just as "effective" as permanent ones.

2. The so-called zero effect view – that consumers ignore the surtax and consume as if it never happened – does not represent the PIH at all. Instead, that theory says that consumers should spend precisely what they would on receipt of a windfall gain (or loss) of $t_1 z$. In the illustrative calculation, this turns out to be the "9 percent effect" view.

9.1.2 Caveats and imperfections

There are several reasons why surtaxes may affect spending more strongly than indicated by pure theory. First, tax-induced income changes that are not consumed must be saved. If windfall gains are used to purchase durable goods, consumer spending may rise much more strongly than consumption;

the converse may happen when there are windfall losses. The magnitude of the marginal propensity to spend windfalls on durable goods is, of course, an empirical question.[3]

Second, some households may be subject to liquidity constraints that are usually ignored by the PIH. If we stay within the certainty context, these constrained households will react strongly to even temporary income changes.[4] Thus the aggregate MPC for a temporary tax is a weighted average of the low MPCs of unconstrained households and the high MPCs of constrained ones. Again, the importance of this phenomenon is an empirical question.

Third, as Okun (1971) pointed out, consumer behavior depends on what people believe rather than on what the government announces. If consumers disbelieve the government when it tells them that a tax hike is only temporary, then the spending response will be greater than that suggested by a naive application of the PIH.[5] Since the perceived duration of the surtax, not the declared duration, is relevant from the standpoint of the PIH, this too raises an empirical issue.

Finally, we must recognize the possibility that households may not do the kind of rational long-term planning envisioned by Modigliani and Brumberg (1954) and Friedman (1957) or, what amounts to the same thing, have very high subjective discount rates. If they are very shortsighted, then temporary fluctuations in disposable income may have substantial effects on spending.

9.2 PREVIOUS EMPIRICAL WORK

Okun's (1971) study opened the empirical debate on this issue. Using the consumption equations of four econometric models, he compared the "full effect" view that the 1968 surtax was just as effective as a permanent tax increase to the "zero effect" view that consumers totally ignored the surtax. While he concluded that the full effect view fit the data better, an intermediate "50 percent effect" view actually does better than either extreme.[6] Springer (1975) criticized Okun's econometric procedures and then performed a similar experiment with a consumption function based on the PIH. He concluded that the zero effect view performed better.

Juster (1977), using a series of savings equations based on the Houthakker-Taylor (1966) model, reached conclusions about the 1975 rebate similar to those of Okun for the 1968 surtax. But Modigliani and Steindel (1977) found that the rebate had very little impact over a horizon of 1 or 2 quarters. Their modified version of the life-cycle model implied, however, a virtually full effect view over a 6-quarter horizon. Modigliani and Steindel assumed that the nonrebate portions of the 1975 tax cuts were treated like permanent taxes and handled the 1968 surtax with dummy variables.

The existing empirical literature thus offers little consensus. The issue seems quite open.

9.3 THE DISTRIBUTED LAG MODEL OF CONSUMPTION

The basic vehicle for investigating the effectiveness of temporary income taxes in this paper is the distributed lag version of the PIH. While this is the standard way of implementing the PIH empirically, the recent literature on rational expectations has seemed to raise doubts about its validity.[7] This section shows how the PIH and rational expectations together lead to an estimating equation very much like the one I use in this paper.

As Muth (1960) pointed out, the PIH is basically a *forward-looking* model of consumer behavior. It states that consumers, in deciding on their current spending, weigh their current asset holdings, their current income from labor, and their expected future income from labor. Specifically, permanent income at time t is defined as:

$$Y_t^p = A_t + \sum_{s=0}^{\infty} \frac{{}_tY_{t+s}}{(1+r)^s} \tag{9.1}$$

where A_t is the stock of real assets at the beginning of period t, Y_t is noninterest income in period t, and ${}_tY_{t+s}$ is the mathematical (i.e., rational) expectation of Y_{t+s} that is formed at time t. (By convention, ${}_tY_t = Y_t$.) However, if the stochastic process generating income can be described by a time-series model such as:

$$Y_t = a_1 Y_{t-1} + a_2 Y_{t-2} + \ldots + a_{n+1} Y_{t-n-1} + \varepsilon_t \tag{9.2}$$

where ε_t is a white noise error term, then the resulting empirical model of consumption will be *backward looking*. For example, if the theoretical consumption function is:

$$C_t = \delta + k Y_t^p + u_t \tag{9.3}$$

then the empirical consumption function will be:

$$C_t = \delta + k A_t + b_0 Y_t + b_1 Y_{t-1} + \ldots + b_n Y_{t-n} + u_t \tag{9.4}$$

To see this, it is only necessary to note that the (rational) expectation of income in period $t+s$ can, in view of (9.2), be based only on the information set $\{Y_t, Y_{t-1}, Y_{t-2}, \ldots\}$. Thus, for example,

$${}_tY_{t+1} = a_1 Y_t + a_2 Y_{t-1} + a_3 Y_{t-2} + \ldots + a_{n+1} Y_{t-n}$$

$${}_tY_{t+2} = a_1 Y_{t+1} + a_2 Y_t + a_3 Y_{t-1} + \ldots + a_{n+1} Y_{t-n+1}$$

$$= (a_1^2 + a_2) Y_t + (a_1 a_2 + a_3) Y_{t-1} + \ldots$$

and so on. Substituting all such expressions into the definition (9.1) and then into the consumption function (9.3), it is clear that (9.4) is derived. As pointed out by Sargent (1978) and others, the coefficients b_i in equation (9.4) will be complicated functions of the coefficients a_i in (9.2).

Suppose then that, as suggested by Dolde (1976), we can distinguish among two or more sources of income whose generating functions (9.2) may differ. The PIH in conjunction with rational expectations then implies that the bs in (9.4) should follow a different pattern for each income source. A simple example will illustrate this point and also give us some feeling for possible magnitudes. Consider several income sources, each of which is generated by a first-order autoregressive:

$$Y_{it} = \rho_i Y_{i,t-1} + \varepsilon_{it} \tag{9.5}$$

Working out the expectations and plugging into (9.1) gives us a simple expression for the permanent income attributable to each source:

$$Y_{it}^p = \frac{1+r}{1+r-\rho_i} Y_{it}, \quad \text{if } \rho < 1+r \tag{9.6}$$

Notice that, despite the long time horizon contemplated by the PIH, consumption depends only on current income. In general, consumption will depend on past income only up to lag n, where $n+1$ is the longest lag considered in equation (9.2).

Now compare two income sources, one of which is entirely permanent ($\rho = 1$) and the other of which is entirely transitory ($\rho = 0$). A \$1.00 increase in the permanent component will, according to (9.6), raise permanent income by $\$(1+r)/r$ and thus raise consumption by $\$k(1+r)/r$. This may imply a very large immediate spending response.[8] By contrast, a \$1.00 fluctuation in the purely transitory component will, again according to (9.6), raise permanent income by only \$1.00 and thus raise consumption by only \$k. The lesson, of course, generalizes and applies far beyond the confines of first-order autoregressives: *income sources deemed to be more permanent will elicit prompter spending responses than income sources deemed to be more temporary.* The application of this principle to permanent versus temporary changes in taxes is apparent and immediate and was elucidated clearly by Lucas (1976). It is the basic notion underlying the empirical model to be developed in the next section.

However, lest confusion arise, I should stress that there is no sense in which the rationality of expectations is either assumed or imposed in the consumption functions estimated here. My point is only that the distributed lag formulation of the PIH is consistent with rational expectations. As Sargent (1978) has emphasized, rational expectations delivers a set of restrictions across equations (9.2) and (9.4) that can be imposed in estimating the two jointly. I have made no attempt to impose these restrictions here because my interest was in getting the best possible consumption function estimates, not in testing rationality. Furthermore, it is well known that quite different models of consumption behavior (*e.g.*, habit persistence) can lead to an estimating equation very much like (9.4). It is not my purpose to discriminate among alternative ways of arriving at (9.4).

9.4 DERIVATION OF AN ESTIMATING EQUATION

The preceding discussion makes it clear that different distributed lag coefficients might be associated with different sources of income. While the actual empirical analysis considered four types of income, the model is most readily explained if I suppose there are only two: income (positive or negative) attributable to temporary tax measures, which I denote as S_t ("special income"); and all other disposable income ("regular income"), which I denote as R_t. The R_t should not be confused with permanent income, since it has both permanent and transitory components. The basic idea underlying the estimating equation is that S_t is identifiably "less permanent" than R_t.

Suppose consumption responds to R_t according to a set of distributed lag weights: $w_j = \partial C_t / \partial R_{t-j}, j = 0, 1, \ldots, n$. Since the w_j depend on the stochastic process generating R_t, it is worth reporting that the deviations of R_t from a logarithmic time trend are well described by the following second-order autoregressive:[9]

$$y_t = 1.28 y_{t-1} - 0.35 y_{t-2} \quad R^2 = 0.91 \; D\text{-}W = 1.86.$$

$$(0.09) \qquad (0.09)$$

When income follows a second-order autoregressive, permanent income as defined in (9.1) is:

$$Y_t^p = A_t + K_t + \frac{(1+r)^2}{(1+r)(1+r-a_1) - a_2} y_t$$

$$+ \frac{a_2(1+r)}{(1+r)(1+r-a_1) - a_2} y_{t-1}$$

if $a_1 + a_2/(1+r) < 1+r$, where K_t is the present value of the trend component of labor income and y_t and y_{t-1} are current and lagged deviations from trend. Given the estimates of a_1 and a_2 above, and for $r = 0.0074$ (a 3 percent annual real interest rate), the implied coefficients are $Y_t^p = A_t + K_t + 13.5 y_t - 4.7 y_{t-1}$. This leads us to expect a very large value of w_0, followed by swiftly declining ws – possibly even turning negative. The empirical results bear this out.

As Lucas (1976) has argued, income changes that are clearly "more temporary" than regular income should get different spending coefficients. To develop a model of the distributed lag response of C_t to S_t, first break down S_t into its components:

$$S_t = S_t^1 + S_t^2 + \ldots + S_t^m \tag{9.7}$$

where S_t^i indicates the income gain or loss in quarter t from the temporary tax. (In the empirical work, $m = 3$.) It will help clarify the treatment of the S_t^i if I define a hypothetical set of lag coefficients β, as the effect on C_t of a \$1.00 pure windfall gain received in quarter $t - j$.

The treatment of S_t^i depends on whether or not the ith temporary tax is still in effect. If it is, I assume that S_t^i is treated as a weighted average of regular and windfall income, so that it gets the distributed lag weights:

$$\gamma_j = \frac{\partial C_t}{\partial S_{t-j}^i} = \lambda w_j + (1 - \lambda)\beta_j, \quad j = 0, 1, \ldots, n \quad 0 \leqslant \lambda \leqslant 1 \tag{9.8}$$

If the temporary tax is no longer on the books, I assume that consumers look upon S_{t-j}^i in retrospect as if it had been a pure windfall and so apply the distributed lag coefficients β_j. By introducing a dummy variable defined as:

$D_t^i = 1$ if the ith temporary tax remains in force in quarter t
  $= 0$ otherwise,

it is possible to combine these two hypotheses into a single expression

$$\gamma_j^i(t) = D_t^i[\lambda w_j + (1 - \lambda)\beta_j] + (1 - D_t^i)\beta_j \tag{9.9}$$

where the notation now indicates that the γ weights depend both on calendar time and on the specific tax under consideration (because of the dummy variable).

An interesting point arises here. Standard pre-rational-expectations approaches to consumption-function estimation would suggest that $\Sigma\beta_j$ and $\Sigma\gamma_j$ be constrained to equal Σw_j, apparently meaning that the "long-run MPC" out of any type of income is identical. However, the PIH-cum-rational-expectations approach suggests no such adding-up constraint. To see this, follow Sargent (1978, pp. 681–2) in rewriting (9.2) in the form $X_t = HX_{t-1} + \eta_t$ (Sargent's equation 8), where:

$$X_t = \begin{bmatrix} Y_t \\ Y_{t-1} \\ \cdot \\ \cdot \\ \cdot \\ \cdot \\ Y_{t-n} \end{bmatrix} \qquad H = \begin{bmatrix} a_1 & a_2 & \cdots & a_n & a_{n+1} \\ 1 & 0 & & 0 & 0 \\ 0 & 1 & & \cdot & \cdot \\ \cdot & 0 & & \cdot & \cdot \\ \cdot & \cdot & & \cdot & \cdot \\ \cdot & \cdot & & 0 & \cdot \\ 0 & 0 & & 1 & 0 \end{bmatrix}$$

$$\eta_t = \begin{bmatrix} \varepsilon_t \\ 0 \\ \cdot \\ \cdot \\ \cdot \\ \cdot \\ 0 \end{bmatrix}$$

and $Y_t = dX_t$, where $d = (1, 0, \ldots, 0)$. As Sargent notes (his equation 9), rational expectations implies $_tX_{t+s} = H^sX_t$, whence $_tY_{t+s} = dH^sX_t$. Substituting this into (9.1) gives the following expression for permanent income:

$$Y_t^p = A_t + \left[\sum_{s=0}^{\infty} \frac{dH^s}{(1+r)^s} \right] X_t$$

which is of the form (9.4) with coefficients:

$$b \equiv (b_0, b_1, \ldots, b_n) = \sum_{s=0}^{\infty} \frac{dH^s}{(1+r)^s}$$

The sum of the b_j has no obvious interpretation. Thus, in a model with several sources of income, there is no particular reason why the various sets of distributed lag coefficients should have a common sum.

Where, then, does the lifetime budget constraint enter? The answer is that (9.4) implies a unitary lifetime MPC for any values of k and the b_j. The proof involves some straightforward but tedious algebraic manipulations of the difference equations (9.4) and:

$$A_{t+1} = (1+r)A_t + Y_t - C_t \tag{9.10}$$

and hence is relegated to Appendix 9.1.

With these preliminaries out of the way, it is easy to explain the estimating equation. If there were no special taxes to worry about, the basic empirical model of consumer behavior would be as follows:

$$C_t = k_0 + k_1 r_t Y_t + \sum_{j=0}^{n} w_j Y_{t-j} + k_2(W_t - A_t)$$
$$+ \sum_{j=0}^{q} k_{3+j} A_{t-j} + u_t \tag{9.11}$$

where r_t is the rate of interest, W_t is consumer net worth at the beginning of period t, and A_t is the market value of stock market wealth at the beginning of period t. The specific way in which assets are entered into the consumption function, including the constraint that $k_3 + k_4 + \ldots + k_{3+q} = k_2$, is suggested by the MIT-Penn-SSRC (MPS) model and is unimportant to what follows.

Now consider the separation of disposable income into its two components:

$$Y_t = R_t + S_t \tag{9.12}$$

The way I have defined the γs means that (9.11) is expanded to:

$$C_t = k_0 + k_1 r_t Y_t + k_2(W_t - A_t) + \sum_{j=0}^{q} k_{3+j} A_{t-j}$$
$$+ \sum_{j=0}^{n} w_j R_{t-j} + \sum_{j=0}^{n} \gamma_j^1(t) S_{t-j}^1 + \ldots + \sum_{j=0}^{n} \gamma_j^m(t) S_{t-j}^m + u_t \tag{9.13}$$

Substituting (9.9) and (9.12) into (9.13), and rearranging terms, gives:

$$C_t = k_0 + k_1 r_t Y_t + k_2(W_t - A_t) + \sum_{j=0}^{q} k_{3+j} A_{t-j}$$

$$+ \sum_{j=0}^{n} w_j (Y_{t-j} + \lambda X_t^j - S_{t-j}) \tag{9.14}$$

$$+ \sum_{j=0}^{n} \beta_j \left[(1 - \lambda) X_t^j + \sum_{i=1}^{m} (1 - D_t^i) S_{t-j}^i \right] + u_t$$

where $X_t^i \equiv D_t^1 S_{t-j}^1 + \ldots + D_t^m S_{t-j}^m$, $j = 0, \ldots, n$. This is not the actual estimating equation because additional income sources were distinguished, because the distributed lag coefficients were constrained in several ways, and because corrections were made for both heteroskedasticity and serial correlation in the error term. Details are spelled out in Appendix 9.2. Nonetheless (9.14) is the most useful form for interpreting the estimated parameters. The model is non-linear because of the parameter λ – the crucial parameter of this study.

As noted above, theory does not imply that $\Sigma w_j = \Sigma \beta_j$. To investigate this further, this adding-up constraint was imposed in (9.14) and its validity tested as follows.[10] Let l denote the likelihood ratio. Then, under the assumption of normality, $-2 \log l = T \log(\text{SSR}_r / \text{SSR})$ is distributed as a χ^2 with r degrees of freedom, where: T = number of observations (= 100 throughout this paper), SSR = minimized value of the sum of squared residuals in the unconstrained regression (equation (9.14) in this case), SSR_r = minimized value of the sum of squared residuals in the constrained regression (obtained by imposing $\Sigma \beta = \Sigma w$), and r = number of restrictions (= 1 in this case). As reported in Table 9.1, row 1, the constraint was rejected at the 10 percent level but not at the 5 percent level. There being no persuasive theoretical rationale for it, the constraint was dropped.

Tacitly, however, (9.14) embodies a number of other constraints that are equally lacking in theoretical justification – constraints that each type of regular income is subject to the same set of distributed lag coefficients. These constraints were tested by a series of likelihood ratio tests, which are described in the balance of this section.

First, "regular" disposable income was disaggregated into its two main components – personal income and "regular" personal taxes:

$$R_t = P_t - T_t^{11} \tag{9.15}$$

Personal income is assumed to be spent according to the lag weights w_j, while regular taxes are assumed to be subject to a different set of lag weights v_j. Special taxes are treated as previously explained, except that the vs replace the ws in equations (9.8) and (9.9). That is, while the tax is on the books, a special tax is treated as a weighted average of a permanent tax and a windfall. Thus the basic consumption function becomes:

$$C_t = k_0 + k_1 r_t Y_t + k_2(W_t - A_t) + \sum_{j=0}^{q} k_{3+j} A_{t-j}$$

$$+ \sum_{j=0}^{n} w_j P_{t-j} - \sum_{j=0}^{n} v_j(T_{t-j} - \lambda X_t^j) \qquad (9.16)$$

$$+ \sum_{j=0}^{n} \beta_j \left[(1-\lambda)X_t^j + \sum_{i=1}^{m} (1-D_t^i)S_{t-j}^i \right] + u_t$$

Since (as explained below) the distributed lag coefficients are constrained to follow a third-degree polynomial with a zero end-point constraint, the null hypothesis that the v_j are equal to the w_j imposes three constraints on equation (9.16). Row 2 of Table 9.1 shows that these constraints were resoundingly rejected by the data ($\chi_3^2 = 12$). However, it turned out that the sum of the v_j was estimated to be almost exactly equal to the sum of the w_j (see row 3 of Table 9.1), so this adding-up constraint was imposed in subsequent estimates.

The final generalization considered was to disaggregate personal income into its two main components – factor income and transfer payments:[12]

$$P_t = F_t + V_t \qquad (9.17)$$

This made the estimating equation:

$$C_t = k_0 + k_1 r_t Y_t + k_2(W_t - A_t) + \sum_{j=0}^{q} k_{3+j} A_{t-j}$$

$$+ \sum_{j=0}^{n} w_j F_{t-j} + \sum_{j=0}^{n} \phi_j V_{t-j} - \sum_{j=0}^{n} v_j(T_{t-j} - \lambda X_t^j) \qquad (9.18)$$

$$+ \sum_{j=0}^{n} \beta_j \left[(1-\lambda)X_t^j + \sum_{i=1}^{m} (1-D_t^i)S_{t-j}^i \right] + u_t$$

Once again, the null hypothesis that the ϕ_j (spending coefficients for transfers) are in fact equal to the w_j (spending coefficients for factor income) was tested by a χ^2 test. And once again it was resoundingly rejected ($\chi_3^2 = 19$; see row 4 of Table 9.1). This time, however, the data also rejected the adding-up constraint $\Sigma \phi_j = \Sigma w_j$, which therefore was not imposed (Table 9.1, row 5). In fact, most of the difference between the ϕ_j and the w_j was in their sums; the time patterns were remarkably similar.

To summarize these tests, we are left with a model that assigns distributed lag weights w_j to factor income, ϕ_j to transfers, v_j to regular taxes, and β_j to windfalls. The Σv_j and Σw_j are apparently equal, but the other sums are not.

Table 9.1 χ tests of constraints

Unconstrained model	Constraint tested	df	Test statistic
1. Eq. (9.14)	$\Sigma\omega = \Sigma\beta$	1	3.67
2. Eq. (9.16)	$v_j = \omega_j$ for all j	3	12.02
3. Eq. (9.16)	$\Sigma v_j = \Sigma\omega_j$	1	Approximately 0[a]
4. Eq. (9.18) with $\Sigma v = \Sigma\omega$	$\phi_j = \omega_j$ for all j	3	19.02
5. Eq. (9.18) with $\Sigma v = \Sigma\omega$	$\Sigma\phi_j = \Sigma\omega_j$	1	12.52
6. Eq. (9.18) with $\Sigma v = \Sigma\omega$	$\lambda = 0$	1	1.32
7. Eq. (9.18) with $\Sigma v = \Sigma\omega$	$\lambda = 1$	1	2.84
8. Eq. (9.18) with $\Sigma v = \Sigma\omega$	$k_2 = 0$	1	17.81

Notes: Critical levels for the χ^2 distribution are:

df	10% point	5% point	1% point
1	2.71	3.84	6.63
3	6.25	7.81	11.34

(a) Due to rounding error, the actual computed test statistic was slightly negative. When this constraint was tested in the context of eq. (9.18), it produced a test statistic of 1.32.

9.5 ISSUES IN ESTIMATION

9.5.1 Data

Following the suggestion of Darby (1975), I used consumer expenditures, rather than pure consumption, as C_t. This seems most appropriate where the focus is on the evaluation of stabilization policy, as it is here, rather than on testing the PIH. Furthermore, it avoids many complicated issues of definition (*e.g.*, which goods are durables? how fast do they depreciate? *etc.*). The cost of this shortcut is that the theoretical interpretation of some of the parameters is lost. For example, k_1 includes the effects of r_t on both pure consumption (which may be positive or negative) and spending on durables (which should be negative). Similarly, the lag weights w_j might be expected to be less smooth than the lag of pure consumption behind income because of the lumpy nature of durables.[13]

Data for the 1968 surcharge were taken from Okun (1971) and converted to 1972 dollars by the deflator for personal consumer expenditures; these comprise S_t^1. Data for the various 1975–6 tax cuts are shown in Table 9.2; they were similarly deflated and segregated into two time series. The S_t^2 series is defined as the explicitly one-shot measures: the tax rebates and the social security bonuses (hereafter referred to as "the rebate"). The rest is considered as S_t^3. Since the 1975 cuts were extended several times and are now a permanent feature of the tax code, an arbitrary decision had to be made as to when they became "permanent."[14] I decided to cut off S_t^3 after 1976:2, because by then the cuts had already been extended once in the Revenue Adjustment Act of 1975 and a second time in the Tax Reform Act of 1976.

Table 9.2 Effects on disposable income of 1975–6 tax cuts and transfers[a]

| Quarter | Taxes[b] | | | Transfers[c] | |
	Tax rate cuts	rebate	social security	earned income	total
1975:2	8.5	31.2	6.7	0	46.4
1975:3	12.3	0	0	0	12.3
1975:4	11.9	0	0	0	11.9
1976:1	14.2	0	0	1.9	16.1
1976:2	14.0	0	0	1.6	15.6

Notes:
(a) In billions of current dollars, at annual rates.
(b) From US Bureau of Economic Analysis (February 1976, March 1977).
(c) Kindly supplied to the author by Joseph C. Wakefield, of the Bureau of Economic Analysis, in conversation.

Data on consumer net worth (W_t), and its breakdown into stock market (A_t) and non-stock market ($W_t - A_t$) components, were taken from the data bank of the MPS model and converted to 1972 dollars. They are based on a number of primary sources, the most important of which is the flow of funds.

Because of the recent findings of Boskin (1978), I thought it important to use a real after-tax interest rate. Since the construction of this series was a fairly involved affair, I explain it only in Appendix 9.3.

9.5.2 Distributed lag estimation

The many distributed lags in equation (9.18) were estimated by an adaptation of the Almon (1965) lag technique, as a method of conserving on parameters. Generally, a third-degree polynomial with a zero constraint at the far end was used. Preliminary tests suggested that these end-point constraints ($w_{n+1} = 0$, *etc.*) could not be rejected. An unconstrained version of one specification, run as an experiment showed that the polynomial constraint had very little effect on the w coefficients but did influence the β_j coefficients.

The distributed lag effects of assets were estimated as follows. In some preliminary regressions, the two components were combined and a cubic distributed lag over n quarters was estimated. Then the two components were disaggregated. These preliminary tests showed quite clearly (*a*) that the coefficients were not the same and (*b*) that the lag was much shorter than n quarters. (As explained just below, n was chosen to be 7.) In the case of non-stock market wealth, an estimated distributed lag over 4 quarters attached virtually all of the weight to the current (start of period) value, so all lagged values were omitted. In the case of stock market wealth, when a cubic was estimated over $j = 0, 1, \ldots, 7$, the coefficients turned out to be almost linear and to be virtually zero after $j = 2$ (a small positive value for $j = 3$

and small negative values for $j = 4, \ldots, 7$). Thus a linear distributed lag over $j = 0, \ldots, 3$ was adopted as the final specification.

The length of the distributed lag, n, was selected by running a preliminary version of the regression for alternative values of n ranging from 6 to 10. A very clear minimum in the sum of squared residuals was found around $n = 7$ or $n = 8$, with the former having a slightly better fit and slightly better coefficients. On this basis, $n = 7$ was selected for all subsequent work.

9.5.3 Treatment of the 1975 rebate

As has been noted already, the model divides the 1975–6 tax cuts into two parts: S_t^2 includes the rebate, while S_t^3 includes all the rest. This makes a strong (and questionable) assumption about how consumers treated the rebate. In particular, it assumes that they treated it just like the 1968 surcharge and the other 1975 reductions: essentially as if a fraction λ of it was a regular increase in income, while a fraction $1 - \lambda$ was a pure windfall. Given the nature of the rebate, this is questionable, to say the least.

An alternative assumption – equally strong as the first – is that consumers treated the rebate as a pure windfall right from the start.[15] While it is not obvious that this is true, since consumers might have anticipated a repeat performance with some reasonable probability, it does seem a plausible working hypothesis. Fortunately, it is not difficult to modify any of the three models to accommodate this alternative hypothesis; all that is necessary is that the lag weights β_j be applied to S_t^2 starting immediately in 1975:2. When this was done in one version of the model, the resulting equation had virtually an identical SSR, almost the same estimated λ, and very similar implications about spending patterns out of the rebate. Thus the conclusions of this study seem insensitive to the treatment of the rebate.

9.6 EMPIRICAL RESULTS

9.6.1 Parameter estimates and interpretation

Estimation was done by the numerical optimization package developed by Goldfeld and Quandt. The results from estimating equation (9.18) on quarterly data covering 1953:1–1977:4 are presented in Table 9.3. The number in parentheses next to each estimated coefficient is its asymptotic standard error (or rather a numerical estimate thereof).

In interpreting the standard error of the regression, it should be mentioned that, as explained in Appendix 9.2, the equation was actually transformed so that the left-hand variable was the average propensity to consume (APC), C_t / Y_t, rather than consumer spending. Thus, the standard error of 0.0038 is relative to a typical value for the APC of about 0.90. This represents an excellent fit.[16] At 1977 income levels, it translates to a standard error of about

Table 9.3 Nonlinear consumption function parameter estimates[a]

k_0	k_1	k_2	λ	ρ
30.1 (7.1)	0.0002 (0.0007)	0.021 (0.005)	0.50 (0.32)	0.54 (0.11)

Distributed lag coefficients[b]

zj	w_j	ϕ_j	v_j	β_j	k_{3+j}	v_j	Rebate
0	0.60 (0.05)	0.50 (0.16)	0.34 (0.09)	-0.03 (0.26)	0.009 (0.002)	0.16	0.16
1	0.16 (0.02)	-0.02 (0.09)	0.14 (0.04)	-0.03 (0.11)	0.006 (0.001)	0.06	-0.03
2	-0.06 (0.03)	-0.20 (0.10)	0.04 (0.05)	-0.01 (0.09)	0.004 (0.001)	0.02	-0.01
3	-0.12 (0.02)	-0.14 (0.08)	0.01 (0.05)	0.03 (0.09)	0.002 (0.0005)	0.02	0.03
4	-0.08 (0.01)	0.04 (0.06)	0.02 (0.03)	0.08 (0.07)	—	0.05	0.08
5	0.02 (0.01)	0.26 (0.07)	0.05 (0.03)	0.11 (0.06)	—	0.08	0.11
6	0.10 (0.02)	0.39 (0.09)	0.08 (0.04)	0.12 (0.08)	—	0.10	0.12
7	0.11 (0.02)	0.34 (0.08)	0.07 (0.04)	0.09 (0.07)	—	0.08	0.09
Sum	0.74	1.17	0.74	0.36	0.021 (0.005)	0.55	0.55

Notes: k_0 = constant, k_1 = coefficient of interest rate, k_2 = coefficient of regular income, ρ = autocorrelation coefficient. Sum of squared residuals = 0.00147, SE = 0.00383, SE of unadjusted errors (without a correction for autocorrelation) = 0.00455, N observations = 100. λ = weight on non-stock market wealth, λ = weight on
(a) Asymptotic SEs are in parentheses.
(b) Components may not add to totals due to rounding.

$3.5 billion in predicting consumer spending. Of course, obtaining a good fit with a consumption function is hardly a notable achievement, and the equation – like most consumption functions – does suffer from some auto-correlation ($\rho = 0.54$).

Turning to the coefficient estimates, the most critical parameter for purposes of this study is λ, the weight attached to regular income in equation (9.8). The point estimate of 0.50 suggests that temporary taxes that are still on the books are treated like 50–50 blends of windfalls and regular taxes. However, the standard error is regrettably large; there are, after all, pitifully few observations that can be used to estimate λ. The null hypotheses $\lambda = 0$ or $\lambda = 1$ can nonetheless be tested by likelihood ratio tests. When these tests were run with equation (9.18) as the unconstrained regression (see Table 9.1, rows 6 and 7), the null hypothesis that $\lambda = 0$ (temporary taxes are regarded as pure windfalls) could not be rejected ($\chi_1^2 = 1.32$). But the null hypothesis that $\lambda = 1$ (temporary taxes are regarded as regular income) could be rejected if we were not too fussy about significance levels ($\chi_1^2 = 2.84$).

I turn next to the distributed lag coefficients of the various income terms. The ws for factor income are very large and positive at first, then turn small and negative, and finally become positive again at the end. This general shape accords well with our expectations.[17] The ϕ_j coefficients for transfer payments follow a similar shape but are much more erratic and less well pinned down econometrically. A notable feature is that their sum is nearly 1.2, indicating "overspending" during the first 2 years after receipt of a transfer payment.

The v_j coefficients for regular taxes also exhibit a characteristic U-shape, but in much more muted fashion. As compared with factor income, spending in the first year after a regular tax cut is apparently substantially less, after which it catches up. This was surprising at first, since Dolde (1976) and Modigliani and Steindel (1977) had suggested that regular tax changes are "more permanent" than regular income.[18] However, it turns out that the following second-order autoregressives describe the deviations from trend of personal income (P_t) and regular taxes (T_t):

$$P_t = 1.32 P_{t-1} - 0.38 P_{t-2}$$
$$ (0.09) \phantom{P_{t-1} - } (0.09)$$

$$T_t = 1.11 T_{t-1} - 0.21 T_{t-2}$$
$$ (0.09) \phantom{T_{t-1} - } (0.10)$$

Using the formulas derived earlier for permanent income, these time-series models imply that "permanent personal income" and "permanent taxes" are given by $P_t^p = 14.9 P_t - 5.7 P_{t-1}$ and $T_t^p = 9.3 T_t - 1.9 T_{t-1}$, so that, contrary to Dolde and Modigliani and Steindel, we should actually expect a stronger short-run response of consumption to fluctuations in P_t than to fluctuations in T_t, which is exactly what I find.

The next column, the β_js, are in some sense out-of-sample extrapolations since there are no "pure windfalls" recorded in the data.[19] Their only use is to form the weighted average $\lambda w_j + (1 - \lambda)\beta_j$, which is reported in the column marked "γ_j." These are the expenditure coefficients for income from a temporary tax that remains on the books for the entire 2 year horizon. To illustrate the opposite extreme, the column marked "Rebate" shows the spending coefficients for a temporary tax that lasts only 1 quarter. These two columns differ in details but are quite similar. There is a moderate spending response in the initial quarter, followed by very little spending over the next 3 or 4 quarters. Most of the spending out of a temporary tax cut, according to these estimates, comes 5 or more quarters after the cut.

The coefficient of assets (0.02) is comparable to what others have estimated, though a bit on the low side. A likelihood ratio test of the null hypothesis $k_2 = 0$ (which, in this constrained form, also implies $k_3 = \ldots = k_6 = 0$) produced a test statistic of 17.8, which is highly significant at any reasonable significance level (Table 9.1, row 8).

If we ignore the fact that income from property is included in the measure of income, the parameter k_2 can be given an interesting theoretical interpretation. In the basic life-cycle model, the consumer maximizes a utility function of the form:

$$\sum_{t=0}^{T} \left(\frac{1}{1+\rho} \right)^t \frac{C_t^{1-\delta}}{1-\delta}$$

subject to a lifetime wealth constraint. It can be shown by straightforward computations that the optimal solution for initial consumption is $C_0 = [(r - g)/(1 + r)] W$, where W is lifetime wealth and g is the optimal growth rate of C_t, defined as $g = [(1 + r)/(1 + \rho)]^{1/\delta} - 1$. This means that k_2 corresponds to the theoretical coefficient $(r - g)/(1 + r)$, which for small values of r and ρ is approximately equal to $r + (1/\delta)(\rho - r)$. Thus for small values of r the estimated value $k_2 = 0.02$ implies that the subjective discount rate, ρ, is approximately 0.02δ or around 2–3 percent per quarter for plausible values of δ.

One striking result, though it is peripheral to the subject of this study, is the tiny coefficient of the real after-tax interest rate.[20] This finding turned up in every specification of the model, including several alternative measures of the rate of interest. (Sometimes the coefficient was trivially negative, sometimes trivially positive, but always trivial.) While it accords well both with my earlier work (Blinder (1975)) and with the work of others, it stands in sharp contrast with Boskin's (1978) recent finding of a strong positive interest elasticity of saving.

9.6.2 Temporary versus permanent taxes

We can now address the principal issue of this study: how effective are explicitly temporary income tax changes as compared to those announced to

Table 9.4 Relative effectiveness of temporary taxes

	Cumulative spending propensities			Ratios	
j	permanent (1)	2-year (2)	rebate (3)	(2)/(1) (4)	(3)/(1) (5)
0	0.34	0.16	0.16	0.47	0.47
1	0.50	0.23	0.14	0.46	0.28
2	0.55	0.26	0.16	0.47	0.29
3	0.56	0.30	0.21	0.54	0.38
4	0.59	0.36	0.30	0.61	0.51
5	0.65	0.46	0.43	0.71	0.66
6	0.73	0.57	0.56	0.78	0.77
7	0.81	0.65	0.66	0.80	0.81

be permanent? Table 9.4 contains the answers derived from the model, using the parameter estimates presented in Table 9.3 to make equation (9.4) operational and using an annual real interest rate of 3 percent in updating wealth according to equation (9.10). It can be seen from column 4 that a temporary tax is about one-half as effective as a permanent tax in the first year, rising to about three-quarters as effective in the second year. Spending out of a rebate is somewhat slower than this. My estimated cumulative spending propensities out of a rebate are larger than those estimated by Modigliani and Steindel (1977) for the first few quarters but smaller thereafter.

These findings carry two important messages to fiscal policy planners. First, and most obvious, is that temporary taxes are less powerful devices for short-run stabilization purposes than are permanent ones. Second, and perhaps almost as important, the short-run relative ineffectiveness of such taxes implies that the impact of these measures in the second year is larger than might be expected. For example, according to Table 9.4, each $1.00 of permanent tax reduction adds $0.25 to spending in the second year, while each $1.00 of a rebate adds $0.45. If the need is for a truly short-run stimulus to aggregate demand, this effect may also be unwanted.

Both of these points can be illustrated by examining what the equations have to say about the 1975–6 episode. First, it is useful to display the observed APCs for this period in Table 9.5. There are two obvious phenomena crying out for explanation in these data. First, why did the APC drop so sharply in 1975:2? Second, why did it thereafter begin a steady climb to what is a truly extraordinary level by 1977:1? (The corresponding personal savings rate was only 4.2 percent – the lowest figure that had then been recorded since the Korean War.)

According to the estimates presented in this paper, the temporary tax cuts of 1975–6 contributed to both phenomena. Using the spending coefficients presented in Table 9.4, Table 9.6 shows the estimated direct (excluding multiplier) effects on consumer spending of the tax cuts of 1975:2 through 1976:2, inclusive.[21] It appears that (1) very little of the rebate was spent in

Table 9.5 Average propensities to consume, 1975–7

	1975	1976	1977
First quarter	0.913	0.914	0.935
Second quarter	0.881	0.918	0.926
Third quarter	0.903	0.922	0.922
Fourth quarter	0.907	0.926	0.925

Source: US Bureau of Economic Analysis (various issues).

Table 9.6 Estimated effects of the 1975–6 temporary tax cuts on consumer expenditures[a]

Quarter	Estimated spending effect
1975:2	5.9
1975:3	1.6
1975:4	2.7
1976:1	4.8
1976:2	6.7
1976:3	6.7
1976:4	7.1
1977:1	6.6
1977:2	7.2
1977:3	7.5
1977:4	7.3

Note:
(a) In billions of 1972 dollars.

1975:2, (2) rather little of the disposable income attributable to the temporary tax cut package was spent during the remainder of 1975, and (3) more spending out of the temporary tax cuts was done in 1976 and yet more in 1977. Both the low APC of 1975:2 and the high APCs of late 1976 and early 1977 are tracked very well by the model. One observation which virtually jumps from Table 9.6 is how very small these estimated spending impacts are relative to the size of the economy they were meant to stimulate (real GNP in the neighborhood of $1,250 billion).

Finally, there is one more question. If, instead of the 1975:2–1976:2 package of temporary measures, the government had cut taxes "permanently" in 1975:2 and then restored them to their original level starting in 1976:3, how large a tax cut would have achieved the same average effect on aggregate demand?[22]

Table 9.7 summarizes the model's answers to this question for three different choices of the horizon over which the "average effect on aggregate demand" might be defined. The first column gives the average direct impact

Table 9.7 Equivalent permanent taxes[a, b]

Horizon	Average impact on spending of actual 1975–6 cuts	Cumulative revenue loss over five quarters of permanent tax cut with equal average impact on spending
4 quarters	3.7	9.5
6 quarters	4.7	12.4
8 quarters	5.3	15.9

Notes:
(a) See text for definition.
(b) In billions of 1972 dollars, at annual rates.

on spending attributed by the model to the 1975–6 tax cuts. The next column shows how much total tax revenue the government would have had to relinquish during the same 5-quarter period (1975:2–1976:2) in order to achieve the same direct impact on spending through a permanent tax cut. Since the total 5-quarter revenue loss from the 1975–6 package was $20 billion, these numbers mean, for example, that a permanent tax cut about half as large ($9.5 billion vs $20 billion) would have had the same first-year effect on aggregate demand. Over a 2 year horizon, however, the 1975–6 package had about 80 percent as much "bang for the buck" as a permanent tax cut.

9.7 SUMMARY

Both economic theory and casual empirical observation of the US economy suggest that short-run spending propensities from temporary tax changes are smaller than those from permanent ones, but neither provides much guidance about the magnitude of this difference. This paper offers new empirical estimates of this difference and finds it to be quite substantial.

The analysis is based on an amendment of the standard distributed lag version of the PIH that distinguishes temporary taxes from other income on the grounds that the latter is "more transitory." This amendment, which is broadly consistent with rational expectations, leads to a nonlinear consumption function.

Though the standard error is unavoidably large, the point estimate suggests that a temporary tax change is treated as a 50-50 blend of a normal income tax change and a pure windfall. Over a 1 year planning horizon, a temporary tax change is estimated to have only a little more than half as much impact as a permanent tax change of equal magnitude, and a rebate is estimated to have only about 38 percent as much impact. The model tracks both the extraordinarily high savings rate of 1975:2 and the extraordinarily low savings rates of late 1976 and early 1977 very well and attributes part of both phenomena to the temporary tax measures of 1975–6. Finally, it is estimated that a permanent tax cut of about $9.5 billion (in 1972 dollars) would have had the same impact on aggregate demand over the first 4 quarters as the $20 billion of 1975–6 tax cuts.

NOTES

1. This is essentially the model introduced by Modigliani and Brumberg (1954).
2. By way of comparison, as $t_1 \to T$, the MPC $\to 5/6$.
3. See, for example, Darby (1972).
4. See Blinder (1976) and Dolde (1978). For a look at one particular type of uncertainty, see Foley and Hellwig (1975), which shows that this result may not carry through to the uncertainty case.
5. This point has rather less cogency with respect to tax cuts; but here too consumers may believe them to be more permanent than the government announces.
6. On this, see Blinder and Solow (1974, pp. 107–9).
7. See Lucas (1976) and especially Hall (1978).
8. Suppose the rate of subjective time discounting is equal to the rate of interest, so that a constant consumption stream is optimal, and that B is the lifetime propensity to consume (i.e., $1 - B$ is the propensity to bequeath). Then k will be $Br/(1 + r)$, so that $k(1 + r)/r$ will be B, which is close to unity.
9. Standard errors are in parentheses. Longer autoregressives, however, give slightly better fits. E.g., if $t - 11$ is the longest lag allowed to enter the regression, significant coefficients are obtained at lags 1, 2, 3, 4, and 11. An F-test for the zero restrictions implied by the second-order model, however, yields an F-ratio of only 1.77, which is well below the critical 5 percent point of the χ_9^2 distribution.
10. See Goldfeld and Quandt (1972, p. 74).
11. In making this separation, I departed a bit from national income accounting conventions by including the employer's share of social insurance contributions in both P and T.
12. For this purpose, both employer contributions and business transfers are considered to be factor income, and the aspects of the 1975–6 tax cuts that are classified as transfer payments in the national income accounts are grouped with temporary taxes.
13. To account for the special features of expenditures on consumer durables, several additional variables were tried in some earlier regressions. Neither the stock of durables, nor the relative price of durables, nor the unemployment rate succeeded in significantly lowering the sum of squared residuals. In several cases, the signs of the coefficients were even the opposite of what theory suggests. It may be that these variables are more relevant to the choice between saving in the form of durables vs. in financial form than they are to the choice between spending and saving.
14. At an early stage of this research, I experimented with a learning model in which a temporary tax gradually came to be considered permanent as it remained on the books longer and longer. This experiment was unsuccessful.
15. Since the rebate was off the books by 1975:3, and hence treated as a windfall in any case, only 1975:2 is at issue here.
16. The standard errors of a comparable equation in Modigliani and Steindel (1977) are 0.0056 with an autocorrelation correction and 0.0065 without.
17. Because of the estimating form, it is unlikely that simultaneity has much to do with the large estimate for w_0. See Appendix 9.2.

18. But see Dolde (1979), where the transitory nature of allegedly permanent tax changes is stressed.
19. I made an attempt, in some early regressions, to treat the National Service Life Insurance Dividends of 1950 in this way, but I was not successful.
20. The specific coefficient in Table 9.3 means that a 1 percentage point rise in r lowers savings by about 0.02 of 1 percent of disposable income – a trivial amount.
21. The reader is reminded that only these 5 quarters are considered temporary cuts.
22. For this calculation I assume that consumers were successfully fooled into thinking that the 5-quarter tax cut would be permanent.
23. See Feige and Pearce (1976).
24. Standard errors are in parentheses. The $D-W$ is the Durbin–Watson statistic. The period of estimation was 1951:3–1977:4, the longest period possible given the need for 17 lagged values of M.

REFERENCES

Almon, S. (1965) "The distributed lag between capital appropriations and expenditures," *Econometrica*, vol. 33 (January), pp. 178–96.
Blinder, A. S. (1975) "Distribution effects and the aggregate consumption function," *Journal of Political Economy*, vol. 83, no. 3 (June), pp. 447–75.
Blinder, A. S. (1976) "Intergenerational transfers and life cycle consumption," *American Economic Review, Papers and Proceedings*, vol. 66 (May), pp. 87–93.
Blinder, A. S., and R. M. Solow (1974) "Analytical foundations of fiscal policy," in A. S. Blinder *et al.*: *The Economics of Public Finance*, Washington: Brookings.
Boskin, M. J. (1978) "Taxation, saving, and the rate of interest," *Journal of Political Economy*, vol. 86, no. 2, pt. 2 (April), S3–S27.
Darby, M. R. (1972) "The allocation of transitory income among consumers' assets." *American Economic Review*, vol. 62 (December), pp. 928–41.
Darby, M. R. (1975) "Postwar US consumption, consumer expenditures, and saving," *American Economic Review Papers and Proceedings*, vol. 65 (May), pp. 217–22.
Dolde, W. (1976) "Forecasting the consumption effects of stabilization policies," *International Economic Review*, vol. 17 (June), pp. 431–46.
Dolde, W. (1978) "Capital markets and the short run behavior of life cycle savers," *Journal of Finance*, vol. 33 (May), pp. 413–28.
Dolde, W. (1979) "Temporary taxes as macro-economic stabilizers," *American Economic Review Papers and Proceedings*, vol. 69 (May), pp. 81–5.
Eisner, R. (1969) "Fiscal and monetary policy reconsidered." *American Economic Review*, vol. 59 (December), pp. 897–905.
Feige, E. L., and D. K. Pearce (1976) "Economically rational expectations: are innovations in the rate of inflation independent of innovations in measures of monetary and fiscal policy?" *Journal of Political Economy*, vol. 84, no. 3 (June), pp. 499–522.

Foley, D. K., and M. F. Hellwig (1975) "Asset management with trading uncertainty." *Rev. Econ. Studies*, vol. 42 (July), pp. 327–46.

Friedman, M. (1957) *A Theory of the Consumption Function*. Princeton: Princeton University Press.

Goldfeld, S. M., and R. E. Quandt (1972) *Nonlinear Methods in Econometrics*. Amsterdam: North-Holland.

Hall, R. E. (1978) "Stochastic implications of the life cycle– permanent income hypothesis: theory and evidence." *Journal of Political Economy*, vol. 86, no. 6 (December), pp. 971–87.

Houthakker, H. S., and L. D. Taylor (1966) *Consumer Demand in the United States*, Cambridge, Mass.: Harvard University Press.

Juster, F. T. (1977) "A note on prospective 1977 tax-cuts and consumer spending," unpublished paper, University of Michigan (January).

Lucas, R. E. Jr (1976) "Econometric policy evaluation: a critique." In K. Brunner and A. Meltzer (eds) *The Phillips Curve and Labor Markets*, Amsterdam: North-Holland.

Modigliani, F. and R. E. Brumberg (1954) "Utility analysis and the consumption function: an interpretation of cross-section data," in K. K. Kurihara (ed.) *Post-Keynesian Economics*, New Brunswick, NJ: Rutgers University Press.

Modigliani, F. and C. Steindel (1977) "Is a tax rebate an effective tool for stabilization policy?" *Brookings Papers on Economic Activity*, no. 1, pp. 175–203.

Muth, J. F. (1960) "Optimal properties of exponentially weighted forecasts," *Journal of American Statistical Association*, vol. 55 (June), pp. 299–306.

Okun, A. M. (1971) "The personal tax surcharge and consumer demand, 1968–70," *Brookings Papers on Economic Activity*, no. 1, pp. 167–211.

Sargent, T. J. (1978) "Rational expectations, econometric exogeneity, and consumption," *Journal of Political Economy*, vol. 86, no. 4 (August), pp. 673–700.

Springer, W. L. (1975) "Did the 1968 surcharge really work?" *American Economic Review*, vol. 65 (September), pp. 644–59.

US Bureau of Economic Analysis, *Survey of Current Business*, Washington: Government Printing Office, various issues.

APPENDIX 9.1

THE LIFETIME BUDGET CONSTRAINT

This appendix demonstrates a result that, to my knowledge, is not very well known: that the long-run MPC corresponding to a consumption function of the form:

$$C_t = kA_t + \sum_{j=0}^{n} b_j Y_{t-j} \tag{A9.1}$$

is unity for any value of k (greater than the real rate of interest) and for any bs.
Proof: Write equation (9.10) in the text as:

$$[1 - (1 + r)L]A_t = Y_{t-1} - C_{t-1} \tag{A9.2}$$

and write (A9.1) as:

$$C_t = kA_t + b(L)Y_t \tag{A9.3}$$

where L is the lag operator and $b(L) = b_0 + b_1 L + \ldots + b_n L^n$. Applying the operator $1 - (1 + r)L$ to (A9.3) and using (A9.2) yields $[1 - (1 + r - k)L]C_t = [kL + [1 - (1 + r)L]b(L)\} Y_t$, which can be written:

$$C_t = B(L)Y_t \tag{A9.4}$$

where:

$$B(L) = \frac{kL + [1 - (1 + r)L]b(L)}{1 - (1 + r - k)L} \tag{A9.5}$$

To obtain the lifetime spending generated by a \$1.00 impulse in Y_t, we must compute the discounted sum of coefficients:

$$\text{MPC} = \sum_{i=0}^{\infty} \frac{B_i}{(1 + r)^i} \tag{A9.6}$$

To simplify the notation, let $\theta \equiv 1 + r - k$. Assuming that $\theta < 1$ (i.e., that $k > r$), (A9.5) can be written: $B(L) = \{kL + [1 - (1 + r)L]b(L)\}(1 + \theta L + \theta^2 L^2 + \ldots)$. This is of the form $B(L) = B_0 + B_1 L + B_2 L^2 + \ldots$, with the following coefficients:

$$B_0 = b_0,$$
$$B_1 = \theta b_0 + [b_1 + k - (1 + r)b_0]$$
$$B_2 = \theta^2 b_0 + \theta[b_1 + k - (1 + r)b_0] + [b_2 - (1 + r)b_1]$$

$$\vdots$$

$$B_n = \theta^n b_0 + \theta^{n-1}[b_1 + k - (1 + r)b_0] + \ldots + [b_n - (1 + r)b_{n-1}]$$
$$B_{n+1} = \theta^{n+1} b_0 + \theta^n[b_1 + k - (1 + r)b_0] + \ldots +$$
$$+ \theta[b_n - (1 + r)b_{n-1}] - (1 + r)b_n$$
$$B_{n+1+s} = \theta^s B_{n+1}, \quad s = 1, 2, \ldots$$

Substitution of all of these into (A9.6), and some truly horrendous grinding, establishes that MPC = 1 regardless of the magnitudes of k and the b_j (as long as $k > 0$). QED.

A brief word on the interpretation of the sum of the b_j in (A9.1) may be in order here. Should Y_t rise permanently by \$1.00 – a statement that is basically meaningless if the autoregressive process assumed in the text (equation (9.2)) really holds – the eventual change in C_t would, by (A9.4), be $B(1) = \sum_{i=0}^{\infty} B_t$. According to (A9.5), this sum is:

$$B(1) = \frac{k - r \sum_{j=0}^{} b_j}{k - r} = 1 + \frac{r}{k - r}\left(1 - \sum_{j=0}^{n} b_j\right)$$

Thus Σb_j controls the size of the spending response to a hypothetical permanent rise in income; it does not influence the lifetime MPC.

APPENDIX 9.2

DETAILS ON THE ESTIMATING EQUATION

This appendix derives and explains the equation that was actually estimated. I begin by repeating equation (9.14) of the text:

$$C_t = k_0 + k_1 r_t Y_t + k_2(W_t - A_t) + \sum_{j=0}^{q} k_{3+j} A_{t-j}$$

$$+ \sum_{j=0}^{n} w_j(Y_{t-j} + \lambda X_t^j - S_{t-j})$$

$$+ \sum_{j=0}^{n} \beta\left[(1 - \lambda)X_t^j + \sum_{i=1}^{m} (1 - D_t^i)S_{t-j}^i\right] + u_t$$

For purposes of reducing heteroskedasticity, the assumption was made that the standard deviation of u_t was proportional to Y_t, so the whole equation was divided through by Y_t to get:

$$\text{APC}_t = \frac{k_0}{Y_t} + k_1 r_t + k_2\left(\frac{W_t}{Y_t} - \frac{A_t}{Y_t}\right)$$

$$+ \sum_{j=0}^{q} k_{3+j}\frac{A_{t-j}}{Y_t} + \sum_{j=0}^{n} w_j(z_{t-j} - q_{t-j})$$

$$+ \sum_{j=0}^{n} \beta_j\left[(1 - \lambda)x_t^j + \sum_{i=1}^{m} (1 - D_t^i)s_{t-j}^i\right] + \varepsilon_t \qquad (A9.7)$$

where:

$z_{t-j} \equiv Y_{t-j}/Y_t$ (note: $z_t = 1$ for all t)

$x_t^j = X_t^j/Y_t$

$s_{t-j} = \dfrac{S_{t-j}}{Y_t}$

$q_{t-j} = s_{t-j} - \lambda x_t^j$

$\varepsilon_t = \dfrac{u_t}{Y}$

To estimate (A9.7), the assumption was made that both w_j and β_j follow third-degree polynomials in j:

$$w_j = a_0 + a_1 j + a_2 j^2 + a_3 j^3$$
$$\beta_j = b_0 + b_1 j + b_2 j^2 + b_3 j^3 \tag{A9.8}$$

The end-point constraints mentioned in the text ($w_{n+1} = \beta_{n+1} = 0$) are thus

$$a_0 + (n+1)a_1 + (n+1)^2 a_2 + (n+1)^3 a_3 = 0$$
$$b_0 + (n+1)b_1 + (n+1)^2 b_2 + (n+1)^3 b_3 = 0 \tag{A9.9}$$

Equations (A9.9) were used to eliminate the parameters a_0 and b_0. The adding-up constraint discussed (and rejected) in the text was thus:

$$\sum_{j=1}^{n} \{a_1[j - (n+1)] + a_2[j^2 - (n+1)^2] + a_3[j^3 - (n+1)^3]\} \tag{A9.10}$$

$$= \sum_{j=0}^{n} \{b_1[j - (n+1)] + b_2[j^2 - (n+1)^2] + b_3[j^3 - (n+1)^3]\}$$

which was used to eliminate the parameter a_1.

Finally, in estimating (A9.7), ε_t was assumed to follow a first-order auto-regressive scheme, $\varepsilon_t = \rho\varepsilon_{t-1} + e_t$, where e_t is white noise. Estimation was by nonlinear least squares, which is equivalent to maximum likelihood if e_t is normally distributed. The function actually minimized was:

$$\sum_{t=0}^{T} \left\{ APC_t - \frac{k_0}{Y_t} - k_1 r_t - k_2 \left(\frac{W_t - A_t}{Y_t} \right) - \sum_{j=0}^{q} k_{3+j} \frac{A_{t-j}}{Y_t} \right.$$
$$\left. - \sum_{j=0}^{n} w_j(z_{t-j} - q_{t-j}) - \sum_{j=0}^{n} \beta_j \left[(1 - \lambda)x_t^j - \sum_{i=1}^{m} (1 - D_t^i)s_{t-j}^i \right] - \rho\varepsilon_{t-1} \right\}^2$$

with all the above-mentioned definitions and parameter restrictions substituted in.

The estimating forms when regular income was further disaggregated were derived in precisely analogous ways from equations (9.16) and (9.18).

APPENDIX 9.3

CALCULATION OF THE REAL AFTER-TAX INTEREST RATE

The real after-tax interest rate is defined as $r_t = i_t(1 - \tau_t) - \pi_t$, where i_t is the nominal interest rate, τ_t is the marginal tax rate, and π_t is the expected rate of inflation.

Nominal interest rate

Four different nominal interest rates were tried: a corporate bond rate, the 4–6 month commercial paper rate, the 3 month Treasury bill rate, and a weighted average of rates received on various time and savings accounts. While all four led to very similar results, the Treasury bill rate gave the best fit and so was adopted.

Marginal tax rate

The marginal tax rate was created from the average tax rate in the following way. Let $T(y)$ be the tax function facing an individual taxpayer, and let $f(y)$ be the frequency distribution of income. The only directly observable tax rate is the aggregate average rate, which is $A = [\int T(y)f(y)dy]/[\int yf(y)dy]$.

Now suppose the whole income distribution shifts to the right with no change in its shape; that is, it shifts from $f(y)$ to $f[y(1-h)]$, where h connotes a "small" multiplicative shift. The average income is then $Y(h) = \int yf[y(1-h)]dy$, so that, for small shifts (h near zero), $dY/dh = -\int y^2 f'(y)dy$. Similarly, average tax payments after the shift are $T(h) = \int T(y)f[y(1-h)]dy$, so that $dT/dh = -\int yT(y)f'(y)dy$. The aggregate marginal tax rate, M, is the ratio of these: $M \equiv [\int yT(y)f°(y)dy]*\{\int y^2 f'(y)dy\}$.

To evaluate these integrals and obtain a closed expression for M/A, I adopted the following functional forms:

$$T(y) = ay^b \qquad (b > 1,\ a > 0)$$

$$f(y) = \gamma e^{-\gamma y} \qquad (\gamma > 0)$$

With these assumptions, the two ratios of integrals work out to be $A = (a\gamma^2/\gamma^{b+1})\Gamma(b+1)$, $M = (a\gamma^3/2\gamma^{b+2})\Gamma(b+2)$, where $\Gamma(n)$ is the "gamma function," namely, $\Gamma(n+1) = n\Gamma(n)$. Hence $M/A = (b+1)/2$, and using a tax elasticity of $b = 1.6$ gives $M = (1.3)A$.

The average tax rate was computed, quarter by quarter, by dividing the sum of federal and state-local personal tax and nontax payments by personal income excluding transfers (an approximation to the tax base). These are all official national income accounts series.

Expected rate of inflation

Inflationary expectations were generated by a model based on what has been called "economically rational" expectations.[23] The idea is that agents, in informing themselves, begin with the data that are cheapest per unit of informational content and then proceed to process more costly data until the marginal cost and (expected) marginal benefits are equated. In this particular application, I assumed that consumers base their expectations of the inflation rate ($\dot{P}_t$) on its own past history and on the history of the growth rate of the money supply ($\dot{M}_t$). Thus I estimated an equation:

$$\dot{P}_t = a_0 + \sum_{j=1}^{J} a_j \dot{P}_{t-j} + \sum_{i=0}^{I} b_i \dot{M}_{t-i} + e_t$$

on actual US quarterly data, using the deflator for personal consumption expenditures for P_t and M_2 for M_t, and assumed that consumers used this equation to generate expectations. In estimation, I used the Almon (1965) lag technique with third-degree polynomials, no end-point constraints, and various choices for J and I. The best results were obtained with $J = 11$ and $I = 17$, namely:[24]

$$\dot{P}_t = -0.60 + \sum_{1}^{11} a_j \dot{P}_{t-j} + \sum_{0}^{17} b_i \dot{M}_{t-i}, \ R^2 = 0.73 \quad D-W = 1.98$$
$$(0.38)$$

standard error $= 1.42$, mean of dependent variable $= 3.35$,

$$\Sigma a_j = 0.67 \qquad \Sigma b_i = 0.27$$
$$(0.10) \qquad\qquad (0.09)$$

10 · SOCIAL SECURITY, BEQUESTS, AND THE LIFE CYCLE THEORY OF SAVING: CROSS-SECTIONAL TESTS

10.1 INTRODUCTION

This paper started out as an effort to use an unusually good source of cross-section data to address two current controversies about savings behavior:

1. Does "social security wealth," that is, the actuarial present value of future social security benefits, displace ordinary assets in individual portfolios?
2. Do people save mostly to finance retirement consumption (or, more generally, to shift consumption over time) or mostly to make intergenerational transfers?

The first question, which was raised originally by Feldstein (1974) and Munnell (1974), is of rather obvious importance for public policy toward the social security system, tax incentives for saving and related issues. Most empirical work on the question to date has been based on time-series data and, perhaps as an inevitable result, has been somewhat inconclusive. This is unfortunate, because the issue basically is a time-series question rather than a cross-sectional one: once general-equilibrium adjustments have taken place, is total national saving reduced by the social security system? Cross-sectional evidence, however, is not irrelevant. If, as Feldstein (1974) claims, social security wealth does displace private fungible wealth in individual portfolios, this effect should show up at the micro level.[1] One purpose of our research was to add to the rather limited supply to cross-sectional evidence on the social security displacement issue.[2]

An answer to the second question – that most saving is for intertemporal reallocation of consumption over the life cycle, not for bequests – was assumed in the original Modigliani–Brumberg (1954) paper, and has characterized most work on the life cycle model ever since. This answer, of course, is not inherent in the model, which is easily extended to include bequests. Tobin (1967), we believe, was the first to ask whether the pure life cycle theory with no bequests could account for aggregate savings in the United States. His answer was in the affirmative; but more recently White (1978) reached the opposite conclusion from a similar simulation model. Diamond's (1977)

This paper was written with Roger Gordon and Donald E. Wise.

analysis of cross-tabulations between assets and income led him to question whether the observed wealth holdings of older people would be sufficient for them to maintain their normal level of consumption – suggesting negative bequests (children supporting their elderly parents). But Mirer (1980) concluded that wealth holdings late in life do not decline as fast as they should if no bequests are intended. The most thorough study of this issue was by Kotlikoff and Summers (1980).[3] Using estimated life cycle patterns of consumption and earnings for individuals, they constructed an estimate of the wealth that those currently alive could have accumulated from their own savings and found that this amount was only a small fraction of total national wealth. The remainder presumably had been inherited – implying that an equivalent amount would have to be bequeathed in equilibrium.

The importance of bequests is relevant to several issues. Bequest behavior is one important determinant of intergenerational mobility in the distributions of income and wealth,[4] and plays a critical role in the debate over whether or not government bonds are net wealth.[5] Both the distributive and efficiency aspects of the choice between a consumption tax and an income tax depend, in part, on the importance of bequests in life cycle saving. Since no consensus has emerged on the relative importance of bequests versus intra-life cycle saving, a second major purpose of this paper was to see what could be learned from cross-sectional data.

Our original research strategy was to investigate these two questions within the framework of the life cycle theory of saving, which has established itself as the pre-eminent theory of saving.[6] However, as the work progressed, our trust in the ability of the life cycle theory to organise the data progressively diminished. In the end, we learned less about the questions that originally motivated the study than we did about the limitations of the life cycle theory itself. And it is the latter message that we now think is the paper's most important contribution.

The life cycle theory is held up in macroeconomics as an exemplary piece of economic analysis. A model with sound theoretical foundations (thanks to Irving Fisher) was given empirical life (through the ingenuity of Ando, Brumberg, Friedman and Modigliani) and subsequently validated many times in empirical tests. However, most of these tests have been conducted on time-series data which, as is well known, often have trouble in distinguishing among competing hypotheses.[7] To our knowledge, the precise implications of the strict form of the life cycle theory (defined specifically below) have never been tested. When we imposed the tight structure of the life cycle model on the data, we found out the following:

1. The model explains very little of the cross-sectional variation in savings behavior. This, in itself, may not be a serious condemnation of the theory since it might still correctly isolate one of many influences on savings. However, we also found that:

2. The critical parameters of the life cycle model are very poorly identified, even in a large cross-sectional sample (over 4,000 observations) with unusually good data on wealth.

3. The data are consistent with the life cycle theory only if it is assumed that people's utility functions shift systematically by age in such a way as to produce an optimal consumption stream with quite low consumption levels late in life.

Each of these is explained more fully later in the paper. Together they suggest to us that the empirical foundations of the life cycle theory are far shakier than was previously thought. More specifically, while the data do not deliver a strong rejection of the life cycle theory, they provide very little support for it.

The paper is organized as follows. The next section explains how we parameterized the strict form of the life cycle theory, and then modified the specification to make it suitable for estimation. After Section 10.3 discusses the data source, Section 10.4 takes a naïve impressionistic look at the data without trying to impose any theoretical structure at all. As we will see, the preliminary look at the data shows broad consistency with the life cycle theory, does *not* suggest that social security displaces private financial assets, and does *not* suggest an important bequest motive for saving. This of course raises a question of whether serious empirical modeling would reverse these rough impressions. The regression results reported in Section 10.5 turn out to be rather unfavorable to the life cycle hypothesis. However, the other two expectations – that the model would suggest neither a quantitatively important bequest motive nor a strong displacement effect of social security wealth – are confirmed. Section 10.6 is a brief summary of the major conclusions.

10.2 THE LIFE CYCLE MODEL: THEORY AND EMPIRICAL IMPLEMENTATION

10.2.1 The pure life cycle theory

The standard life cycle theory envisions an individual with a flow of earnings through time, E_t, and an initial endowment of wealth, A_0, choosing a consumption path, C_t, to maximize lifetime utility:

$$\sum_{t=0}^{T} \theta(t) U(C_t) + B(A_T) \tag{10.1}$$

where $U(C_t)$ is the one-period utility function, $\theta(t)$ is a weighting factor, and $B(A_T)$ is the utility of terminal assets. (Throughout the paper t is the individual's age and is assumed to run from 0 to T.) Normally $\theta(t)$ is specified as:

$$\theta(t) = \frac{1}{(1 + \rho)^t} \tag{10.2}$$

and $U(C_t)$ and $B(A_T)$ are assumed to be isoelastic:

$$U(C_t) = \frac{C_t^{1-\delta}}{1-\delta}, \quad B(A_T) = b \frac{A_T^{1-\delta}}{1-\delta} \tag{10.3}$$

While these specific assumptions are not inherent in the principle that individuals formulate life cycle plans, some such assumptions are necessary if the theory is to be made operational. If $\theta(t)$ is allowed to follow *any* arbitrary path, then no data can refute the theory. In this study we make the standard assumptions equations (10.2) and (10.3).

In a certain world with a perfect capital market, the only constraint on the maximization of lifetime utility is the lifetime budget constraint:

$$\sum_{t=0}^{T} \frac{C_t}{(1+r)^t} + \frac{A_T}{(1+r)^T} = A_0 + \sum_{t=0}^{T} \frac{E_t}{(1+r)^t} \equiv A_0 + Y_0 \tag{10.4}$$

where r is the rate of interest (assumed constant over time) and Y_0 is life-time discounted earnings, expressed in the dollars of $t = 0$. Maximizing equation (10.1) with respect to equation (10.4) under the specific assumptions (10.2) and (10.3) leads, as is well known, to:

$$C_t = C_0(1 + g)^t \tag{10.5}$$

$$A_T = \hat{\beta}C_0 \tag{10.6}$$

where g is positive if the rate of interest exceeds the rate of time discounting and negative otherwise,[8] and where $\hat{\beta}$ is a taste parameter.[9]

To adapt this to the case of a family consisting of N_t adult equivalents when the head is of age t, it is convenient to assume that family utility is:

$$N_t U(C_t/N_t)$$

where C_t now stands for *family* consumption. In words, family utility is the utility of the family's consumption per adult equivalent multiplied by the number of adult equivalents. In this case, it is readily shown that equations (10.5) and (10.6) are replaced by:

$$C_t = \left(\frac{N_t}{N_0}\right) C_0(1 + g)^t \tag{10.7}$$

$$A_T = \hat{\beta}\left(\frac{C_0}{N_0}\right) \tag{10.8}$$

Almost no cross-sectional data set has good data on consumption by age; ours is no exception. To move toward a testable equation, we must draw out the implications of the model for current holdings of assets A_t. Let Y_t be the present discounted value (in time t dollars) of earnings from time t *forward*, viz.:

$$Y_t = \sum_{s=t}^{T} \frac{E_s}{(1+r)^{s-t}}$$

where T, the length of life, is assumed for the present to be known. The budget constraint from time t forward implies that the sum $A_t + Y_t$ must be equal to the discounted present value of future consumption plus the planned bequest. Thus:

$$A_t + Y_t = \sum_{s=t}^{T} \frac{C_s}{(1+r)^{s-t}} + \frac{A_T}{(1+r)^{T-t}}$$

Using equations (10.7) and (10.8) this can be written:

$$A_t + Y_t = \sum_{s=t}^{T} \left(\frac{C_0}{N_0}\right) N_s \frac{(1+g)^s}{(1+r)^{s-t}} + \frac{\hat{\beta}}{(1+r)^{T-t}} \frac{C_0}{N_0}$$

or:

$$A_t + Y_t = (1+r)^t \frac{C_0}{N_0} \left[\sum_{s=t}^{T} (1+\mu)^s N_s + \beta \right] \tag{10.9}$$

where $1+\mu \equiv (1+g)/1+r$ and $\beta \equiv \hat{\beta}(1+r)^{-T}$. By setting $t=0$ in equation (10.9) we derive the lifetime budget constraint:

$$A_0 + Y_0 = \frac{C_0}{N_0} \left[\sum_{s=0}^{T} (1+\mu)^s N_s + \beta \right] \tag{10.10}$$

which can be used to solve for C_0/N_0. Substituting the result back into equation (10.9) gives the basic life cycle equation that we would like to estimate:

$$A_t + Y_t = \frac{\left[\sum_{s=t}^{T} (1+\mu)^s N_s + \beta \right]}{\left[\sum_{s=0}^{T} (1+\mu)^s N_s + \beta \right]} (\hat{A}_0 + \hat{Y}_0) \tag{10.11}$$

where $\hat{A}_0 + \hat{Y}_0$ is initial (non-human plus human) wealth expressed in time t dollars, that is, $\hat{A}_0 + \hat{Y}_0 = (A_0 + Y_0)(1+r)^t$.

The ratio of the two sums in equation (10.11) has a straightforward intuitive interpretation. The denominator is the number of adult equivalent years of consumption (properly discounted, and embodying any desired trend in consumption) in the family's entire life cycle, including an allowance for planned bequests. The numerator is similarly interpreted as the number of adult equivalent years of consumption still remaining when the head is age t. The equation then states that the fraction of total lifetime resources still available, $A_t + Y_t/\hat{A}_0 + \hat{Y}_0$, is equal to the fraction of adult equivalent years of life still remaining.

Notice two features of this specification. First, the units for β are years of adult equivalent consumption. Thus an estimated β of 5, say, would imply that the average family leaves a bequest equivalent to five adult-years of consumption. Second, equation (10.11) is *very* tightly parameterized according to the life cycle theory. Apart from whatever parameters constitute β (which we specify below), there is only *one* parameter to be estimated in equation (10.11). In particular, the dependence of asset holdings on age follows the very specific (and highly non-linear) functional form dictated by the strict form of the life cycle theory. This is very different, for example, from regressing assets on age and age squared.

We can make the specification a little more flexible, and at the same time provide a test of the rational planning calculation inherent in the life cycle model, by adding a parameter γ in front of the sum in the numerator of equation (10.11). That is:

$$A_t + Y_t = \frac{\left[\gamma \sum_{s=t}^{T} (1+\mu)^s N_s + \beta \right]}{\left[\sum_{s=0}^{T} (1+\mu)^s N_s + \beta \right]} (\hat{A}_0 + \hat{Y}_0) \qquad (10.12)$$

If people arrive at age t (which in our sample ranges from 60 to 65) with the level of assets implied by the life cycle theory, then γ should be equal to unity, as in equation (10.11). If, however, people systematically under-provide for their consumption at older ages, then γ will be less than unity. Thus testing whether γ differs from unity is a way of testing the life cycle model.[10]

10.2.2 Empirical implementation

Several additional assumptions were required before equation (10.12) could be confronted with data.

Uncertainty and family composition
The theoretical model just sketched assumes that the length of life, T, and the size of the family at each t, N_t, are known with certainty from the beginning. To point out that such knowledge is not available is trite. Knowing what to do about this uncertainty is less obvious, since a full-blown theoretical development of the model under uncertainty is very difficult. We have therefore adopted several simplifying assumptions.

First, we assume that individuals have access to a competitive annuities market – either directly or through pension plans (including, importantly, public pensions through social security). As Yaari (1965) has shown, the optimal life cycle plan in such circumstances is basically the same as in a world of certain lifetimes: the individual just needs to provide for his *expected* lifetime consumption by purchasing the requisite annuities.[11]

Second, we assume that future wage income and the dates of marriage and having children are known with certainty at the outset. Uncertainty over future income and family size would probably raise, rather than lower, saving. So if we find (as we do) that savings are lower than called for by the life cycle theory with certainty, then they must be lower than what an uncertainty model would predict.

Under these assumptions, it makes sense to adopt the following empirical proxies for the variables N_s in the theoretical model. Let Δ denote the husband's age minus the wife's age, and define:

$P_m(s, t)$ = probability that a male of age t survives to age s;
$P_f(s, t)$ = probability that a female of age t survives to age s.

Then our empirical proxy for N_s in the *denominator* of equation (10.12) was:

$$N_s = \begin{cases} 2 \text{ with probability } P_m(s, 17)P_f(s - \Delta, 17) \text{ (both partners living)} \\[4pt] 1 \text{ with probability } [1 - P_m(s, 17)]P_f(s - \Delta, 17) \\ + P_m(s, 17)[1 - P_f(s - \Delta, 17)] \text{ (one partner living)} \\[4pt] 0 \text{ with probability } [1 - P_m(s, 17)][1 - P_f(s - \Delta, 17)] \\ \text{(neither partner living)} \end{cases}$$

where survival probabilities are drawn from standard life tables.[12] Similarly, we replaced N_s in the *numerator* by:

$$N_s = \begin{cases} 2 \text{ with probability } P_m(s, t)P_f(s - \Delta, t - \Delta) \\[4pt] 1 \text{ with probability } [1 - P_m(s, t)]P_f(s - \Delta, t - \Delta) \\ + P_m(s, t)[1 - P_f(s - \Delta, t - \Delta)] \\[4pt] 0 \text{ with probability } [1 - P_m(s, t)][1 - P_f(s - \Delta, t - \Delta)] \end{cases}$$

Note the updating of the survival probabilities to ages t and $t - \Delta$.

Children had to be treated differently since, except for those still supported by their parents (a rarity in a sample where fathers ranged in age from 60 to 65 years), we did not know how many years of support each child had claimed. We decided arbitrarily that each child had been supported for 18 years, and that this support cost the family 18α adult equivalent years of consumption, where α is a parameter to be estimated. Thus, if we define:

NKIDS = number of children ever born;
NSUP = sum of (18-age), summed over any children still
        supported,

our approach was to add α_1NSUP to the numerator of equation (10.12) and

$18\alpha_2$ NKIDS to the denominator. We allowed α_1 to differ from α_2 on the grounds that, if intergenerational transfers are made *inter vivos*, adult sons and daughters might have received some of their inheritances but minor children would not have. This suggests that α_2 might exceed α_1.

Taste for bequests

An obvious determinant of the taste for bequests, and the only one we considered, is the number of children ever born. We therefore specified that β in equation (10.12) was given by:

$$\beta = b_0[b_1 + b_2 \text{NKIDS} + b_3 (\text{NKIDS})^2]$$

Thus, we look for a bequest motive by looking for an association between asset holdings late in life and number of children.

The seemingly redundant parameter b_0 was included originally to allow for possible nonlinearities in bequest behaviour (*i.e.* a wealth elasticity of bequests different from unity). To this end, we specified that:

$$b_0 = 1 + b_4(\hat{A}_0 + \hat{Y}_0)$$

so that a negative b_4 would signify a wealth elasticity of bequests below one and a positive b_4 would signify a wealth elasticity above one.[13] In the strict life cycle model, b_4 is zero (*i.e.* indifference curves are homothetic).

Finally, lacking any information on inheritances received ($\hat{A}_0$ in equation (10.12)) we simply assumed $A_0 = 0$ for everyone in the sample. If A_0 were typically positive, our equation should systematically understate asset holdings. In fact, it overstates them.

After all these modifications, equation (10.12) became:

$$A_t + Y_t = \left[\frac{\gamma P_t + \alpha_1 \text{NSUP} + \beta}{P_{17} + 18\alpha_2 \text{NKIDS} + \beta} \right] \hat{Y}_0 \qquad (10.13)$$

where:

$$P_t \equiv \sum_{s=t}^{110+\Delta} (1+\mu)^s \{ 2P_m(s,t) P_f(s-\Delta, t-\Delta)$$

$$+ [1 - P_m(s,t)] P_f(s-\Delta, t-\Delta) \qquad (10.14)$$

$$+ P_m(s,t)[1 - P_f(s-\Delta, t-\Delta)]$$

$$\beta = (1 + b_4 \hat{Y}_0)[b_1 + b_2 \text{NKIDS} + b_3 (\text{NKIDS})^2] \qquad (10.15)$$

Notice that apart from the parameters γ and b_4, this equation adheres scrupulously to the strict parameterization implied by the life cycle theory. It has a very specific (and highly nonlinear) structure, and includes only eight parameters.

So far, however, we have said nothing about one of the critical variables of our study: social security wealth (henceforth, SSW). As written in equation (10.13), the model *assumes* the validity of Feldstein's hypothesis that

SSW displaces private fungible wealth on a dollar-for-dollar basis, that is, if total lifetime resources are held constant, equation (10.13) implies that:

$$\frac{\partial A'_t}{\partial \text{SSW}_t} = -1,$$

where A'_t is financial assets. But there are a number of reasons why this might not be true: social security provides an annuity that cannot be bequeathed, SSW is an illiquid asset that is not fungible, SSW cannot be used as collateral on loans, social security benefits are indexed, and so on. For similar reasons and some additional ones (*e.g.* lack of vesting, worries about the financial reliability of the employer), private pension wealth may also be a less than perfect substitute for other wealth (and also for SSW). Similarly, there are many reasons why the net asset value of one's house may not be a perfect substitute for financial assets. To allow for these phenomena, we added the following three parameters to the model:

$$\lambda_1 \equiv -\frac{\partial A'_t}{\partial \text{SSW}_t}, \quad \lambda_2 \equiv -\frac{\partial A'_t}{\partial \text{PPW}_t}, \quad \lambda_3 \equiv -\frac{\partial A'_t}{\partial \text{RE}_t}$$

where SSW_t is the actuarial discounted value (in time t dollars) of the future social security benefits to which the individual is entitled;[14] PPW_t is private pension wealth, the analogous concept for private pension benefits; and RE_t is the net value of real estate owned. This led us to amend equation (10.13) as follows:

$$A'_t + \lambda_1 \text{SSW}_t + \lambda_2 \text{PPW}_t + \lambda_3 \text{RE}_t + Y_t$$

$$= \left[\frac{\gamma P_t + \alpha_1 \text{NSUP}_t + \beta}{P_{17} + 18\alpha_2 \text{NKIDS} + \beta} \right] (\hat{Y}_0 + \lambda_1 \text{SSW}_t + \lambda_2 \text{PPW}_t + \lambda_3 \text{RE}_t)$$

Notice that the concept of lifetime resources on the right-hand side of equation (10.16) is augmented in the same way as the assets variable on the left-hand side – each different type of asset gets its own λ. Equation (10.16), along with the definitions in equations (10.14) and (10.15), constitutes the model we originally set out to estimate.[15] Unfortunately, this task turned out to be surprisingly difficult.

10.3 DATA AND CONSTRUCTION OF VARIABLES

10.3.1 Data source and sample selection

The basic sampling frame was white men other than the self-employed in the 1971 wave of the Longitudinal Retirement History Survey (LRHS). This survey began with 11,153 individuals (both sexes, all races) between the ages of 58 and 63 in 1969, and reinterviewed those who survived and could be located at two year intervals through 1977.[16] Detailed information on asset holdings, earnings histories, pensions, and various socioeconomic traits was collected from each individual. Though our assets data came from the 1971 wave, information from the 1969, 1973, and 1975 interviews and from the related social security earnings histories was used in constructing several of the variables.

The potential sample of over 6,700 white men still living in 1971 was pared to only 4,130 observations for a variety of reasons:

1. When the asset data were incomplete, the observation was dropped.
2. All individuals who reported having an investment in a business were dropped. Due to some unfortunate wording in the questionnaire, the reported value of this investment was unreliable.
3. Lifetime earnings were constructed for each individual and his spouse by a procedure sketched below and described in detail in Appendix 10.1. When respondents did not supply enough information to construct it, they were dropped from the sample.[17]
4. When the husband was reported to be 20 or more years older than the wife, or more than 15 years younger, we dropped the observation. Most of these cases seem to be clear errors in the data.[18]
5. For a few cases, the reported value of the house net of the mortgage was negative. Sceptical about such a possibility, we dropped these cases.

10.3.2 Lifetime earnings data

The variable $\hat{Y}_0$ in equation (10.16) is the actuarial discounted present value from age 17 forward (converted to 1971 dollars) of the earnings of *both* the husband and the wife. The variable Y_t is the same variable, but including only earnings from age t forward. To construct these variables, it was necessary to generate for each husband and wife a lifetime profile of both wages and hours. Since this is a complex calculation, we sketch it here and relegate the details to the appendix.

Wage rates of the husband
Our procedure for generating a wage profile for men began by gathering all possible observations on past wages available in the LRHS surveys. This provides us with *at most* four wage observations: the wage reported for the first job, the wage reported for the "last job" as of the 1969 interview, and the wages reported for the "current jobs" in the 1969 and 1971 interviews.[19] The gaps between observed wage rates were "filled in" by using estimates derived from a wage equation discussed in Gordon and Blinder (1980), as explained in the appendix.

Hours of work for the husband
There is a fairly obvious endogeneity problem between assets and hours of work late in life. Differences in assets can cause differences in labor supply

and/or retirement age. To purge the data of this potential endogeneity, we used an *estimated* labor supply profile, rather than the *actual* profile observed in the data. From an econometric point of view, this can be thought of as using an instrument for $\hat{Y}_0$.

Specifically, we assumed that typical hours are always 2,000 per year until retirement and zero thereafter,[20] which reduces the problem of constructing a typical hours profile to one of estimating the probability of being retired at each age. For this purpose, we used the retirement probabilities derived and presented in Gordon and Blinder (1980) to generate for each individual a predicted probability of being retired at each age between 58 and 85 based on his wage rate and personal characteristics. Retirement before age 58 was assumed never to occur, and every individual was assumed retired after age 85 even if our equations gave them some small probability of still being at work. Hours for individual i in year t were set equal to $2,000\,(1 - p_{it})$, where p_{it} is the estimated probability that individual i is retired in year t.

Having thus estimated both wages and hours in each year of life, the implied earnings for each year were discounted or accumulated to 1971 using a 2 percent real interest rate to arrive at $\hat{Y}_0$ for the husband. Predicted wages and hours from 1971 *forward* were used to construct Y_t in precisely the same way. Table 10.1 reports the means and standard deviations of both of these constructed variables. In terms of expected discounted present value, these men have on average less than 6 percent of their lifetime earnings still ahead of them. Notice also that while Y_t is very small relative to Y_0, it is much more widely dispersed. (The coefficient of variation of Y_0 is 0.9, while the coefficient of variation of Y_t is 1.8.) This is as expected because of individual differences in retirement decisions.

Earnings of the wife

Most of the men in the sample were married. The presence of a wife is relevant both as an additional claim on the resources of the family (as explained earlier) and as an additional contributor to the family's resources through her own earnings. Lifetime earnings measures for wives were constructed in much the same way as for husbands. However, a few extra problems arose, and are explained in the appendix.

Table 10.1 shows that the computed lifetime earning figures for women are on average about 10 percent of the corresponding figures for men, and are

Table 10.1 Selected data on lifetime earnings (in 1971 dollars)

		Mean ($)	Standard deviation ($)
Husbands	Y_0	445,514	493,057
	Y_t	24,207	48,183
Wives	Y_0	43,666	64,569
	Y_t	5,772	13,521

also much more variable. Both of these are as expected, given the spotty work histories of women of this age cohort. It is also not surprising that the wives have a much larger percentage of their total lifetime earnings still ahead of them – over 13 percent versus less than 6 percent for husbands.

The variable $\hat{Y}_0$ used in the regression consisted of the sum of the estimated lifetime earnings of the husband and wife. Its mean is about $482,000.

It is worth comparing the numbers in Table 10.1 with the corresponding figures from a recent paper by Feldstein (1980), which uses the 1969 wave of the LRHS, since a sharp difference emerges. The mean of lifetime earnings in Feldstein's sample is only $244,566, barely more than half of ours. That Feldstein uses 1969 dollars while we use 1971 dollars requires some small adjustment to put his numbers on an equal footing with ours, and his numbers should also differ on account of excluding single men (which should make his mean higher) and government employees. But we imagine that the largest source of difference is that Feldstein's estimates of lifetime earnings were derived from social security records. The earnings figures he uses therefore will be systematically too low because of the following:

1. Earnings prior to 1936 are excluded, and people in this sample were already 25–30 years old by 1936.
2. Social security records include only *covered* earnings, and coverage of the system was far from complete in its early years. For example, in 1939 and 1955 only 55 percent and 76 percent respectively of all civilian employees were in covered employment.[21]
3. Only the simple *sum* of earnings between 1936 and 1950 appears in the social security records. By necessity, the accumulated (at compound interest) earnings over this 15 year period must exceed this simple sum.

10.3.3 Assets data

The LRHS offers unusually detailed information on asset holdings by type of asset. The variable A'_t in equation (10.16) was constructed as the sum of the following components of net worth (each expressed in 1971 dollars).[22]

1. *Net financial assets*: the sum of all bank account balances, plus the market value of any stock, bonds, or life insurance, minus any outstanding loans. The market value of life insurance was estimated as the reported face value of the policy multiplied by:

$$\sum_{s=t}^{100} \frac{P_m(s, t)}{(1 + r)^{s-t}} \tag{10.16}$$

2. *Net value of real estate*: the market value of an owner occupied house or any other real estate owned, minus the outstanding mortgage balance.

The other two assets considered in the study are as follows:

3. *Social security wealth*: the actuarial discounted present value of future social security benefits. This is an important asset for older people, and earlier studies have been plagued by the absence of a reliable estimate of its value.[23] To estimate an individual's social security benefits at retirement, we applied the social security benefit formula to the earnings history that we estimated for him using the procedure described in Appendix 10.1. Estimated rather than actual earnings were used to avoid any endogeneity problems between hours of work and assets. However, in any year for which an individual's covered earnings were much smaller than our estimated earnings, we assumed his main job was not covered by social security, and set his covered earnings to zero. The individual's yearly benefits, assumed to be indexed to prices and to grow in real terms by 2 percent per annum, were then actuarially discounted back to the present to arrive at our measure of social security wealth. The effect of using estimated, rather than actual, social security benefits was to change the mean of SSW very little, but to reduce its standard deviation by about 25 percent.

4. *Private pension wealth*: a similarly constructed measure of the actuarial present value of expected future benefits from private and/or government pensions. For individuals reporting their expected pension benefits, we treated the reported flow as a fixed *nominal* amount (unlike social security benefits, which are indexed), and discounted by the nominal interest rate. For people reporting a pension but not knowing the amount of their future benefits, we made an imputation based on regressing pension benefits on wages for those who reported their future benefits.

Even before any statistical analysis is performed, it is interesting to look at the amount of assets of various types held by people in our sample.[24] Table 10.2 shows the means and standard deviations for each category of net worth. A few striking facts emerge immediately. First, social security wealth is by far the most important source of wealth for the average person in the sample. Second, however, in accounting for the variance of wealth across people, SSW is probably of minor importance because it is so equally distributed as compared with any of the other sources of wealth. Third, mean holdings of financial wealth – which here include the market value of life

Table 10.2 Selected data on wealth holdings, 1971

Asset type	Mean ($)	Standard deviation ($)
Financial	17,159	36,116
Real estate	15,888	26,662
Social security	34,527	8,270
Pensions	6,383	12,970

insurance – look so small compared to lifetime resources (whose mean is over $500,000) as to suggest irrationally low savings. However, total non-human wealth is about four times as large as financial wealth – about $70,000 for the average family, or one-seventh of total lifetime resources. In addition, most of these families still have some unused "human wealth" (discounted present value of expected future earnings) as well – amounting on average to about 6 percent of lifetime resources according to Table 10.1. It is far from obvious that reserving one-fifth of lifetime resources for use after age 60–65 (including any planned bequests) constitutes "too little" saving.

Again, comparisons with Feldstein's (1980) tabulations with the same data source are instructive. The per capita (or per couple) wealth totals are very similar (his is roughly $69,000) but the distribution across components is quite different. His estimated social security wealth per couple – about $45,000 – is far higher than ours, mainly because Feldstein excluded government employees, whose SSW is zero. Offsetting differences appear in non-pension wealth, where Feldstein's mean is $23,682 and our sum of mean financial wealth plus mean real estate is $33,062, even though we eliminated from the sample all business assets. Finally, Feldstein does not attempt to estimate private pension wealth for the individuals in his sample.

10.4 DETERMINANTS OF ASSET ACCUMULATION: A PRELIMINARY LOOK

Before proceeding to explain the difficulties that arose in attempting to estimate equation (10.26) and to present the estimates, it is worth pausing to consider what we are looking for in the data. Such an initial look will teach us much that maximizing a likelihood function with 8 parameters and 4,130 observations conceals.

Our version of the life cycle theory makes asset accumulation depend essentially on the ages of the husband and the wife and on the number of children (which we use as a proxy for the bequest motive). The theory implies a very particular rate of decline with age of a comprehensive concept of wealth, $A_t + Y_t$. Specifically, denote the ratio of $A_t + Y_t$ to $\hat{A}_0 + \hat{Y}_0$ by the symbol R_t. Then, in the case $\gamma = 1$, the theory implies:

$$\frac{R_{t+1}}{R_t} = \frac{P_{t+1} + \beta}{P_t + \beta}$$

when there are no dependent children in the household.[25] If the parameter μ is close to zero (as it should be), and both husband and wife are alive both in period $t + 1$ and period t, then $P_{t+1} = P_t - 2$, so the rate of decline of R_t is:

$$\frac{R_{t+1} - R_t}{R_t} = \frac{-2}{P_t + \beta} \tag{10.17}$$

In our sample, a value of P_t near 30 is about average, so equation (10.17) implies that R_t should fall about 6.7 percent per year if $\beta = 0$ or about 5 percent per year if $\beta = 10$.

Do the data display this predicted behavior? On the surface, they seem not to, as Fig. 10.1 indicates. The bottom line in Fig. 10.1 plots the age profile of financial assets, A'_t, relative to lifetime income. There is not a hint that this ratio declines with age. However, it is worth stressing that the theory predicts a declining age profile only of a much more comprehensive measure of wealth: $A'_t + RE_t + SSW_t + PPW_t + Y_t$. Since the last three items on this list must decline with age, we might see a decline in a broader wealth concept that does not appear in A'_t. The remaining lines in Fig. 10.1 investigate successively more comprehensive definitions of wealth by adding additional assets to A'_t, more or less in order of liquidity. Thus, the second line adds the value of real estate to financial assets; still there is no trace of a negative slope. When pension assets (both SSW and PPW)–which, by their method of construction are virtually guaranteed to decline with age[26] – are added to wealth, a slight tendency toward a declining wealth profile does emerge. (The ratio of all non-human assets to lifetime income drops only 8 percent between ages 60 and 65, and is almost the same at age 64 as it is at age 61.) However, when the present value of future earnings is added to non-human assets, a very pronounced declining age profile appears. On average, the ratio of (human plus non-human) assets to lifetime income falls by 6.3 percent per year between ages 60 and 65 for the people in our sample. As noted, this is broadly consistent with the prediction embodied in equation (10.17).

In sum, if a broadly-defined concept of wealth that includes expected future earnings is used to measure current assets, the data do show the sort of pattern prescribed by life cycle theory. In terms of the specific model in equation (10.16), then, there is nothing in this crude look at the data to warn us that the estimated γ will stray far from its theoretical value of unity.[27]

The second thing we are looking for in these data is a systematic dependence of assets on the number of children, either increasing with children due to bequest, or decreasing due to the expenses of child rearing and/or intergenerational transfers given *inter vivos* rather than at death. Figure 10.2 plots the same four concepts of wealth (all normalized by lifetime income) against the number of children.[28] A clear relationship does emerge: with few exceptions, assets (no matter how defined) are *decreasing* in the number of children. Now this, of course, does not disprove the existence of a bequest motive. But it does indicate that the factors leading assets to decline with the number of children dominate any bequest motive that may exist. Our statistical specification in equation (10.16) is designed precisely to separate out the effects of the bequest motive (which is captured by the bs) from the effects of child-rearing expenses (which are captured by the αs). But even before estimation, Fig. 10.2 should give pause to believers in a strong bequest motive. Of the assets considered here, financial assets and real estate seem

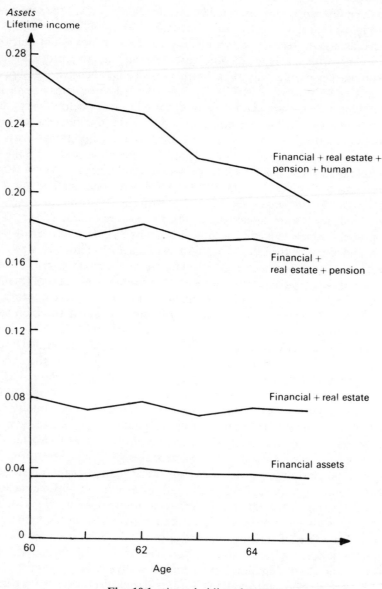

Fig. 10.1 Asset holdings by age

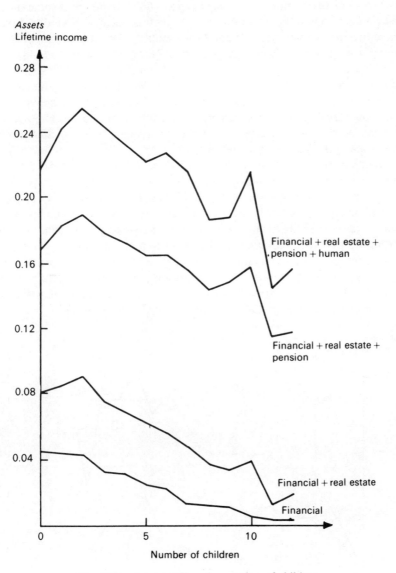

Fig. 10.2   Asset holdings by number of children

most suited for bequests, yet the pattern of decline of $A'_t + RE_t$ with the number of children is marked.

Let us next turn the glare of crude empiricism on the hypothesis suggested by Feldstein: that families with a high ratio of SSW to lifetime income should have a correspondingly low ratio of A'_t to lifetime income. Figure 10.3 plots these two ratios against each other[29] on a graph that should produce a slope of −1 if the Feldstein hypothesis is correct. This pattern most certainly does not appear in the data. If anything, both A'_t and $A'_t + RE_-^{[}Efdt$ relative to lifetime income look to be *increasing* with SSW$_t$ relative to lifetime income over most of the range. The dotted lines in Fig. 10.3 indicate where most of the people are located, with social security wealth between 3 and 11 percent of lifetime income. In this range, A'_t looks relatively independent of SSW$_t$, while RE_t apparently is strongly increasing.

Once again, we must emphasize that these plots are only indicative of *simple correlations*. It could be that once we control for other pertinent influences (such as age and number of children) evidence that SSW displaces A' will emerge. This is why we need to estimate a statistical model. Nonetheless, in view of Fig. 10.3 it would be quite surprising if the data provided strong support for Feldstein's displacement hypothesis.

To sum up, this preliminary look at the data makes it seem reasonable to try to use the life cycle model of consumption to organize the data, but does not give any reason to expect the estimated model to turn up a strong bequest motive or a strong displacement effect of social security wealth.

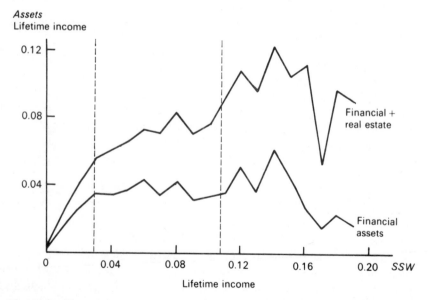

Fig. 10.3 Financial assets versus social security wealth (both normalized by lifetime income)

10.5 ESTIMATION PROBLEMS AND EMPIRICAL RESULTS

As everyone knows, the distribution of wealth is incredibly skewed. This makes it important to estimate equation (10.16) by weighted least squares, for otherwise a handful of very rich families may dominate the results.[30] We assumed that the error variance was proportional to the square of $(Y_0 + SSW + PPW)$ and hence divided both sides of equation (10.16) by this quantity to arrive at the estimating equation:

$$\frac{A_t' + \lambda_1 SSW_t + \lambda_2 PPW_t + \lambda_3 RE_t + Y_t}{\hat{Y}_0 + SSW_t + PPW_t}$$

$$= \left[\frac{\gamma P_t + \alpha_1 NSUP_t + \beta}{P_{17} + 18\alpha_2 NKIDS + \beta} \right] \tag{10.18}$$

$$\times \left[\frac{\hat{Y}_0 + \lambda_1 SSW_t + \lambda_2 PPW_t + \lambda_3 RE_t}{\hat{Y}_0 + SSW_t + PPW_t} \right] + \varepsilon_t$$

Estimation was by nonlinear least squares, using the Davidson–Fletcher–Powell algorithm as programmed in the GQOPT package. However, we quickly learned that the model as originally posited was statistically unidentified, even with over 4,000 observations.

Some of the reasons are easy to explain by referring to equation (10.18). Consider first the parameter b_4 in β (see equation (10.15) for definition of all the bs), which was designed to estimate the wealth elasticity of bequests. Obviously it is very hard to distinguish b_4 from the other parameters pertaining to bequests (b_1, b_2 and b_3).[31] Similarly, the functional form shows that the growth rate parameter, μ in equation (10.14), will probably be a good substitute for the multiplicative parameter, γ, at least in a sample with limited variation in ages such as ours; that is, raising one while lowering the other will have very little effect on the sum of squared residuals (or on the predictions of the model). Thus it became quite clear very early in the research that neither μ nor b_4 could be estimated with any precision. Fortunately, the initial point estimates of both b_4 and μ were extremely close to zero, so little was lost by constraining them both to be zero. Setting $b_4 = 0$ imposes the usual linearity assumption of the life cycle model, and setting $\mu = 0$ imposes $g = r$. These constraints raised the sum of squared residuals hardly at all, and improved the precision of the other estimates somewhat (though they were still not estimated very precisely).

What was more surprising, and more distressing, was that the α parameters in equation (10.18) were so hard (really impossible) to pin down empirically. Recall that these parameters are designed to distinguish between child-rearing expenses (plus gifts *inter vivos*) and bequests at death as conflicting influences on asset accumulation of people with different amounts of children.

The reason for the lack of identification of the α_1 in the numerator is clear enough: very few people in this age range still have dependent children. However, the α_2 in the denominator also proved impossible to estimate, despite very considerable cross-sectional variation in NKIDS. The reason in this case is that α_2 whose presumptive sign is positive, cannot be distinguished from b_2, the linear term in the bequest function (whose presumptive sign is also positive). Included in the denominator of equation (10.18) is a term that is essentially $(b_2 + 18\alpha_2)$NKIDS; and the presence of b_2NKIDS by itself in the numerator is apparently not enough to identify α_2 and b_2 separately. Some experimentation showed that the sum of squared residuals (henceforth) SSR function was essentially flat over a wide range of α_2 values, so we arbitrarily set $\alpha_2 = 1$.

Even after making all these additional restrictions, the estimates we obtained were disappointing. The point estimates of equation (10.18) along with their asymptotic standard errors are presented in Table 10.3, and it can be seen that they are regrettably imprecise.

Let us start with γ, the parameter designed to test whether people were following the age-assets pattern dictated by the life cycle theory. The estimate of γ (0.45) is significantly below its theoretical value of unity, which means that assets do not decline fast enough with age. This is not what Fig. 10.1 suggested to us earlier. Apparently, controlling for other variables (such as wife's age) changes things dramatically.

Turning next to the bequest parameters (the bs), we find very little ability to pin down any systematic effect of the number of children on asset accumulation, even after constraining $\alpha_2 = 1$. The standard errors of b_1, b_2 and b_3 are all very large relative to their point estimates. Taken at face value, the point estimates do suggest a bequest motive, but a rather weak one. Table 10.4 uses the point estimates to tabulate the total, marginal and average bequest as a function of the number of children. The point estimates imply that the marginal effect of an additional child on the planned bequest is positive up to

Table 10.3 Parameter estimates, constrained model

Coefficient	Estimate	Standard error
γ	0.45	0.19
λ_1	0.39	0.45
λ_2	−0.30	0.54
λ_3	−0.34	0.10
μ	0	Constrained
α_1	0.10	1.45
α_2	1.0	Constrained
b_1	−2.67	4.19
b_2	1.98	2.56
b_3	−0.10	0.47
b_4	0	Constrained

Standard error of the regression = 0.101

Table 10.4 Estimated planned bequests (in years of consumption)

Number of children	Fraction of sample	Total bequest[a]	Marginal bequest[b]	Average bequest[c]
0	0.16	−2.7	—	—
1	0.18	−0.8	1.9	−0.8
2	0.24	0.9	1.7	0.4
3	0.17	2.3	1.5	0.8
4	0.10	3.6	1.3	0.9
5	0.06	4.6	1.0	0.9
6	0.03	5.4	0.8	0.9
7	0.02	6.1	0.6	0.9
8	0.01	6.5	0.4	0.8
9	0.01	6.7	0.2	0.7
10	0.005	6.7	—	0.6

Notes:
(a) Computed as $-2.67 + 1.98(NKIDS) - 0.10(NKIDS)^2$.
(b) Computed as $1.98 - 0.10[(NKIDS)^2 - (NKIDS - 1)^2]$.
(c) Computed as $\dfrac{-2.67}{NKIDS} + 1.98 - 0.10 NKIDS$.

10 children, and that the bequest per child is constant at just under 1 year's worth of adult consumption over much of the relevant range. Thus, despite the fact that Fig. 10.2 showed assets *decreasing* as the number of children increased, there is some weak evidence here of a bequest motive. But it is weak indeed, and gives no reason to think that the desire to leave a bequest is a major motive for saving. (The estimated mean bequest in the sample is only 1.25 years of consumption.)

The other question of interest was the displacement effect of social security wealth. Our point estimate states that each \$1 of social security wealth leads people to decrease their financial wealth by 39¢. This does not seem an unreasonable number, and is in fact better than we might have expected after looking at Fig. 10.3. However, the standard error of this estimate is so large (0.45) that we can reject neither $\lambda_1 = 0$ nor $\lambda_1 = 1$. One other remark should be made about λ_1. In experimenting with minor changes in the specification (principally constraining different subsets of $(\gamma, \alpha_2, \lambda_2, \lambda_3)$ to be unity), we found that the estimate of λ_1 was highly unstable – as is only to be expected from the large standard errors.[32]

The other λs are much worse. The weight for private pension wealth (λ_2) has the wrong sign, though it is not significantly different from zero. The weight on real estate wealth (λ_3) is also incorrectly signed, and is highly significant as well. These estimates suggest that PPW and RE may be capturing some aspects of lifetime income that we missed in our constructed proxy $\hat{Y}_0$.

10.6 SUMMARY AND CONCLUSIONS

The pattern of asset holdings by age that is found in our sample of data is not on its face inconsistent with the strict form of the life cycle theory of saving. However, when the parameters of the life cycle model are estimated we are forced to conclude either that the taste for consumption is systematically weaker in old age than in earlier years, or that people are underproviding for their retirement consumption. In addition, the parameters of the model appear to be very poorly identified, even with an extensive cross-sectional data set. Some parameters could not be estimated at all while others could be estimated only with very large standard errors.

Though some weak evidence (not statistically significant) was turned up for the existence of a bequest motive, there is nothing in these data to suggest that the desire to leave a bequest is an important motive for saving. A few remarks are needed to put this finding into proper perspective. First, there is an untested hypothesis that underlies this research: that if there is a strong bequest motive, it ought to show up in asset holdings late in life being higher for people with more children. This seems a reasonable hypothesis to us, though it remains untested. What we actually find in the data is that once we control for other pertinent influences, families with more children have only slightly higher assets.[33]

Second, this finding does not say that intergenerational transfers are trivial because transfers *inter vivos* might be important. Third, in the real world, unlike in our model, the actuarially fair indexed annuities of the Yaari (1965) model are not available (except for those households whose social security wealth is large enough to meet their entire demand for annuities). As a result, actual bequests will be more variable than planned bequests, with those who die earlier than expected leaving larger bequests than they had planned.

Finally, even though the data show that people with higher social security wealth (relative to lifetime income) have higher financial assets (relative to lifetime income), our model does suggest that there may be some "displacement" of private savings by social security once other things are held equal. Unfortunately, the point estimate – that each $1 of social security wealth displaces 39¢ of private financial wealth – is too imprecise (and too unstable) to draw any conclusions.

NOTES

1. A demonstration that social security wealth displaces private wealth at the micro level, however, does not establish that a similar displacement takes place at the macro level. Even if social security has no effect in the aggregate, those who receive unusually high benefits may save less while those who receive unusually low benefits may save more.
2. See Feldstein and Pellechio (1979), and Feldstein (1980).

3. See also related work by Darby (1979) and Atkinson (1971).
4. Blinder (1976a), Shorrocks (1979), Menchik (1979).
5. Barro (1974, 1976), Feldstein (1976).
6. For our purposes, there is no important difference between the life cycle theory of Modigliani and Brumberg (1954) and the permanent income theory of Friedman (1957).
7. In time series, the characteristic implication of the life cycle theory is that assets, in addition to income, influence consumption. For the permanent income version, as usually implemented, it is that lagged as well as current income influences consumption. It is not hard to think up entirely different models of consumption that have the same implications. Hall (1978) offers a more stringent test which, interestingly enough, supports the theory on time-series data but rejects it in cross-section (Hall and Mishkin, 1980).
8. Specifically, $1 + g \equiv \left(\dfrac{1+r}{1+\rho} \right)^{1/\delta}$
9. Specifically, $\beta = (b)^{1/\delta}(1 + r)^{T/\delta}$.
10. An alternative interpretation of $\gamma < 1$, which we do not find very satisfying, is that θ_t shifts systematically with age in such a way that average consumption at ages beyond 60–5 is lower than $C_0(1 + g)^t$. As stated earlier, if arbitrary changes in θ_t over time are permitted, *any* data are consistent with the life cycle theory.
11. Unfortunately, the requisite annuities are *indexed* annuities, which normally are *not* available apart from social security.
12. Age 17 is assumed to be the age of economic adulthood. We assumed marriages took place when the younger partner was 17; for years in which only one partner was over 17, N_s set equal to 1, not 2.
13. For reasons why this is an important parameter, see Blinder (1976b), or Menchik and David (1979).
14. Our SSW measure is *gross* social security wealth since payroll taxes are deducted before computing earnings.
15. This is not quite true. When we started the work we had more confidence in the life cycle theory, and hence constrained $\gamma = 1$. We also constrained $\alpha_1 = \alpha_2$ at first.
16. Survival is assumed random, so that no selectivity problems arise.
17. We also dropped a few observations where the various reported wage rates were dramatically at odds with one another, suggesting an error on the original data tape.
18. Our model of asset holdings depends heavily on the ages of the couple, so would be very sensitive to reporting errors in these ages.
19. We had in addition wage information on the current jobs reported in 1973 and 1975, but did not use these data because of potential endogeneity between current assets in 1971 and future labor supply decisions.
20. This may seem an extreme assumption, and perhaps it is. However, evidence presented in Gordon and Blinder (1980) suggests that it is a tolerably accurate description of the labor-supply behavior of men in this sample.
21. See *Social Security Bulletin*, Statistical Supplement, 1975, Table 7, page 44.
22. Throughout the study, whenever it was necessary to discount or accumulate sums at compound interest we used a 6 percent nominal or a 2 percent real rate of interest.
23. See, for example, Munnell (1974), Feldstein and Pellechio (1979).
24. Our data set does not report information on the value of consumer durables, hence this asset is omitted.
25. The definition of P_t is provided in equation (10.14).
26. In calculating SSW and PPW, we assumed individuals initially claimed benefits at

age 65, so that no one in our sample would yet have drawn on their benefits. We thus underestimate any decline in the value of this component of wealth with age.

27. When the parameter γ is introduced, equation (10.17) becomes: $\dfrac{R_{t+1} - R_t}{R_t} = \dfrac{-2\gamma}{\gamma P_t + \beta}$ so an estimated γ well below unity would imply that assets were not falling "fast enough."

28. The graph is truncated at 12 children even though a few families in our sample had more because the tiny sample sizes lead to erratic behavior in the upper tail.

29. Specifically, the ratios of SSW to lifetime income for each person are grouped as follows: numbers between 0 and 0.009 are considered as zero in the figure; numbers between 0.01 and 0.019 are considered as 0.01, and so on. For each such class, the mean of assets divided by lifetime income is calculated and plotted in Figure 10.3.

30. We have in our sample, for example, one observation for which assets are 252 times as large as lifetime earnings.

31. Identification of b_4 hinges precariously on the presence of the constant 1.0 in equation (10.15).

32. The estimates of the bs were also highly unstable. However, we never obtained a set of point estimates of b_1, b_2 and b_3 that suggested an important bequest motive.

33. It is apparently important to control statistically for "other things.". Without such controls, Fig. 10.2 showed clearly that families with more children have lower assets.

REFERENCES

Atkinson, A. B. (1971) "The distribution of wealth and the individual life cycle," *Oxford Economic Papers* (July), vol. 23, no. 2, pp. 239–54.

Barro, R. J. (1974) "Are government bonds net wealth?," *Journal of Political Economy*, vol. 82 (November–December), pp. 1095–117.

Barro, R. J. (1976) "Reply to Feldstein and Buchanan," *Journal of Political Economy*, vol. 84 (April), pp. 343–9.

Blinder, A. S. (1976a) "Inequality and mobility in the distribution of wealth," *Kyklos*, vol. 29, fasc. 4, pp. 607–38.

Blinder, A. S. (1976b) "Intergenerational transfers and life-cycle consumption," *American Economic Review*, vol. 66 (May), pp. 87–93.

Darby, M. R. (1979) *The Effects of Social Security on Income and the Capital Stock*, Washington: American Enterprise Institute.

Diamond, P. A. (1977) "A framework for social security analysis," *Journal of Public Economics*, vol. 8, pp. 275–98.

Feldstein, M. S. (1974) "Social security, induced retirement, and aggregate capital accumulation," *Journal of Political Economy*, pp. 905–26.

Feldstein, M. S. (1980) "Social security benefits and the accumulation of preretirement wealth," NBER Working Paper no. 477 (May).

Feldstein, M. S. and A. Pellechio (1979) "Social security and household wealth accumulation: new microeconomic evidence," *Review of Economics and Statistics*, pp. 361–8.

Friedman, M. (1957) *A Theory of the Consumption Function*, Princeton: Princeton University Press.

Gordon, R. H. and A. S. Blinder (1980) "Market wages, reservation wages, and retirement decisions," *Journal of Public Economics*, vol. 14, pp. 277–308.

Hall, R. E. (1978) "Stochastic implications of the life cycle– permanent income hypothesis: theory and evidence," *Journal of Political Economy*, vol. 86 (December), pp. 971–87.

Hall, R. E. and F. S. Mishkin (1980) "The sensitivity of consumption to transitory income: estimates from panel data on households," NBER Workings Paper no. 505 (July).

Kotlikoff, L. J. and L. H. Summers (1980) "The role of intergenerational transfers in aggregate capital accumulation," NBER Working Paper no. 445 (February).

Menchik, P. L. (1979) "Inter-generational transmission of inequality: an empirical study of wealth mobility," *Economica*, vol. 46 (November), pp. 349–62.

Menchik, P. L. and M. David (1979) "The effect of income distribution and redistribution on lifetime savings and bequests," mimeo, University of Wisconsin (November).

Mirer, T. W. (1980) "The dissaving behavior of the aged," *Southern Economic Journal* (April), pp. 1197–205.

Modigliani, F. and R. Brumberg (1954) "Utility analysis and the consumption function: an interpretation of cross-section data," in K. K. Kurihara (ed.), *Post Keynesian Economics*, New Brunswick, NJ: Rutgers University Press.

Munnell, A. H. (1974) *The Effect of Social Security on Personal Savings Behavior*, Cambridge, Mass.: Ballinger.

Shorrocks, A. F. (1979) "On the structure of inter-generational transfers between families," *Economica*, vol. 46 (November), pp. 415–25.

Tobin, J. (1967) "Life-cycle saving and balanced growth," in W. Fellner (ed.), *Ten Economic Studies in the Tradition of Irving Fisher*, New York: Wiley, pp. 231–56.

White, B. B. (1978) "Empirical tests of the life cycle hypothesis," *American Economic Review*, vol. 68 (September), pp. 547–60.

Yaari, M. E. (1965) "Uncertain lifetime, life insurance and the theory of the consumer," *Review of Economic Studies*, vol. 32 (April), pp. 137–50.

APPENDIX 10.1

THE ESTIMATION OF LIFETIME EARNINGS

As explained in the text, lifetime earnings were generated by modeling separately the time profiles of hours and wages. The former was explained in the text. The latter required a good deal of interpolation and extrapolation using an estimated wage equation reported in Gordon and Blinder (1980). Figure A10.1.1 illustrates the construction of Y_0 in the case of an individual whose record supplied the maximum number of wage observations–four. The observations are plotted as points A, D, F and G. The wage observation from 1928 (point A) is the wage the individual reported receiving on his first full-time job. The wage observation for 1952 (point D) is the wage the individual reported earning when he left his last job (at the time of the 1969 interview). The 1969 observation (point F) is the current wage as of the time of the 1969 interview and the 1971 observation (point G) is the current wage as of the 1971 interview. We now turn to our method of filling in the gaps between these wage observations.

The first gap we need to fill is the one between 1928 and 1942, which is the year that the "last job" began. This time period may cover more than one job. We know (except when data are missing) the starting and ending dates of the first job, the starting date of the last job (1942), and whether the individual's "longest job" intervened between these two. Figure A10.1.1 illustrates a case in which the period was entirely spent on the first job. To fill the gap between 1928 and 1942 we adjust the constant term generated by our wage equation for each individual so that we estimate the 1928 wage rate exactly, and then forecast the remainder of the period (through 1942) on the basis of the estimated wage equation. The path from A to B shows the predicted wage profile resulting from this step of the process.

The second gap to be estimated is the one from 1942 to 1952 – the period of work on the last job reported on the 1969 survey. In this case, we do not know the starting wage, but rather the wage the head received when he *left* the job (point D). So, instead of having to forecast this gap, we backcast it from point D by a procedure conceptually identical to that used to forecast the first wage gap. The path from D back to C illustrates the result of this projection. (In this example we have predicted that the individual took a reduction in the wage rate when he changed jobs in 1942.)

The final gap, between 1952 and 1969, is handled in the same fashion. We adjust the constant term to make the profile pass through point F exactly and backcast the market wage equation over the period to point E. The wage in 1970 is assumed to be the average of the 1969 and 1971 wages. This gives us an estimate of each individual's lifetime earnings profile from the beginning of his first full-time job through 1971. Future earnings are estimated by adjusting the constant of the wage equation to make it pass through point G (the observed 1971 wage), and forecasting wages forward through age 85, the oldest age at which it was assumed anyone could work. All wages are expressed net of payroll tax. Figure A10.1.1 illustrates a completed wage profile constructed by this method.

So far, we have assumed that the individual reported the maximum number of wage observations. This, of course, was not always the case. For those individuals who held only one job during their lifetime, and there were

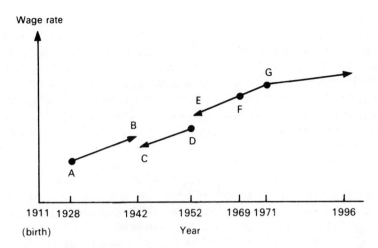

Fig. A10.1.1 Constructing the lifetime wage profile

a number of them, we backcast their 1969 wage rate to the beginning of their work history. If we also had the wage when they started their first job, which in this case was the same as their current job, we had two wage observations for the same job. This enabled us either to take the 1969 observation and *backcast* wages to the beginning of the job or to take the starting wage and *forecast* wages to 1969. We chose to do both and to take a weighted average of the two sets of estimates, using weights that vary linearly with age to force the profile through the two observed wages. Figure A10.1.2 shows an example of an individual for whom this procedure was used.

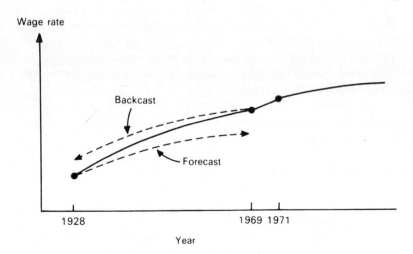

Fig. A10.1.2 Method used for interpolation

In other cases, we knew that the individual had a job, but he did not report the wage rate he earned. In this case we constructed an estimate of the wage rate from our wage equation without any adjustment of the constant term.

Since both the data and the work histories were scantier for wives than for husbands, the construction of lifetimes earnings for wives was more problematic. We began by taking whatever wage observations we could from the LRHS surveys, forecasting and backcasting earnings by use of the wage equation estimated for husbands. In doing this, we implicitly assumed that women's earnings profiles are generated by the same mechanism that generates the earnings profile for men. The reader who is incredulous about this assumption should recall that we always adjusted the *levels* of the wage profiles up or down to conform with the observed wage rates at various points in time. Our assumption therefore introduces error only in so far as women's earnings profiles differ in *shape* from men's.

An additional difficulty arose in attempting to generate earnings profiles for women: wage rates were frequently unavailable. For example, we might have a wife whom we knew held a job between 1930 and 1935, after which she left the labor force for a protracted period (probably to raise a family) before reentering the labor force in, say, 1955. At the time of the 1969 interview, the woman may not remember the wage she earned during the earlier job. Estimating that wage rate with our wage equation would clearly be incorrect, however, since our equation was estimated for men only. How then do we estimate wage rates for such women? There were too many cases of missing data on women's wage rates to discard these observations from the sample. So instead we imputed a woman's wage as 70 percent of the average wage in the industry in which she worked.

Hours of work were treated in the same way as for men; in particular, the probability that a wife would be retired in any given year was assumed equal to the probability that her husband would be retired. This seems a reasonable assumption when husband and wife are close in age (the vast majority of cases), but is probably totally unreasonable in (the small minority of) cases in which the two ages differed dramatically. This was another reason why we eliminated such couples from the sample.

11 · THE LIFE CYCLE PERMANENT-INCOME MODEL AND CONSUMER DURABLES

11.1 THE LIFE CYCLE MODEL AS A THEORY OF CONSUMER SPENDING

In the 1950s, Modigliani and Brumberg (1954) and Friedman (1957) turned the abstract Fisherian model of intertemporal maximization into an operational model of consumption. The model they developed,[1] which drew the crucial distinction between consumption and consumer expenditures and applied only to the former, has three main empirical implications about consumption at the microeconomic level:

1. Consumption at every age is proportional to permanent income, *i.e.* to the present value of expected lifetime resources.
2. Consumption is insensitive to transitory fluctuations in income that do not affect permanent income.
3. Under the usual assumption that the utility function is CES, consumption grows or shrinks at a rate $(r - \alpha)/b$, where r is the rate of interest, α is the rate of subjective time discounting, and b is a taste parameter.

Item 1 on this list was, of course, the empirical observation that motivated the theory. Item 2 is the distinguishing characteristic of the theory. Both of these apply to aggregate as well as to individual consumption. Item 3 points out an implication of the particular utility function needed to derive item 1; but it does not survive aggregation.[2]

The LCH/PIH is often held up as a model of good economics, and rightly so. A puzzling set of empirical phenomena was explained by a theory based on maximizing behavior. That theory was then translated into econometrically estimatable equations and subjected to a battery of empirical tests – with generally favorable results. Yet, from a business cycle perspective, the model has at least one serious shortcoming: it applies only to consumption, not to consumer expenditures, while spending on durables accounts for most of the cyclical variability. Thus the PIH needs to be supplemented by a model of expenditures on consumer durables (and also, of course, by a way to translate durable stocks into the service flows required by the theory). The usual way to do this is by the stock (partial) adjustment model.

The stock adjustment (SA) model assumes the presence of convex adjustment costs that give rise to a lagged adjustment of actual to "desired" stocks. Each period a constant fraction γ of the gap between the desired and actual stock is closed:

$$K_{t+1} - K_t = \gamma(K_{t+1}^* - K_t) \tag{11.1}$$

where the parameter γ, $0 \leqslant \gamma \leqslant 1$, is called the "speed of adjustment." K_t denotes the durable stock at the beginning of period t and K_t^* is the desired stock at that time. On the further assumption that depreciation is proportional to the stock, gross expenditures are given by:

$$E_{t+1} = \gamma(K_{t+1}^* - K_t) + \delta K_t \tag{11.2}$$

where δ is the per period depreciation rate. According to the LCH/PIH, the desired stock will be proportional to permanent income. But the existence of adjustment costs ($\gamma < 1$) results in a deviation of the actual stock, and thus the service flow of durables, from the desired level.

Despite the SA model's wide acceptance, it has some obvious theoretical and empirical drawbacks.

The first pertains to its microfoundations. It has been known for a long time (Holt, Modigliani, Muth and Simon (1960)) that the SA model can be justified rigorously by quadratic costs of adjusting durable stocks. But this assumption is counterintuitive. There is no apparent reason why it should be less costly to adjust durable holdings in several small steps rather than all at once. In an attempt to rationalize the assumption of quadratic adjustment costs, Bernanke (1985) claimed that "it takes time to shop for and acquire a new car." That is no doubt true, but it implies the existence of *transactions costs*, not *adjustment costs*. With lumpy transactions costs, we show below, consumers either fully adjust by replacing their old durable good or do not adjust at all. The SA model implies, instead, that they will partially adjust, *i.e.* purchase successively better durable goods over several consecutive periods. Even if partial adjustment at the aggregate level is conceivable (more on this below), it is hard to accept the conclusion for individuals.

Second, it is well known that an important property of demand for durables is that the purchasing decision can be advanced or postponed. This, many people suspect, is why spending on durables is so volatile. It is difficult to integrate this idea into the SA framework.

Third, the SA model is really a model of expansion demand. Replacement demand is simply grafted on as a fraction of the current stock. But the separation between expansion and replacement demands is an artificial one; consumers make one decision about durable purchases and do not distinguish between the "replacement" and "expansion" parts. In addition, actual data on durables expenditures lump the two components together; unfortunately for the theory, most of the demand is the unmodelled, replacement part.

Fourth, it is generally assumed that the speed of adjustment is constant and independent of any economic variables. In principle, this ought not to be the case; some variables, like credit rationing, interest rates, supply constraints, should affect γ. However, "in the simple stock-adjustment framework, desired stocks are the only channel through which economic variables can act" (Deaton and Muellbauer (1980), p. 353).

Finally, when the SA model is estimated empirically, the estimated adjustment speeds are very low; in most cases below 30 percent per quarter.

These problems all suggest that there is room for improvement. In particular, we will derive here a model in which the underlying microeconomics makes better sense, in which postponement/advancement decisions and depreciation are integrated, and in which aggregate behavior is not necessarily a blowup of individual behavior. Instead, the model distinguishes between the individual dynamics, which may be quite discontinuous, and relatively smooth aggregate dynamics.

11.2 MICROFOUNDATIONS OF THE (S, s) MODEL

11.2.1 Discrete versus smooth adjustment

In deriving a new model of the demand for durable goods, we begin by solving for the decision rule of a single consumer. This decision rule will then be aggregated to yield the consumption behavior of the whole economy, which may be very different from that of any single consumer.

The underlying assumption is that the market for durables is characterized by important lumpy transactions costs. The possible origins of these costs are many. Sometimes transactions costs are large and explicit (*e.g.*, in buying a house). Alternatively, since durable goods are characterized by a variety of characteristics, potential buyers must spend time and effort finding the right combination for their purposes. So search costs, whether described as time costs, utility costs, or financial costs, may be heavy. A third source of transactions costs is asymmetric information between buyers and sellers of durable goods – which gives rise to the "lemons" principle (Akerlof (1970)). As a result, the buyer suffers a lumpy cost – in the form of a loss of a fixed percentage of value – as soon as he takes the durable home.

Another property which distinguishes durables from nondurables is non-combinability (Lancaster (1979)), which means, for example, that two used cars cannot be combined to make one new car. Noncombinability implies that if a consumer wants to increase his flow of durable services, he will probably have to replace his old "car" rather than buy a small addition to it. And, because of the "lemons" effect, each replacement will involve a lumpy cost which is a fraction of the purchase.

Despite the apparent similarity between adjustment costs and transactions costs, the two are very different, both in nature and in their empirical implications. The combination of lumpy transactions costs and noncombinability implies that durable purchases will be made infrequently. If the deviation between actual and desired stocks is small, people will not find it worthwhile to pay the transactions costs necessary to change their durable good. Instead, they will wait until the deviation is large enough to justify the costs involved in the transaction. Quadratic adjustment costs imply the opposite dynamics. Even if the discrepancy between desired and actual stocks is small, the old "car" should be "replaced" by a slightly better one. Moreover, this should not be done in one shot, but rather spread over several periods.

It is obvious that people purchase durable goods infrequently and, when they do, the additions to their stocks are significant. Unfortunately, lumpy transactions costs are much more difficult to model than the quadratic adjustment costs that underly the SA model. Yet modeling them properly is worth the effort because similar theoretical and empirical problems arise in so many areas of economics.

For example, partial adjustment is often unthinkingly grafted on to models of the demand for money, which then display puzzlingly low speeds of adjustment. But this makes little sense. What possible reason can there be to assume that it costs four times as much to make twice as large a change in one's money holdings? Is it not more likely that marginal adjustment costs are decreasing, or even zero? The same reasoning applies, more generally, to all portfolio adjustments. Contrary to naive theory, investors do not adjust their portfolios continuously, and for good reasons: because there are fixed costs of doing so. Similarly, government officials and business executives may be reluctant to pay the fixed costs of decision-making until they are convinced that their current policy is far from optimal. Quadratic adjustment costs have been used to rationalize the Q-theory of investment (see Abel (1980)). But here, just as with consumer durables, lumpy adjustment costs are far more plausible. Is it believable that it costs a firm 49 times as much to install seven new drill presses as it costs to install one? We think not.

Indeed, we find it hard to imagine any application in which the (commonly made) assumption of quadratic adjustment costs is more reasonable than the (rarely made) assumption of lumpy transactions costs. Economists' standard theory of gradual adjustment seems to need rethinking. Fortunately, there is a well-known body of analysis in the inventory literature that applies to the case of fixed transactions costs. It leads to the so-called (S, s) or two-bin policy. The basic idea of this approach, which we apply here to consumer durables, is that the optimal plan is defined by a target point S and a trigger point s. If the stock (of money, inventories, or durable goods) falls below level s, an order to restore the stock to level S is made; otherwise, no order is made. We now show how the (S, s) rule applies to the demand for durable goods with lumpy transactions costs.

11.2.2 An (S, s) rule for durables

Suppose that a consumer consumes two commodities: a perishable good X and a durable good K which depreciates at a constant exponential rate μ.[3] Denote by $q < 1$ the ratio of the selling price of durables to the purchasing price; thus the lumpy transactions cost is a fraction $(1 - q)$ of the purchase price, as suggested by the "lemons" principle. We would like to see what effect this parameter has on the consumption plan of a consumer who maximizes lifetime utility subject to a lifetime budget constraint. Assume that the instantaneous utility function is of the standard LCH/PIH form:

$$u(K_t, X_t) = aK_t^k + bX_t^k, \quad k < 1 \tag{11.3}$$

where we assume, as is usual, that the flow of services from durables is proportional to the stock. Assuming time separability and an infinite horizon, the consumer wants to maximize:

$$U = \int_0^\infty u(K_t, X_t)e^{-\alpha t}\,dt \tag{11.4}$$

where U is lifetime discounted utility and α is the rate of subjective time discounting.

It is obvious that, because of the lumpy transactions costs, durable purchases will take place only occasionally, for continuous replacement implies infinite transactions costs. Denote by S_n the durable stock immediately after the nth durable purchase which takes place at time t_n. That good will be replaced at time t_{n+1}, when it has deteriorated to a value s_n given by:

$$s_n = S_n \exp[-\mu(t_{n+1} - t_n)] \tag{11.5}$$

Thus the discounted utility obtained while the nth "car" is held will be:

$$\int_{t_n}^{t_{n+1}} u[S_n \exp(-\mu(t - t_n)), X_t]e^{-\alpha t}\,dt \tag{11.6}$$

Summation over all lifetime purchases of durables and use of the specific functional form (11.3) yields the following expression for lifetime utility:

$$U = [a/(\mu k + \alpha)] \sum_{n=1}^{\infty} [\{\exp[-(\mu k + \alpha)t_n] - \exp[-(\mu k + \alpha)t_{n+1}]\}$$

$$\times (S_n e^{\mu t_n})^k] + b \int_0^\infty e^{-\alpha t}(X_t)^k\,dt \tag{11.7}$$

which is homogeneous of degree k in its arguments S and X.

In order to derive the budget constraint, assume that the nondurable good X is the numeraire and that the relative price of durables to nondurables is constant. Denote the purchase price of one "unit" of the durable good by p; therefore the resale price is qp. The discounted cost of the nth durable good is:

$$pS_n \exp(-rt_n) \tag{11.8}$$

where $r > 0$ is the interest rate. The discounted income from selling this "car" at time t_{n+1} will be

$$qpS_n\exp[-rt_{n+1} - \mu(t_{n+1} - t_n)]$$ (11.9)

The difference between (11.8) and (11.9) is the net expenditure on the nth car.[4] Summation over all durable transactions and inclusion of spending on nondurables yield the following lifetime budget constraint:

$$W = p\sum_{n=1}^{\infty}\{[e^{-rt_n} - q\exp[-rt_{n+1} - \mu(t_{n+1} - t_n)]]S_n\}$$

$$+ \int_0^{\infty} e^{-rt}X_t dt$$ (11.10)

where W denotes total (human and nonhuman) lifetime wealth. Notice that the budget constraint is homogenous of degree 1 in its arguments X and $S_1, S_2, \ldots$

The intertemporal optimization problem of the consumer is maximization of total discounted utility subject to the lifetime budget constraint. The solution consists of a plan for nondurable consumption, X_t, and two infinite series of trigger points $(S_1, S_2, \ldots)$ and $(s_1, s_2, \ldots)$ which denote the stocks immediately after the purchase and just before resale, respectively. However, the homogeneity of lifetime utility and the linearity of the budget constraint simplify the solution significantly and reduce the infinite number of parameters in the s and S series to only three: S_1, S_{n+1}/S_n and s_n/S_n. Similarly, the nondurable consumption plan X_t is characterized by only two parameters: the initial consumption and a constant exponential growth rate. Moreover, the growth rates of the consumption plans of both goods are the same, which reduces the total number of parameters to four. All this is summarized in the following theorem:

THEOREM 11.1. *The optimal consumption plan (S, s, X) exhibits the following properties:*[5]

1. *X_0, all the S_n, and all the s_n are proportional to total lifetime wealth.*
2. *The ratio s_n/S_n defined by (11.5) is constant, so the interval between purchases, τ, is constant.*
3. *The ratio S_{n+1}/S_n is constant and equal to $e^{\tau g}$ where*

$$g = \frac{r - \alpha}{1 - k}.$$

4. *The growth rate of nondurable consumption is constant and equals the growth rate g in (3).*

The inclusion of lumpy transactions costs in the durable goods market changes the durable transactions plan substantially from a continuous to a discrete one. Except for isolated points in time at which a purchase is made, the consumer will not be active in the market for durables. Do the key features of the PIH/LCH still hold with transactions costs? The answer is that these properties do hold in the "long run", but not in the "short run." Specifically, the pattern of durables stock, and therefore the service flow from durables, follows a ratchet path, as shown in Fig. 11.1. This path, of course, differs in details from the predictions of the strict PIH. However, the envelope curve which connects the S_i levels (and s_i levels) in Fig. 11.1 does follow the PIH/LCH predictions: it is proportional to permanent income; the rate of growth of consumption (g) is identical to that implied by the PIH; and transitory income affects consumption only insofar as it changes permanent income.[6] Thus in the short run, between purchases, there are deviations from the strict PIH/LCH predictions, deviations which are larger the larger are transactions costs. However, in the long run these deviations are rectified and the consumption plan returns to the PIH/LCH path. Notice also that since each purchase of a durable good involves a lumpy transactions cost, each change lowers the value of lifetime wealth. Thus total lifetime wealth, W, will follow a discontinuous ratchet pattern. At a time of a durable purchase, when the durable stock jumps up, wealth jumps down.

It is of interest to compare the predictions of the (S, s) model with those of the SA model. The inclusion of transactions costs increases the number of

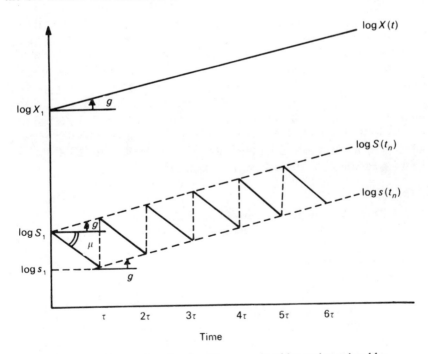

Fig. 11.1 Time paths of expenditures on durables and nondurables

choice variables from one (the "desired" stock) to two, S and s – a change which has considerable implications for the microdynamics. To see this, assume that the rate of time discounting (α) equals the discount rate (r) so that the trigger points, S and s, do not change unless new information is received. The SA model implies that the individual will hold a constant durable stock by replacing the depreciated amount each period. The (S, s) dynamics, by contrast, follow a ratchet path. Even with no new information the stock in different periods may be different, and durable purchases will not be made each period. If an unanticipated income shock takes place, the SA model predicts a smooth exponential convergence toward the new desired stock. No such smooth partial adjustment is predicted by the (S, s) model. Everyone adjusts either fully or not at all. Thus unanticipated changes may induce large contemporaneous changes for those consumers who adjust right away. But, for other consumers, no adjustment whatsoever will be observed for some time.

The microdynamics are therefore not the smooth paths described by the SA model. The "speed of adjustment" may vary considerably among individuals, depending on their initial durable stock. Thus explicit aggregation over the entire population is necessary in order to find the aggregate adjustment speed. Note also that, although the dynamics implied by the (S, s) model are more complicated than those of the SA model, the underlying theoretical basis is more solid. The postponement/advancement decision is naturally integrated into the model. By optimizing over the choice variables S and s, the consumer decides not only *how much* to spend on durables (as in the SA model), but also *when* to spend; when the durable stock hits the level s, he spends $p(S - qs)$. In principle, every piece of relevant information is taken into account in determining the levels S and s. This means that such important timing factors as intertemporal price substitution and variable interest rates are in principle captured by the model.[7] Another advantage relative to the SA model is that the (S, s) model envisions one unified decision about how much to spend on durables; this avoids the artificial distinction between expansion and replacement expenditures.

11.3 FROM MICROFOUNDATIONS TO MACRO IMPLICATIONS: AGGREGATION

Clearly, individuals do not "partially adjust" to "desired" stocks. Does the aggregate economy? In order to aggregate over the population, assume that all consumers have the same lifetime income but differ in their durable stocks, *i.e.* their position between the (common) levels S and s. An unexpected change in income will set in motion the following dynamics. Consumers who find themselves outside their (new) desired (S, s) region will react by moving into that region.[8] This is the short-run effect. These rescheduled purchases will also change the distribution of durable stocks in the population, which will lead to long-run dynamics.

Assume that consumers monitor their durable stocks continuously while the econometrician observes the data only periodically, at intervals of length θ. Denote the depreciation rate for one observation period by δ; thus $\delta = 1 - e^{-\mu\theta}$. Durable goods that depreciate to the new trigger point, s_t, within the period will be replaced. The following is the decision rule:

$$\begin{cases} \text{If } K_t(1 - \delta) < s_t, \text{ buy } S_t - qs_t \\ \text{If } K_t(1 - \delta) \geq s_t, \text{ buy nothing} \end{cases} \tag{11.11}$$

where K_t is the stock at the start of a period.

Hence the number of consumers N_t who purchase a durable good during period t is:[9]

$$N_t = \int_{s_{t-1}}^{s_t/(1-\delta)} f_t(K_t)dK_t = F_t(s_t/(1-\delta)) - F_t(s_{t-1}) \tag{11.12}$$

where $f_t(K_t)$ is the density function of durables at the beginning of period t and $F_t(K_t)$ is the corresponding cumulative density function. Those who buy a new "car" during period t spend:

$$C_t = S_t - qs_t \tag{11.13}$$

where we have normalized $p = 1$.

Denote by E_t the average economy-wide expenditure on durables during period t. E_t is the product of C_t times N_t, or:

$$E_t \equiv C_t N_t = (S_t - qs_t)\left[F_t\left(\frac{s_t}{1-\delta}\right) - F_t(s_{t-1}) \right] \tag{11.14}$$

At this point a simple example may be helpful. In the steady state, the number of durable goods purchased is the same each period (except for a possible trend). Hence the age distribution of cars is uniform. If cars are held for at most T periods we have:

$$f(h) = \begin{cases} \dfrac{1}{T} & \text{for } 0 \leq h \leq T \\ 0 & \text{otherwise} \end{cases} \tag{11.15}$$

where h is the age of the car. To derive the density of K_t from that of age, recall that:

$$f(K) = f(h)\left|\frac{dh}{dK}\right| \tag{11.16}$$

and that K and h are related by:

$$K = Se^{-\mu h} \quad \text{for} \quad 0 \leq h \leq T \tag{11.17}$$

Equations (11.15), (11.16) and (11.17) yield the following expression for the density function of the durables stock:

$$f(K) = \begin{cases} 1/(\mu TK) = 1/[K(\ln S - \ln s)] & \text{for} \quad s \leqslant K \leqslant S \\ 0 & \text{otherwise} \end{cases} \tag{11.18}$$

since $s = Se^{-\mu T}$.

The function $f(K)$ is depicted in Fig. 11.2. Although the age distribution is uniform, the distribution of stocks is monotonically decreasing due to exponential depreciation. The distribution in (11.18) implies that the average stock is:

$$\bar{K} = \frac{S - s}{\ln S - \ln s} \tag{11.19}$$

It is clear from the fact that the distribution is skewed towards the lower end that $\bar{K}$ is below $(S + s)/2$. For example, if $S = 10$ (thousand dollars), $\mu = 0.2$ and $T = 5$ then $s = 3.68$ and $\bar{K} = 6.32$, even though the midpoint of the (s, S) range is 6.84. The cumulative distribution function corresponding to the density function (11.18) is:

$$F(K) = \begin{cases} 0 & \text{for} \quad K \leqslant s \\ \dfrac{\ln K - \ln s}{\ln S - \ln s} & \text{for} \quad s \leqslant K \leqslant S \\ 1 & \text{for} \quad K \geqslant S \end{cases} \tag{11.20}$$

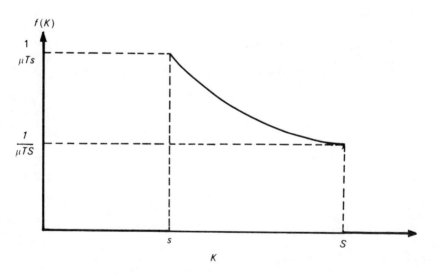

Fig. 11.2 Density function of durables stock

Since $\ln S - \ln s = \mu T$ and $\ln(1 - \delta) = -\mu\theta$, equations (11.14) and (11.20) yield the following simple expression for average expenditures on durables at period t:

$$E_t = \frac{\theta}{T}(S_t - qs_t) \qquad (11.21)$$

If, for example, the average durable good is held for $T = 5$ years, and the observation period is a quarter ($\theta = 1/4$), then about 5 percent of the cars are replaced each period in the steady state ($\delta = 0.049$). If $S = 10$ (thousand dollars), $s = 3.68$, and $q = 0.7$, average expenditure per capita is \$371.

Returning to the general case, we would like to understand the dynamics implied by equation (11.14), and in particular whether the standard implications of the PIH/LCH hold for aggregate expenditures on durables. The contemporaneous effect of a permanent income change on E_t is:

$$\frac{dE_t}{dy_t^p} = \left[F\left(\frac{s_t}{1-\delta}\right) - F(s_{t-1}) \right] \frac{d(S_t - qs_t)}{dy_t^p}$$

$$+ (S_t - qs_t) \frac{1}{1-\delta} f\left(\frac{s_t}{1-\delta}\right) \frac{ds_t}{dy_t^p} \qquad (11.22)$$

The first term represents the increase in expenditures per consumer (C_t) times the number of buyers (N_t). The second term is the average expenditure per buyer times the increase in the number of buyers. Recall from Theorem 1 that both S_t and s_t are proportional to permanent income y_t^p. Therefore, the difference $(S_t - qs_t)$ is also proportional to permanent income. That means that $S_t - qs_t$ is unit elastic with respect to y_t^p. So the first term in (11.22) is:

$$\frac{d(S_t - qs_t)}{dy_t^p} \left[F\left(\frac{s_t}{1-\delta}\right) - F(s_{t-1}) \right] = \frac{S_t - qs_t}{y_t^p} \left[F\left(\frac{s_t}{1-\delta}\right) - F(s_{t-1}) \right]$$

$$(11.23)$$

Similarly, the second term in equation (11.22) simplifies to:

$$(S_t - qs_t) \frac{1}{(1-\delta)} f\left(\frac{s_t}{1-\delta}\right) \frac{s_t}{y_t^p} \qquad (11.24)$$

Adding (11.23) and (11.24), and converting to an elasticity of aggregate expenditures on durables with respect to permanent income yields:

$$\frac{dE_t}{dy_t^p} \frac{y_t^p}{E_t} = 1 + x_t \frac{f(x_t)}{F(x_t) - F(s_{t-1})} \equiv 1 + \eta_t > 1 \qquad (11.25)$$

where $x_t \equiv \dfrac{s_t}{1-\delta} \geqslant s_t > 0$.

Thus the elasticity of durable expenditures with respect to permanent income is larger than one, rather than the unit elasticity normally associated with the PIH/LCH. The actual number depends on the density function.

However, if the distribution of durables is close to its steady state, the elasticity must be much larger than 1. For example, consider again the case of a uniform age distribution. Using the previous expressions, the second term in (11.25) becomes:

$$x_t \frac{f(x_t)}{F(x_t) - F(s_{t-1})} = \left[\ln\left(\frac{s_t}{(1-\delta)s_{t-1}} \right) \right]^{-1} = \frac{1}{\mu\theta}$$

where the last equality results from assuming a steady state ($s_{t-1} = s_t$). This gives the following (large) elasticity:

$$\frac{dE_t}{dy_t^p} \frac{y_t^p}{E_t} = 1 + \frac{1}{\mu\theta} \tag{11.26}$$

For an annual depreciation rate of 20 percent ($\mu = 0.2$) and quarterly observations ($\theta = \frac{1}{4}$), the elasticity will be 21, meaning that a 1 percent increase in permanent income yields a short-run increase of 21 percent in durable expenditures!

What is the reason for this very large elasticity? Look at the two terms in equation (11.22). The first term, the increase in expenditures per transaction (C_t), is unit elastic to permanent income because both S_t and s_t are. The second term describes the increase in the number of purchasers, which might be very large because of advancement of the purchasing decision. In the case of a periodical depreciation rate of $\delta = 0.05$, 5 percent of the population are replacing their durable good each period in the steady state. If permanent income now rises by 1 percent, the trigger point s will increase by 1 percent. This temporarily raises the percentage of the population buying cars from the normal 5 percent up to 6 percent. Thus the increase in the *flow rate* of transactions is 20 percent (6 percent instead of 5 percent of the population). The other 1 percent comes from the larger purchase size.

This discussion shows why breaking the data on durable expenditures into C_t and N_t is important. The average transaction size C_t describes the behavior of a single consumer. As such it should satisfy the predictions of the PIH/LCH; and, in fact, C_t is proportional to permanent income, is not sensitive to transitory income, and the growth rate of C_t is identical to that implied by the PIH.[10] The number of transactions N_t may vary widely in the short run with changes in permanent income. Since changes in aggregate durable expenditures E_t are dominated by variations in N_t, we cannot expect E_t to be proportional to permanent income. In the next section we shall make an empirical test of the different theoretical predictions for C_t, N_t and E_t. Although aggregate expenditures are not described very well by permanent income on a period by period basis, E is proportional to y^p in the long run. To see this, recall that:

$$E_t = (S_t - qs_t)\left[F_t\left(\frac{s_t}{1-\delta} \right) - F_t(s_{t-1}) \right] \tag{11.14}$$

In the long run $\left[F_t\left(\dfrac{s_t}{1-\delta}\right) - F_t(s_{t-1}) \right]$, the proportion of the population purchasing durables in a certain period, equals the steady state level – which is independent of permanent income. Thus in the long run E_t changes only with $C_t = (S_t - qs_t)$, which *is* proportional to permanent income.

The conclusion is that durable expenditures will exhibit a very high short-run income elasticity and a long run elasticity of unity. What can be said about the dynamics between these two extreme cases? The aggregate demand for durables depends crucially on the initial distribution of stocks and, in particular, on the lower tail of that distribution. An increase in permanent income leads to advancement of purchases, and hence to a change in the distribution. The echoes may reverberate for a long period and are not easy to characterize. We can, however, get a rough idea about the nature of these subsequent changes in the distribution of stocks. After a rise in y^p, there are more "new cars" and fewer "old cars". So the density in the lower tail will be smaller and fewer people will purchase new cars. Thus an unexpected income increase will lead to the following dynamics. Initially, there is a large short-run increase in durable expenditures. If the initial distribution is uniform, then the distribution after the income shock will not be uniform anymore. Then there is a long period in which expenditures may change as the distribution of stocks adjust. Spending will tend to be low until convergence to the long-run steady state is achieved, which might take a long time.

These dynamics are quite different from those implied by the stock-adjustment model, which predicts smooth, exponential convergence of actual to desired stocks. The closest analogue to the "desired" stock in the SA model is the mean of the steady-state distribution in the (S, s) model. But according to the (S, s) model, the mean of the actual distribution does not converge smoothly to this "desired" level. For example, we have just noted that if the initial age distribution is uniform, then the average stock will "overshoot" the "desired" level. Subsequently, it will fluctuate in long damped oscillations around the steady state until convergence is achieved.[11] Thus the SA and (S, s) models imply very different micro and macrodynamics.

At this point, it may be useful to summarize the aggregate implications of the (S, s) model:

1. The variable which is most closely related to the PIH/LCH is average expenditure per transaction, C_t. This variable should satisfy the key properties of the PIH. However, total expenditures on durables E_t should not be predicted very well by standard results of the PIH. The reason is that the typical application of the PIH is based on a representative consumer. This abstraction can capture only one dimension of the consumption decision: how much to spend. But because of the existence of transaction costs, there is another dimension: when to spend. This advancement/postponement decision cannot be captured by a model of a representative agent.

2. The average durable stock, K_t, and total expenditures, E_t, will not necessarily be proportional to permanent income; neither will they follow the growth rate implied by the PIH. Instead, changes in permanent income might lead to very large changes in durable expenditures with echo effects which might last for a long time. Only the long-run, steady-state levels of expenditures and stock will follow the predictions of the PIH. This means that the market for durable goods is inherently more volatile than the markets for nondurable goods and services. Even with no new information, E_t and K_t might vary across periods. Only when there are no surprises *and* the distribution of stocks is in a steady state will durable expenditures and stocks not fluctuate.

3. The high short-run income elasticity of expenditures implied by the (S, s) model opens up an avenue through which small impulses in perceived permanent income may lead to large business cycles. Suppose a small, negative innovation to income leads people to write down their estimated permanent incomes by small amounts. By the logic of the (S, s) model, spending on durables may fall by a much larger percentage than permanent income, thereby kicking off a recession. (Supposing, of course, that prices and wages are not perfectly flexible.)[12]

4. The empirical implications of the SA and (S, s) models differ in a number of ways, of which three are worth mentioning.

    (a) In the SA model, but not in the (S, s) model, the average stock of durables converges monotonically to the "desired" stock following a shock.

    (b) In the (S, s) model, but not in the SA model, the age distribution of the stock affects spending. Specifically, the model implies that older durables are more important determinants of expenditures than are newer durables. Note that standard estimates of the aggregate stock of, say, cars, give less weight to older cars than to newer cars because their market values are lower. The (S, s) model implies that this is precisely the wrong weighting.[13]

    (c) The SA model, but not the (S, s) model, implies symmetric reactions of net investment to positive or negative income shocks. According to the (S, s) model, positive shocks pull S and s up, putting many consumers below s, and triggering purchases. Negative shocks push S and s down, putting many consumers above S. However, lumpy transactions costs may preclude selling durables to get below S. Instead, consumers may wait until depreciation does the job for them.

11.4 PRELIMINARY EMPIRICAL TESTS

The analysis of the former section suggests that the average transaction size, C_t, but not the number of transactions, N_t, will follow closely the predictions of the PIH/LCH as enunciated by Hall (1978). To see this, recall from Theorem 1 that the target stock S_t and the trigger s_t are both proportional to permanent income:

$$\begin{cases} S_t = a_1 y_t^p + u_t \\ s_t = a_2 y_t^p + v_t \end{cases} \tag{11.27}$$

where u_t and v_t are stochastic terms which represent factors that are not included in the analysis. The amount spent on durable purchases C_t is, in real terms:

$$C_t = S_t - q s_t = \Omega y_t^p + \varepsilon_t \tag{11.28}$$

where the coefficient Ω is defined by $\Omega \equiv a_1 - q a_2$, q is the ratio of selling to purchasing price, and the transitory component ε_t satisfies $\varepsilon_t \equiv u_t - q v_t$. Equation (11.28) is the conventional way of modeling the PIH. (See, for example, Flavin (1981), p. 978.) It states that, apart from transitory consumption, consumption is proportional to permanent income.

In order to estimate the number of purchases, N_t, begin with equation (11.12). The integral can be approximated by using The Theorem of the Mean for Integrals which states that if $f(x)$ is a continuous function on a closed interval $[a, b]$, then there is a number c, $a < c < b$, such that

$$\int_a^b f(x) dx = f(c)(b - a)$$

Applying this theorem to (11.12) yields:

$$N_t = f_t(\hat{K}_t)[s_t/(1 - \delta) - s_{t-1}] \tag{11.29}$$

where $s_{t-1} \leqslant \hat{K}_t \leqslant s_t/(1 - \delta)$.

Equation (11.29) is exact because no approximation was involved in its derivation. However, it is not operational since the theorem does not specify the exact location of the point $\hat{K}_t$. In general $f_t(\hat{K}_t)$ depends on the distribution of stocks in the lower tail. The simplest assumption to permit empirical work is that $f_t(\hat{K}_t)$ is constant through time. Call that constant B. Using the approximation $1/(1 - \delta) \simeq 1 + \delta$ for $\delta \ll 1$, we get:

$$N_t = \delta A y_t^p + A(y_t^p - y_{t-1}^p) + (1 + \delta) B v_t - B v_{t-1} \tag{11.30}$$

where $A \equiv B a_2$. Notice that N_t depends not only on y_t^p, but also on y_{t-1}^p.

In his influential (1978) paper, Hall pointed out that if the PIH holds then lagged information other than lagged consumption will be useless for predicting consumption. In order to see if this result is robust to the inclusion of transactions costs, difference equation (11.30) to obtain:

$$N_t = N_{t-1} + A(1 + \delta)(y_t^p - y_{t-1}^p) - A(y_{t-1}^p - y_{t-2}^p)$$
$$+ (1 + \delta) B(v_t - v_{t-1}) - B(v_{t-1} - v_{t-2}) \tag{11.31}$$

And similarly equation (11.28) implies:

$$C_t = C_{t-1} + \Omega(y_t^p - y_{t-1}^p) + \varepsilon_t - \varepsilon_{t-1} \tag{11.32}$$

Equation (11.32) is Hall's well-known result. Expenditures per transaction follow a random walk process if we assume away the transitory element, or ARMA (1, 1) without this assumption. However, equation (11.31) implies that the number of durables sold, N_t, is far from a random walk. Even ignoring the moving average error term, ΔN_t depends on both Δy_t^p and Δy_{t-1}^p. So past income does have a value in predicting N_t, and thus future consumption expenditures.

We test these implications with quarterly US data on automobile purchases because good data are available on both the average price of a new car, C_t, and the number of new cars purchased by consumers, N_t.[14]

First, following Hall, we ask if E_t can be predicted by its own past values other than E_{t-1}. The result is (with t-ratios in parentheses):

$$E_t = 28.52 + 0.571 E_{t-1} + 0.387 E_{t-2} - 0.113 E_{t-3} - 0.067 E_{t-4}$$

$$(3.44) \quad (5.66) \qquad (3.35) \qquad (-0.98) \quad (-0.68)$$

$$R^2 = 0.635; \quad DW = 1.987; \quad F(3,98) = 3.799 \tag{11.33}$$

The F test rejects the omission of longer lags at the 2 percent level, and the equation makes it clear that it is E_{t-2} that matters. According to our theory, the rejection should come from N_t, not from C_t. That turns out to be the case, as the following two regressions show.

$$C_t = 11.01 + 1.017 C_{t-1} - 0.025 C_{t-2} + 0.094 C_{t-3} - 0.086 C_{t-4}$$

$$(0.11) \quad (10.22) \qquad (-0.18) \qquad (0.71) \qquad (-0.87)$$

$$R^2 = 0.956; \quad DW = 2.006; \quad F(3,98) = 0.265 \tag{11.34}$$

$$N_t = 533.7 + 0.583 N_{t-1} + 0.414 N_{t-2} - 0.124 N_{t-3} - 0.041 N_{t-4}$$

$$(2.76) \quad (5.76) \qquad (3.55) \qquad (-1.07) \qquad (-0.41)$$

$$R^2 = 0.687; \quad DW = 1.984; \quad F(3,98) = 4.511 \tag{11.35}$$

Longer lags are inconsequential in the C_t equation, but N_{t-2} matters in the N_t equation. (The F-statistic for omitting the longer lags rejects the null hypothesis at well below the 1 percent level.)

Next, again following Hall, we ask if lagged values of disposable income can predict expenditures on autos. The result is:

$$E_t = 38.14 + 0.622 E_{t-1} + 0.642 y_{t-1} - 0.244 y_{t-2} + 0.234 y_{t-3} - 0.615 y_{t-4}$$

$$(4.02) \quad (7.87) \qquad (1.90) \qquad (-0.54) \quad (0.52) \qquad (-1.83)$$

$$R^2 = 0.621; \quad DW = 2.350; \quad F(4,97) = 1.856 \tag{11.36}$$

or, if only y_{t-1} is allowed to enter the equation:

$$E_t = 28.80 + 0.737 E_{t-1} + 0.013 y_{t-1}$$

(3.23) (11.12)   (0.724)

$$R^2 = 0.594; \quad DW = 2.340; \quad F(1, 100) = 0.534 \tag{11.37}$$

In both (11.36) and (11.37), the null hypothesis that all lagged ys can be excluded cannot be rejected. In this case, the failure to reject characterizes both the equation for the number of cars and the equation for average expenditure per car:

$$C_t = 22.02 + 0.978 C_{t-1} - 0.043 y_{t-1} - 0.313 y_{t-2} + 0.604 y_{t-3} - 0.223 y_{t-4}$$

(0.24) (28.44)   (−0.18)   (−0.93)   (1.78)   (−0.94)

$$R^2 = 0.958; \quad DW = 1.970; \quad F(4, 97) = 1.295 \tag{11.38}$$

$$N_t = 952.4 + 0.751 N_{t-1} + 0.796 y_{t-1} - 0.338 y_{t-2} + 0.280 y_{t-3} - 0.795 y_{t-4}$$

(3.65) (11.82)   (1.06)   (−0.32)   (0.26)   (−1.02)

$$R^2 = 0.659; \quad DW = 2.487; \quad F(4, 97) = 1.088 \tag{11.39}$$

We conclude that lagged disposable income is of no use in predicting expenditures on cars. In the case of (11.39) this is contrary to our model. A similar conclusion was obtained by Hall, and also by Mankiw (1982), who tested Hall's hypothesis using data on total expenditures on durable goods.

Finally, we ask whether lagged wealth has any predictive power. In this case, the answer is significantly yes (at a 1 percent level) for E_t and N_t, but barely so (significant at 10 percent, but not 5 percent level) for C_t:

$$E_t = 34.64 + 0.692 E_{t-1} + 0.234 W_{t-1} - 0.381 W_{t-2} + 0.330 W_{t-3} - 0.182 W_{t-4}$$

(3.73) (10.80)   (3.53)   (−2.78)   (2.41)   (−2.69)

$$R^2 = 0.657; \quad DW = 2.462; \quad F(4, 97) = 4.621 \tag{11.40}$$

$$C_t = 64.22 + 0.930 C_{t-1} + 1.300 W_{t-1}$$

(0.70) (22.10)   (2.41) \hfill (11.41)

$$-2.196 W_{t-2} + 1.483 W_{t-3} - 0.451 W_{t-4}$$

(−1.98)   (1.33)   (−0.83)

$$R^2 = 0.960; \quad DW = 1.924; \quad F(4, 97) = 2.283$$

$$N_t = 1213.6 + 0.738 N_{t-1} + 4.828 W_{t-1}$$

(4.30) (12.52)   (2.97) \hfill (11.42)

$$-8.20 W_{t-2} + 7.243 W_{t-3} - 4.128 W_{t-4}$$

(−2.44)   (2.16)   (−2.49)

$$R^2 = 0.699; \quad DW = 2.573; \quad F(4, 97) = 4.480$$

which echoes Hall's finding. It is pretty clear that the strongest rejection of the PIH comes from N_t, not from C_t.

These results hardly can be said to support the (S, s) model. More exacting tests of some of the implications mentioned in the previous section are necessary for that. But they are encouraging in that rejections of the simple PIH/LCH using data on durables do seem to stem more from the behavior of N_t than from the behavior of C_t, which is what out model predicts.

11.5 SUMMARY

We have presented here an extension of the life cycle permanent-income model of consumption to the case of a durable good whose purchase involves lumpy transactions costs. The micro-theoretic foundation of the model is a particular application of what might be called "the general optimality of doing nothing" in that fixed costs of decision-making generally make it optimal to make large changes in behavior at sporadic intervals, but to do nothing most of the time.

Where individual behavior is concerned, the implications of the model match those of the PIH/LCH in some respects, but not in others. Specifically, rather than choose an optimal *path* for the service flow from durables, the optimizing consumer will choose an optimal *range* and try to keep his service flow inside that range. When the durable good deteriorates to the bottom of the range, s, he will buy enough to restore the stock to the top of the range, S; he will not "partially adjust" toward some "desired level" of the durable stock. The (S, s) range itself, however, evolves precisely as prescribed by the PIH/LCH, as does the consumption of nondurable goods and services. The model naturally integrates replacement and expansion investment in a unified framework, and also automatically takes account of the opportunities to postpone or advance purchases that may make expenditures on durables so volatile.

Because there is no "representative consumer" in the (S, s) model, aggregation is more difficult than in the standard PIH/LCH. Building from microfoundations to macro aggregates suggests separate treatment of the number of durable goods purchased and the purchase size. According to the theory, the latter follows the implications of the PIH. The former displays higher-order dynamics and a potentially huge short-run elasticity to changes in permanent income (despite a long-run elasticity of unity).

Empirical tests of the sort suggested by Hall (1978), carried out on quarterly data on new purchases of automobiles by US consumers, generally produce results that are in line with the predictions of the theory. In particular, the time series behavior of the number of cars purchased differs substantially (and in the predicted way) from that of the average purchase size. However, these are not very powerful tests for discriminating between the (S, s) model and the stock adjustment model. Much more detailed empirical work is necessary before anyone can really say that the data support or reject the (S, s) model.

NOTES

1. For the purposes of this paper, the differences between the life cycle hypothesis (LCH) and the permanent income hypothesis (PIH) are inconsequential.
2. There is much confusion on this point. If population is constant and the age distribution is uniform, then the LCH/PIH implies that aggregate consumption is constant regardless of the time profile of individual consumption, that is, regardless of r and α.
3. This section is an extension of earlier work by Flemming (1969).
4. The implicit assumption is that each consumer holds one "car" only. However, the number of units of this durable good, *i.e.* its size and quality (and therefore also its price), is a continuous variable. Hence the levels S and s can be chosen continuously as well.
5. For the proof, see Blinder and Bar-Ilan (1987). The consumption plan depends also on the initial durable stock. The solution stated in Theorem 11.1 and described in Fig. 11.1 holds when the consumer adjusts his initial stock immediately to level S. This will be the case, for example, when the initial stock is zero. However, if the initial stock is different from zero, there is a possibility that the optimal policy is not to purchase anything for some time. In this case the first holding period may be different from the other periods. Hence property (2), Theorem 11.1, holds only after the first purchase of durables had been made.
6. In an uncertainty model an innovation to permanent income will induce a consumer to advance his purchase and spend more on durables. Both of these effects will be larger the more permanent the income shock.
7. However, in practice analytical solutions for S and s are hard to obtain; so implementing these features analytically is difficult.
8. Either immediately, by making a durable transaction, or by letting their "excessive" durable stock depreciate to the new region.
9. $N_t = 0$ when $S_t/(1 - \delta) < s_{t-1}$.
10. C_t is depicted in Fig. 11.1 by the difference between the upper and lower envelope curves. Since both curves grow at the same rate, this is also the growth rate of C_t. Notice that unlike the discrete purchasing behavior of a specific consumer, C_t is observed every period and its growth path is continuous, *i.e.* the predictions of the PIH hold each period and not only right after a purchase by a specific individual (as was the case in the former section).
11. The convergence is guaranteed when the depreciation is stochastic. For a more rigorous analysis of the dynamics in the case of stochastic depreciation, see Bar-Ilan (1985).
12. The stock-adjustment model can also produce a large short-run income elasticity, though for very different reasons. In the SA model, the short-run elasticity arises from the stock/flow distinction; each consumer's *flow* rate of expenditure depends on his desired *stock*, and the desired stock may be very large relative to the flow of expenditures. In the (S, s) model, the high short-run elasticity arises naturally from the postponement/advancement decision.
13. This is very similar to the explanation given by Bils (1985) to the countercyclical aggregation bias in computing average real wage. Since the income of low income people is most volatile, they should be weighted highly in studying the cyclical behavior of wages, not given the low (or even zero, when they are unemployed) weight assigned to them automatically by their income.

14. The data are unpublished and were kindly furnished by the Bureau of Economic Analysis. The period of observation is 1958:1 through 1984:3, and all data are seasonally adjusted. C_t is average expenditure per new car purchased by consumers. N_t is retail sales of new passenger cars to consumers (business and government expenditures are excluded). E_t is the product $C_t N_t$.

REFERENCES

Abel, A. B. (1980) "Empirical investment equations: an integrative framework," in K. Brunner and A. H. Meltzer (eds) *On the State of Macroeconomics*, Carnegie-Rochester Series on Public Policy.

Akerlof, G. A. (1970) "The market for lemons: qualitative uncertainty and the market mechanism," *Quarterly Journal of Economics*, vol. 84, pp. 488–500.

Bar-Ilan, A. (1985) "Optimal decision rules and fixed transactions costs," unpublished PhD Dissertation, Princeton University.

Bernanke, B. (1985) "Adjustment costs, durables and aggregate consumption," *Journal of Monetary Economics*, vol. 13, pp. 41–68.

Bils, M. J. (1985) "Real wages over the business cycle: evidence from panel data," *Journal of Political Economy*, vol. 93, pp. 666–89.

Blinder, A. S. and A. Bar-Ilan (1987) "Consumer durables and the optimality of usually doing nothing," mimeo.

Deaton, A. S. and J. Muellbauer (1980) *Economics and Consumer Behavior*, Cambridge: Cambridge University Press.

Flavin, M. A. (1981) "The adjustment of consumption to changing expectations about future income," *Journal of Political Economy*, vol. 89, pp. 974–1009.

Flemming, J. S. (1969) "The utility of wealth and the utility of windfalls," *Review of Economic Studies*, vol. 36, pp. 55–66.

Friedman, M. (1957) *A Theory of the Consumption Function*, Princeton, NJ: Princeton University Press.

Hall, R. E. (1978) "Stochastic implications of the life cycle–permanent income hypothesis: theory and evidence," *Journal of Political Economy*, vol. 86, pp. 971–87.

Holt, C. C., F. Modigliani, J. Muth and H. Simon (1960) *Planning Production, Inventories and Work Force*, Englewood Cliffs, NJ: Prentice-Hall.

Lancaster, K. (1979) *Variety, Equity, and Efficiency*, Columbia: Columbia University Press.

Mankiw, N. G. (1982) "Hall's consumption hypothesis and durable goods," *Journal of Monetary Economics*, vol. 10, pp. 417–25.

Modigliani, F. and R. E. Brumberg (1954) "Utility analysis and the consumption function: An interpretation of cross-section data," in K. K. Kurihara (ed.) *Post-Keynesian Economics*, New Brunswick, NJ: Rutgers University Press.

INDEX